At Play in the Tavern

STYLUS
Studies in Medieval Culture

Mirabile Dictu: Representations of the Marvelous in Medieval and
Renaissance Epic, *by Douglas Biow*

Ami and Amile: A Medieval Tale of Friendship, Translated from the
Old French, *translated by Samuel N. Rosenberg and Samuel Danon*

At Play in the Tavern: Signs, Coins, and Bodies in the Middle Ages, *by
Andrew Cowell*

This interdisciplinary series is devoted to that millennium of Western
culture extending from the fall of Rome to the rise of Humanism that
we call the Middle Ages. The series promotes scholarship based on the
study of primary sources and artifacts within their social and discursive
contexts. With its emphasis on cultural studies, the series favors
research that considers how the psychological, ideological, and
spiritual dimensions of the medieval world converge in expressions of
individual experience and in perceptions of material events.

At Play in the Tavern

Signs, Coins, and Bodies
in the Middle Ages

Andrew Cowell

Ann Arbor

THE UNIVERSITY OF MICHIGAN PRESS

2002   2001   2000   1999   4   3   2   1

A CIP catalog record for this book is available from the British Library.

Library of Congress Cataloging-in-Publication Data

Cowell, Andrew, 1963–
    At play in the tavern : signs, coins, and bodies in the Middle
Ages / Andrew Cowell.
        p.   cm.   — (Stylus)
    Includes bibliographical references (p.   ) and index.
    ISBN 0-472-11007-1 (acid-free paper)
    1. French literature—To 1500—History and criticism. 2. Taverns
(Inns) in literature. I. Title. II. Series.
PQ155.T38   C68   1999
840.9'355—dc21   98-40266
                                                                  CIP

Acknowledgments

I would like to briefly thank all of my friends, colleagues, and mentors who have been generous enough to read all or parts of this book, whether at the University of California–Berkeley, the University of Colorado, or elsewhere. These include Carolyn Dinshaw and Joseph Duggan, who were so valuable in the early stages of this work; Andrea Frisch, Bruce Holsinger, Jann Purdy, and Michelle Warren for many useful comments; and Beth Robertson for her very much appreciated help in making revisions. Special thanks go to Howard Bloch, without whose teaching, advice, inspiration, and assistance this book would never have been conceived and certainly would never have reached this final form. His influence will be visible here far beyond the various specific footnotes and comments. Of course, the flaws and shortcomings in this book are purely my own. I would also like to thank everyone at the University of Michigan Press for their interest and assistance in this project.

Part of the discussion of *Courtois d'Arras* in chapter 3 appeared in *Symposium* 50 (1996): 16–27, and I am grateful to the journal and to Heldref Publications for permission to reprint. Parts of chapters 3 and 4 were presented at the University of Miami conference "Medieval Renaissance Baroque" in 1996, at the "Journée de travail sur les Fabliaux" at Columbia University in 1997, and at the Medieval Institute Conference in Kalamazoo in 1998.

Contents

Introduction   1

Chapter 1. Charity, Hospitality, and Profit   14

Chapter 2. *Le Jeu de Saint Nicolas* and the Poetics of the Tavern   54

Chapter 3. The Moral Economy of the Tavern   111

Chapter 4. Autobiography and Folly   180

Conclusion   241

Bibliography   251

Index   265

Introduction

This book is about the tavern, inn, and brothel in medieval France. More generally, it is about the French "comico-realist" literary tradition—the fabliaux, Rutebeuf, drama, various short *dits* and contes, as well as the poetry of the goliards, all of which contain numerous tavern scenes. The extraordinary number of appearances of the tavern in comico-realist texts was in fact the starting point of this project. Along with its associated institutions, the inn and brothel, from which it was scarcely distinct in the High Middle Ages, it is the single most important locale of the thirteenth-century dramas from the city of Arras—*Le Jeu de Saint Nicolas, Courtois d'Arras,* and *Le Jeu de la Feuillée*—as well as of Rutebeuf's so-called poems of misfortune. It is one of the two or three predominant locales of the fabliaux and of the poems of the goliards, one of whose most famous texts is "In taberna quando sumus." And it appears endlessly in both parodic and moralizing texts with colorful titles like "Le credo au ribaut," "Li proverbe au vilain," "Les deux bordeors ribauds," and "La devise au lecheor."[1] Indeed, the tavern scene and its associated thematics constitute one of the strongest bases for isolating a comico-realist tradition and provide a privileged entry to this tradition (though this book will also demonstrate that this tradition, while quite comic, is hardly realist).[2]

---

1. Barbazon, *Fabliaux et contes,* 4:445–51; Langlois, *La vie française au Moyen Age,* 1:27–46; Faral, *Mimes français,* 106–11; Méon, *Nouveau recueil de fabliaux et contes,* 301–8.

2. The identity and indeed existence of such a tradition is problematic, and this book will suggest that this tradition is both more and less than it seems. The tradition has been defined by the common presence of several features, most important of which are (1) the relative absence of "courtly" themes; (2) a neglect of the feudal aristocracy in favor of the peasant, the "bourgeois," and the priest; (3) a decided tendency toward satire, parody, and pedantry; and (4) a "low" style, often featuring slang, obscenity, and "popular" elements. The tradition thus typically excludes the genres of epic, courtly romance, the poetry of the so-called courtly love tradition, and Latin literature directed toward learned elements of the church. Its most cele-

But most generally of all, this is a study of the origins of the Western notions of profit and of play in the Middle Ages. Comico-realist literature, and more specifically the tavern/inn/brothel, is the crucial site for the medieval elaboration of these two concepts as necessarily interrelated phenomena. Furthermore, the conjunction of these two concepts formed the basis for entirely new models of sign theory in the Middle Ages—models that reflected the participation of new voices in the discourse of medieval culture. I seek in this study to locate the forms of medieval literature within a deep cultural matrix, which the comico-realist texts not only reflect but help constitute. The central components of this matrix engaged by comico-realism are, as the terms *profit* and *play* already suggest, those of economics and of bodily desires. This work thus draws inspiration from that of a number of scholars who have worked on questions of economics and the social status of carnal desire in the Middle Ages and the relation of both of these factors to the sign.[3]

Profit, Play, and the Sign

The tavern and inn, as both literary and historically recorded institutions, began to flourish in France for the first time in the twelfth century. They rose to prominence not long after the birth of a true vernacular literary culture in France (not including older oral forms, such as the epic) and at

---

brated exemplars are the drama, the fabliaux, the poetry of Rutebeuf, and numerous variously moral and immoral *dits,* or short rhymed narratives, all of which I will treat in this book, and fables and *Le Roman de Renart,* which I will not.

The tradition has a long history: Petit de Juleville split his history of medieval French literature into two volumes, the second of which roughly covers the comico-realist, or more broadly "popular," tradition (*Histoire de la langue et de la littérature française,* 1896). More explicitly, Gustave Lanson's 1938 *Histoire de la littérature française* is divided into two sections, one on heroic and chivalric texts and one on "la littérature bourgeoise." Despite the growing awareness of the pitfalls inherent to criteria of audience and style in the Middle Ages, recent books continue this distinction: Daniel Poirion's *Précis de la littérature française du moyen age* (1983) covers the tradition in two chapters, one on "the town" and the other on "the comic (le rire)," while Michel Zink's *Littérature française du moyen age* (1992) covers epic, troubadour lyric, romance, prose romance and chronicles, allegory, and finally "la dramatisation et le rire"—almost exactly matching the classic comico-realist tradition. Such distinctions are sometimes less clear in American and British analyses, where hierarchical divisions of this type are less common, but they still form an important—and sometimes misleading—paradigm of medieval studies.

3. In particular (with representative works), R. Howard Bloch *(Etymologies and Genealogies),* Eugene Vance *(Mervelous Signals),* Alexandre Leupin *(Barbarolexis),* Judith Kellogg *(Medieval Artistry and Exchange),* R. A. Shoaf *(Dante, Chaucer, and the Currency of the Word),* and Marc Shell *(The Economy of Literature).*

the time when the first true urban centers were gaining importance. Their appearance roughly coincided with the coming into being of the market-place as a widespread economic phenomenon. They witnessed the early rise of the profit motive in northern France and Flanders and the beginnings of a form of protocapitalism.

Their birth was also the time of the decline of "Romanesque" models of sign theory in the Middle Ages, a sign theory marked by an Augustinian Neoplatonism and an emphasis on models of "charitable" intention that might ultimately lead to a process of "theosis"—the experience of the divine immanence of God in language and the world. Monastic modes of reading began to lose their dominance as both vernacular and Latin literature expanded their audiences to address the growing urban populations and the new ethical issues that their social and economic lives posed.

The twelfth and thirteenth centuries were thus, in many ways, about the confrontation between a centuries-old ecclesiastical model of living and of reading (itself strongly influenced by the rural, aristocratically dominated lifestyle of medieval western Europe) and a new model of the way in which signs, money, texts, and bodies might be used. The tavern, inn, and brothel, as will become clear in this book, were represented as the central point of this confrontation by the twelfth and thirteenth centuries. The tavern is portrayed as the birthplace of profit—not just economic, but also corporal, textual, and ultimately semiotic. By the word *profit* I mean here the idea that signs—which at this time included not only words but coins and bodies as well—could produce an excess of meaning or value that became not problematic and socially disruptive but desired. This profit found its concrete realization in forms as varied as prostitution, usury, gambling, "la folie," and the creation by the jongleur of comico-realist literature itself. In a battle of insults between two rival jongleurs entitled "Les deux bordeors ribauds," one says to the other, "Ja n'est il nus hom qui Dieu croie / Qui en moustier entrer te voie. / Tu as toute usée ta pel / en la taverne et au bordel" (There is no man who believes in God who has ever seen you enter a church. You have worn out your hide in the tavern and the brothel).[4]

What is finally most interesting about the tavern, inn, and brothel, however, is that the literature of these locales frames all of the other illicit activities associated with them in terms of literary practice. In simpler terms, gambling, prostitution, folly, and usury are repeatedly used as metaphors

---

4. Faral, *Mimes français,* 106–11, vv. 135–39.

for writing (producing) and reading (consuming) texts in medieval French literature. Gambling with dice, to take one example, becomes emblematic of a particular ludic aesthetic and poetics in *Le Jeu de Saint Nicolas*. Likewise, the disruptive effects of poetic language are linked to the linguistic, psychological, and corporal disruption resulting from drunkenness. One goliard poem notes, "ita bibas absque pare / ut non possis pede stare / neque recta verba dare" (thus you drink without ever getting enough so that you cannot remain on your feet nor correctly speak).[5] The phrase "recta verba" recalls the classical definition of grammar as the art of *recte loquendo,* while the "feet" can be read as those of Latin meter. Both the body and the body of language are disrupted by drink—the same drink of which the Archpoet writes, "tales versus facio, / quale vinum bibo" (how I write is governed by the kind of wine I swallow).[6] The representations of all of these activities contribute to the elaboration of a new model of the essential nature and social function of literature, a model that posits not theosis but semiotic play and overproductivity—profit—as the central feature of literature. And most crucially, the two notions of profit and play are linked in comico-realism in a unique way. The profit was generated by—and was the expression of—forms of gratuitous play, of nonutilitarian exchange. In these texts, semiotic profit is not, in the final analysis, a calculated form of gain but the outgrowth of forms of play that escape such calculating maneuvers.

Yet the tavern is not just the site where a number of economic and ethical practices are reduced to metaphors for a new vision of literature and the sign. It is also the site where such a new vision of the sign is extended in support of a new vision of social and economic activities—in particular, those of the profit-seeking, urban merchant and those involving the gratuity of the body. Many of the tavern texts offer both the earliest model and the earliest apology that can be found in western Europe for play, profit, and a release of semiotic practices in all forms from the constraints of the Augustinian, Neoplatonic model, whether it be in the merchant's usurious lending or in the joyous freedom of drink.

Two Visions of the Sign: The Word and the Coin

In a certain sense it is not surprising that the many features of the tavern can be read as a series of representations of the practice of literature, the

5. "Potatores exquisiti," vv. 26–28 (*CB* 644–46); the translation is my own.
6. *Hugh Primas and the Archpoet,* 118, stanza 18.

semiotic act par excellence. The fundamental "semioticity" of the Middle Ages has been widely noted.[7] Eugene Vance writes, for example: "The major thread of coherence in medieval culture was its sustained reflection . . . upon language as a semiotic system—more broadly, upon the nature, the functions and the limitations of the verbal sign as a mediator of human understanding."[8] While one might suggest that this was *a* major thread rather than "the major thread," I concur with the broad import of this statement, and it is certainly true in the case of the tavern. Over the last two to three decades, much attention has been paid to the changes in sign theory, and in hermeneutic models, within the medieval ecclesiastical context, from monastic symbolic reading through twelfth-century Neoplatonism to scholastic models of authority in the thirteenth century.[9] The relations between this evolution and the milieu of the tavern will be discussed more fully later. But in carefully reading the literature centered around the tavern, a more fundamental epistemic transition can be detected. While the changes between monastic and scholastic ideas on sign theory and hermeneutics play an important role within the history of medieval ecclesiastical culture, and of "high" culture in general, the tavern offers the point of entry for theories of the sign that were at least partly elaborated under the influence of urban, vernacular culture. An entire realm of social, economic, and semiotic practice that had previously lacked any representation in medieval culture found a voice in the High Middle Ages in the tavern, inn, and brothel. This domain not only offered new visions of the sign and its use but proposed a new "master signifier." In place of the linguistic sign that dominated ecclesiastical culture, the literature of the tavern proposed money and the coin—the central concern of urban, vernacular, mercantile culture—as the model through which all signs and their use

---

7. See Zumthor, *Speaking of the Middle Ages,* 30. See also in particular Gellrich, *The Idea of the Book;* Sturges, *Medieval Interpretation;* Nichols, *Romanesque Signs.* Indeed, the sign as a central thematic vehicle has motivated many of the most influential recent studies of medieval literature. See in addition Bloch, *Etymologies and Genealogies;* Burns, *Arthurian Fictions.*

8. Vance, *Mervelous Signals,* x.

9. Alastair J. Minnis' *The Medieval Theory of Authorship* is perhaps the clearest examination of the turn away from allegorical exegesis toward a greater emphasis on the literal meanings of texts and from divine to human intentions in those texts—a trend that dominated the twelfth century. See also Wetherbee, *Platonism and Poetry in the Twelfth Century,* and Chénu, *Nature, Man, and Society,* in particular the authors' remarks on Hugh of Saint Victor as an early exponent of the importance of the literal level of the Bible as the foundation of all other interpretation, and also in particular Chénu's discussion of the "evangelical awakening" (chap. 7).

could be conceived. Thus, for example, the model of the linguistic sign was used by the church to theorize the way monetary signs should work (which explains much of the difficulty with accommodating usury), while vernacular comico-realist literature used the potential profitability of the economic exchange as a model for the literary exchange of writer, text, and reader, even suggesting a model of hermeneutics based on the vagaries of the market. Thus an at least semipopular voice enters the medieval discourse of the sign for the first time and, in so doing, introduces a new form of cultural criticism and dissent into medieval life.

Situating the Rhetoric of Dissent in the High Middle Ages

While the tavern was a key medieval site of profit, play, and a new semiology, its status was complicated by the fact that it was also a key tool of religious writers for locating all that was evil in medieval society. It was used as an icon not only by the dissenters but by those against whom they dissented. As such, the tavern and its competing representations can be used as a model for understanding the more general interaction and competition of discourses in the Middle Ages and, most crucially, for their final interdependence.

In *Criticism and Dissent in the Middle Ages,* Rita Copeland rightly questions the scholarly tendency to formulate "monolithic" versions of the church and of clerical or monastic reading practices. She notes the way in which "stable ideological articulations" are often used as "backdrops" for readings that locate dissenting voices of multivocity in one or another text, and she criticizes the failure of historians to recognize dissent and critique as "inevitably constitutive of [the established] orders themselves." But at the same time, she notes that medieval representations of such stable ideologies could be seen as a "radical rhetorical effect" (2–3). The terms "rhetorical" and "radical" carry in them the notion of an agonistic confrontation, a confrontation that moreover involves not just a scholastic exercise in dialectic but a will to truly "dissent" and reform. Certainly modern readers should avoid blindly reconstituting such monoliths, as Copeland suggests. Yet the deeper question raised by these remarks is really, it seems to me, whether medieval dissent must always be read through a series of rhetorical effects.[10] These "effects" would act to consti-

---

10. Along with the semioticity of the Middle Ages, there is the widespread recognition of its "rhetoricity," particularly in one of the genres under discussion here, drama. See Enders, *Rhetoric and the Origins of Medieval Drama.*

tute a stable "ideology" against which they could then operate. However, they would also thereby constitute the grounds of their own resistance, as the original ("stable") ideology obliquely defines the alternative. Thus the clearest evidence of mutual constitution of discourses is perhaps to be found in the rhetorical effects.

This book is in a sense a study of one radical rhetoric—that of profit and play. In the interstices of the texts, however, this rhetoric constitutes its stable ideological opponent. That opponent, as will become clear, is epitomized in a Neoplatonic discourse of "charitable intentionality" elaborated initially by Saint Augustine and expanded by John Scotus Eriugena with his conception of the world as the Book of God, to be read in Christian terms.[11] The suggestion that all high medieval literature enacts a drama of charitable and cupidinous intention as part of an essential allegory of reading has been (rightly in my opinion) questioned in recent years. More recently, however, a number of scholars, most notably perhaps Stephen Nichols in *Romanesque Signs,* have stressed the wide extension in the eleventh and twelfth centuries of such general ideas as divine immanence in language, the notion of the sign as a utilitarian vehicle that should lead to extrinsic meaning rather than having any intrinsic value, and the importance of proper intention in order for signs to function effectively. But in contrast to D. W. Robertson, who argues for the dominance of Neoplatonic sacred exegesis to the extent that the drama of the text would be the choice of cupidity or charity, made within the framework of orthodox hermeneutics, Nichols underlines the importance of the possibility of a rival hermeneutics as the central implicit drama of many texts.[12] The representation of this possibility is itself, however, a "radical rhetorical effect" on the part of ecclesiastical writers. The hermeneutic rival is a devil that, once depicted, can be triumphantly slain in the end and revealed as a false ideology.

---

11. D. W. Robertson's *Preface to Chaucer* is perhaps the most famous study of the techniques of sacred exegesis as a cross-cultural medieval phenomenon. Of course there was no single "orthodox" hermeneutics, even in the twelfth century. Chénu, among others, has examined the vast differences between the Augustinian sign and the Pseudo-Dionysian symbol, for example (*Nature, Man, and Society,* 124–26). Yet at the same time, he notes certain dominant features of the interpretive thought of this century, all sharing basic Neoplatonic features (51–52). These include an opposition between the intelligible and sense-perceptible worlds, with the goal of humans being to move from the latter to the former, and eventually to God himself, via a fundamentally interpretive process (whether via signs or via symbols), with the assurance that this is possible due to the presence of the Creator in all reality.

12. Nichols, *Romanesque Signs,* 39.

Most important for our purposes, a key part of this particular "effect" in church moral and didactic writing was to define the tavern as the central locus of transgression against proper sacred hermeneutics in both its literal and metaphorical forms. One of the fundamental, entangling ironies of the medieval representation of the tavern is in fact that it began precisely as a locus of transgression, being defined as such within a broadly popular ecclesiastical discourse.

Certainly any attempt to arrive at broad characterizations of dominant social discourses is fraught with hazards. This book is not an attempt to examine the history of medieval Latin exegesis and sign theory in detail. Such debates, as many members of today's academy are aware, often go on more or less removed from the ongoing production of vernacular texts, even as the discussion inevitably filters into general cultural discourse (and is affected by it). Similarly, in the High Middle Ages there was a series of generalized cultural "commonplaces" and discourses located figuratively somewhere between the University of Paris and the local marketplace— fluid, dynamic, and varied certainly, but retrievable.[13] In fact, the tavern as antichurch finds its central role not in the most elevated levels of scholastic debate but in the world of vernacular texts, sociopolitical conflict, clerical or clerically educated secular authors trying to engage with diverse social elements, and "commonplace" cultural perceptions.[14] This is the level of culture where the complexities of the monastic, "scholastic," or "academic" debate often give way to more generalized and schematized representations, and it is in this space that the extension of certain commonplaces of a Neoplatonic sacred hermeneutics appear to reach their strongest extension into the domains of ethics, economics, and so forth, even as these ideas lost their dominance within the domain of medieval theology and philosophy.

Thus the tavern began its representational life as a rhetorical effect—an

---

13. My project here might be compared to that of Aron Gurevich in *Medieval Popular Culture,* where he seeks to study a popular religion that he calls a "vulgarized" version of Christianity (xiv). Here, however, I am less interested in the popular contaminations of official religion (Gurevich's principle concern) than in the way in which the official religion filtered into the secular world of the urban inhabitants.

14. For this reason, I have tried to choose Latin and religious writers who were of unquestioned centrality (i.e., Augustine), who had broad popularity throughout medieval ecclesiastical circles (Peter Lombard and Honorius d'Autun, to take two later examples), and/or who were closely engaged with contemporary social issues (in particular, Peter Cantor and his circle, active in northern France in the late twelfth and early thirteenth centuries, and closely studied by John Baldwin in *Masters, Princes, and Merchants*).

icon of transgressive ideology—which served in turn to obliquely reinforce a popular religious discourse of Augustinian charity. It was then appropriated by writers who were themselves most probably either clerics or at least clerically trained (Latin textual models lie at the base of several of the vernacular texts to be considered). It subsequently became the locus of a new semiotic practice that turned the tables by positing the "charitable" discourse as the stable ideology against which this new semiotic practice was elaborated. The end result was that the tavern became the site of a discursive knot, where secular economic practice in part shaped the scholastic discourses on usury, purgatory, and other issues, while Neoplatonic hermeneutic practices were used as extended models for the ethics and economics of the urban mercantile classes. In this light, the tavern is a key locus for examining the interpenetration of these discourses—for appreciating how sin began to be economically quantified such that purgatory could be viewed as a labor market, or for appreciating how the commonplaces of Neoplatonic sign theories were used to argue against the practice of speculative investment. In other words, the tavern was not just a locus of opposition. It was also the site where the confrontation of opposites was discursively played out. Clearly, this introduces a tension into the site of the tavern, which will run throughout this book. Is the tavern finally, fundamentally, a site of cultural resistance and dissent, distanced from that which it critiques, or a site both determining and determined by an engagement of discourses that defeat the final, full triumph of the new semiotic practices in question?

The fundamental implication of this question, and an important point of this book, is that the literature of the tavern is not the unadulterated voice of the market, nor does it engage directly with theoretical issues of theology and philosophy in a Robertsonian sense. I hope to escape the either-or trap of either insisting that medieval literature be read strictly in light of religious exegesis or conversely arguing for an overly secularized literature in an era when virtually every (literate) author had received clerical training and when the only vocabulary of the sign was that offered by the traditions of grammar and rhetoric as part of a fundamentally religious education. The tavern is really the privileged point of contact between the sacred and the secular, the Latin and the vernacular, the high culture of church philosophy and theology and the popular urban realities of markets and profit. Perhaps no other site in medieval literature is the focus of either so much moral didacticism and reprobation or so much gratuitous play. Its voice should be added to the voices of the church, the court, and the castle as a fundamental constituent of the culture and literature of the Middle Ages.

Contents

Chapter 1 of this book examines how the tavern was specifically determined within "charitable" literature as the central site of transgression against proper sacred hermeneutics, whether in economic, ethical, or literary terms. Jongleurs, after all, were the "ministri Satani" according to the twelfth-century cleric Honorius d'Autun,[15] and the tavern commonly gained the status of the "church of the devil." Chapter 1 offers a sense of the fundamental unity of the tavern as a conceptual space. Once this is accomplished, it is then possible to nuance the reading of the tavern and its characteristic activities in order to investigate how the generalized semiotic discourse can be reread in terms of the specifics of economics, ethics, and literature. In essence, chapter 1 examines the way in which diverse social, religious, and cultural issues are represented through the medium of the dominant discourse of sacred hermeneutics, as well as the ways in which the more specific discourses interact with (and are deformed by) this dominant one. Dice playing, for example, can be read not only in terms of a certain ludic poetics but as a metaphor for the economic practice of usury. It also raised important issues within the medieval religious ethics of utility and gratuity; and as figures of Fortune, dice pose important teleological issues. These were all important medieval issues of their own, not merely coded debates over signs and sign use. Yet each of these issues was addressed ultimately in terms of the sign.

Chapters 2–4 explore the ways in which this image of the tavern is appropriated in order to carry out a broad sociosemiotic rethinking. In these chapters, comico-realist literature can be seen as what might be called in Bakhtinian terms a protonovelistic space, a genre defined by its polygeneric and polydiscursive engagement with virtually every facet of medieval culture.[16] Chapter 2 begins with an exploration of general church views of profit and usury in the twelfth century. Then it focuses on *Le Jeu*

---

15. Faral, *Les jongleurs,* app. III, no. 29.

16. This polygeneric characteristic has been noted by Per Nykrog *(Les fabliaux)* for the fabliaux, and Jean-Claude Aubailly's study of medieval theater *(Le théâtre médiéval profane et comique)* strongly argues this point as well. Both approaches tend to see comic literature as largely "parasitic" (in a parodic sense) on other genres, however. I will argue for a more equal engagement, on a discursive as well as generic level.

de Saint Nicolas, examining the ways in which the play appropriates the previous representations of the tavern and ironically refigures it as a locus of positive economic and linguistic profit. When one customer remarks to the tavern keeper that he is certainly quick to "compter" but also to "mescompter" his affairs, playing on the Old French *(mes)compter* (to [mis]count) and *(mes)conter* (to [mis]recount a tale), he succinctly evokes the linguistic and monetary revaluations that are the central drama of the play.[17] This leads to a concept of usury as an economic, linguistic, and finally semiotic practice and suggests that the play may ultimately be read as an apology for this practice in both economic and poetic terms within the context of the urban market center of Arras, its place of origin. Chapter 2 also raises the issue of the "tavern piece" as a medieval genre of its own, whose development I follow through two centuries.

Chapter 3 starts with an examination of the semiotic status of the body within Neoplatonic orthodoxies. In that chapter, I am particularly interested in the female body (mostly in the person of prostitutes) as an especially problematic locus in medieval culture. I examine how the tavern, the brothel, and the female body serve to challenge medieval conceptions of specifically masculine authority, identity, and intentionality, while at the same time locating the origin of comico-realist literature in the linguistic "gaps" that render such masculine (according to the Middle Ages) conceptions of language so problematic. When Courtois d'Arras says, for example, in the play of the same name that he "can be identified by his purse" and assures that his word can be trusted because he "speaks with a full purse" (evoking a common medieval pun on the scrotum and testicles), what then are the full implications of the fact that he is robbed by two prostitutes, who propose a usurious economic deal to him in a language replete with double and triple entendres, some of which play on his own name and reduce it to a nominal commodity? (They remark that there appears to be much "courtoisie" in Courtois for example.)[18] I examine both prostitutes and usurers as comico-realist author figures. Chapter 3 concludes with a reading of certain fabliaux as part of a protocapitalist economy of the sign, where semiotic value does not lie in language per se

On a theoretical level, these remarks obviously evoke the work of Bakhtin. On a more applied level, Kathryn Gravdal's work on medieval parody *(Vilain and Courtois),* though not necessarily strictly Bakhtinian, offers an exemplary examination of parody as a creative rather than "destructive" phenomenon, as play rather than critique. This approach has influenced several of my readings.

17. Vv. 691–92 of Bodel, *Le Jeu de Saint Nicolas,* ed. Albert Henry (1981).

18. Vv. 88, 183–84, and 167, respectively, of *Courtois d'Arras.*

but is rather a function of the market exchanges of reading and writing that occur in the tavern. In this context, the tavern can be read as the actualizer or source of comico-realist literature itself.

In light of this emphasis on the sources of literary creativity, chapter 4 considers the rise of artistic subjectivity in the thirteenth century, in particular in the guise of ostensibly "autobiographical" forms of representation, and connects it to the phenomena of guilt culture, confession, and penitence. Through an examination of the figure of the fool and *folie,* which both Rutebeuf and Adam de la Halle locate in the tavern, I examine the limitations of such subjectivity. In fact, both poets ultimately reveal the semiotic bases for the impossibility of autobiography in the Middle Ages. Rutebeuf's claim that he begins his poetry with "povre estoire, povre sens et povre memoire" raises important issues regarding the potential inadequacy of language, authority, and self-identity, for example.[19] And by ending their texts with themselves trapped in the tavern, both poets suggest equally important limitations in the possibility of complete self-knowledge, penitence, and confession.

The conclusion examines the links between the tavern and the theater as metageneric locales of both cultural contestation and cultural play that nevertheless ironically refuse, in a kind of exemplary poststructuralist fashion, the possibility of disengagement from the discourses of the sign with which both genres engage and play. As such, tavern and theater extend the limits of medieval subjectivity into the broader realm of language and culture as a whole, suggesting the limits of cultural contestation and dissent in the Middle Ages.

I add a final remark about my own methodology in this book. Though I have used the word *semiotic* on several occasions in this introduction, this word should be taken simply as the adjective of the noun *sign* and not in the context of any narrowly understood branch of "semiotics" per se (Sausurrean, Piercean, etc.). I am in fact interested less in classical semiotic theory than in the relation of literature and culture in the High Middle Ages. While it so happens that the sign constituted the master discourse of this particular culture (whether in its linguistic or economic manifestations), this is not always the case. For example, for the aristocratic/oral subculture of medieval Europe that produced the early epic, I would suggest that the body, not the sign, constituted the "master discourse," to the

---

19. Vv. 9–10 of "La griesche d'yver" (*OC* I:184–89).

extent that this term is applicable.[20] Thus I view the generalized social priority of hermeneutic models in the Middle Ages as a historically contingent phenomenon. A second term that I use in this book is *semiology,* by which I mean not the French equivalent of "semiotics" but rather a particular ideology of the sign; thus the early High Middle Ages feature a Neoplatonic semiology, for example. Note that the semiology describes not actual sign use from a modern linguistic perspective but rather the normative ideological representation of sign use by the culture itself.

Beyond the sign, my interest is in one specific literary and historical moment in medieval history and in one subset of that moment as found in the tavern and in comico-realist literature. Throughout the book, I seek to identify precisely some of the sociohistorical factors that determined the use of the tavern as an emblem of cultural and epistemic evolution. The book thus attempts to offer a kind of archaeology of the tavern and of comico-realism that is finally an archaeology of profit and play in the Western tradition.

A note on translations: Due to the varying style and quality of the translations available for the texts discussed in the book, I have chosen to provide my own translations for passages cited in the original. All translations may be assumed to be by me except where translated editions are listed in the bibliography.

---

20. It is in this sense that my approach in this book differs from that of Jean-Joseph Goux, who has perhaps gone the farthest in theorizing the link between language and money, and more generally in suggesting that all exchanges in society are fundamentally homologous (see *Freud, Marx*). While I am also interested in homologous structures, I suggest that these are as much representational strategies as historically determined results of modes of production and exchange. Goux himself recognizes the historically contingent nature of the particular "matière" that constitutes the privileged sign of exchange ("chef, phallus, langue, monnaie," 101), but he insists that each functions fundamentally as a monetary symbol (98). Thus "argent" (as opposed to "monnaie," the physical coin) lies always at the base of the isomorphic exchanges that he examines. I do not agree either that the monetary symbol is always the "master signifier" of social exchange or that there is one such single, transhistorical master signifier. This book is more a study of why one such signifier was chosen at one particular moment.

There is actually an amazing amount of isomorphism between Marxism, especially as expressed by Goux in relation to Freudianism, and medieval monastic and scholastic thought on economics, sign theory, and the body.

Chapter 1

Charity, Hospitality, and Profit

Miracle and Condemnation: The Church and the Tavern

This chapter examines the important place of the tavern within the iconography of medieval moral discourse. It also argues that this place is an expression of the deeper semiotic status of the tavern. For this reason, I would like to begin this chapter with an examination of one particular miracle narrative that exemplifies the tavern's status within medieval representations of proper hermeneutics as they appeared in a popular, vernacular context.

The text with which I wish to begin is by an author named Jean le Marchant.[1] In *Le livre des miracles de Notre-Dame de Chartres,* the twentieth miracle tale in the narrative relates the story of two companions, "dont l'un fust gari et l'autre non" (of whom one was cured and the other not). One of the two is described as "aveugle" (blind), though the tale reveals him to be one-eyed, while the other is unable to hear or speak. The one-eyed man is a "lecheor" (lecher), "mauparlier" (ill-speaker), and "jangleor" (jongleur), and one day for a joke—a "borde," for he is also "bordierres"—he decides to challenge the supposed power of Our Lady of Chartres. He proposes to the mute man that they go to Chartres on a short pilgrimage to try and be cured. We are informed that "cil le dist par derision; / Li autre o bone entencion / les dis dou gabeor recut" (this one said it derisively; The other with good intention heard the joker's words) (113). On arriving at Chartres, the mute man hurries off to the church with the best of intentions, to pray for his cure.

---

1. Jean [Jehan] le Marchant, *Le livre des miracles de Notre-Dame de Chartres,* 112–19. I am indebted to Howard Bloch for bringing this text to my attention.

La langue mue se tesoit
Mes la foi qui au cor pleisoit
Oureit et la bone pensee
Qui ert dedens le cor celee.

(116)

[His silent tongue was quiet
But the faith that pleased the heart
Did its work and (revealed) the good thoughts
That were hidden in the heart.]

Meanwhile the one-eyed "menestrel"

de boivre estoit plus curieus
Et de hanas de vin voier. . . .
si que tantout com il vint la
Tot droit en la taverne ala
Si com toz jours fere soloit.

(115)

[was more interested in drinking
and in emptying cups of wine . . .
so that as soon as he arrived in town
he went straight to the tavern
as he was accustomed to doing every day.]

The mute man, thanks to his faith, devotion, and good intentions, does in fact receive his voice back. However, with it comes an overwhelming sensation of pain and nausea, and he races out the front door of the church. A bystander asks him what is the matter, and he relates that when his tongue was first returned to him, he was afraid that "le cuer ne li menti" (his heart might lie to him) (117). Upon confessing this fact, his pain disappears and he is completely cured. The whole town goes running to see the miracle, and news of it reaches the one-eyed jongleur, still tossing down drinks in the tavern. Impressed by the unexpected cure, he hurries off to the church as well, to pray for his own cure, but since "il ne pria fors que de bouche" (he only prayed with his mouth) (119), his prayers remain unanswered.

This miracle clearly enacts a conflict between the church and the tavern.

Yet the full implications of one aspect of the conflict—the fact that the two men are pilgrims—is not immediately apparent. In reality, the tavern and particularly the inn are represented in numerous medieval texts as being the locale where the pilgrim is victimized at the figurative expense of the church. Such victimization reached the point that in 1205 the city of Toulouse felt obliged to pass a statute specifically to protect pilgrims from the rapacity of tavern keepers and innkeepers. These overaggressive merchants were warned to stop forcing pilgrims to enter their establishments by seizing them by their clothes or by seizing their horses' reins. The merchants were not allowed to lock pilgrims in the inns once they had entered or to compel them to buy their food and drink only from the inns where they were sequestered.[2]

The church, of course, offered free lodging to pilgrims (and indeed to all travelers) at monasteries along the pilgrimage routes. The rivalry between free hospitality, especially for pilgrims, and commercial lodging ultimately reached iconic status in medieval texts, as representative of a larger conflict between a ritualistic economics of Christian charity and noble gift giving, on the one hand, and an economics of profit, on the other, with the tavern becoming the icon of a new profit-oriented urban economy. The choice, on the part of the pilgrims, between tavern and church in this miracle story is thus symbolic of an entire cultural confrontation and will be considered more fully later in this chapter.

The inn and the profit motive are expressions of a larger medieval weakening of religious, class, and finally textual communities in favor of an individual search for profit. The simultaneous breakdown of religious and textual community is thematized in the miracle story by the fact that though the one-eyed minstrel intends his remarks as a blasphemous joke, they are entirely misunderstood by the pious deaf-mute. As the tale of the miracle opens, there is neither communication nor community, only the potential of winners and losers in a tricky game of individual competition.

A second salient point of note is that the tavern is particularly opposed to the church in its resolute carnality. The "bons vins" (good wines) are described as "clers, seins, nes et delicieus" (clear, healthy, sharp, and delicious). The "lecheor, glouton et beveor" (lecher, glutton, and drinker) is unconcerned to "voair" (see) virtue, as the text plays on his blindness. But at the same time he is a devotee of the mouth as an organ of carnality: "Car trop avoit la bouche tendre / de bons vins et de bons morsiaus" (For

---

2. See Henri Gilles, "Lex Peregrinorum."

he had a very tender mouth accustomed to good wines and tasty morsels) (115). The mouth rather than the heart is triumphant, and with it the flesh rather than the spirit. The bad pilgrim is blind to God's intellectual light. The tavern is also clearly a world of illicit desire—of the antiutilitarian, gratuitous enjoyment that Saint Augustine, for example, finds so objectionable. "'Cupidity' is the motion of the soul toward the enjoyment of one's self" (*DDC* III.x.16), Augustine writes, and the jongleur is clearly out to enjoy himself, "curieus" (desirous) to drink all that he can.

Such a representation of the tavern as not only economically but morally antithetical to the church is common in the Middle Ages. In *Courtois d'Arras,* a dramatization of the parable of the prodigal son, Courtois exclaims in the tavern, at the height of his prodigality, "Or Dieus i viegne et Dieus i soit! / Caiens fait plus biel k'an mostier" (Now let God come here and let him remain here! In here it's more beautiful than in a church) (vv. 124–25). In a famous exemplum about Saint Louis, it is related that a particular tavern was directly across the street from the church and that people often left the church to go and drink at the tavern, so that Saint Louis was forced to issue edicts against the tavern.[3] Here, as in the miracle story already discussed, the tavern is elevated to the status of a general locus of the carnal and the sinful—on the road to hell rather than to paradise.

Though *Courtois d'Arras* uses the tavern and brothel to pose fundamental moral questions concerning guilt and salvation, the moral rivalry between church and tavern is pursued in a more humorous vein in "Le Credo au ribaut," where the "ribaud," or scoundrel, states, "Creatorem qui tant cria / ai renoié . . . Mes tant com je poi m'acordai / A la taverne et au vin cler" (I have rejected the creator who created so much . . . but as much as I could I followed the tavern and fine wine).[4] These texts echo a third important detail of Jean le Marchant's miracle in that the "bordeor" or "jongleur," and by extension the literature associated with these figures, is situated in the tavern. Jean's miracle serves to locate at least some literature, as well as food and wine, in the realm of carnal desire.

In fact, another of Jean's terms for the jongleur is "lecheor." The term captures in its very etymology the two natures of the jongleur as both illicit consumer of wine and illicit composer of verse: it derives from Germanic sources and most immediately from the Frankish *lekkon,* meaning "to lick." The term nicely combines the orality of gluttonous consumption

3. Le Goff, *Your Money or Your Life,* 14.

4. Barbazon, *Fabliaux et contes,* 4:445, vv. 65–66, 70–71.

with the orality of medieval poetry and gives deeper resonance to Jean's concentration on the mouth, eating, drinking, and the sense of taste in the tavern. Thus the carnality so characteristic of the tavern extends not just to the enjoyment of the body but also to the enjoyment of the sign, recalling Saint Augustine's remark that "it is a carnal slavery to adhere to a usefully instituted sign instead of the thing it was designed to signify" (*DDC* III.vii.11). Among the spiritually useless things Augustine mentions, interestingly enough, is mimetic art (II.xxv.39). If the tavern is the antichurch, or the church of the devil, then the jongleurs "sunt ministri Satanae" (are the ministers of Satan), in the words of the twelfth-century cleric Honorius d'Autun, and "ideo Deus sprevit eos . . . quia derisores deridentur" (God scorns them so . . . in order to mock those who mock others).[5]

The semiology of the tavern involves ultimately an idolatry of the sign—not used to represent and to communicate socially, but rather revalued and commodified for the sake of private gain, at community expense. The tavern and the church are the two sides of a semiotic dichotomy of prayer and transgression. Though the specific conjunction of economic, poetic, and moral discourses expressed in the literature of the tavern is unique, the larger dichotomy of proper and improper uses of the sign that they address was a dominant intellectual feature of the High Middle Ages. The "official" or "ordained" semiology of the Catholic Church at this time, while never entirely unitary, was nevertheless in its basic outlines an inheritance from Saint Augustine, and his *De doctrina Christiana,* from which I have already quoted, can be taken as the single best exemplar of this semiology. Jean's miracles can in fact be read as a rewriting of the *De doctrina Christiana* in which Jean allows Augustine to address the semiotic menace of the tavern.

Though both Augustine and medieval theorists realized that language could potentially become disseminatory and refuse stable meaning, they offered a normative Neoplatonic theory of the operation of the sign that could in principle prevent this possibility, at least in sacred contexts.[6] In fact, Jean's miracle enacts such a normative process of communication—more specifically, that which has been termed "theosis" by Stephen

---

5. Honorius d'Autun *Elucidarium* MII.58, in Kleinhans, *Lucidere,* 476.

6. See Sturges, *Medieval Interpretation,* 6ff. The concept of a normative, prescriptive semiology is very important, for it is in this normative prescription, rather than in actual practice, that much of the unity of "proper semiology" lies. For the implications of this within the educational system, see Irvine, *The Making of Textual Culture,* 49, 55–57, 88–91, 118–21, 160–61, and see also Suzanne Reynolds' recent argument that this factor was a fundamental determinant of glossing in the thirteenth century (*Medieval Reading*).

Nichols. Nichols has examined the process of theosis specifically in the context of a Romanesque-era response to "the spectre of a rival hermeneutics," but the concept is not limited to this period. Theosis is actually the general response of Augustine to the same basic problem—how to guarantee correct reading in the face of signs that allow for multiple interpretations.[7] As elaborated in his *De doctrina Christiana,* his response involves communication governed by divine grace and human charity, such that correct intention is guaranteed and truthful communication can occur: "Rooted and founded in charity, we may be able to comprehend, with all the saints, what is the breadth, and length, and height, and depth, which things make up the Cross of Our Lord," writes Augustine (*DDC* II.xli.62).[8] However, Nichols' examination of the specific enactment of theosis in medieval texts of the eleventh century is especially relevant to this narrative. Augustine had noted that "by following certain traces [the reader] may come to the hidden sense without any error" (prologue.9). In medieval texts, according to Nichols, proper communication signals its authenticity by the presence of three such traces: "the speaker's struggle to intellectualize divinity" (i.e., to have an understanding of God that transcends the limits of sensory experience and the expressions of carnal signs); "an image of that struggle in some form or another"; and a "condition of discourse [that] is based upon a triad of . . . subjects"—the speaker, God, and a human addressee, where God's grace and the listener's charity constitute the theosis.[9]

In Jean's miracle, the good pilgrim's struggle to intellectualize divinity is in fact already accomplished for him by his muteness; his own expression and knowledge of God are framed not in terms of the carnal signs of the voice but in the silent understanding of the heart. He accepts his fellowman's proposal (offered through gestures, emphasizing the corporeal nature of the signs) with the best of divinely oriented charitable intentions, just as Augustine argues that we must assume that the interpretation of any difficult statement conforms to the content of the Scriptures (*DDC* III.x.14). But more importantly, he is himself able to surpass any corporeal expression of faith, in words or images, due to his "devocion pure et fine." As we saw earlier, the tongue is silent while he communicates "par-

7. Nichols, *Romanesque Signs,* 11 (theosis), 39 (rival hermeneutics).

8. See *DDC* II.xlii.63 for a more detailed description of the process of preparing to read, as detailed by Augustine, and for the fundamental role of "charity" or goodwill in the reader for proper interpretation of spiritual texts, particularly the Bible.

9. Nichols, *Romanesque Signs,* 39.

feitement" with God "de cuer verai qui pas ne ment" (with a true heart that does not lie) (*Le livre des miracles de Notre-Dame de Chartres,* 116). His prayer to God is purely intellectual.

Yet upon receiving his voice, he is plunged into the world of the corporeal sign and faces a struggle to reintellectualize God. The voice becomes an automatic, carnal temptation to lose the theotic relationship with God, a relationship that has been symbolized by the grace of the miracle. This gift of God actually reenacts on a smaller scale God's gift of the body to humans at the time of creation, for the Creation is the moment when he plunges all humans into the temptations of the flesh, including those of the sign, which is specific to "living creatures" who are carnal and mortal (*DDC* II.iii.3). The struggle of the good pilgrim to continue to intellectualize divinity is represented in the "enmerteur" (pain) that he now feels in his mouth, "don la douleur au cuer tocha" (whose pain touched his heart) (*Le livre des miracles de Notre-Dame de Chartres,* 117)—the carnal threatens the soul ("le cuer"). The pilgrim, like Augustine, recognizes the degraded nature of the flesh and of the sign—itself a form of the flesh—and their potential for abuse.[10] Ironically, because of the miracle, the pilgrim can now use the carnal sign to thank God for his grace but for other purposes as well, and accordingly we are told that "la douleur le tint einsi qu'il ot poour qu'il ne vomist" (the pain was so great that he feared he might vomit) (116). The mouth can now, potentially, literally pour forth degraded carnality into the sanctity of God's realm, the church. In a sense, the pilgrim is invaded from within by the contamination that is symbolized by the tavern. Not only do tavern-frequenting jongleurs pour forth "degraded" literary creation, but the gluttony and drunkenness of the tavern are the more typical producers of nausea.

The pilgrim flees from the church, followed by the human addressee who will complete the triad of theosis. This man can be identified as sharing in the spirit of charity necessary for communication, since he issues forth from the church, listens sympathetically to the miracle's "hero," and immediately recognizes the status of the event as a miracle. He asks the pilgrim why he has fled, and the pilgrim responds, primarily to God but secondarily to the man, that he felt the "enmerteur"

---

10. Augustine notes, "In order that what we are thinking may reach the mind of the listener through fleshly ears, that which we have in mind is expressed in words and called speech" (*DDC* I.xii.12). The word may then be further carnally embodied in the letter (*DDC* II.iv.5), and Augustine argues, "nor can anything more appropriately be called the death of the soul than that condition in which the thing that distinguishes us from beasts, which is the understanding, is subjected to the flesh in the pursuit of the letter" (*DDC* III.v.9).

Qu'a poi le cuer ne li menti.
Vomir cuida [en es le pas].
Et por ce qu'il ne vouloit pas
Que si hau lieu seintefiez
Fust ordaiez ne conchiez
De vomissement ne d'ordure,
Porce toust et grant aleure
De l'iglise hors s'en issi.

(117)

[Such that his heart almost lied to him.
He thought he would vomit then and there.
And since he did not wish
That such a sacred place
Be soiled or stained
By vomit or filth,
For this reason as fast as he could
He ran out of the church.]

Though the tongue has almost led the heart to lie, he affirms before both God and this witness his desire not to allow his tongue, "de novelle char" (of new flesh) (117), to be used for degradation, and the pain vanishes. He is then able to return into the church and verbally give his thanks to God and the Virgin without pain or worry. Augustine insists that "the things that are to be enjoyed are the Father, the Son, and the Holy Spirit" (*DDC* I.v.5) and that "charity" is "the motion of the soul toward the enjoyment of God" (III.x.16). All other things, including signs, are to be used only in facilitating this enjoyment of God (I.xxii.20), and "if we who enjoy and use things . . . wish to enjoy those things that should be used, our course will be impeded and sometimes deflected, so that we are retarded . . . or even prevented altogether, shackled by an inferior love" (I.iii.3). The pilgrim successfully resists the temptation to enjoy his newfound speech, instead putting it to immediate use praising God. Thanks to God's immanent presence in speaker, listener, and the world as a whole, correct interpretation and communication are assured, both in the success of the good pilgrim's prayers and in the failure of those of the bad one.

This miracle is hardly alone in the Middle Ages in its representation of the dominant Romanesque (pre-twelfth-century) medieval theory of the sign as a purely utilitarian, telementational vehicle. That is, the sign possesses no value in and of itself, but serves always to refer beyond itself to a transcendental referent, the idea of which it "transports" from the mind of the speaker to that of the listener.[11] Nor is it unique in its representation of the necessity of charity (good public intentions) for proper communication with humans and God or in its insistence on the need for humans to avoid all "superfluous" carnal and earthly elements that do not lead to the enjoyment of God. This same consecrated semiology is represented over and over in medieval texts, and indeed the very cultural and literary omnipresence of this semiology explains its detailed elaboration and the ability of writers of widely varying quality and intellectual preparation to make use of the complex thematics that surround it in such profound and effective ways.

Yet all is not well in the miracle—as the need for a "miracle" itself points out. Implicitly, the miracle raises the question of whether intentionality in language can always be guaranteed. Are all men of good intention to be potentially victimized by the "bordes" of a tavern-frequenting "janglior mauparlié" (if not for the continued immanence of God), and how can the "Truth" be determined? As noted earlier, the action of the miracle is initiated by a joke that is intended to deceive the mute man. In the end, however, the seemingly deceived victim profits despite this fact. Thus he could be taken as an example of Augustine's scriptural reader who,

> if he is deceived in an interpretation which builds up charity, which is the end of the commandments, he is deceived in the same way as a man who leaves a road by mistake but passes through a field to the same place toward which the road itself leads. But he is to be corrected and shown that it is more useful not to leave the road, lest the habit of deviating force him to take a crossroad or a perverse way. (*DDC* I.xxxvi.40)

The miracle can be seen in this light as a lesson on proper "reading" for the audience of the miracle text, whether it is read or heard. It is the map illuminating the road to the church and away from the tavern. Yet there is a

---

11. "Conventional signs are those that living creatures show to one another for the purpose of conveying, insofar as they are able, the motions of their spirits or something that they have sensed or understood. And there is not any other reason for signifying, or for giving signs, except for bringing forth and transferring to another mind the action of the mind in the person who makes the sign" (*DDC* II.ii.3). The system of signs exists so that "by means of corporal and temporal things, we may comprehend the eternal and spiritual" (*DDC* I.iv.4). "No one should consider them [signs] for what they are but rather for their value as signs that signify something else" (*DDC* II.i.1).

recognition of the deviant path—of a mode of reading by the mute man or of writing by the jongleur and of general behavior—which is posited as counter to Augustine's theosis and thus as anti-Platonic. Jean's miracle raises the specter of the competition that moved Augustine to write the *De doctrina Christiana* and of which Nichols speaks—the general turning away from charity toward individual indulgence for individual enjoyment and profit. The existence of such an anti-Platonic semiology within the minds of medieval thinkers—that is, the representation of a choice between two dichotomous paths—is an important feature of medieval thought. Clearly, the suggestion that all medieval society truly exhibited one of two basic semiologies, or that its literature exhibited one of two basic poetics, is untenable. A close reading of medieval literature will reveal a multiplicity of poetics, and it must be recognized that all literature exhibits the fundamental poetic characteristics that are represented as illicit in the Middle Ages. Yet it seems that medieval thinkers and authors like Alain de Lille themselves thought in terms of such broad poetics.

We have already seen that Augustine wrote of "deviation" and "deflection" from one's "course." The influential twelfth-century cleric Alain de Lille, in *De planctu Naturae,* states that Nature has given the writing pen to Venus so that

> She might trace the classes of things, according to the rules of my orthography, on suitable pages that called for writing by this same pen . . . so that she might not suffer the same pen to wander in the smallest degree from the path of proper delineation into the byways of pseudography. (*DPN* 156)

Despite this hope, he finds it necessary to "excommunicate from the schools of Venus certain practices of Grammar and Dialectic" (162). Clearly many poets, like the "menestrel" of our miracle, have strayed from the pilgrim's (the believer's) correct path, wandering to the tavern on their way to the church. In fact, in the *De planctu Naturae,* Nature finds it necessary to cause the poet to vomit forth his own fantasies and desires in order to purify him for his role as her secretary (157). The image echoes exactly the nausea felt by the ex-mute in Jean's miracle.

The miracle thus enacts in the tavern and the church a vision of sign usage dominated by carnal intentions in one case, divinely oriented in the other. It also establishes the tavern as both locus and source of carnal desires and intentions and suggests that these desires are themselves intimately associated with the carnal idolatry of the sign that constitutes literature as practiced by the jongleur. Indeed, the initial joke of the jongleur—which seems to be simply an excuse to go to Chartres and visit the tavern—can be read as the very incarnation of the transgressive literary act, specifically the comico-realist act. The joke certainly contains an explicit challenge to divine authority. Yet in the very nature of the speech act in question—the use of language not for sincere communication but for the production of gratuitous amusement—the Joke embodies all that was supposedly wrong with the practice of literature in the eyes of high medieval moralists. The same joker, or jongleur, is either implicitly or explicitly the focus of the many comico-realist texts considered in this book, and literature—as far as it is associated with the tavern—becomes the single dominant semiotic transgression at stake in these texts. The tavern is the place where one intends to play with signs.

Indeed the tavern in many cases is representative of the place where divine immanence is lacking. It is used to enact many of the same dramatizations of fears—but also celebrations—of the loss of immanence that romance texts portray in the crisis of the judicial oath and combat, most notably in Isolde's famous ordeal scene. In the largest sense, the tavern is used to address—and contest—the place of God in medieval language and society. In the majority of the texts considered in this book, the jongleur, however, not the pilgrim, emerges triumphant. And with the jongleur's triumph comes that of the merchant and investor as well.

The Gift of Hospitality and Social Class

While "charity" was an important concept within medieval hermeneutic discourse, it was also a central element of the economic thinking of the church. And if the practice of charity is broadened to the general realm of the "gift," then it was central to the medieval aristocracy as well. In both the aristocratic and church setting, the gift of lodging played an important role. Yet the tavern and inn arose as an alternative form of lodging in the High Middle Ages. In fact, in the context of medieval economic discourse, these institutions came to occupy a place quite similar to that occupied within the hermeneutic discourse. They were emblems of the rejection of ritualistic charity in favor of personal profit and desire for the sign (of money). This rejection was first criticized (in the texts considered in this section) but was later valorized as well.

Arriving in a medieval city, the first place one would seek out might well have been the tavern, functioning as an inn.[12] Often it was simply a private home or series of adjacent private homes converted to a new use. A main room on the lower level served for reception of guests, eating and drinking, cooking, and so forth. A series of bedrooms occupied the upper levels, each equipped with several beds, each bed in turn accommodating two or more people. The establishment might contain a single room with only a couple of beds as an adjunct to a private house or might hold up to forty beds. There would also typically have been a stable and a warehouse for the goods of traveling merchants. The tavern keepers were often foreigners in the town and often catered particularly to foreigners from their own homeland. Each inn or tavern was equipped with a sign called an *enseigne,* typically with a particular animal or plant, a sword, a cart, or any number of other emblems depicted on it. Finally, both ancient and medieval taverns often featured a branch or bunch of foliage outside them for identification. However, one would probably have been lucky to have the leisure to search out these emblems, because the tavern keeper or a hired crier would have often been outside, enticing in clients or dragging them in by the cloak if necessary. Jean Bodel's *Le Jeu de Saint Nicolas* offers an example.

> Le vin aforé de nouvel,
> A plain lot et a plain tonnel,
> Sade, bevant, et plain et gros,
> Rampant comme escuireus en bos,
> Sans nul mors de pourri ne d'aigre.
> Seur lie court et sec et maigre,
> Cler con larme de pecheour;
> Croupant seur langue a lecheour;
> Autre gent n'en doivent gouster.
>
> (vv. 649–57)

> [Wine newly opened in its cask,
> Glassesful and barrelsful,
> Smooth, tasty, full and strong,
> Running like a squirrel in the woods,
> With no trace of rot or sourness.
> It runs dry and heady,

---

12. The most complete work on the inn in the European Middle Ages is Peyer, *Gastfreundschaft, Taverne und Gasthaus.*

Clear like the tears of a sinner;
Crouching on the tongue of the gourmand;
No one else should have a taste.]

Of course there would have probably been a monastery or *hospitalium* too, where charitable monks offered food and lodging for free. The choice was between charitable hospitality and the profit seekers. (Henceforth in this book, I will use the term *hospitality* to refer specifically to the offering of free lodging and provisions without expectation of compensation in any form. The equivalent, often encountered German term in the literature is *Gastfreundschaft.*)

Saint Augustine, in *De doctrina Christiana,* understands cupidity and charity as fundamental models of general conduct, not just of textual interpretation.[13] He sees correct reading as simply a subset of correct ethical comportment, and he considers reading, writing, and communication in general to be fundamentally ethical acts. This view is really not surprising, since Augustine sees the sign as a fundamentally social product (see *DDC* II.ii.3, II.xxiv.37) and as a telementational vehicle for the exchange of ideas within society. In his view, linguistic communication is only one among many forms of social interactions and exchanges, all of which are governed by the general ethical principles of charity: economics is another. This was particularly true for the Cistercians, whose spiritual and temporal life was essentially organized around the concept of "caritas."[14] The twelfth century, which is the focus of this chapter, was in many ways the Cistercian century, and Cistercian culture developed in many of the same areas of northeastern France as did the vernacular comico-realist tradition. (The later chapters focus more on the thirteenth century and on the influence of canon law, urban preaching, and the mendicant friars.) The broad influence of concepts of charity and community in Christian thought of this century owes much to the Cistercians. Their exegetical practice was fundamentally Augustinian and, especially as applied to the Song of Songs, held crucial importance for the formation of community.[15] At the same time, their economic ideals, if not always their practice, were

---

13. He notes that "Scripture teaches nothing but charity nor condemns anything except cupidity" (*DDC* III.x.15).

14. See Newman, *Boundaries of Charity;* Bynum, *Jesus as Mother,* especially 59–81.

15. On their Augustinianism, see Newman, *Boundaries of Charity,* 82–83; on the general Augustinian roots of monastic exegesis of the twelfth century, see Chénu, *Nature, Man, and Society.* On the formation of Cistercian textual community, see Stock, *The Implications of Literacy,* especially 405–8, 451–54.

founded on charity as well. Thus many of the ideas attributed in this chapter to the medieval church as a whole have a more properly Cistercian—and secondarily, Benedictine—coloring, though none are limited to these groups only.

It should be noted that the term *charity* is used here not to designate the actual practice of economic exchange in the early High Middle Ages but for the medieval representation of proper economic activity as inherited from biblical, patristic, and other sources.[16] As an idealizing, normative construction, it corresponds in many ways to Neoplatonic sign theory. Despite this concern with idealizing constructions, this section of this chapter will also isolate certain elements of social reality to elucidate the socioeconomic bases for the specific cultural and literary representation of the tavern. It was, in fact, chosen as an icon of the entire profit economy because of its dominant position in that developing economy. In particular, its position in the lodging "industry" thrust it into direct conflict with the Catholic Church in a way not characteristic of other business activities.

As the Bible says, Mary and Joseph laid Jesus in a manger "because there was no place for them in the inn" (Luke 2:7). The very birth of Christianity inaugurates the opposition between the church and the inn and tavern, though in reality medieval (and many modern) readers seem to have misunderstood the actual sense of the text.[17] The story of the Good Samaritan is one of the great exemplars of charity in the Bible, yet while the Samaritan ministers freely to the victim found by the roadside, he must provide payment to an innkeeper to continue the care once he goes on his way (Luke 10:30–37).

While such biblical stories must have exercised an influence on medieval readers, there appears to have been little or no actual continuity between the taverns of the Greco-Roman era and the lodging alternatives that arose in the Middle Ages. However, the terminology of the ancient institutions, as well their representation in various literary and historical texts, exercised a strong influence on the medieval conception of the inn and tavern and on their representation in the Middle Ages.

The Greeks had a two-tiered lodging system based on class distinctions, which was mirrored in the Middle Ages. Ancient Rome shared a similar

---

16. The Cistercians offer a good example of this phenomenon. Much recent work has revealed that their representation of their economic practice was often an after-the-fact idealization and that they were heavily involved in the market economy. See Newman, *Boundaries of Charity,* especially chap. 3; Bouchard, *Holy Entrepreneurs.*

17. See Hiltbrunner, "Gastfreundschaft and Gasthaus in der Antike."

system, with the wealthy and noble being welcomed into the households of their peers and provided for as members of the family in a *Gastfreund-schaft* system, while others paid an innkeeper for their lodging in locales known as *cauponae* or *tabernae*.[18]

These institutions were rarely highly regarded. They were typically associated with such social vices as drunkenness, prostitution, and gambling. Theodosius simply equates the inn with prostitution, and any woman associated with an inn was automatically assumed to be a prostitute. In fact, Roman laws excluded all women who lived or worked in inns from the laws against prostitution, thus marginalizing them and their locale, placing it outside the scope of society's normal rules. The innkeeper himself was likewise excluded from the strictures and protection of normal civil law. During the excavation of Pompeii, an inn was unearthed whose walls still bore the paintings with which they were decorated. The four walls featured depictions of prostitution, gambling, drinking, and a brawl, respectively. Thus ancient and medieval images of the inn and tavern tended to thematize virtually the same features, which tended to place the institutions in a morally dubious light.[19]

A second reason for the inn's low regard was that it was seen as prostituting hospitality in the name of avarice. This view must certainly have been strengthened by the very existence of the two-tiered, class-based sys-

---

18. See Hiltbrunner, "Gastfreundschaft and Gasthaus in der Antike." Wealthy private citizens *(xenokdos)* lodged higher-class visitors free of charge and provided them with all the necessities, so that the guests were considered part of the household during their stay. The less highly considered *pandokeus* was obliged to accept anyone who demanded lodging, and he in turn demanded payment. The *pandokeion* was in effect a commercial inn, used by those lacking the status or social connections necessary to benefit from hospitality.

Neither of the terms *taberna* and *caupona* made a distinction between a place simply to drink and a place to spend the night, though the latter could be explicitly indicated by the term *taberna deversoria* (Hiltbrunner, op. cit., 12). In both ancient and medieval eras, it is often impossible to distinguish the two through the terms used by a given source (if there even is a source).

It does seem, however, as a general rule, that there were several times more establishments offering only drink and food as compared to the number offering lodging. See, for example, Hiltbrunner, op. cit., 13, which gives a ratio of 6 to 1 for Pompeii, and see Clark, *The English Alehouse*, which comes to similar conclusions for medieval Britain.

Around the time of Cicero, in an effort to euphemize their profession, innkeepers adopted the terms *hospes* and *hospitium* as well, which originally applied only to free hospitality (Hiltbrunner, op. cit., 13). In addition, the terms *deversorium* and *stabulum* were sometimes used.

19. The Code of Hammurabi refers to a place that was either a tavern or brothel or perhaps both, the lack of distinction being perhaps the most revealing feature of the reference (White, *Palaces*, 2). See White, *Palaces*, 18 (on Theodosius), 24 (on Roman law and Pompeii).

tem. Plato attacked commercial lodges for this reason in the second book of his laws. The text is interesting because it speaks consistently of three activities: "retail trade, commerce, and inn keeping."[20] Plato thus gives inn keeping a relatively high profile position in the spectrum of all commercial activity, far more so than would be the case today. The passage under discussion here is actually a general attack on commerce of all types; yet Plato chooses later in the discussion to single out the innkeeper as exemplary of the most emblematic and egregious abusers of the profit motive, for "instead of treating [guests] as comrades and providing friendly gifts . . . [the innkeeper] holds them ransom."[21] While the Bible elevates the inn to the antithesis of charitableness, Plato elevates it to a general symbol of the commercial profit motive. The tavern and inn thus came to the Middle Ages already heavily weighted with ideological implications, of which Plato's *Laws* are simply one example.

The social and material conditions of the medieval institution were probably at least as important in explaining its literary and social image as any scandalous reputation drawn from ancient sources. (To this point, I have tended to speak of "inns" and "taverns." Terminological difficulties are a major problem in this area of historical study.[22] Henceforth, I will use *tavern* as a general, neutral term where an aforementioned distinction

---

20. Plato *Laws* II.xi.918.

21. Plato *Laws* II.xi.919. Aristotle of course also was partially hostile to commerce in general, including inn keeping, and in the *Politics* he denies full citizenship to those who practice arts and crafts (*Politics* VII.1328b). The general antimercantile bias of Roman letters is well known. Cicero, for example, noted that petty retailers were chronically guilty of lies and thieving. See Baldwin, *Masters, Princes, and Merchants,* 262.

22. Noel Coulet especially remarks on the difficulty of distinguishing "aubergier" from "tavernier," and he notes, for example, that Italian legal documents "ne font pas toujours une distinction très rigoureuse entre les deux mots" ("Les Hôtelleries," 166). The most exhaustive study of this problem of medieval terminology (Gerster, "Beitrag zur Geschichte") arrives at the conclusion that we should, ideally, consider the tavern as a provider of food and drink and the auberge as a provider of lodging or in some cases of food, drink, and lodging, but the study admits that the terminology is very slippery. In reality, it is common to find the word *tavern* referring to a place for both lodging and eating and drinking. In the thirteenth-century "Gautier d'Aupais," the title character is returning home after a tournament, "Et quant ce vint au vespre, si s'est a l'ostel trais, / Dedenz une taverne ou granz fu li bobais / De la gent du païs que li vins ot atrais" (And when it began to get dark, he went to look for lodging, in a tavern where there was much merriment among the people of the region whom the wine had attracted) (vv. 18–20). The text then goes on to say that Gautier lodged there, that the host took his horse to the stable and fed it, and that there was plenty of food, as well as gambling. *Courtois d'Arras* also features a "tavierne" (v. 99) that contains "cambres pointes et soef lit" (decorated rooms and soft beds) (v. 134), indicating lodging in the tavern. "Ostel" can mean any lodging place at all and is not particularly used for inns or taverns.

between lodging, eating, or drinking is not or need not be made, while I will prefer the term *inn* where the primary function being discussed is that of lodging. In the same sense the métier itself and even the entire industry, if it could be so-called, are marked by a fluidity and lack of specificity that seem to escape traditional classifications. This is all the more remarkable in an era that saw the rise of guilds and the rigorous control of much commercial endeavor. The inn and tavern act as a central focus that draws on several different métiers and where the tavern keeper himself is forced to assume several different roles. It thus differs from the strictly defined métier, being more of a public locus that draws from throughout the public sector. Thus in his study of lodging in medieval Italy, Thomas Szabo shows numerous instances where the tavern keeper or innkeeper came into conflict with other guilds for usurping their economic domain and, in the opposite sense, situations where the innkeeper was courted and/or coerced into joining several different guild groups successively, such as the bakers, the wine merchants, and so forth, since his job overlapped the domain of these different guilds.)[23] The Middle Ages adopted a two-tiered lodging system similar to that employed in Greece and Rome, the common traveler relying on the church, while a continuation of the Greco-Roman *Gastfreundschaft*—or to be more precise, a native Germanic version of it—came to serve the noble classes more and more as the period progressed (though the distinction was never entirely rigid, since nobles and even kings often availed themselves of church hospitality).[24]

The ancient German custom of *Gastfreundschaft* is described by Tacitus in chapter 21 of his *Germania* and certainly long predates that work. The duty of hospitality is also specifically prescribed in the great Germanic law compilations of the early Middle Ages.[25] It required of all men, not just the wealthy or noble, that they receive any visitor and provide him with food, lodging, and protection. This reception was surrounded by a series of ritual acts, such as the guest being met on arrival by the host, his surrendering his weapon on arrival, his receiving the seat of honor at the host's table, formal inquiry being made as to his name and origin, the host's accompanying him for a certain distance upon departure, and so forth.

23. Szabo, "Xenodochia," 85–86.

24. Schuler, "Gastlichkeit" gives a good description of the varieties of monastic hospitality offered the typical traveler and the noble.

25. The *lex Gundobarda* states: "Quicumque hospiti venienti tectum aut focum negaverit, trium solidorum inlatione multetur" (*Mon. Germ. Hist., Hist. Leg. Nat. Germ.*, ed. Salis, 2:69). See also the Frankish laws (*Mon. Cap. Reg. Franc,* ed. Boretins, 1:96, 144) and the Burgundian Laws. All are cited in Peyer, *Von der Gastfreundschaft,* 37.

The effect of these ritual acts surrounding lodging was to emphasize the bond established between host and guest, echoing Plato's emphasis on the comradeship between guest and host. This ritual bond was so strong that both host and guest were required to take blood vengeance for the other should this be necessary, and should the guest die during his stay (a maximum of three days) without testament or known heirs, the host was considered his heir. In addition, should hospitality be refused, the refuser was to be treated as a thief according to early Germanic law.[26]

This primitive Germanic system had already begun to change somewhat by the time of the great migrations of the fourth through eighth centuries (e.g., providing of food was no longer required). In addition, the details always varied from place to place and time to time.[27] Yet the broad outlines of the system remained essentially intact into at least the eleventh century,[28] and they can be found depicted in detail in the courtly romances of Chrétien de Troyes in the late twelfth century. In verses 3103–87 of *Erec et Enide,* a count's squire sees Erec, goes out to meet him, greets him, offers to arrange lodging where he can lay down his arms and rest and where his horses will be taken care of, then himself proceeds to remove Erec's armor and serve him food and drink, making it plain to Erec that "ne rien nule ne vos demant" (v. 3113). Erec, however, "cortois et larges fu" (v. 3144) and offers him a gift in exchange for his services, allowing him to choose one of his horses. In this theoretically free exchange of gifts, a ritual bond is established between Erec and his host.

As mentioned earlier, this free hospitality became more and more the province of the upper classes as time progressed, so that incidences of the noble taking in the poor man were worthy of being reported in miracle literature in the High Middle Ages. In fact, the function that the bonding between guest and host had in solidifying class membership and unity remained a crucial aspect of the practice. This bonding would eventually serve in the twelfth and thirteenth centuries to create a dichotomy between nobility and free hospitality, devoid of monetary considerations, on the one hand, and the bourgeoisie and its commercial lodging practices, concerned with monetary profit, on the other. The ritual and indeed joyous

---

26. Peyer, *Gastfreundschaft und kommerzielle Gastlichkeit,* 3–4, 7.

27. Idealizing German historians of the nineteenth century tended to ignore the variations of the system in favor of a simplistic repetition of Tacitus' descriptions. A major critique and revision of the concept of *Gastfreundschaft* has in fact recently begun to occur. See in particular the introduction to Hellmuth, *Gastfreundschaft und Gastrecht bei den Germanen.*

28. Peyer, *Von der Gastfreundschaft,* 41.

aspect of this form of hospitality, with its celebration of largesse and class solidarity, appears clearly in *Yvain* as well.

> Si li dïent: "Bien soiez vos,
> biax sire, venuz antre nos,
> et Dex vos i doint sejorner
> tant que vos an puisiez torner
> a grant joie et a grant enor."
> Des le plus haut jusqu'au menor
> li font joie et formant s'an painnent;
> a grant joie a l'ostel l'en mainnent.
>
> (vv. 3811–18)

> [They said to him: "May you be
> Welcome, sire, here among us,
> And may God grant that you stay here
> Until you can leave
> With great joy and great honor.
> From the mightiest to the least of them,
> They took great pains to welcome him;
> With great pleasure they led him to lodgings.]

Indeed, one could argue that scenes of hospitality are a fundamental feature of courtly romance.[29] Their function at the beginning of so many episodes is to establish a community between characters in the text and between text and audience. They are the emblems of largesse, the value that forms the economic basis of the noble class. They also provide important interpretive clues, and initial failures of hospitality essentially predict the anticourtly adventures that are to follow. Yet, while hospitality is often linked not only to social and economic communities but also to textual communities, certain fabliaux suggest the way in which the desire for profit tends to weaken or destroy not only the Christian community of charity but textual "communities" as well.

The fabliau "Le prestre et le chevalier," for example, marks the conflict of class and values as commerce replaced hospitality and tavern replaced

---

29. For a more general question of the relation between hospitality and medieval courtly narrative, see Bruckner, *Narrative Invention in Twelfth-Century French Romance;* Esposito, "Les Formes d'Hospitalité dans le Roman Courtois." Esposito notes the importance of the Benedictine Rule and the Cluniac and Cistercian reforms for high medieval hospitality.

monastery in the twelfth and thirteenth centuries, evoking the rage of the knight at being subjected to the profit seeking of his lodger.[30] The satirical effect is heightened by the fact that the profit-seeking host is a priest, "Riche, manant et asasé" (powerful, wealthy, and comfortable) (v. 45). In contrast to the nobles' joyous ritual welcoming, the priest "mout ert fel et de put estre, / Petit ot en son cuer de joie" (is very treacherous and despicable and has little benevolence in his heart) (vv. 124–25) when the potential guest arrives. "Fel" is of course the classic epic adjective for the traitor, who betrays the values of the chivalric world. The priest refuses to lodge the knight initially but finally relents after an episode of commercial negotiation leads to an acceptable bargain: "Vous me donrés / De tous les mes dont vous gerés / Servi cinc saus par convenanche" (You will give me, for each dish which is served to you, five sous each) (vv. 214–16). The chevalier is then served a handsome dinner but is dismayed to find that the bargain turns out to be a gouging, as he is charged for every single item, including the salt, the pepper, and the table: he is held to ransom as are guests in Plato's critique of the inn. The tale ("le conte") dissolves into a bill ("un compte"): "Vos conterai cinc saus au pain" (I'm charging you five sous for the bread), begins the priest (v. 353), as the fabliau becomes a list of items and prices (vv. 352–77).

In this particular case, at least, the knight ultimately gains his revenge for the avariciousness of the priest. Just as the priest has twisted the language of the commercial agreement to suit himself, the knight twists his own initial demand—that the priest provide everything he ask for—in order to demand the right to sleep with first the priest's niece, then his mistress (the priest's house becomes an ironic version first of a tavern and then of a brothel), then the priest himself.[31] The priest is willing to give up his niece and mistress but draws the line at himself, thereby breaking the bargain. His willingness to treat his niece and mistress as commodities, drawing the line only at himself, reveals both a lack of (family) community and his purely individualistic self-interest. The tricky, slippery, indeterminate nature of the economic agreement and its language, always lending itself to abuse and deceit by one of the parties and therefore to an unequal exchange, is particularly interesting. The desire for profit is expressed by a

---

30. Noomen, *Nouveau recueil,* IX:67–124.
31.   C'a mon talent servis serai
       De tous les mès que je saurai
       Que vous arés en vo baillie.

(vv. 226–28)

potentially unequal economic exchange—a gap in value—and this is replicated in linguistic gaps of understanding. But ironically, the failures of understanding result from the extreme literalism that both parties eventually apply to the contract. Economic profit, at least here, is linked to a refusal of the "spirit" of the letter. The gap is really between what should be understood in a charitable community and what literally could be understood by a profit-seeking individual. And since there is no Notre' Dames de Chartres here, the situation is redeemed not by a final triumph of the spirit of the letter but by the knight's use of the same profitable literalness that the priest adopts. Although the fabliau seems initially to offer a moralistic critique of the priest, the means of critique and redemption suggest that a deeper crisis of language and community is at stake here.

The practice of free hospitality can be understood in the larger context of the medieval gift economy. Plato in fact speaks in his *Laws* of the "gifts" that should be provided to the guest. Relying on the work of Marcel Mauss and others, Georges Duby analyzes medieval society of the eleventh and early twelfth centuries as an interlocking vertical and horizontal system created and sustained by gift giving.[32] This system in fact surpassed the bounds of the aristocracy; the Cistercians, for example, used the practice of gift giving to establish bonds of community with their surrounding aristocratic neighbors.[33] In the example of Erec and the squire, the key aspect of the gift is that it creates the obligation—both financial and moral—of a later reciprocation, thus binding giver to receiver, though the gift is never considered as actual payment for a service. Gifts are looked on by the recipient not as a source of profit but rather as something to be given away again in turn, and the giver sees the gift not as a loss but as largesse that will be returned in the future. The gift has no precise value: this is the key to the concept of largesse. The basic principle of commercial exchange, in comparison, is monetary measure, or more precisely measurability in general, which is typically expressed in monetary terms. Thus Erec is described as "cortois et larges" (courtly and generous) when giving his gift and leaves its exact value open to the squire, who will choose the horse he wants.

It is implicit in Duby's analysis that just as the gift creates bonds, so the

---

32. Mauss, *The Gift;* Duby, *La société aux XIe et XIIe siècles.* See also Duby's subsequent work, especially *The Early Growth of the European Economy,* as well as Bataille, "The Notion of Expenditure." On the explicit connections of gift giving and hospitality among the Norse, see Gurevich, *Categories of Medieval Culture,* 215ff., 226ff.

33. See Bouchard, *Holy Entrepreneurs.*

withholding of the gift from the outsider or its limitation to a certain group not only binds that group together but also excludes those who do not receive, leading to the dichotomy between noble and bourgeois. The idea that the aristocracy engaged in a number of practices to further class solidarity in the face of rising economic and social threats, particularly in the late twelfth and early thirteenth centuries, has been suggested by a number of scholars, perhaps most notably by Erich Köhler.[34] He points, for example, to the valuation of "largesce" in Old French romance as less an ethical than an economic virtue, to ensure the continued functioning of the gift economy and prevent the impoverishment and disenobling of the lower nobility, though it is presented in the texts in terms of social ethics.

Work on the early tavern has shown that these establishments were quite often just a private home or series of adjoining homes converted to this new use. It seems likely that much paid lodging was simply provided by bourgeois families within their own houses, perhaps often as a secondary contribution to their income, and involving no more than two or three visitors at a time. This would appear to be the case in Jean Bodel's fabliau "De Gombert et des deus clers," for example: two clerks on their way back home from school "ostel pristrent ches un vilein" (sought lodging in the house of a townsman)—though the fabliau suggests that they are not paying very much.[35] In contrast to Erec's lodging with a nobleman, when he lodges with a bourgeois host, the issue of monetary expenditure and precise reckoning of value is explicitly raised. In this instance, the bourgeois has offered to lodge him only in the hope of betraying Erec for the host's own monetary gain. Upon leaving, having foiled the host's plans, Erec explicitly pays the host for his services.

> . . . "Sire, de mon despans
> n'avez ancores rien conté.
> Enor m'avez feite et bonté,
> et molt i afiert grant merite.
> Por set destriers me clamez quite."
>
> (*Erec et Enide*, vv. 3468–72)

> [. . . "Sir, you have as yet
> made no reckoning of my expenses.
> You have shown me honor and kindness,

---

34. See in particular Köhler, *Ideal und Wirklichkeit in der höfischen Epik*, chap. 1.
35. Noomen, *Nouveau recueil*, IV:279–302. v. 5.

and that deserves a rich reward.
Let me be quit for seven chargers.]

The scathing irony of Erec's words and the avariciousness of the bourgeois, who is quite happy with the "don" (gift) (v. 3475), only serve to heighten the ethical and social judgment of the passage, where the class distinction is made so clear by the fact of a payment.

While true gifts include and bind, the payment excludes and disengages the two men and their classes from each other. The word "conté" (v. 3469) is of particular importance because it emphasizes the precise accounting of payment, whereas the value of the gift remains always theoretically uncalculated. The assigning of precise value is part and parcel of the rise of the profit economy.[36]

When Lancelot wants to escape notice and not be recognized, he chooses to stay in a "taverne" (v. 5538), which is depicted as the very antithesis of noble hospitality: "La ou il jut si povrement" (while he was lying in this hovel) (v. 5535) "en un lit qu'il molt po prisoit, / qu'estroiz ert" (in a rather uncomfortable bed, which was too narrow) (vv. 5530–31). One wonders if "estroiz" consciously echoes in this passage its etymological opposite *larges.* King Arthur likewise, in a celebration of aristocratic joy and largesse, closes down the inns and hospitality of the bourgeoisie, at least some of which must have been of a commercial variety, so that all comers will lodge free with him.

> Tant est gentix et frans li rois
> qu'il a fet ban a ses borjois,
> si chier con chascuns a son cors,
> que prodom qui viegne de hors
> an lor meisons ostel ne truisse,
> por ce que il meïsmes puisse
> toz les prodomes enorer
> qui leanz voldront demorer.
>
> (vv. 5439–46)

> [The king is so noble and gracious
> that he has made a proclamation to his burghers
> that, if they value their lives,

---

36. For further implications of this, see Little, *Religious Poverty,* 4–5; Vance, *Mervelous Signals,* 116; Kellogg, *Medieval Artistry and Exchange,* 149.

no nobleman who comes from outside
may find lodging in their houses,
so that he himself may
honor all the noblemen
who want to stay in the town.]

Thus the bourgeoisie, with its paid lodging and services, comes to represent the antithesis of noble hospitality, and this conflict of modes of lodging becomes a part of the larger representation of the conflict between two worlds—the noble world of ritual gift exchange and largesse, with its emphasis on the creation of bonds of interdependence and solidarity, and the bourgeois world of monetary, market transactions motivated by profit, in which each individual seeks only his own personal gain.[37] A confrontation framed in terms of the ethics of class is also an economic dichotomy fundamental to medieval culture. Similarly, Rutebeuf notes in his "La complainte de Constantinople" (*OC* 1:355–66):

De Grece vint chevalerie
Premierement d'anceserie,
Si vint en France et en Bretaingne.
Grant piece i at estei chierie.
Or est a mesnie escherie,
Que nuns n'est teiz qu'il la retaingne.
Mort sunt Ogiers et Charlemainne.
Or s'en vont, que plus n'i remaingne.
Loyauteiz est morte et perie:
C'estoit sa monjoie et s'ensaingne,
C'estoit sa dame et sa compaingne
Et sa maistre habergerie.

[Chivalry came from Greece,
Who was the first of its ancestors,
And arrived in France and Brittany.
It was long cherished there.
Now its followers are depleted,
And there is no one who still honors it.
Ogier and Charlemagne are dead.

---

37. The bourgeois could, however, occasionally offer "noble" hospitality, as in Marie de France's "Eliduc." See Jacques Le Goff, *The Medieval Imagination,* 164–65.

They have departed now, and nothing of chivalry remains.
Loyalty is dead and gone:
She who was chivalry's glory and emblem,
Chivalry's lady and companion
And her principal abode.]

Chivalry's figurative locale is, and is represented by the act of, "haber-gerie." The decline in hospitality is to be seen not only in the context of the death of the great epic heroes and the death of the fundamentally chivalric virtue of loyalty but as one element in the disruption of a *translatio imperii*—of an entire sociohistorical worldview.

The Monastery and the Inn: The Brotherhood of Charity

The religious duty of *hospitalitas* was part of the general requirement of Christian charity and had theological as well as social implications. The idea was based on exemplary biblical passages involving, for example, Abraham and Lot,[38] as well as on Deuteronomy 10:18–19:

> He [the Lord] executes justice for the fatherless and the widow, and loves the sojourner, giving him food and clothing. Love the sojourner therefore; for you were sojourners in the land of Egypt.

Numerous other writings of the early Christian era also supported this idea, and Charlemagne explicitly prescribed this duty for both clerics and laypeople in 789.[39] Christianity combined the sacred sanction of the church with the Germanic sanction of clan loyalty and solidarity, so that the ideological underpinnings of the concept of free lodging were extremely powerful.

Despite general expectations, the duty of hospitality fell especially to the monasteries. The Benedictine Rule required that monasteries welcome all travelers, though pilgrims and believers were singled out as deserving particular welcome.[40] Once again, it was especially the Cister-

---

38. See Genesis 18:1–8 on Abraham and Genesis 19:1–3 on Lot.

39. See Schmugge, "Pilgerverkehrs," especially 39, and from the Aachen Synod of 816–17, "Laicus enim unum aut duos suscipiens implevit hospitalitatis officium . . ." (quoted in Schmugge, op. cit., 39–40).

40. "Et omnibus congruus honor exhibeator, maxime domesticis fedei et peregrinis" (*Benedicti Regula,* ed. Hanslick, 53.2).

cians who were noted for their adherence to this rule.[41] All arriving guests were to receive a reception at the gates, where their specific identity could be determined, and after they had laid aside their weapons, they were to be escorted to their appropriate quarters, with quarters provided for their animals as well. This ceremony had many parallels to the primitive rites of *Gastfreundschaft* in its emphasis on ritual honoring of the new guest, and indeed it served to underline the universal brotherhood of Christians—a brotherhood defined not by class in this case but by a shared moral injunction to practice an economics of charity. This difference was marked by the addition of such specifically Christian rituals as the symbolic washing of the feet of the poorer guests.[42] Nevertheless, in both cases, it is the host who guarantees the safety and comfort of the lodger and, in so doing, integrates the lodger into the larger group. The fact that the guest does not pay places no explicit obligation on him, but it nevertheless binds him to the system from which he has benefited.

In extremely frequented locales, entire separate institutions known as a *xenodochium* were established to care for the flow of pilgrims.[43] These establishments continued to be founded in relatively large numbers in France at least to the end of the twelfth century.[44] This was, for example,

---

Interestingly enough, despite the preceding injunction, the monasteries preserved in their own way the traditional two-tiered, class-based system of lodging that characterized Greek and Roman custom. In theory monasteries were supposed to provide three separate types of lodging—one for the wealthy traveling bishops and nobles, one for the monks who lived in the monastery on a regular basis, and finally one for the less wealthy, typical traveler.

41. See Newman, *Boundaries of Charity*, 125.

42. The biblical injunctions against usury also invoke the idea of brotherhood, of lending freely to a brother without interest. We will see in chapter 2 that usury was closely associated with the new bourgeois class, so that it too could be seen as breaking the universal Christian brotherhood in the same way that charging for hospitality tended to sever social bonds.

43. At the same time, between the ninth and eleventh centuries virtually every monastery had attached to it a *hospitale pauperum* devoted to the care of the old, the sick, and the poor. As the Middle Ages continued, the distinction between the pilgrim, the sick, the poor, and the general itinerant wanderer lost some of its importance. As a result, the functions of the *xenodochium* and the *hospitale* gradually faded together, so that the *hospitale*, or *hospitalium*, became the general institution charged with caring for all of the aforementioned categories of people. The term *xenodochium* began to be replaced by *hospitale* in the eleventh century and was definitively replaced by the time of the twelfth century. However, the institution itself had already merged with that of the *hospitale* to form a general place of welcome for all. These general institutions thus remained unchanged—the bipartite naming system was simply replaced by the single term. See Szabo, "Xenodochia"; Gerster, "Beitrag zur Geschichte."

44. Schmugge, "Pilgerverkehrs," 42–43.

the case in Toulouse, at the crossroads of several pilgrimage routes. Several different *hospitalia* were established there.[45]

The connection between Christian hospitality and pilgrimages should be particularly stressed. The great network of welcome was established primarily for the holy purpose of sheltering these pilgrims. The Christian duty of hospitality could equally well be considered as simply a duty toward the pilgrim, and this duty was enshrined in laws of the church—it was not a mere favor.[46] In *Le guide du pèlerin de Saint-Jacques de Compostelle,* a mid-twelfth-century travel guide for pilgrims, the author makes clear that

> Pilgrims, poor or rich, who are coming from or going to Saint Jacques, must be received with charity and veneration by all. For whoever receives and lodges them with solicitude will have as his guest not only Saint Jacques, but Our Savior himself, as he said in the Evangel: "Whoever receives you receives me." Numerous are those who once incurred the wrath of God because they did not wish to receive the pilgrims of Saint Jacques nor the indigent. (123–25)

As a result, a challenge to this system of feeding and lodging could be considered as a more general challenge to the possibility of pilgrimage and in particular to its legal and economic foundations as a privileged and protected activity integral to the nature of the medieval Catholic Church. The ideological underpinnings of the Christian system of hospitality thus placed it at the heart of the concerns of the church.

One can easily imagine that the reality of the situation sometimes failed to match the theory, but it seems that this system did function rather successfully for an appreciable part of the Middle Ages.[47] By the twelfth century, the church as well as noble society had established a huge network of lodging, available at least in the church's case to virtually all comers, and offering shelter to both man and beast at no charge. Yet just as this network was reaching its greatest development, an entirely new institution, the inn and tavern, was rising to prominence, and this new institution

---

45. See Jugnot and de la Coste-Messeliere, "L'accueil des pèlerins à Toulouse." For a general discussion of this matter, see Schmugge, "Pilgerverkehrs."

46. On this point, see Jugnot, "Les Chemins de pèlerinage dans la France Médiévale," 78–79.

47. On the question of theory versus reality in this system in the period before the rise of the inn and tavern in the twelfth and thirteenth centuries, see, for example, Schuler, "Gastlichkeit"; Lekai, *The Cistercians,* especially 381.

would react to the increasing strains placed on the existing system and quite rapidly replace it in the course of the two centuries from approximately 1150 to 1350.

The earliest reference to a private commercial inn is from Florence in 1065,[48] but inns under the control of either monasteries or local nobles seem to have existed as early as the 900s.[49] However, it is generally agreed that the institution blossomed primarily in the last half of the twelfth century and, particularly, in the early years of the thirteenth century. It is at this point that inns enter the record of municipal and legal documents.[50] It is basically clear that the church system of lodging was quite simply overstrained in the High Middle Ages by the increasing number of travelers.[51] The eleventh and twelfth centuries witnessed a rapid expansion in the number of *hospitalia,* which must certainly be seen as a response to the increase of traffic, and the twelfth century in particular provides us with many examples of monasteries facing an increasing burden in accepting

---

48. Szabo, "Xenodochia," 78.

49. There is comparatively little information on the crucial era that witnessed the birth of the tavern and the disappearance of the church as free provider, during what Marc Bloch considers to be the period of transition from the first feudal age to the second. While there is substantial evidence for the tavern in the late twelfth and early thirteenth centuries (both in literature and from municipal, historical, and legal sources), in the case of the origins of the institution in the eleventh and twelfth centuries, documentation is lacking.

After explicitly evoking "les rares travaux consacrés aux auberges avant le XIVe siècle . . . ," Noel Coulet elaborates on some of the other problems to be pursued: ". . . il resterait à suivre les progrès de l'individualisation du métier, en examinant ses relations avec d'autres professions voisines, taverniers, marchands de vin, courtiers. Il resterait aussi à voir comment, et jusqu'à quel point, s'affirme la spécificité de l'activité hôtelière, face aux particuliers et aux institutions qui, regulièrement ou à l'occasion, logent et nourissent les gens de passage" ("Les Hôtelleries," 165–66).

50. See the statutes of Volterra of 1223, the statutes of Trévise of 1231, and the consular establishment of Toulouse of 1205, cited in Coulet, "Les Hôtelleries," 66. Coulet sees the inn as taking over the primary lodging function from the monastery and hospital in the course of the twelfth and thirteenth centuries. Peyer (*Gastfreundschaft und kommerzielle Gastlichkeit,* 7ff.) sees the transition from guest hospitality to commercial lodging as occurring in the early twelfth century. In Italy many hospitals were built well into the twelfth century, but as the century went on, church hospitality apparently diminished, so that by the thirteenth century the hospital served almost entirely the poor and the sick (Szabo, "Xenodochia"). Jugnot (Jugnot and de la Coste-Messeliere, "L'accueil des pèlerins à Toulouse") have pinpointed the early thirteenth century as an era of conflict between the innkeeper and the pilgrim.

51. Important historical questions are to what extent this strain was due simply to an increasing number of pilgrims and to what extent it was caused by additional users of the system, such as merchants, whose numbers increased dramatically throughout the eleventh through the thirteenth centuries, as is well known. Schmugge ("Pilgerverkehrs") and Szabo ("Xenodochia") attribute the great increase in church *hospitalia* to the rise of pilgrim traffic in that time.

travelers.[52] By the late twelfth and thirteenth centuries, the church hospitality system had become so inadequate that even pilgrims were often forced to stay at the incipient commercial establishments.

In fact, one can surmise that the growth of pilgrimages itself fueled the growth of the taverns. The aforementioned guide to Compostela describes the city thus:

> After the fountain is a walled enclosure. It's pavement is of stone. It is there that one sells to the pilgrims. . . . One meets also on the road toward France money changers, innkeepers, and various merchants. (*Le guide du pèlerin de Saint-Jacques de Compostelle* 97)

There was an increasing series of complaints on the part of these pilgrims about the conditions involved in this commercial hospitality, centering around unfair prices and attempts to rob, cheat, and otherwise deceive the gullible traveler. In 1205 the city of Toulouse promulgated the series of restrictions that I mentioned in the introduction.[53] The guide to Compostela provides a vivid picture of abuse and exploitation of pilgrims by innkeepers, concentrating in particular on cases of substituting low-quality wine and food for the high-quality items that the pilgrims believed themselves to be buying, as well as cases of trickery in monetary exchanges where the exchange was unequal and the innkeeper profited handsomely. Undoubtedly these abuses occurred with all customers, but it is the pilgrims who are consistently singled out as victims.[54] In a poem from the *Carmina Burana,* "Denudata veritate" (*CB* 616–20), which is a debate between wine and water, water explicitly links wine and the tavern with a variety of evil men and deeds.

> Et qui tuus est amator
> homicidia, fornicator,
> Davus, Geta, Byrria;
> tales tibi famulantur
> tales de te gloriantur
> tabernali curia.

(vv. 55–60)

---

52. See, for example, Lekai, *The Cistercians,* 381; Schuler, "Gastlichkeit."

53. For more on the strife and exploitation of pilgrims, see Jugnot, "Les Chemins de pèlerinage dans la France Médiévale," 81 and the notes referenced there. On the statutes of 1205, see Gilles, "Lex peregrinorum," 183–84; Jugnot and de la Coste-Messeliere, "L'accueil des pèlerins à Toulouse," 130.

54. See Peyer, *Von der Gastfreundschaft,* 57.

[Who is your companion?
Homicide, fornication,
David, Geta, Byrria;
These are your servants,
These are glorified by you,
These devotees of the tavern.][55]

Meanwhile, the pilgrim is absent from the tavern, heading rather to celestial palaces, and drinks water rather than the wine symbolic of the tavern.

Potum dono sitienti,
ad salutem me querenti
valde necessaria;
quia veho peregrinos,
tam remotos quam vicinos,
ad celi palatia.

(vv. 67–72)[56]

[I give refreshment to the thirsty,
Who come to me seeking health,
Which is so necessary;
For I lead pilgrims
Both from near and afar
To the palaces of the heavens.]

We have already seen another example of the tavern as the antithesis of the proper locale for pilgrims in Jean le Marchant's miracle, where the two pilgrims who go to Chartres divide paths both literally and spiritually, one choosing the church, the other the tavern. To cite a final example, in Adam de la Halle's "Li jus du pelerin"[57] we find a meeting between the pilgrim and a "vilains." The *vilains* tells the pilgrim:

. . . je t'en voeil desmentir
. . . .

---

55. See the vernacular equivalent of this poem, "La desputoison du vin et de l'iaue," in Jubinal, *Nouveau recueil,* 1:293–311.

56. Vollmann gives only the first three verses in his text, but Whicher *(The Goliard Poets)* gives all six cited here. This is reasonable since otherwise all the strophes are six verses long except the final one, which is nine verses in Vollmann.

57. In Adam de la Halle, *Die dem trouvère Adam de la Hale Zugeschriebenen Dramen,* 12–15.

Vous aries ja plus chier a sir en le taverne
que aler au moustier . . .

(vv. 16–19)

[. . . I want to warn you
.   .   .   .
It will cost you much more to lodge in the tavern
Than if you go to the church . . .]

He later warns him:

. . . vilains fuies de chi
Ou vous seres mout tost loussies et desvestus
a l'ostel seres ja autrement revestus.

(vv. 48–50)

[. . . Flee from here, mister
Or you will soon be robbed and divested
You'll be clothed in a whole new fashion at the tavern.]

The command to flee from the tavern is quite appropriate here, for what is really at stake is not simply the presence of the pilgrim in a dangerous locale but his presence in the economy of that locale. As I noted earlier, in 1205 Toulouse promulgated written laws to protect the pilgrim from the tavern keeper, illustrating the breakdown of the ritual that had characterized hospitality. Interestingly enough, several of the laws were really designed to protect the pilgrim not just from ethical and economic abuse but from being forced to enter the economic world of profit at all, even though—and because—pilgrims did become a significant part of the traveling economy.[58] The pilgrim was not even to be touched by the innkeeper or forced to buy anything from him other than lodging, and he could not be made to buy lodging unless he agreed to do so. Contamination from the pursuit of profit is maximized in these laws. Another legal document stated that pilgrims would be exempt from the normal duties and fees on commerce and transport and that the innkeeper would not receive his normal percentage for transactions involving pilgrims.[59] The pilgrim was thus to be protected from the economic exploitation that was

58. See Cohen, "Roads and Pilgrimage."
59. Quoted in Gilles, "Lex peregrinorum," 172.

at the center of much conflict between pilgrims and tavern keepers—conflict that was simply a mirror of the general "horror of the market" that is found in some church sources of the era.[60] Indeed some of the most vital elements of the church in the twelfth and thirteenth centuries—the Cistercians and the mendicant orders, respectively—were founded explicitly on models of nonparticipation in the world of the cash economy. The Cistercians were (ideally) devoted to the concepts of manual labor and agricultural production, and both Dominicans and Franciscans went so far in their early days as to forbid their members to even touch money.[61] The moral and ethical concerns voiced on behalf of the pilgrim clearly have a strong economic component.

Hospitality, a "gift" arising out of the Christian duty of charity toward the brotherhood of men, was replaced by the bourgeois innkeeper or tavern keeper out to make a profit in the process of economic exchange, motivated by no other interests than his own. Given the classical stigmatization of the inn, it is not surprising that when it began to become a challenge and threat to the church's system of lodging and, in a larger sense, to the vital concerns of the church relating to pilgrimage and charity, it was stigmatized in a more general sense. The connection between the tavern, a general monetary, profit economy, and a larger attack on cultural values is perhaps most explicit in "L'image du monde."[62] According to that text, "monnoie" was invented by the ancient philosophers so that they could travel about the world and instruct themselves. It got its name because one can "mène" (lead, carry) it on the "voie" (road). However, now money has been corrupted because people try to hoard it and charge the poor philosophers for their lodging, which "le droit corrompent de nature" (corrupts the natural order of things) and impedes the philosophers' instruction. Money, lodging, and profit are connected in a general disruption of charity, order, and even the *translatio studii* once again.

---

60. See in particular Lekai, *The Cistercians,* 26—the Cistercian order's *Institutes of the General Chapter* contained specific rules regarding buying and selling by monks. Lekai likewise states (311) that the frequentation of markets was considered "dangerous and unbecoming" for the religious man. In a larger sense, one can also consider the monastic reforms, the founding of the Cistercians, and the rise of the mendicant orders as a kind of withdrawal of the church from the "market"—that is, from the world of economic exchange—as far as possible. (In reality, however, the Cistercians were soon heavily involved in the market, and their antipathy, it has been argued, was more toward the city than the market per se. See Little, *Religious Poverty,* 96; in general, Bouchard, *Holy Entrepreneurs.*)

61. Little, *Religious Poverty,* 84–93, 164. Peter Damian even went so far as to oppose all exchanges, even the gift (Little, op. cit., 72).

62. Langlois, *La vie française au Moyen Age,* 3:191–93.

As a center of vice and a social disrupter of Christian brotherhood and charity, the tavern was ideally suited to be a kind of hell on earth for the church.[63] On many occasions in the literature, the tavern is explicitly placed in rivalry with the church, as was clear in the case of Jean le Marchant's miracle. The tavern was of course also forbidden to priests and clerks by numerous authorities and councils throughout the Middle Ages.[64] These same priests often used the tavern in the sermons that were preached more and more often to the urban inhabitants of France as part of the thirteenth-century revival of popular religion. The tavern is commonly found in the exempla used to illustrate these sermons, which were, like the tavern itself, closely linked to the new urban bourgeois milieu.[65] In one case, the tavern is the "templum" of gluttony, the crier who advertises the wine is the "campana," the altar is the "mensa splendida," and the tavern keeper is the "sacerdos"; Bernard of Cluny compares the "lofty temples of God" filled with light to the "dank tavern."[66] In summary, just as was the case with the aristocracy, the lodging conflict becomes one element of a larger economic confrontation. Whereas the aristocracy framed this conflict in the ethical and social terminology of class distinctions, the church did so in terms of traditional religious morality. Despite the moral attacks, the concern with an economic system based on private profit rather than public, charitable solidarity lies at the root of many representations of the tavern.

Ritual, Class, and Profit

In modern terms then, the inn is the icon of a general new economic orientation. Interestingly enough, inn keeping becomes in the Middle Ages what it was for Plato in his *Laws*—a privileged symbol for commercial activity and profit seeking. It seems unlikely that Chrétien de Troyes or

---

63. For a later example, see Bronislaw Geremek's work on marginal society in Paris. The association of inn, tavern, *otium,* crime, gambling, and prostitution is pervasive in the sources quoted by Geremek. In the words of one magistrate, a certain criminal "se tint long temps sanz rien fere ou ouvrer, jusques ad ce que tout l'argent qu'il avoit fu despendu tant au jeu de dez comme en la taverne, comme aus filletes de vie." Geremek notes that Parisian taverns and brothels were a particular attraction for wintering gangs of criminals (*The Margins of Society in Late Medieval Paris,* 130).

64. Peyer, *Von der Gastfreundschaft,* 79–80.

65. For examples of the tavern in sermons, see Welter, *La Tabula Exemplorum,* 23, 31, 109, 122. For an excellent general introduction to the exempla, see Bremond and Le Goff, *L'exemplum;* see especially 55–56, for the links between exempla and urban bourgeoisie.

66. Welter, *La Tabula Exemplorum,* 31; Bernard of Cluny, *De contemptu mundi,* 111.

other writers of the twelfth century had direct access to Plato's text, but the cultural continuity is striking in its detail, though hardly surprising in a more general sense. In the Middle Ages, this profit orientation was of course promoted by the urban bourgeois class who ran the inns. Opposed to the social, economic, and moral interests of the church and nobility, and largely outside the realm of the peasants, the inn and tavern are both explicit exemplars and suitable general symbols of that profit-oriented economy. The tavern itself was of course a commercial enterprise, a part of the new middle-class economy, often characterized by absentee owners who invested in the property and franchised the management to the tavern keeper. Figures in fact suggest that it was one of the principal new commercial activities.[67] Thus a broad identity was established between the tavern and inn and the new mercantile middle class of the twelfth and thirteenth centuries. Whenever authors needed to localize the sins of the monetary, profit-oriented economy—its individualizing, legalizing, and deritualizing of the world—the tavern became perhaps the most common icon and geographical locus of avarice, greed, and profiteering in medieval literature.[68]

Indeed, the geography of the tavern seems to correspond to the geography of the mercantile middle class. As both lodging and entertainment centers, taverns were largely confined to the cities, which appears to have been the case specifically for northern France.[69] In addition, the other obvious location for the inn/tavern was the important mercantile travel

---

67. See van Houtte, "Herbergswesen und Gastlichkeit im mittelalterlichen Brugge"; Szabo, "Xenodochia." The degree of importance of the inn and tavern can also be grasped by the fact that "the third largest group of traders serving as London aldermen between 1200 and 1340 were vintners, a number of whom were doubtless taverniers" (Clark, *The English Alehouse*, 10).

68. The tavern's association with the particular social villains of the moment transcended its connection with the bourgeoisie in twelfth- and thirteenth-century France. David Aers has shown that in the later instance of *Piers Plowman*, the tavern is associated with the working class, who are criticized by the more privileged for their unwillingness to work cheaply following the drastic depopulation of the Black Death (*Community, Gender, and Individual Identity*, 38–40).

69. For example, Coulet writes, "Dans l'espace, il s'agit surtout ici des hôtelleries urbaines" ("Les Hôtelleries," 167), although he admits that "l'auberge n'est pas pourtant un monopole de la ville." See also Ladurie, *Montaillou*, 399. Le Roy Ladurie concludes that "d'une façon générale dans les villages purement ruraux . . . la taverne n'existe que sous forme embryonaire" (though later an extensive network of village and purely rural establishments came into being). He limits true taverns to "les petites villes, dans les bourgades ou dans les lieux d'échange et de trafic" (399–400). On northern France, see Coulet, "Inns and Taverns," 469.

routes, especially between Italy and Flanders. We will see in chapter 3 an ironic Bédieriste twist on literary origin in relation to the geography of the tavern. Just as Joseph Bédier argued that the monasteries and pilgrimage roads were the loci lying at the origin of the epic, we will see that the tavern, situated along the travel routes of the bourgeois merchants, is often presented as the source of much so-called bourgeois comico-realist literature.

The geography of the tavern within the medieval city itself repeats these associations. The inns and taverns were located along the main trade roads in and out of the city, especially at the point where the roads passed through the city gates and around the central marketplaces. They were also especially found in the suburbs—centers of economic activity within the larger city, typically inhabited by merchants, and primarily founded around city gates or across the bridges from the city.[70] It is certainly not just by chance that Chaucer's pilgrims in the *Canterbury Tales* set off from a tavern, for as the tales suggest, it was the point where the diverse medieval population came together.

Finally, on the most microgeographic level, the tavern itself might often be the site of economic transactions. The gradual appearance of the tavern at roughly the same time as the European economic revival has been noted by historians, who have found that the tavern could at times in fact be at the origin of a market, as a site for transactions.[71] It could even facilitate the enforcement of market rights and would thus be a preferred market location. The innkeeper in such circumstances functioned as a middleman for business affairs. In the *Moniage Guillaume,* which features a scene in a "taverne," the tavern keeper tells a jongleur who has spent all his earnings, "Querrés aillors ostel, / Que marcëant doivent ci osteler" (Look elsewhere for lodging, for some merchants are going to stay here); Guibert de Nogent notes that a certain riot was so severe that the innkeepers exposed nothing for sale.[72] It is important to appreciate fully the importance of the

---

70. Coulet, "Inns and Taverns," 469.

71. Peyer, in the introduction to his volume on the tavern (*Gastfreundschaft, Taverne und Gasthaus,* xii), notes that the tavern could function "als eine Art Markt." Wilfried Kerntke (*Taverne und Markt*) posits the tavern as the center and origin of local markets in Germany, and Irena Rabecka-Brykczynska ("Die Taverne im fruhmittelalterlichen Polen") and Kerntke ("Taberna, Ortsherrschaft und Marktentwicklung in Bayern") have studied the same phenomenon in medieval Poland and Bavaria.

72. The passage in the *Moniage Guillaume* begins at v. 1248, and the citation is from vv. 1262–63. The citation is from the second redaction. For Guibert, see Benton, *Self and Society in Medieval France,* 172.

innkeeper and the inn as a market for exchanges. These exchanges produced profit not only for the two parties directly involved but also for the innkeeper, and the profitable exchanges were now legally regulated. Francis Garrisson studies the rise of laws regulating such situations, beginning in the late twelfth century.

Lodging alone sufficed to establish close relations between the host and his client . . . the host indicated to the stranger the commercial customs of the town, put him in contact with the merchants of the city, and assisted him in his buying and selling . . . and served him directly as an intermediary.[73]

The host then received a tax on each transaction, known as the *hostellagium*. In addition, Garrisson notes that "the house of the host was considered a public place, open to all."[74] The host enjoyed not only the *hostellagium* but a "droit de participation" that allowed him to profit from any bargains obtained by his clients: the inn could become a veritable brokerage house. In fact the word *taverner* later came to mean both "to sell goods in a tavern" and, by extension, "to sell goods in general."[75]

Of interest here as well is the fact that these exchanges were now legally regulated by written statutes, for just as ritual was significant to the gift economy, so legal statutes were to profit making. Throughout France and Italy, a large body of law grew up concerning the reciprocal duties of the tavern keeper and innkeeper and the guest merchant. The existence of such bodies of written law also implicitly underlines the lack of any ritual component of exchange in this new economy. In addition to laws governing all exchanges, as the medieval economy expanded, contractual obligations defined in writing replaced ritual, oral agreements in the context of each individual exchange as well.[76] In *Le miracle de Theophile*, Theophile sells his soul to the devil, but this merchant of souls is not satisfied with

---

73. Garrisson, "Les Hôtes et l'hébergement des étrangers au moyen age," 200 (my translation).

74. Garrisson, "Les Hôtes et l'hébergement des étrangers au moyen age," 201 (my translation).

75. Godefroy, *Dictionnaire de l'ancienne langue française*, s.v. "taverner."

76. This is of course just one small aspect of the great medieval shift from an oral, customary legal system ultimately dependent on tradition and the immanence of God, assured through ritual, as a guarantor of the proceedings, to a system derived from Roman law and based on witnesses, testimony, and written documents. See in particular Bloch, *Medieval French Literature and Law*. See also Clanchy, *From Memory to Written Record*.

Theophile's ritual "hommage" (v. 242): "Saches de voir qu'il te convient / De toi aie lettres pendanz" (Be advised that you must provide me with a written promise) (vv. 249–50), he says, and Theophile replies, "je les ai escrites" (I've got it all written up) (v. 255). An area of medieval civilization that has been insufficiently investigated is the relation between oral culture and the barter economy, on the one hand, and the monetary profit economy with its attendant written implements of exchange, on the other.[77] Certainly scholars, such as Brian Stock, have noted the parallel rise of literacy and a monetary economy in medieval France,[78] but the deeper semiotic connections between these two events remain unclear.[79] It seems that money, by its very nature as a secondary sign of value, calls forth the urge to profit—to introduce a gap into the exchange—via symbolic manipulations,[80] and in the following chapters we will see that this urge is paralleled in the tavern by an urge to do likewise with the linguistic sign. The tavern, it turns out, not only is a locus of moral and economic sin but also partakes in the spreading cultural literacy of the High Middle Ages, with literacy understood here in the broadest terms, as the modes of thought characteristic of literate societies, whether or not a given individual is actually literate. In any event, the tavern certainly witnesses the end of ritual, whether that ritual is primarily concerned with class, ethics, religion, economics, or language. And of course ritual is itself at base an invocation of solidarity and charity.

As the words of the crier in Le Jeu de Saint Nicolas (649–57) cited earlier in this chapter make clear, the tavern is about not solidarity or charity but seduction. The choice to enter is a choice to leave behind the "autre gent"—the common folk, probably staying in the monastery—and accept one's special place as a "lecheour," who desires more than the simple dictates of bodily necessity allow. The wine served here is not that of the Christian Communion. Rather than being transubstantiated, it is held on the tongue, not even swallowed, an emblem of carnal desire in the tavern.

---

77. For a discussion of this issue, see Shell, The Economy of Literature.

78. Stock, The Implications of Literacy, 83–85.

79. See Cowell, "The Fall of the Oral Economy"; Goux, Freud, Marx.

80. One of the specific parallels that Stock notes in pp. 83–85 of The Implications of Literacy is that both literacy and a monetary economy involve concrete external signs that express desire and mediate exchanges (The Implications of Literacy, 85). In both barter economies and oral communication this is not the case, because there the signs, especially oral language, are considered more internal to the speaker—a product of the speaker—and never attain a concrete externalization. In both literate and monetary economies, the external signs are subject to measure, and it is specifically this external measuring that allows fraud in economic exchanges.

Vois con il mengüe s'escume,
Et saut et estinchele et frit!
Tien le seur le langue un petit,
Si sentiras ja outrevin.

(655–58)

[See how it bubbles,
And leaps and sparks and chills!
Hold it on your tongue a moment
And you'll taste a fine wine indeed.]

Personal enjoyment here replaces a ritual of community and charity.

In the "Songe d'enfer" of Raoul de Houdenc, the author, who was him-self quite possibly a noble of limited means,[81] makes a journey to hell, stopping along the way at inns; at "Vile Taverne," whose tavern keeper is "Roberie"; and at a brothel. Asked by "Foimentie" to describe the moral state of the world at the time, he replies:

Tolirs est biaus et renommez;
N'est pas chetis ne recreüs,
Ainz est et granz et parcreüs.
De cuer, de cors, de braz, de mains,
Est granz assez; Doners est nains.

(vv. 130–34)

[Taking is esteemed and renowned;
He is neither wretched nor cowardly,
But rather is great and most powerful.
His heart, his body, his arms, his hands
Are all quite large; Giving is a dwarf.]

This said, he goes on his way to the tavern. "Tolirs" could easily be read as "profit," though the literal translation would be "acquisitiveness," and "Doners" of course evokes the early medieval gift economy. The challenge to the noble lodging system becomes a moral challenge to the noble class, and that challenge is ultimately an attack on the gift economy. The chal-

---

81. See the introduction of Mihm's edition of the *Songe d'enfer,* for a discussion of Four-rier's hypotheses that Raoul was the nephew of Peter Cantor (who will be met again in chap-ter 2) and was part of a landless noble family.

lenge to the church lodging system becomes a challenge to Christian charity, and that challenge is ultimately an attack on the economy of charitableness. The already mentioned similarities in the ritual of welcoming as well as the mutual use of gift giving by both monasteries and nobles to create community underline the fundamental similarities of these two economies. In both cases, economies that are nonprofit and whose purpose is the establishment of ritual solidarities are challenged by an economy whose goal is clearly profit for an individual.[82]

In the same light, another interesting example of a journey to hell featuring stops at taverns is Rutebeuf's "Voie de Paradis" (*OC* 1:305–53). In the poem, the poet receives hospitality from "Pitié," "mais li renons / est petiz, toz jors amenuise" (but her fame is small, and everyday getting smaller) (vv. 116–17). He then meets "Envie," who "met discorde es freres" (sows discord among brothers) (v. 351)—the bonds of charity and brotherhood are broken. It is "Gloutonnerie" who runs the tavern, where she lodges the bourgeois who are on their way to hell because of their acquisitiveness and excessive indulgence (vv. 403ff.).

Whereas the early medieval economy, as ideally understood by church and nobility, could be interpreted as nothing more than a series of ritual exchanges—as a ritual itself—the profit economy of the middle classes was an individualizing, fragmenting, socially disruptive system whose exchanges occurred under the aegis of secondary representations—money and writing.[83] We will see in the next chapter that the tavern serves to underline and exploit the imperfections—gaps—inherent in these systems of representation, dramatizing the loss of community that results from the individual exploitation of the imperfect sign for private profit. Just as the gift and the ritual both find their betrayal in the tavern, the literature of ritual and community solidarity—the epic, hagiography, moral, and didactic texts; the liturgically inspired drama—finds its foe in the literature of sec-

---

82. In reality there were ritual forms of bonding between merchants as well. The guilds were of course one example, though these were oriented more toward craftsmen than toward traders and bankers. Another was the drinking rituals engaged in by merchants, most probably occurring in taverns, fittingly enough (see Duby, *The Early Growth of the European Economy*, 243). However, this aspect of merchant activity is virtually unrepresented in the tavern scenes of high medieval French literature, and it plays no part in the general thematics of the tavern. Indeed, drinking in general often has such a ritual function, but in the tavern, drinking as ritual serves to establish private bonds and to separate the drinkers from the larger community, as will be seen in *Le Jeu de Saint Nicolas*. It is thus consistent with the larger thematics of the tavern.

83. For more on this ritual aspect of medieval economy, see Duby, *The Early Growth of the European Economy*, 50–56.

ular comico-realism. We will see that this literature, like the economic practices of the urban mercantile economy, alternately celebrates and laments the process of fragmentation, subjectivization, and privatization of the social system.

Chapter 2

Le Jeu de Saint Nicolas and the Poetics of the Tavern

The Unity of *Le Jeu de Saint Nicolas*

Chaiens fait bon disner, chaiens!
Chi a caut pain et caus herens,
Et vin d'Aucheurre a plain tonnel.

[In here you'll dine well, in here!
We've got warm bread and warm herring,
And wine from Auxerre, by the barrelfull.]

These three lines open the first tavern scene in Jean Bodel's miracle play, *Le Jeu de Saint Nicolas* (vv. 251–53).[1] The *boniment,* pronounced by the tavern keeper, serves to entice both the customer and the reader into the tavern. He promises, "Je n'en serai a nul fourfait / Ne du vendre ne du mestrait" (I'll be liable to no one neither in the selling [price] nor in the measuring of quantity) (259–60). The implicit promise to the customer as reader lies in the word "mestrait," which derives from the Old French verb *mestraire. Traire* could mean either to draw out or measure out or to draw out and tell a tale. The tavern keeper thus assures his audience of both his financial and narrative honesty in these lines. Yet his first customer, after having finished his drink, protests, "Chis hanas n'est mie parfons: / Il fust bons a vin assaier!" (This goblet isn't very deep: it was only good for trying a taste) (270–71). The protest suggests the inadequacy of the tavern keeper's economic dealings, as well as the inadequacy of his word in his earlier claims. Though the tavern keeper may sell his wine "au ban de le

1. I cite the third revised edition edited by Albert Henry.

vile" (at the fixed price of the town) (v. 258), the measure or quantity of wine is inadequate to the fixed price, and the customer receives less than he expected. At the same time, the tavern keeper's own claims on price and measure seem to amount to both more and less than they ought: in light of the subsequent multiple deceptions of the play, his assurance "Je n'en serai a nul fourfait / Ne du vendre ne du mestrait" ambiguously suggests that he may actually never fail to measure out incorrectly or to misrepresent himself in his "accounts." Such ambiguity both doubles the possible meanings of the passage (to the tavern keeper's profit) and reduces the adequacy of its expression (to the loss of the customer). Economic profit and linguistic profit of sense and meaning are intimately allied in the tavern keeper's claims, along with concomitant losses on the part of the customer, who is himself a reader of the tavern keeper's rhetorical text.

This is just one instance in Jean Bodel's play of the same gaps in economic exchange that we have already witnessed in the tavern. More interestingly, we will see that these gaps consistently find their equivalents in the linguistic gaps that characterize the poetics of the tavern scenes, as one inadequacy produces the other: the play constitutes a long series of linguistic ambiguities enabling an equally long series of problematic economic transactions. Ultimately, poetics and economics coincide in a homologous amplification and commodification of the sign.

At the same time, the opening of the first tavern scene is merely a *mise en abyme* of the larger play and in particular of the prologue of the play. The prologue, which I will discuss in more detail later, offers a standard preview of the events to come. Yet it offers both more and less than the play actually delivers. To take just one example, the prologue talks of a pagan king who attacks Christian forces (vv. 9–10), yet the play deals with Christian troops invading a Saracen land. In the course of the work, Bodel radically reformulates the legend of Saint Nicolas (for consistency, I will use the Old French spelling *Nicolas* throughout) at the expense of the standard events that one finds in "lisant" (reading) (v. 8) the authorities, just as the economics of drink are reformulated at the expense of the public "ban de le vile." In the light of the play as a whole, both the advertisement of the tavern keeper and the literary advertisement of the prologue raise the question of the relation of the entrepreneur—tavern keeper and author—to public authority. This authority seeks to constrain and govern their personal, private reformulations of the rules of public *traditio*—"passing on" or "exchange"—in both the linguistic and economic domains, though it fails to do so successfully in the play. *Le Jeu de Saint Nicolas* is not only about semiotic multiplicity, disruption, and play but about the relation between the players involved and the cultural forces of the late twelfth and early thirteenth centuries that tended to resist such forms of semiosis in favor of a functional theory of both money and language that supported the maintenance of Christian linguistic and economic community in the face of social change and, in the eyes of church moralists, social disruption. Jean Bodel, however, offers a more positive view of the changes in question: both merchant and author can be read as exemplars of a new economic and textual freedom and creativity that herald the continuing rise of both the market economy and a secular, vernacular literary culture.

Le Jeu de Saint Nicolas, dating from the first decade of the thirteenth century, was performed in the northern French city of Arras—one of the principal commercial and literary centers of the time. The play opens with the invasion of a Saracen kingdom by crusaders, who are massacred by the Saracens. The only survivor is an old man discovered kneeling and praying before an image of Saint Nicolas. He claims that Saint Nicolas is his protector and that the saint will safeguard any treasure if his image is placed upon it. The amused Saracens drag him before their king, who decides to try out this guarantee on his own treasure, with the assurance that a horrible death will be inflicted on the old man if Saint Nicolas fails to come through.

The action then moves to a tavern, and for the next several hundred lines, in the middle of the supposed miracle play, we witness three thieves arguing and playing dice, trying to decide who will pay the overdue bill for the excessive amount of wine they have recently consumed. In the midst of a chaos of obscure gambling terms and colorful insults, the king's crier arrives to announce quite pointedly that henceforth the king's treasure will be left unguarded except by the image of Saint Nicolas. The thieves hurry off and steal the king's gold.

The old man, on the point of execution, returns to his jail cell and begins praying to Saint Nicolas. This being a miracle play, his prayers are answered. Saint Nicolas miraculously appears before the thieves in the tavern, issues dire warnings, and forces them to return the treasure, which is discovered the next day back in place and doubled in value. (This doubling is a typical topos of such tales and is in fact parodied in one of the fabliaux.)[2] The king then converts, forcing his unwilling admirals to join him, while the thieves flee the city.

---

2. "Brunain et la vache au prêtre." See Noomen, *Nouveau recueil,* 5:39–48.

Although this play corresponds in its broad outlines to the general themes and style of medieval miracle literature, it has many aspects that do not fit into this miracle pattern. The most obvious and important of these are the tavern scenes, which occupy fully half of the entire play. Many critics have traditionally been troubled by the length of these scenes and by their seemingly extraneous details. Bodel has been explained away as simply another medieval author who lacked a sense of unity or proportion. Readers have been troubled by the willingness of the king to gamble his whole fortune on proving the old devotee of Saint Nicolas wrong, to the point of encouraging the theft of his gold. The thieves are hardly contrite at the end of the play; they are simply upset that their theft has not worked out. Their parting words to each other are "Pincedés, or du bien pinchier!" (Pincedés, now on to good thieving!) (v. 1375), to which comes the reply "Dieus nous ramaint a plus d'avoir" (God grant us better success next time) (v. 1376). Finally, the king, still a nonbeliever, receives a very handsome "return" on his "investment" in that he gets back double what he risked. As I noted, this doubling is typical of miracle literature, but normally doubling occurs when someone gives away his fortune out of charity—as a reward for being a good Christian. Here, the king, like the one-eyed jongleur and *bordeor* in Jean le Marchant's miracle discussed in chapter 1, invests his time and money in combating the efficacy of Christian doctrine. Yet unlike the *bordeor,* he is rewarded for his very effrontery. For these and other reasons, one of the more important articles on this drama (by Alfred Adler) is entitled "*Le Jeu de Saint Nicolas:* Édifiant, mais dans quel sens?"

More recently a number of readers have pointed to a fundamental link between the tavern and the Saracen palace where the other half of the play occurs, recognizing the importance of the profit motive for the play as a whole, as well as the fundamental role of *engan* (trickery). One reader has noted that the courtiers are "no less consistently reckless than the thieves in their devotion to their own particular variety of the games of chance," since they gamble treasure, fate, and life on the claims of the "preudom."[3] Profit seeking, trickery, and gambling become the unifying features of the play.

---

3. Raybin, "The Court and the Tavern", 187. On the dual spaces, see, for example, Robertson, "Structure and Comedy in *Le Jeu de Saint Nicolas*"; Lemke, "The Angel in *Le Jeu de Saint Nicolas*"; Carolyn Dinshaw, "Dice Games and Other Games in *Le Jeu de Saint Nicolas.*" Dinshaw sees this link between tavern and palace in the concept of the "game"—in the ludic nature of the text in both spaces. For her, the ludic behavior of the thieves is mirrored in the behavior of the king.

More specifically, Henri Rey-Flaud recognizes that the tavern keeper engages in usury, and he raises the problem of usury in general in the tavern: "Le jeu, comme l'usure, c'est de l'argent qui produit de l'argent."[4] While he does not develop this idea further, in reality the concept of usury provides the key metaphor for understanding the poetics and the economics of the Saracen palace as well as the tavern and for understanding the relation between the poet and the bourgeois merchants with whom the tavern's economics can be identified. As my earlier choice of vocabulary has suggested, the king in the play can actually be seen as a speculative investor, who encourages the thieves in the play to "borrow" his money and then gets the money back at an interest rate of 100 percent. As was noted, this return can in no way be seen as heaven-sent or justifiable. The king's economic gamble is against Nicolas specifically and, by implication, against Christianity. The king, like the tavern keeper, is in fact that greatest of medieval economic sinners—a usurer. (Speculative activity purely for the sake of profit was considered a form of usury in the Middle Ages.) The thieves, as receivers of the loan, are likewise complicit in his usury. This connection between king, thief, and tavern keeper, each engaged in the transgression of usury, is fundamental to the play, and the unity provided by the concept of usury is the key to a reading of the entire drama. By the term *usury* I intend here not only the actual economic practice of lending money at interest but a broader and more metaphorical definition as well, which can be extended to the medieval sign in all its manifestations—not just monetary, but especially linguistic and poetic. This leads finally to the concepts of poetic usury and, most broadly, semiotic usury. However, to extend appreciation for why such a metaphor is appropriate and justified, I will first discuss briefly the status of strictly monetary usury in the Middle Ages.

The ultimate origin of medieval prohibitions against usury lay in the Bible, in such frequently cited passages as Deuteronomy 23:19 20.[5] This

---

On the centrality of profit, see Raybin, "The Court and the Tavern." Henri Rey-Flaud likewise finds that money is the "véritable sujet et enjeu du jeu" (*Pour une dramaturgie,* 12), and he notes that the concepts of profit and *jeu* are fundamental to the play (86). See Raybin, op. cit., on trickery as well.

4. Rey-Flaud, *Pour une dramaturgie,* 107, 86 (for the quote). Likewise, he recognizes that wine produces a kind of "new language" as a result of drunkenness (119), a language that mirrors the commerce of wine—both characterized by trickery and deceit (105, 124).

5. Non foenerabis fratri tuo ad usuram pecuniam,
   nec fruges, nec quamlibet aliam rem: Sed alieno.
   Fratri autem tuo absque usura, id, quo indiget,
   commodabis . . .

was reinforced by the writings of the early church fathers and the edicts of the church councils.[6] Despite these theoretical condemnations, strong sanctions against the offender were proclaimed initially only against the cleric. In fact, the stigma of usury was not nearly so strong in the early Middle Ages as it would later become; the relatively small quantities of actual coinage that circulated in this era rendered usury a de facto nonissue. In addition, early theorists considered usury to be not a crime against justice but rather "a form of avarice or uncharitableness."[7] It was often labeled "turpe lucrum," and restitution was not an obligation of justice. Usury was thus in a sense only a sin against oneself, and the fact of an exchange with a second party was less important. Finally, the most common lenders of the tenth and eleventh centuries were actually the monasteries.[8] The Benedictine monks, living on the cusp of economic revolution, not only failed to appreciate the degree to which this revolution would challenge traditional church ideas on economics and morality but actually plunged wholeheartedly into the revolution, thus helping precipitate the monastic reform movements that would give birth to more strenuous objections to usury and allied economic activities, primarily on the part of the reformist Franciscans and Dominicans.[9] Usury was therefore not a prevalent theoretical or practical concern of the church—despite the faithful repetitions of traditional prohibitions—until the end of the eleventh century.

From this date on, however, usury dominated theorists' attention, and the concept itself underwent intense scrutiny, redefinition, and expansion.

[You shall not lend upon interest to your brother,
interest on money, interest on victuals, interest on
anything that is lent for interest. To a foreigner you
may lend upon interest, but to your brother you shall
not lend upon interest . . .]

6. The most important ecclesiastical documents were the papal epistle "Nec hoc quoque" and a canon passed by the Council of Nicea, both contained in the collected canons of the *Hadriana.* Early Christian prohibitions are also strongly echoed in the capitularies of Charlemagne, which were the first secular documents to forbid usury. See Noonan, *Usury,* 15. Other early sources are the edicts of the Paris Synod of 829. See also Le Goff, *Your Money or Your Life,* 23.

7. Noonan, *Usury,* 17.

8. For more on this point, see Noonan, *Usury,* 14; Lekai, *The Cistercians;* Little, *Religious Poverty,* 7. The monasteries were also, especially prior to the twelfth and thirteenth centuries, the proprietors of a number of taverns and inns. This is a good example of the fact that usury and taverns were not necessarily objectionable to the church per se; rather, due to their latent objectionableness, they could quickly be recruited as icons for a larger debate on the proper nature of economic activity during the great commercial revolution of the eleventh through thirteenth centuries. See also Ibanès, *La Doctrine de l'église et les Réalités Economiques.*

9. See Little, *Religious Poverty,* 61–69.

This was also the period of greatest economic expansion during the Middle Ages. With the rise of a truly vigorous monetary economy and a vastly increased money supply, money lending and usury became major economic activities.[10] A static, localized, largely barter economy was replaced by a dynamic, trade-oriented monetary economy that severely damaged the fortunes of the rural feudal aristocracy, to the advantage of a new, urban, merchant middle class.[11] In addition, the Catholic Church, which had earlier been an important lender of funds, became in many cases a victim of the usurer—the newly moneyed bourgeois. The rising indebtedness of the Cistercians in the later twelfth century has been well documented, for example; and Innocent III initiated curtailment of usury partly to expedite the crusades and prevent Venetian loan gouging, after Eugenius III had first made the link between the crusades and usury in a papal bull of 1145.[12] Caesarius of Heisterbach tells a tale in which a usurer is explicitly placed in a tavern, where he scorns the church's departing crusaders, preferring to stay home, keep his money, and make his fortune; here tavern, usury, avarice, and an anticharity attitude are all nicely combined.[13]

Thus church theorists began a renewed campaign against usury as part of a larger resistance to the new economic developments that began in the eleventh century.[14] Saint Anselm of Canterbury (1033–1109) was the first to take the important step of equating usury with theft of private property, so that it became a sin against justice: "Non ex rapinis et usuris, vel fraudibus acquirere debemus" (We must not enrich ourselves through theft and usury or by fraud), he writes (*PL* 158.659). In the mid–twelfth century, Peter Lombard writes in his hugely influential *Liber sententiarum* that "usura prohibetur, quae sub rapina continetur" (Usury is prohibited and is to be considered a form of theft) (*PL* 192.832). For the first time

---

10. For information on the nature and timing of this increase in the money supply, see Spufford, *Money and Its Use in Medieval Europe*. Spufford (99) dates the major increase in silver supply to 1160.

11. The classic discussion of this development is Duby, *La société aux XIe et XIIe siècles*.

12. On Cistercian debt, see Bouchard, *Holy Entrepreneurs,* 60. On the bull, see Nelson, *The Idea of Usury,* 7. The papal bull of Eugenius is in *PL* 180.1064. Of course, this conflict was neither a sole nor a primary cause of the renewed church opposition to usury but was simply a contributing irritant that nevertheless allowed the problem to be conveniently cast in terms of "the crusades versus the usurer," in much the same way that the economic issues of hospitality could be cast in the simpler and more visceral terms of "the pilgrim versus the tavern keeper and innkeeper."

13. Le Goff, *Your Money or Your Life,* 61.

14. The eleventh century also witnessed a great increase in venality satire within Latin literature—just another example of the increasing concern with profit and avarice. See Wolterbeek, *Comic Tales,* 22, 105.

there is an obligation of restitution by the thief, and usury is no longer just a personal sin but concerns the larger society as a whole. The gain of the one becomes the loss of the others. In an anonymous didactic poem entitled "Les Vers de la Mort," we find the following:

> Li useriers dist: Je sai bien,
> Ce k'ai reubé n'est mie mien.
> Pecieres sui et desloiaus
> Quant en contre raison retieng
> Ce c'autrui est, u je n'ai rien.[15]

> [The usurer says: I know very well
> That what I have stolen is not mine.
> I am a dishonorable sinner
> Because I keep, against the law,
> That which belongs to another, in which I have no part.]

Pope Alexander III then expanded the definition of usury to include sales on credit at a higher price than those for cash. For the first time, New Testament texts were cited to uphold the usury prohibition.[16]

Around 1185, Pope Urban II emphasized that "intention to gain alone will constitute usury."[17] Not only is illicit profit stigmatized, but so is the simple intention of gaining. This is a major extension of usury, but it also reflects a more general medieval development that will be of especial interest later in this book. Usury, like so many other crimes and sins, is rethought according to the general rise in the emphasis on intentionality that characterizes legal analysis of the late twelfth and early thirteenth centuries. We will see in chapters 3 and 4 that questions of intention and desire come to dominate the discussion concerning proper use of signs. Furthermore, Rutebeuf and especially Adam de la Halle ironically reveal the manner in which the idea of intentionality eventually renders sign use so problematic that the entire possibility of a successful role for signs is put into question.

---

15. Cited in Ungureanu, *La bourgeoisie naissante*, 92.

16. On credit sales, see Noonan, *Usury*, 19. For the New Testament, see especially Luke 6:35: "But love your enemies, and do good, and lend, expecting nothing in return . . ." Note that the Old Testament prohibition of usury in the case of one's brother is now implicitly extended to one's enemy as well—the acceptable bounds of usury are increasingly restrained.

17. Quoted in Noonan, *Usury*, 20.

This two-century period thus witnessed the weight of greater and greater authorities placed behind the prohibition of usury, as well as an increase in the gravity of the sin involved. This culminated in a situation on which John Noonan remarks that "by a strict application of the early [i.e., high medieval] theory in capitalist cities . . . nearly the whole community is involved in usury."[18] The key words of this quote are evidently "capitalist cities." In its broadest application, usury became synonymous with contract sales, loans, credit—all the monetary instruments necessary to operate a monetary economy based on trade, urban production centers, and the profit motive. The concept of usury was enlarged so that it became a tool for the general critique of a profit-oriented market economy. The men and women who essentially operated this economy—the urbanized middle classes—become labeled virtually as an entire class as usurers. In fact, in a sermon in which the celebrated urban preacher Jacques de Vitry identifies each social group with a particular sin, he identifies the characteristic sin of the bourgeoisie as usury. The same identity occurs elsewhere in Old French literature as well.[19] Thus just as the inn and tavern became emblematic of the bourgeois economic world in imaginative literature, usury becomes emblematic of the bourgeois economic world in theological and philosophical literature. The church's struggle against usury during these two centuries, which witnessed the rise of the bourgeoisie, can to a certain degree be seen as nothing less than a struggle against the economic theories and realities implicitly embodied in the profit-oriented activities of this class, in exactly the same sense that the criticism of the inn was part of a larger resistance to the profit-oriented monetary economy.[20]

Closer to home, Arras itself was one of these "capitalist cities," the principal industrial center of the Artois region, and the center of the cloth

---

18. Noonan, *Usury,* 81. See also Little, *Religious Poverty,* 39–41.

19. On Jacques de Vitry, see Schmitt, *Prêcher d'exemples,* 62. See also "Li mariages des filles au diable" in Jubinal, *Nouveau recueil,* 1:283–92.

20. Historians, such as John Noonan, have in fact directly tied papal efforts to suppress usury to the rise of trade and commerce in Italy (Noonan, *Usury,* 13), to take one example. Noonan, however, sees this as part of an effort to insure liquidity for capital to aid economic expansion, thus evoking the tensions and ambivalence that characterized the church's overall response. In fact, the latter half of the thirteenth century witnessed a move in the opposite direction by canonists—toward a greater and greater apology for usury, which broadened the realm of acceptable economic practice to a large degree (see Noonan, op. cit., in particular, as well as Baldwin, *Masters, Princes, and Merchants*). This trend largely postdates the texts discussed in my second and third chapters, however.

industry.[21] As an urban "metropolis" with twenty thousand inhabitants, it boasted a large middle-class population and was the most visible representative of the new, profit-oriented economics of the time. Not surprisingly, Arras and avarice became virtually synonymous.[22] Arras was also the northern European banking center and therefore a hotbed of usury. The financiers of Arras seem to have enjoyed a particularly powerful political and economic position in the thirteenth century, even in comparison to other similar cities, and usury was openly tolerated in the city.[23] A letter from Innocent III to the bishop of Arras notes that "so many usurers are said to have appeared in your city and diocese that if the censure issued by the Lateran Council against these people was applied against them all, the churches would have to be closed entirely."[24]

This capital of avarice and usury could not fail to attract the attention of church moralists and reformers. Most active in their opposition to usury were a group of scholars associated with Peter Cantor, including Peter Lombard, Jacques de Vitry (whom we have just met), Foulques de Neuilly, Robert Courson, and others, who flourished between 1190 and 1210.[25] The sermons and exempla of these and other urban reformers were often addressed primarily to bourgeois audiences.[26] Significantly, Courson and Stephen Langton are believed to have engaged in an extensive preaching campaign against usury in the city of Arras in the year 1213.[27] In a

---

21. The best texts on the history and social conditions of Arras are Dufournet, *Adam de la Halle à la recherche de lui-même;* Lestocquoy, *Aux origines de la bourgeoisie; Etudes d'histoire urbaine;* and Berger, *Littérature et société arrageoises.*

22. Dufournet, *Adam de la Halle à la recherche de lui-même,* 273ff.

23. See especially Ungureanu, *La bourgeoisie naissante,* 30–38. As early as 1100, Guibert de Nogent had taken note of the usurers of Arras, and the especially open tolerance of the practice resulted in plentiful documentation; it is known, for example, that the typical annual interest rate was 12–14 percent (Ungureanu, op. cit., 33). See also Jean Alter, *Les origines de la satire anti-bourgeoise,* 44ff. and 102, for a discussion of the literary notoriety of Arras and other towns of the region, such as Metz and Reims, as centers of usury.

24. "Usurarios qui tantum in civitate ac diocesi tua excrevisse dicuntur, quod si censura in Lateranensi concilio prodita contra tales proferretur in omnes, omnine claudi ecclesias pare multitudine oporteret" (quoted in Dufournet, *Adam de la Halle à la recherche de lui-même,* 216). Likewise, Lestocquoy notes: "on finit par se représenter Arras comme une vaste rue Quincampoix. Tout le monde trafique, tout le monde prête de l'argent . . ." (*Etudes d'histoire urbaine,* 161).

25. For a complete discussion of the circle of Peter Cantor and that circle's views on merchants and usury, see Baldwin, *Masters, Princes, and Merchants.*

26. See in particular Bremond, *L'exemplum,* 55–56, on the relation between preaching and the bourgeois milieu.

27. Baldwin, *Masters, Princes, and Merchants,* 20–21.

short literary text from this period entitled "Le Patenostre a l'usurier,"[28] Robert Courson is specifically mentioned as one of the enemies of usury, and Foulques de Neuilly is likewise named. Thus usury was a dominant issue in Arras at roughly the time of Bodel's play, and Peter Cantor's circle of reformers seems to have targeted Arras as their *bete noire,* bringing the conflict between doctrinal and illicit economics to the forefront.

Usury and the Sign

One must still ask why usury was chosen as the icon of an entire class and indeed an entire economic system. Among the many types of exchange, it occupied a unique position in that it involved a purely monetary transaction without the exchange of any other material goods. Herein lay the difficulty: accounting for the practice of usury required a theory of the nature and function of money that was radically different from the theory commonly in use at the time.

As we will see when we discuss in more detail the medieval theory of money, theorists of the time considered it to be a sign and treated it like any other sign within the framework of contemporary sign theory—in this particular case, as a mediator for all economic exchanges. Unfortunately, money does not actually function like a linguistic sign, and the effort to harmonize the two produced a great deal of grief for the theoretician, not to mention the merchant. The practice of usury was thus a threat to the standard theory of money and, by extension, to virtually all economic doctrine. Given these issues, it is not surprising that one authority has stated that for the Middle Ages "the problem of interest is the central issue in economic investigation."[29] I will briefly detail exactly how usury violated medieval monetary theory. This may seem to take us far afield from Jean Bodel, but in reality, because this analysis will allow an appreciation both of the true horror of usury for the medieval theoretician and, consequently, of the reasons for its choice as icon of the "new economics," it will also allow an appreciation of the full extent of the usury practiced in the tavern of Bodel's play.

Though the details of monetary theory varied, Saint Thomas Aquinas can be taken as representative of the thirteenth-century view: money was a measure of the value of some commodity. It had no value itself but only signified the value of the commodity. Money supposedly functioned just

---

28. Barbazon, *Fabliaux et contes,* 4:99–106.
29. Gordon, *Economic Analysis,* 141.

like a linguistic sign—always referring beyond itself to the idea or object or value that it represented. Aquinas himself quotes Aristotle.

All other things from themselves have some utility; not so however money. But it is the measure of the utility of other things. (Aristotle *Ethics* 5.9)

Like any measure, money had to have a fixed value (its face value), just as a word supposedly had a fixed meaning. A given face value always had to refer to the same "real" economic value and utility. As a signifier of value, money's function was to commute between two different commodities. Money was thus understood as a sort of convenient intermediary to avoid the actual physical exchange of the two commodities, as would occur in a pure barter economy. However, the exchange was still seen to be analogous to a barter exchange. Aquinas says of money that it was invented "ut sint quasi mensura quaedam rerum eanalium" (so that it might be the measure of common things) and that this invention was "chiefly for exchanges to be made."[30]

In the thirteenth century, money was considered a fungible that had to be consumed to obtain utility, just as did a bushel of wheat. It differed fundamentally from a nonfungible fertile field, which could be used to grow crops on more than one occasion, producing a profit (the crop to be sold) while the ownership of the land was retained. All fungibles were sterile and incapable of producing a surplus value—a profit: they could only be either physically consumed or exchanged for something else of equal value. Money was sterile—this is a fundamental truth of medieval monetary theory. Pope Innocent III stated that "money bears no fruit," and Aquinas maintained this as well.[31] This aspect of money is simply a result of its function as a sign. According to traditional medieval semiotics, all signs must be fungibles in that they must be sterile, producing no profit or surplus meaning or value.

Usury violated all of these principles. In a loan, money ceased to refer to the value of a commodity: rather it became a commodity, an object of exchange. It also became fertile, the money itself creating excess value in the form of the interest paid on the loan. And finally, the value of this sign

---

30. Aquinas *Summa Theologica* Ia, IIae, q. 2, art. 1; IIa, IIae, q. 78, art. 1.

31. Innocent is cited in Noonan, *Usury*, 50. The idea was a medieval commonplace. For reference to Aquinas, Saint Bonaventure, and others, see Le Goff, *Your Money or Your Life*, 29.

that supposedly had fixed value changed, since a quantity of money M became M + interest. Usury involved revaluation, commodification, and unnatural fertility of the sign. Likewise, speculative buying—a form of usury—reversed money's normal role, turning the commodity into the intermediary term, with money as the object of exchange.

In addition, usury separated the use and ownership of money. This separation was not theoretically possible for money as it was for, for example, a wheat field. Thus usury had to be treated as "selling that which is not."[32] As such, usury was in many cases viewed as a kind of "unnatural" gain (in addition to being an unnatural distortion of the sign, as we saw earlier), and in the early thirteenth century, William of Auxerre considered usury a violation of natural law.[33] Only such commodities as cattle and fields were considered "natural wealth," which in Aquinas' words "subvenitur ad defectos naturales tollendos; sicut cibus, potus, vestimenta . . . et alia hujusmodi" (are supplied to fulfill natural wants, such as food, drink, clothing, . . . and other things of this type), while those that "secundam se natura non juvatur, ut denarii, sed ars humana eos adinvenit propter facilitatem commutationis" (in themselves do not serve nature but were invented by human agency to facilitate exchange) were considered "artificial wealth."[34] Not only is this distinction echoed throughout the Middle Ages, as in *The Romance of the Rose*'s contrast of the "Golden Age," when wealth consisted of food, clothing, and shelter, to the symbolic wealth of gold and precious stones of the later degraded ages (vv. 8355–9527), but Aquinas' suggestion that money is a tool invented for the use of human society, to allow commutation of commodities, exactly parallels Augustine's conception of the invention and purpose of the linguistic sign.

Thus, as Aquinas said, "When money is acquired not by means of natural things but out of money itself, this is against nature."[35] (I will return to this concept of "unnatural" gain in my discussion of contemporary rhetorical issues as well.) In addition, usury was often interpreted as selling the time during which the money was used in exchange for the interest received on its return. Thus usury constituted a selling of time, which of course belonged only to God. And since the usurer sold what was not his,

---

32. Quoted in Noonan, *Usury,* 55.

33. Noonan, *Usury,* 42–44. See also Langholm, *Economics in the Medieval Schools,* 71.

34. Aquinas *Summa Theologica* Ia, IIae, q. 2, art. 1.

35. From his comments on Aristotle's *Politics* in *III primos libros politicorum* I.57, quoted in Gordon, *Economic Analysis,* 170–71.

he was ultimately a thief from God, using God's own time for his personal profit. In sum, usury violated the normal rules of the sign as they were applied to money, and consequently it violated medieval ideas of justice and just exchange of property, it violated natural law, and it was a direct theft from God. It is therefore not surprising that usury should attain iconic status in relation to profit economics and the bourgeoisie.

Interestingly enough, both usury and speculative buying were equated with gambling.[36] As late as the sixteenth century, we find in a French economics treatise the following remark, regarding merchants who buy low abroad and return to France during the wars of religion to sell very high and exploit the peasants.

> Ce sont là des contrats illegitimes, en l'espece des aleatoires, ou hazardz plus participant des contractz de sort & ieux de dez, que de juste commutation, plus digne d'estre mis entre les illusions de taverne, que entre les contractz civilz et politiques . . .[37]

> [These are illegitimate transactions, of a chance nature, or wagers resembling more closely contracts of fortune and games of dice than just commercial exchanges, and they are more worthy of being placed among the illusions of the tavern than among civil and social contracts . . .]

Here the tavern is a particular locus not simply of profit economics in general but more specifically of the most negative aspects of this economics: fraud, theft, and usury.

There is ample medieval evidence to substantiate this suggestion. We will see that the tavern boy in *Le Jeu de Saint Nicolas* favors certain customers when he serves the wine—filling some glasses more than others, and shortchanging many. In both *Le Jeu de Saint Nicolas* (1028–30) and *Courtois d'Arras* (vv. 126–27) there is the suggestion that the tavern keeper typically cheats his customers, either by charging too much or by watering down the wine. Arras had a municipal "ban" to fix a just price for wine,

---

36. It should be clarified, however, that there was no actual denunciation of simply reselling a commodity at a later date for a different price—it was recognized that prices could legitimately change. Rather, the buying and selling either of the same or of different commodities with the express intent to profit by the selling were condemned. Again, intentionality is the key issue.

37. The citation is from Charles Du Moulin's *Tractatus contractuum et usurarum* of 1542, provided via personal communication by Terence Cave, April 1992.

but as we have already seen, this nominal price could easily be shifted for excess profit through pouring more or less wine for a "pint." Medieval churches often featured stereotypical depictions of wine sellers in hell for overcharging their clients.[38]

Of course the tavern keeper was himself a merchant, engaged in the typical behavior of the bourgeois merchant, including specifically usury. The tavern keeper in *Le Jeu de Saint Nicolas* both loans money (vv. 815–17) and offers drink on credit after he is informed of the great treasure that the thieves are going to steal, though the credit price, since it is higher, is itself a form of usury as well as a selling of time.[39] Furthermore, the dice with which the thieves play, in addition to representing usurious speculative investing, constitute an illegitimate economic activity. Making money gambling at dice involves making money from money, without working, in exactly the same way as usury does. Though the Middle Ages may not ever have arrived at a strict labor theory of value, medieval economic writing broadly implies that a commodity could not increase in value unless additional work was invested in the commodity.[40] Thus the product of a harvest represented the work put into the plot up to that harvest. The origins of the idea can be found in Genesis 3:17–19, where the necessity of labor is linked to the Fall.[41] Whereas before the Fall the amount of labor was not necessarily commensurate with its output, after the Fall "man's standard of consumption is now linked to his productive activity in a way which did not pertain before the Fall": in other words, after the Fall one cannot get something for nothing; yet this is exactly what the (winning) dice players

---

38. See F. J. Warne's edition of *Le Jeu de Saint Nicolas*, note to v. 258.

39. For this same behavior, see also *Courtois d'Arras*, vv. 108–13. For a detailed discussion of what was and was not permissible in the area of credit sales, mortgages, contract sales, and so forth, see Baldwin, *Masters, Princes, and Merchants*, 273ff. As the thirteenth century proceeded, the canonists developed a massive body of theory attempting to circumscribe the exact limits of usury.

40. On the merchant and his activities, see especially Baldwin, *Masters, Princes, and Merchants*, chap. 14. Labor is cited over and over in the Middle Ages as the fundamental justification for a profit (Baldwin, op. cit., 271). The usurer is therefore often depicted as a transgressor against the labor theory of value, since the usurer makes money even while sleeping. Additional information on medieval concepts of labor can be found in Langholm, *Economics in the Medieval Schools*, 44, 52.

41. "And to Adam he said, 'Because you have listened to the voice of your wife, and have eaten of the tree of which I commanded you, "You shall not eat of it," cursed is the ground because of you; in toil you shall eat of it all the days of your life; thorns and thistles it shall bring forth to you; and you shall eat the plants of the field. In the sweat of your face you shall eat bread until you return to the ground . . .'"

propose to do.[42] The dice players correspond to the merchant, who was seen as selling goods for a profit that he did not himself produce. Dice and usury are explicitly linked by Philippe de Beaumanoir when he writes of the traditional laws of Normandy, "Autres convenances y a encore qui ne sunt pas a tenir, si comme se je convenance a paier detes du jeu des des ou d'usure."[43]

In summary, the tavern is a general locus of fraud and a specific locus of usury, enacted both in the commercial behavior of the tavern keeper and in the gambling of the customers. We have already seen that the Saracen king of *Le Jeu de Saint Nicolas* is also a usurer, abetted by the thieves. Usury was a theft from God, and fittingly the play features a literal theft from God on the part of the three thieves who steal the king's money. The money has been personally guaranteed by the saint and is therefore a sign of the greatness and power of God or, at the very least, of his saintly representative, Saint Nicolas. Upon hearing of the money's availability, the thieves exclaim "les granges Dieu sont aouvertes" (God's storehouses are open) (v. 773). They then appropriate this divinely sanctioned sign for their personal use and profit. In sum, the play features, first, a king who acts as a merchant in that he invests his money in a speculative venture, literally gambling it on the bet that Saint Nicolas is wrong, behavior befitting a tavern; and, second, three thieves who spend their time gambling in a tavern and act as the king's accomplices in that their theft "fertilizes" the money and allows interest to be accrued on it, however ironically, in this literal theft from God. (In fact, the thieves' use of the term *grange,* which normally would indicate a place for storing agricultural commodities, implicitly suggests that the king's artificial and sterile monetary wealth may actually be more natural and fertile than medieval monetary theory

---

42. The citation is from Gordon, *Economic Analysis,* 74. Isidor of Seville bases his origin for dice playing on classical references: he claims that the game was invented during the Trojan War by a soldier named Alea, to while away leisure time during periods of inactivity (see Tauber, *Das Wurfelspiel im Mittelalter,* 10). Dice are thus contaminated by their association with *otium:* their very production arises at an unproductive moment. In the tavern texts we have seen, dice are in fact symbolic of this state of otium (the characteristic state of the usurer, who does no real "work"), which is diametrically opposed to the proper state of work, the only source of true production of value and profit.

43. Beaumanoir is quoted in Semrau, *Wurfel und Wurfelspiel im alten Frankreich,* 19. As was the case with usury, gains made at dice were considered illegitimate and had to be returned to the victim; otherwise the winner was guilty of theft. Again, a slightly later example illustrates this point: "Car qui y jeue, rendre doit / Ce qu'il gaigne, selon de droit / Divin, sans en rien retenir" (Eustache Deschamps, cited in Semrau, op. cit., 19).

would allow.) Taverns, gambling, illegitimate merchant use of money, profit seeking, and theft are the rule in both the half of the play that occurs in the tavern and the half that takes place in the king's palace—itself a kind of figurative tavern.[44] The tavern scenes and ultimately the play as a whole thematize the issue not just of money and usury but of general semiotic transgression (at least in the church's eyes); this is the constant theme of the drama.

Poets and Thieves

Certainly this play can be read through the eyes of the church. It was almost certainly commissioned by a religiously oriented *confrérie*, and its most obvious meaning is that of the traditional saint's play.[45] But below this obvious surface lies a much more intriguing look at the status of language and money.[46] The biggest thief of all is perhaps Jean Bodel himself, who appropriates the Saint Nicolas legend to create a picture of a successful economic and poetic investment—an investment that leads to a text far richer and more ambiguous, more usurious even in its meanings, than any previous saint's play.

Bodel, in writing this play for a bourgeois audience in Arras, can be seen as an ally of the bourgeoisie just as the three thieves are the allies of the Saracen merchant king. He offers an ambiguous endorsement of a new economics and semiology, an endorsement placed under the aegis of the saint's play. The final result, on one level, is religion's consent to profit and usury—ultimately seen to be in the service of God, since everyone converts in the end, all the richer.

The association of poetics and economics, of jongleur/poet and bourgeois usurer, is particularly appropriate for the case of *Le Jeu de Saint Nicolas* since Arras was especially noted for its literary associations combining poets and the bourgeoisie—the *puy* and the *confrérie*. Writers were

---

44. The parallels of palace and tavern can be developed much further. Both the tavern and the palace feature criers, for example, who entice the audience to the respective locales with similar *boniments* (vv. 649–57 for the tavern, vv. 225–38 for the palace). See in particular Arens, *Untersuchungen zu Jean Bodels Mirakel,* for an analysis of the linguistic and structural parallels between the tavern and the palace on an extremely minute level. Such parallels have been widely noted, though not in the specific sense that I present here. See, for example, Joseph Dane, *Res/Verba.*

45. See Albert Henry's 1965 edition of *Le Jeu de Saint Nicolas,* 38–39, for a brief summary of the interpretations of all the play's major critics.

46. The closest reading to mine in terms of recognizing the two-faceted nature of the text is that of Roger Dragonetti ("Le *Jeu de St. Nicolas* de Jean Bodel"). He speaks of the dissimulation "du désir 'sarrasin' . . . sous les couleurs d'une rhétorique de l'orthodoxe" (371).

in general given particularly high standing in the town and allowed to join numerous bourgeois organizations, a rather unique situation for the Middle Ages. This was in part due to a local legend that the city had been saved from an epidemic when the Virgin appeared to two jongleurs to reveal to them how to end the sickness. Yet Bodel's drama suggests that the two groups shared more fundamental interests at the semiological level. The uniquely close association of the two groups in Arras could only have helped emphasize this fact.

The parallel between the thieves and the poet (and the alliance of the poet and the bourgeois merchant, himself bordering on a thief) suggests that the three thieves in the tavern represent the inscription of the poet into the play. In reality, the language of the thieves provides an alternate problematization of traditional semiotics. Economic usury is one means of implicitly questioning dominant sign theories. The thieves offer a second means, through their poetic version of the sign. They can be seen as exemplars of a usurious, illicitly profitable, and excessively meaningful poetics. The alliance of poet and merchant is the alliance of a new poetics and economics in a single anti-Platonic semiology.

We can begin by examining more closely a few of the exchanges that occur in the tavern scenes between the thieves, the innkeeper, and the crier. To start, we must strongly suspect that the thieves are at least tipsy, if not excessively drunk, as they spend much of the play actively drinking. And like all drunks, they mix up words, mispronounce them, and turn language into nonsense. At one point, one of them tries to reply to the tavern keeper with the proverb "En autre bus gist li lievre" (The rabbit is in another bush) but instead says, "En autre lievre gist li bus" (The bush is in another rabbit) (v. 822). On another occasion, one of them replies angrily to the crier, who is named Connart, that "Tous jours sont connart bateïç / ja n'ierent liet s'on ne les bat" (Connards are always fit for a beating and they'll never be happy if you don't beat them) (vv. 619–20). Here, the thief plays on the alternative meaning of *connart* as a reference to the female sexual organs, evoking the act of sexual intercourse and the suggestion of insatiable sexual desire.[47] In the first example the signs of language cease to refer to their proper referents but instead turn on themselves in their non-

---

47. The initial confrontation between the two criers, Connart and Raoulet, has itself been seen as the confrontation between two worlds—that of the palace and that of the tavern (Dufournet, "Variations sur un motif"). Connart is in fact treated much as Courtois will be in *Courtois d'Arras*: the play on his name by the thieves serves to empty the name of content and reduce it to a nominal form. In the latter play, it is two prostitutes who play on the name *Courtois* and the word *courtoisie*. It is clearly the "courtly" character who is victimized in both cases.

sense, while in the second example the wordplay produces an excess of sense beyond the proper signification. The excess, potentially limitless fertility of language is of course especially emphasized by the particular reference to the female sexual organs.

Certainly, a few puns or slips of the tongue in a text do not themselves constitute the formation of a poetics of revalued or reified signs. Yet the particular choice of puns here insistently draws our attention to the linguistic phenomena in question and begins a thematization of these phenomena of revaluation and reification of the sign. The dislocation of language by drink is a common medieval theme, and more important, we will see in chapter 3 that the Latin goliard tradition offered examples of explicit *mise en question* of the problem of inadequate signs via drunken speech. Similarly, in the case of the pun on multiple meanings and semiotic fertility via reference to the reproductive organs, not only does the pun itself explicitly point to the themes in question, but this same pun is used in the same way over and over in the fabliaux. Punning and transfer of meaning when referring to the sex organs and sex act become in the fabliaux an explicit problematization of the nature of metaphor and of a poetics where the sign consistently fails to refer univocally and "transcendentally."[48]

Among other examples of revaluation of the sign are those that occur when Auberon, one of the king's messengers, arrives in the tavern. Joseph Dane has noted that Auberon arrives using the discourse of the palace but that his words are consistently redefined in the new discourse of the tavern (and note that they are typically redefined toward monetary meanings, emphasizing the commodification of the sign, since we have seen that money is a resolutely commodified sign in the tavern).[49] Thus "partir," meaning "to depart," is redefined to mean "a round of dice" (v. 281) (modern French "une partie"), and "vostre affaire" (v. 293), a reference to the messenger's official business, becomes a reference to his business at the dice board. Dane notes that in verses 251–57 the messenger's arrival ("venir") becomes first "vendre" and then "vin."

Not only are the messenger's words redefined, but if we take the messenger as himself the embodiment of his language, then his own stay in the tavern emphasizes the fact that language there is turned from communication to gratuitous circularity. In his last words on leaving the palace, he

---

48. See, for example, "La Dame qui Aveine demandoit pour Morel," "L'Esquiriel," "La Damoisele qui ne pooit oir parler de foutre," "La Grue," "La sorisete aus Estopes," and "Porcelet," among others.

49. Dane, *Res/Verba*, 59–69.

promises, "nus cameus une lieue / N'est tant isniaus de courre que je nel raconsieue" (No camel can run a league so swiftly that I will not catch him) (248–49), yet he is immediately waylaid in the tavern, where his mission is forgotten for the sake of a glass of the "wine from Auxerre." While his function is to use his voice to proclaim the king's decrees, his words in the tavern are only used for fruitless argument over his bill—public performance turns to private indulgence.

In a number of places in the text, there are words that are either unknown slang or apparently made-up nonsense based on slang, so that we have not just the semantic nonsense of the mixed-up proverb but a total lack of signification: the linguistic sign, which should properly refer beyond itself, becomes entirely a physical commodity. Verses 701–4 are especially interesting because of their obscurity. This passage occurs during a drinking episode where the thieves have been complaining of the cutthroat attitude of the tavern keeper's assistant, Caignés. One of them, Pincedés, tastes the wine and praises its quality, remarking that the tavern keeper could sell the wine for even more if he wanted. The following dialogue then ensues.

Clikés.   Santissiés pour le marc dou cois
           Et pour sen geugon qui l'aseme!

Pincedés. Voire, et qui maint bignon li teme,
           Quant il trait le bai sans le marc.

Although there are many troublesome instances in the text where a given word or expression remains obscure, this passage stands out from all the others in the play due to the extreme amount of obscure slang employed— the meaning of virtually every noun and verb in these four lines remains open to question. It has been suggested that the passage is not pure nonsense but only indecipherable to the modern critic, and Michel Dubois provides one quite possible interpretation for the majority of the passage.[50] He proposes that "geugon" means "garcon de taverne," finding two citations in Guesnon; he considers "santissiés" a form of "centissier," meaning "se taire" (for which he finds one citation); and he claims that "marc dou cois" means "maitre de la taverne," based on the forms "coys" and "cowes" in Villon for "maison" and on "bai" as a form of Villon's

---

50. Dubois, "Sur un Passage obscur du *Jeu de St. Nicolas.*"

"bay," meaning "vin." He translates the lines as "Taisez-vous à cause du maître de la taverne et de son valet qui . . ." and "Oui, et qui lui . . . quand il tire le vin sans le maître." Albert Henry translates them as "Boucle-la, pour le singe du caboulot et pour son larbin qui le grignote!" and "Oui, et qui lui pelote maint baricaut, quant il tire le rouge sans galette." Clearly, the passage is still not entirely elucidated. Given the preceding context, the full sense is most likely "Be quiet and don't let the tavern keeper hear you, because his valet is doing us a favor" and "True, the helper robs his profits when he pours a little extra when the host isn't looking." Alternately, the assistant could be pouring the glasses short as well. In either case, the passage simply offers a more intriguing and more explicit example of the rhetoric of the tavern. For if our interpretation is correct, then the discussion here involves inexact measures of wine offered by the tavern boy to certain customers. "A glass of wine" does not mean the same amount of wine for everybody. The glass of wine is nominally still a "glass" (with "glass" being a specific measure), but the real contents are in fact a surplus or deficit of wine in this case. The "glass" as a sign is still a glass for all, but for some the contents (the referent) are different than for others. Another way of saying this is that the publicly assigned *proprietas* of the sign has been altered for private advantage in the exchange. This is of course simply a variation on the watering down of the wine: when the thieves return to the tavern loaded down with their loot, the host suddenly assures them, "Arés vous, onques n'en doutés, / Et vin qui n'est mie boutés" (Don't doubt it, you'll have wine that is not in the least adulterated) (vv. 1028–29). Evidently this was not the case before. The tavern keeper is in both cases abusing public expectation and propriety.

I introduce this notion of *proprietas* because I would like to return briefly to economic theory and draw a parallel between economic transgression against *proprietas* and linguistic transgression against this same notion. The medieval ideas of the "just" price and "just" linguistic exchanges were intimately connected: both of these concepts involved an attempt to stabilize the meaning or value of signs for the entire semiotic community. And the conflict of public and private centered around the notion of *proprietas* raises fundamental issues concerning the medieval idea of poetic production as a distribution of "truth" rather than a "creative" activity.

What is today termed economics was conceived of in medieval canon law as the question of the just exchange of personal property. Private property was typically viewed as a necessary evil of the Fall, resulting (much as the world's different languages did) from a loss of human universality and perfect communal existence and understanding.[51] Yet once property was admitted, it was imperative to insure that each person's *proprietas* remain rightfully his own and that no one be "robbed" through unequal exchange. All medieval economic writings can be considered as attempts to arrive at ways of guaranteeing just exchange of personal property—in other words "economic justice."[52] In the same line of thought, William of Auxerre states that "if it is strictly used, justice is the value by which to each one is rendered what is his own, because it is his own."[53]

This notion of the alteration of *proprietas* as an infringement on justice is of vital importance, for in the most pessimistic of church writings, all economic activity was held in suspicion because it was believed that there would always be an unequal exchange—that all economics was an attempt to cheat the opposing party. Tertullian, in *De idolatria,* considers all business to involve the sin of covetousness and to be a type of idolatry. He linked all commercial practices with deceitful behavior. Roman law had already recognized that in buying and selling, "each party is allowed to outwit the other." Bernard of Cluny, among others, echoes this attitude in the Middle Ages, noting that "The merchant conducts nearly all his business by deception."[54]

This suspicion was the basis for the medieval doctrine of the just price. The just price was an attempt to ensure fair economic exchanges—to avoid the deceit and outwitting that could occur. The idea was that a fixed price for commodities could be established based on community evaluation of the commodity's worth. The just price was to be an objective price, which

---

51. A classic example is the fall from the "Golden Age" to the "Age of Iron" in *Le Roman de la Rose.* In the Golden Age, there is no property and all possessions are communal; property arrives with the decline of the Golden Age. In v. 8448, describing the Golden Age, we read of the people, "Ne rien propre aveir ne voulaient." For more on this postlapsarian idea of property, see Langholm, *Economics in the Medieval Schools,* 20–26, 72–76.

52. This approach to economic analysis was essentially the same as that found in Roman texts, where "economic issues are explored to the extent felt necessary to elucidate the manners in which institutional justice might be achieved in particular areas of human intercourse" (Gordon, *Economic Analysis,* 123). The real basis of economic thought is thus considered by Gordon to arise from the concern for law, justice, and social order. See also Langholm, *Economics in the Medieval Schools,* 20–26.

53. *De justitia in generali* fol. 176r:b, quoted in Noonan, *Usury,* 31.

54. For more on the antimercantile attitudes of late Roman and early Christian writers, including Cicero, Tertullian, and Jerome, see especially Baldwin, *Masters, Princes, and Merchants,* 262. The citation of Roman law is from *Digesta* 19.2.22, quoted in Gordon, *Economic Analysis,* 128. The original quotation from Bernard is "Institor omnia pene negotia fraude volutat" (*De contemptu mundi,* 97).

should not be altered by the needs of a particular seller or to the advantage of a particular buyer.[55] The evaluation could of course only occur in an atmosphere of free competition among all buyers and sellers. The great fears were that some buyer or seller could artificially monopolize the market and fix prices contrary to those of the greater community and that goods could be fraudulently represented.

Interestingly, the economic deceptions were considered to be most often accomplished by linguistic means: the fraudulent commercial exchange was intimately associated with the fraudulent linguistic exchange.[56] Rutebeuf echoes this view in his description of merchants in "L'estat du monde" (*OC* 1:77–87).

> Je vous [le] dis bien vraiement
> Ils font maint mauvais serement
> Et si jurent que leurs denrées
> Sont et bonnes et esmerées
> Tell(e) fois que c'est mensonge pur;
> Si vendent à terme, et usure
> Vient tantôt et termoierie
> Qui sont de la même mainie;
> Alors est le terme acheté
> Et plus cher vendue la denrée.
>
> (vv. 125–34)

> [I tell you truthfully,
> Many times they take false oaths
> And swear that their wares
> Are both excellent and pure
> When this is sometimes a total lie;
> And they sell on credit, and usury

---

55. For further discussion of the complexities of community evaluation, see Gordon, *Economic Analysis,* 128ff.; Noonan, *Usury,* 88. On the just price in general, see Noonan, op. cit., 87–88; Baldwin, *Medieval Theories of Just Price;* Salin, "Just Price."

56. For Tertullian's remarks, see Baldwin, *Masters, Princes, and Merchants,* 262. Baldwin's discussion also covers such figures as Saint Jerome and Cicero, who considered all merchants to be inveterate liars and thieves, thus providing another example of the link of economic exchange and lying. Hugh of Saint Victor writes that "commerce . . . is beyond all doubt a peculiar sort of rhetoric . . . for eloquence is in the highest degree necessary to it" (*Didascalicon* II.23), though he takes a more favorable attitude toward the subject than many others.

Appears quite often and credit sales,
Which are all of the same family;
Thus time is bought
And the wares more dearly sold.]

The lie, usury, and credit sales are all equally illicit inflations of value, though the first alters initially linguistic and subsequently economic *proprietas,* while the second and third alter economic *proprietas* directly.[57]

In addition, we have already seen (in chap. 1) the fraudulent economic exchange in "Le prestre et le chevalier," where the priest's monopoly on hospitality in the village is repeated in the fraudulent linguistic exchange wherein the priest abuses the community understanding of the word *met* for his own profit. There is, in the dynamics of this exchange, the suggestion of a parallel between the conditions for "just" economic exchange (the avoidance of private monopoly on goods and services) and the conditions for "just" linguistic exchange (the avoidance of a private monopoly on the truth or on the meaning of a given word). Thus attempts to establish objective monetary prices immune to individual reinterpretations are parallel to the Neoplatonic desire for the transcendent linguistic signifier, for guaranteed "vertical" referentiality, functioning equally well for all members of the community in conveying meaning and intention. Such signs must also be immune to individual redefinitions: an attempt to establish a privileged monopoly wherein certain parties have special understanding of signs, breaking the larger community into smaller semiotic—or, to use Brian Stock's widely employed term, textual—communities, would constitute a kind of linguistic fraud or monopoly. The conditions for just economic exchange parallel those for just linguistic exchange.

Usury was fundamentally a sin against the *proprietas* of the sign: unjust profit and loss are the by-products of one individual's revaluation of the sign for his private gain. But the loss here is not only private but public, since the private revaluation (to one individual's profit) violates not just the economic *proprietas* of another individual but, in a larger sense, the public system of *proprietas* embodied in the sign as public measure. Money was considered public property—minted by the ruler for public use, and

57. See also Honorius d'Autun *Elucidarium* DII.55 and MII.55, in Kleinhans, *Lucidere,* 474: the disciple asks,"Quam spem habent mercatores?" (What hope do merchants have [for salvation]?), to which the master replies: "Parvam. Nam fraudibus, perjuriis, lucris omne pene quod habent acquirunt" (Little, for they acquire almost all they possess through fraud and lies).

theoretically always having an objective public value. It was widely interpreted as a symbol of a ruler's prestige and of public order in general.[58] Language was likewise a public medium for the exchange of ideas, as we saw in discussing Augustine in chapter 1.[59] Usury was thus a private attack on the public—a case of an individual destabilizing the communal semiotic system for his own personal profit.

Such communal property ultimately belonged to God and was to be used only in his service, being provided by him for human benefit and to aid in serving him. The author of the moralizing text "Miserere" asks the wealthy man: "Cuides ke Dieus te doinst les fruis / De le tere por toi soul paistre? / Tu as en ton grenier tans muis, / Et li greniers ton proisme est vuis" (Do you believe that God gave you the fruits of the earth for you alone? Your storehouses are so full, and those of your neighbors are empty).[60] In the ideal public economy of the Catholic Church, all exchanges were for utilitarian purposes, to aid the survival and development of man, the servant of God; money was "only meant to be used in purchasing."[61] The patristic writer Hermas noted: "Riches are properly of God—exercised correctly, command over resources can yield spiritual benefits to the administrator while it serves the material needs of society as a whole."[62] Thus we have the traditional exhortation "Lend only for God, and from charity."[63] Trade and commerce in general were widely regarded as being legitimized only by the needs of individuals to make up for shortfall or in cases where the buyer planned to distribute goods into areas where they were scarce. When such commerce ceased to have such utilitarian benefits, it ceased to be legitimate in the eyes of theologians.[64] The thirteenth-century development of an apology for the activity of the merchant was based primarily on this concept of distribution.[65] Yet this idea of distribution was the basis for the legitimacy not only of the merchant but of the poet as well, and it is this concept that is violated so often

---

58. See Duby, *The Early Growth of the European Economy*, 64–66.

59. Aquinas himself noted that "human society could not endure without just buying and selling and just price" (*Summa Theologica* IIa, Iae, q. 95, art. 4).

60. Langlois, *La vie française au Moyen Age*, 2:165.

61. The quotation is from the *palea* "Ejiciens," quoted in Noonan, *Usury*, 38.

62. Quoted in Gordon, *Economic Analysis*, 99.

63. Quoted in Noonan, *Usury*, 32

64. See Duby, *The Early Growth of the European Economy*, 107–8, for an interesting formalization of this idea from the *Capitularia Regum Francorum*, decreed by Charlemagne.

65. See Baldwin, *Masters, Princes, and Merchants*. See also Little, *Religious Poverty*, especially 24–27 on the idea of distribution and the manipulation of signs (as opposed to labor). See his chapter 10 for more on the developing apology for commerce.

in *Le Jeu de Saint Nicolas,* where linguistic "truth" is not distributed but illegitimately "created" in the form of poetic "surplus." The thieves rob the "granges" (or *greniers*) of God himself, despite the admonitions of the "Miserere."

The idea of distribution reveals a fundamental fact about medieval conceptions of wealth and truth: that they were part of a system wherein exchanges were always a zero-sum game. In other words, if someone profited, someone else had to lose. This is the reason for the obsession with the process of exchange, the attempts to guarantee equal exchange, and the attempts to remove pilgrims, monasteries, and others from this process as much as possible. The only way that humans could actually create wealth was through proportionate labor: there was no possibility of doing so in the process of exchange. Except for the value added by labor, the total quantity of value was considered fixed: only God could create wealth ex nihilo.[66] In this system, any profit entails loss by another individual, but in a larger sense, any individual private profit must entail a corresponding loss by the rest of the public community as well. In this Neoplatonic view of the purpose and functioning of the sign, the transgression of the jongleur was to turn language from its function as aid for the survival of Christian society to purely private ends and thus to rob from humanity. Significantly, Peter Cantor noted that only the jongleurs, among all professions, had no function or role on the earth and were totally without utility. In the *Verbum abbreviatorum,* in the chapter "Contra dantes histrionibus" (Against giving to *histrions* [jongleurs]), he states: "Nullum genus hominum est, in quo non inveniatur aliquis utilis usus . . . praeter hoc genus hominum, quod est monstrum, nulla virtute ademptum a vitiis" (There is no type of person in which some useful purpose is not found . . . except for this type of persons, who are monsters, whom no virtue rescues from their vices) (*PL* 205.154). The struggle over the idea of profit (in all senses) is really a struggle over the injection of the private individual into the public system of exchange, over his intention to revalue part of that system for his private benefit, and a struggle to maintain a "brotherhood" of society in the face of its increasing individualization, whether that be the Christian brotherhood of charity discussed in chapter 1 or the "brothers" to whom the Bible forbids lending at interest, whose number the church attempted to make as large as possible in the Middle Ages. This brother-

---

66. See Chénu, *Nature, Man, and Society,* 40ff., for more on humans as "artisans" versus God as "creator."

hood, as Augustine and Aquinas make clear through their emphasis on signs as mediums of exchange, is defined by a series of shared public signs.

Similarly, in regard to Aquinas' discussion of the book, Jane Burns has noted: "there is an essential distinction to be made between the preverbal existence of God and a linguistic system that necessarily involves mediation. This distinction is used typically to explain why only God has the power to create, whereas the artist using words can merely represent."[67] Augustine himself states this claim in a slightly different form: "For no one should consider anything his own, except perhaps a lie, since all truth is from Him who said, 'I am the truth'" (*DDC* prologue.8). Truth is a kind of universal community property, which the individual cannot own or create but can only reproduce in a mimetic fashion.[68] Yet in economic terms, valuable production cannot come without the requisite labor, and the same could be said of linguistic value, as is clear from Burns' discussion of Aquinas. Neither language nor money should create something entirely new "'out of the void,'" as God did at the time of the Creation: they should only refer to what already exists. "The person who narrates," says Augustine, "simply points out an existing truth" (*DDC* II.xxxii.50).

While Augustine clearly predicts Aquinas, his remarks contain, in the concept of the lie, a further limitation of human representational activity. The poet not only can represent but must do so to act licitly; otherwise the poet lies. As we saw in the introduction, Augustine claimed that the only proper use of signs was as representational, telementational vehicles (*DDC* II.ii.3). The poet should always be implicated in an act of reference when using language: language is not free and without incumbent referentiality. Thus signs are constrained within a double bind, for they must always refer, and always only refer, to preexisting, essential reality. In this way, a rigorous homology is established between reality and language. Faced with illicit creativity in the form of nonreferring signs, or signs that created their own value independently of reference to real truths, traditional thought had no option but to claim that such creativity did not exist but was rather a theft of someone else's goods, as in usury, or was a lie, as Augustine suggests and as many medieval theorists reiterated. Alain de Lille, speaking of the art of painting, though he could equally well be discussing poetry, says:

---

67. Burns, *Arthurian Fictions,* 21–22.
68. Hugh of Saint Victor, for example, in *Didascalicon* I.3, notes that God creates, Nature brings into actuality what is latent in creation, and the artificer can only imitate Nature.

What can have no real existence comes into being and painting, aping reality and diverting itself with a strange art, turns the shadows of things into things and changes every lie to truth.[69]

A Private Superabundance

The larger issues that are ultimately at stake in verses 701–4 of *Le Jeu de Saint Nicolas* and in the play as a whole are issues of public and private and of the creative surplus that robs the public to benefit the individual. The private cheating on the contents of the nominal public unit of consumption, the private betrayal of the public unit of measure by the thieves/jongleurs, is appropriately paralleled by their use of language in this passage. They violate just economic exchange and just linguistic exchange. Meaningful or not, the vocabulary of verses 701–4 is clearly chosen by the thief to obscure meaning for the general public in the tavern, especially for the innkeeper. The public tool of communication is taken over as a private tool to insure private profit; words are chosen that are known only to some of those present, so that the conditions of linguistic exchange are not equivalent and the speaker holds a kind of linguistic monopoly. He thus draws unfair linguistic advantage (excess meaning) from his use of these private signs, and this linguistic profit corresponds to the monetary profit he makes by getting extra wine for his money. The thief is finally the exact equivalent of the usurer, who alters the stability of the public monetary sign for his own profit.

This fragmentation of the public linguistic space into various private spaces occurs not only for the characters in the tavern but for at least the modern reader as well and possibly for at least some of the contemporary viewers of the play. The linguistic fragmentation of the tavern thus parallels an additional fragmentation of literary space, as verses 701–4 potentially become a wink or an aside to a certain privileged audience who might understand—an effect that reaches its greatest development in the tavern poems of François Villon using the dialect of the "Coquillage."[70] Verses 701–4 briefly signal the end of the general, shared, public literary language and space of the epic, as does the play in general with its depiction of the defeat of the epic crusaders in its opening verses— their world inadequate to the challenge of the times. It is the comic

---

69. Alain de Lille, *Anticlaudianus*, 49. See also *DPN* 138–41.
70. See Guiraud, *Le jargon de Villon*.

equivalent of Charlemagne tugging fitfully on his beard at the end of *The Song of Roland.* Finally, as with the other passages mentioned, these four verses seem to insistently draw our attention to the poetic phenomena in question and to thematize the issue of the private abuse of the sign—as I noted, the four lines stand out from all others in the text for their apparently willful obscurity. The author, Jean Bodel, is doing to his audience with these four lines exactly what the thief in the play is doing to *his* audience in the tavern, and the inscription of the poet into the play becomes all the clearer.

This crisis of the public sign actually dominates the entire structure of the play. The tavern sections feature three broad movements, each of which begins with a quantity of money in question, and each of which then devolves into a dispute over that money where two or more individuals attempt to lay private claim to the sum in question. And the dispute is in each case enacted through a game of chance: first the king's crier Auberons and the thief Clikés gamble to decide who will pay Auberon's bill (vv. 251–314); then the three thieves Rasoirs, Pincedés, and Clikés gamble again to decide who will pay their own bill (vv. 836–958); then they play at the dice game "hasard" with the loot stolen from the king (vv. 1053–1183).

The insistence on a private partitioning rather than mutual ownership, use, and responsibility converts each of these arguments into a question of individual profit and loss and thus into a metaphor for all commerce according to the medieval point of view discussed earlier. Someone is always trying to come out a little ahead of equal, fair, and just. This metaphor is only strengthened by the use of dice to effect the partitioning, evoking as it does the image of commercial speculation. The church might argue that the fate of the thieves is in a certain sense the future fate of the society as a whole: endless bitter dispute over a fixed sum of money, where someone always wins and someone else must lose, and where the basis of labor no longer provides a rational means of sharing resources. The only solution to this problem in the play is to fragment the shared resource. The tavern keeper solves the dilemma thus.

Par foi! Or sommes nous yevel:
Comme devant resoit communs.
Or en prengne se part chascuns!

(1175–77)

[By my faith, now we're quits [equal]:
As before, no more debts.
Now let each take his own share!]

Through this fragmentation, the community of the thieves is shattered like the other communities of the play. Indeed, they split up in the end, as the poetic, economic, and semiotic logic of their position demands: "Que chascuns voit hui mais par lui; / Li quels que soit iert ëuereus" (Let each one go his own way; may each find his own happiness) (1357–58).

Thus the poetics of the tavern corresponds closely to its usurious economics. The referential value of both linguistic and monetary signs is consistently revalued, and they fail to function as intermediaries between commodities and ideas of equal value and meaning. Rather, they are themselves commodified, becoming valued for themselves rather than as referrers. They both become fertile producers of surplus value and sense—profit. The objective public sign, intended for public utility, is rendered subjective and private for the sake of private profit. This poetics is furthermore enacted primarily by the three thieves and secondarily by the tavern keeper and crier. The three thieves in particular are the key linguistic performers of the play as well as the prime agents of the action, and they "fertilize" not only the king's money but language as well. Thus we can speak of a usurious poetics as well as of a usurious economics.

The particular poetics of this tavern scene, as well as the inscription of the poet as thief, are far from unusual.[71] In fact, the medieval jongleur is portrayed time and again in the twelfth and thirteenth centuries as a kind of thief of language, a linguistic speculator or gambler who uses language in tricky or deceitful ways to produce excess sense or to turn language away from its rightful purpose of referring, toward a self-referential condition as commodity. The jongleur was quite often associated with the tavern as well. We have seen this already in Jean le Marchant's miracle and in the citations I have given in the introduction. Rutebeuf portrays himself as a gambler and tavern frequenter, François Villon is a thief and a visitor of taverns and brothels, and the fabliaux often portray or inscribe the poet as

---

71. See Nykrog, *Les fabliaux,* 130–31, for a discussion of the link between the tavern and the thief in the fabliaux ("Ils sortent la nuit, ayant une taverne mal famée comme port d'attache et son tavernier comme receleur . . ."). He follows this discussion with remarks on the jongleur, the thief and jongleur constituting the two principal "rebuts de la société médiévale" appearing in the fabliaux. This conjunction can hardly be considered an accident.

both gambler and thief, as in the case of "St. Pierre et le jongleur," to take one example—we will see others in chapter 3. The jongleur was himself often condemned as an inveterate sinner doomed to hell, as by Peter Cantor (quoted earlier), so the association of poet and tavern—the antichurch—is entirely fitting.[72] The three thieves in the tavern and their particular brand of language can be seen in the larger context of the representation of the poet in the comico-realist genres of medieval French literature. Just as this tavern in particular and the tavern in general are characterized by illicit economics (usury), so the tavern of *Le Jeu de Saint Nicolas* is reflective of the tavern in general in high medieval French literature as a locus of illicit poetics.

Clearly, almost any medieval literary text would reveal some instances of usurious poetics: it is important to stress once again that Bodel's text explicitly allies the two forms of usury in question and pointedly emphasizes the failure of the Neoplatonic sign. There are two important points to be made: first, the early Middle Ages had developed a normative semiology that insisted that the above usurious process should not occur and that signs could attain to something resembling fixed, transparent reference; second, medieval texts that question the efficacy of the sign often do so specifically in relation to this specific, deep-seated cultural semiology of the Neoplatonic or Augustinian sign. Many medieval texts may be the product of a poetics that contradicts Augustinian sign theory: it could hardly be otherwise, since from a modern linguistic and semiotic point of view, this theory clearly fails to account adequately for the functioning of signs. This contradiction itself is often of little value in interpreting medieval texts: some of the most complex linguistic play can be found in such texts as Gautier de Coinci's *Miracles de Notre Dame,* though this text hardly seems otherwise to represent itself as semiotically transgressive. My particular interest lies in the cases where such texts as this one thematize their semiological oppositions.

In *Le Jeu de Saint Nicolas,* we have already seen that in several cases an illicit poetics is used to produce illicit economic gain for the characters in the tavern. This occurs so often that one must recognize the insistence

---

72. One of the classic statements of condemnation is that of Honorius d'Autun: the disciple asks, "Habent spem joculatores?" to which the master replies: "Nullam. tota namque intentione sunt ministri Satanae, de his dicitur: 'Deum non cognoverunt; ideo Deus sprevit eos, et Dominus subsannit eos, quia derisores deridentur'" (*Elucidarium* DII.58 and MII.58, in Kleinhans, *Lucidere,* 476). For another good example of the jongleur in the tavern, see Faral, *Les jongleurs,* app. III, no. 102.

with which Bodel underlines this theme of the general illicit use of the sign to produce a semiotic "profit": in fact, many instances of linguistic ambiguity serve to provide monetary profit for the speaker, and others are framed in terms of double meanings, with at least one instance having a monetary sense. For example, after one false addition, one of the thieves replies to Caignes: "Au conter n'iés tu point laniers, / N'au mesconter, s'on te veut croire" (You're no slouch at adding the bill, or in misadding, if you're to be believed) (vv. 691–92). These lines play on the homophony between "conter" meaning "to tell a tale" (i.e., to use language) and *compter* meaning "to settle one's account, pay the bill," as well as on "croire," which could mean either "to believe someone's words" or "to accept someone's monetary credit." There is a shifting of the value of both linguistic and monetary signs. Likewise, at one point Clikés says to Caignes, "De gage prendre et de mestraire / N'a ten pareil jusques au Dan!" (In taking insurance and in miscounting you have no equal to the ends of the earth!) (vv. 1331–32). "Mestraire" can mean both "to lie or tell a false tale" and "to engage in a false economic reckoning." Profit comes in many forms.

An earlier scene (vv. 272–83) features an argument over the price of certain types of wine and the total bill owed.

Auberons.   Dites, combien doi je paier?
              Je faç que faus, qui tant demeure.

Li Tavreniers. Paie denier et a l'autre eure
              Aras le pinte pour maille.
              C'est a douze deniers, sans faille:
              Paie un denier ou boi encore.

Auberons.   Mais le maille prenderés ore
              Et au revenir le denier!

Li Tavreniers. Veus tu faire ja le panier?
              Au mains me dois tu trois partis:
              Ains que de chi soies partis,
              Sarai bien a coi m'en tenrai.

[*Auberon.*   Tell me, how much must I pay?
              I'd be wasting my time to stay here any longer.

The Tavern Keeper.   Pay one denier and the next time
You'll get a pint for one maille.
It costs twelve deniers [for eight glasses]
Pay one denier or have another glass.

Auberon.   You take the maille now
And you'll get the denier the next time!

The Tavern Keeper.   Do you want to cheat me?
You owe me at least three bits [one and a half
mailles].
Before you leave here,
I'll have my share.]

One denier is equal to two mailles. In the preceding dialogue, the wine costs one and a half mailles for one pint or three mailles for two pints. However, since the maille is the smallest denomination of French coin in existence, it is impossible to pay precisely for a pint of wine. (One could pay exactly for two, which is what the innkeeper hopes the customer will drink.) The ensuing argument is then over how the customer will pay for his one pint of wine—will he pay two mailles now and receive a later pint for one maille (the innkeeper's preference), or will he pay one maille now and two mailles later (the customer's preference)? The same argument may well have been common in medieval French taverns, as suggested by the proverb "Avoir la maille à fendre," which Auberons echoes in his remark "Ne me puis a vous awillier, / Se une maaille en deus ne caup" (I can't make arrangements with you, unless I cut a maaille in two) (288–89).[73]

The situation would have been familiar to the audience and would certainly have produced smiles of recognition. Yet, given the many related scenes, it also seems to be a comic meditation on the inadequacy of the monetary sign, even where values are not open to debate. The pint has a fixed, nominal value, yet in the real world there is a gap between the supposed value of the commodity and the ability of the actual monetary sign to express this value. (This scene immediately follows that with which I opened this chapter, wherein the tavern keeper assures that he sells his wine "au ban de le vile" but his customer complains that he has nevertheless been shortchanged because the goblet is too small.) The sign here fails

---

73. See Foulet and Foulon, "Les scènes de taverne et les comptes du tavernier."

to signify fully and adequately in the real world: there is always a deficit or surplus, always a gap. Or perhaps one could say more precisely that there is always the potential for such a gap in the imperfect world of signs; after all, it is the tavern keeper who has manipulated the price to produce such a gap. The argument is as virulent as it is because both the innkeeper and the customer know that, unlike regular customers, the king's crier will probably not be back. The real question, then, is who will make a profit off the inadequacy of the sign—who will effect a de facto shift of the value of the pint to one or two mailles from one and a half. The sign, through its inadequacy and the tavern keeper's self-serving manipulation of it, becomes a battleground for personal profit rather than a medium for just exchange of equal value.

These conjunctions of linguistic and monetary themes and signs are perhaps the strongest indicator of the thematic dominance of sign in the play: Bodel's drama in particular and the tavern genre in general consistently engage in such a thematization in terms of both language and money. The dual themes of the tavern as locus of illicit economics and as locus of illicit rhetoric already existed when Bodel wrote his play. The great originality of *Le Jeu de Saint Nicolas* lies in its establishing for the tavern scene a coherent series of economic and poetic themes in the vernacular: many of the examples that I cited to show Bodel's place in the tradition of the tavern scene probably postdate his work. In regard to both economics and poetics, his play adopted the themes of earlier tradition and elaborated them far beyond their previous level. In so doing, he established a powerfully attractive model of the tavern scene that, along with that of the contemporaneous *Courtois d'Arras,* formed the basis for all future elaborations of what came to constitute a true genre of its own. It is the very strength and depth of this model that allow texts such as Jean le Marchant's miracle tale to connote such deep meanings through its use of the tavern.

Despite this feat, the even greater originality of Bodel lies in the degree to which he successfully integrated the two thematics of illicit poetics and illicit economics, using the concept of usury to produce a general meditation on the nature of the sign. That such a meditation should be framed in terms of money and usury is actually less surprising than it might seem. Boethius, in the year 513, had already supplied the basis for an explicit linking of language and money as representational signs in his widely read commentary on Aristotle's *De interpretatione.* The consideration of the failure of the sign, especially the linguistic sign, through the use of monetary motifs is actually quite widespread in the Middle Ages, and R. A. Shoaf in particular has written extensively on this topic with regard to Chaucer and Dante.[74] An interesting earlier example of such a thematization from a literary text is the poem "Manus ferens munera" from the *Carmina Burana,*[75] where money is linked to the corruption of grammatical cases.

Tale fedus hodies
defedat et inficit
nostros ablativos,
qui absorbent vivos,
moti per dativos
movent genitivos.

(vv. 55–60)

This text has been translated as "Greed for money now disgraces / And infects grammatical cases: / Our 'takers away,' the ablative, / Rogues that deserve suppression, / Prey upon our datives, 'those who give,' / While genitives keep possession."[76] The poet neatly posits a virtual gift economy of grammar, whose disruption is simultaneously moral, economic, and linguistic. Proper relations, he suggests, are gradually being defrauded by the avarice of the ablative, that most ill defined and wide-ranging of tenses. Like money, it threatens always to substitute itself for a more proper, precise relation, thereby reducing everything (linguistic) to a common, unstable denominator. The stability of values—moral, linguistic, and economic—is at stake.

The turn of the thirteenth century was an especially propitious moment for raising such issues. Following an explosion in the availability of silver beginning around 1160, a great profusion of mints arose throughout Europe, all minting deniers. The value of the metal in these deniers varied widely, to the point that a denier from Toulouse was equivalent to four denier from Le Puy. Such a situation furnished a perfect model for a crisis in the value of the sign, since the nominal, signified face value of all the deniers was always one "denier." This crisis of nominal value replicates exactly the crisis of the nominal "glass" of wine discussed earlier. Appro-

---

74. Shoaf, *Dante, Chaucer, and the Currency of the Word.* See pp. 9–11 on *De interpretatione.*

75. *CB* 10–13.

76. Whicher, *The Goliard Poets,* 146–47.

priately enough, the height of this monetary crisis corresponded to the exact moments of the composition and performance of Bodel's play.[77] The play in fact shows an overall fascination with multiple and arbitrary determinations of value that extends beyond the slippery pricing and unsettled bills in the tavern. The various admirals who arrive at the king's palace to wage war on the Christians come from lands where, in one case, "li chien esquitent l'or" (the dogs shit gold) (v. 363) and, in another, "n'a monnoie / Autres que pierres de moelin" (there are no coins except millstones) (vv. 376–77). Such images underline the lack of any general stabilizing system of value in the world.

But usury was a concern at the time not merely in terms of money and the problem of stable monetary values but in any sort of exchange whatsoever, including those involving goods and services. Peter Lombard writes in the *Liber sententiarum,* "accipe quod dedisti, et nihil superfluum quaeras; quia superabundantia usura computatur" (receive that which you gave [loaned], and ask for nothing in addition, for any excess must be considered usury [interest]) (*PL* 192.832). He then goes on in the same passage to further emphasize that it is this "superabundance"—not just monetary interest—that is at the heart of the matter.

Putant aliqui usuram tantum esse in pecunia; sed intelligant usuram vocari superabundantiam, scilicet quidquid est si ab eo quod dederit plus est.

[Some think that usury involves simply money; but let it be understood that usury should be called superabundance, that is to say, the part that is more than that which was given.]

In fact, there were precedents for expanding the idea of usury to cover both rhetoric and spirituality. We will see one such example in chapter 3.[78] Lombard's use of the term "dederit" would seem to allow for the extension

---

77. Spufford, *Money and Its Use in Medieval Europe,* 99–105.

78. There was in fact precedent in tradition not just for a linking of the coin and the sign but also for a linking of economic and verbal usury. Such links can be found in the Islamic tradition as well as in the Talmud (Shell, *Money, Language, and Thought,* 49), where there are references to "writers of usury" and "verbal interest," respectively, and also in the medieval *Glossa ordinaria* (*PL* 113), where "spiritual usury" is considered in discussing the parable of the talents (Shell, op. cit., 75). In fact, the parable of the talents is a key text for generating debate in the Middle Ages on the proper use of the sign (see the discussion of Guillaume le clerc de Normandie later in this chapter). See also Cowell, "Deadly Letters," for more on the *Glossa ordinaria,* the parable, and Marie de France.

of the model of usury to cover any domain where exchange occurs—whether economics, language, or any other realm. Though this may not have been the intended import of this particular passage, it is, I argue, what occurs in Arras in the thirteenth century and indeed more generally in the Middle Ages. As such, *usura* may be read as "semiotic superabundance." I do not suggest in employing the term *usury* that questions of language—or ethics, to take an example from chapter 3—are considered as variants of a fundamentally economic framework. Rather, language, ethics, and economics are all understood and represented in terms of a single, Neoplatonic sign theory. Usury in the narrow sense concerns economics, but in a broader sense it is simply a convenient term, borrowed from one of these domains, for what is really a question of the nature of proper semiosis. It is in this broader sense that I intend the term *usurious poetics*.

That the tavern scene and the concept of usurious poetics did constitute a fully elaborated medieval textual and poetic model within the comico-realist domain can be additionally illustrated by a text mentioned earlier when discussing the campaign against usury in Arras in the year 1213. "Le patenostre a l'usurier," which mentions several figures involved in this preaching campaign, is one of a number of medieval farcical amplifications of the church creed and paternoster, several of which are assigned explicitly to either usurers or jongleurs *(ribauds)*. The text in question, as was typically the case, amplifies, dislocates, and redefines the religious discourse of the standard paternoster for the sake of parody.

> "Pater noster," biaus sire Diex,
> Quar donez que je soie tiex
> Que je puisse par mon avoir
> Et le los et le pris avoir
> De gaaignier et d'amasser
> Tant que je puisse surmonter
> Trestoz les riches usuriers
> Qui onques pretaissent deniers.
> "Qui est in coelis," mult me poise
> Que je n'i fui quant la borgeoise
> Voloit emprunter les deniers.

(vv. 27–37)

> ["Pater noster," fair Lord,
> Grant that I be such

That I may through my wealth
And my good sense and my worth
Be able to gain and amass
So much that I can surpass
All the rich usurers
Who ever lended money.
"Qui est in coelis," it greatly worries me
That I wasn't there when the townswoman
Wanted to borrow money.]

"Le patenostre a l'usurier" is itself usurious not only in its subject but also in its poetics of revaluation and amplification. It gains ironic revenge on Courson and Neuilly, the anti-usury preachers, by making them participants in this act of rhetorical usury, as it names them and redefines their roles in the affair: the author states at the beginning of the text that he is simply going to "rimoier et . . . conter" a sermon already pronounced by Courson in Paris (vv. 6–9). Not only is the sacred text of the paternoster revalued, but so is that of Courson, since his straightforward depiction of the usurers' sins is retold in a heroic and admiring tone. The poet asks, "Qui est cil Robers Torchon" (v. 124), playing with several puns on Courchon's name; for example, the word *rober* means "theft" (though it is the usurer whom Courchon accuses of theft).[79] The text furnishes yet another example of the explicit linking of illicit economics and illicit poetics, both serving, I argue, to raise the question of illicit semiology. The text's awareness of the connection between the illicit activities was seemingly shared by Peter Cantor himself, the leader of the circle of anti-usury moralists. We have already seen earlier in this chapter Cantor's critique of the jongleur in economic terms as having no utility in the world, no useful role or function.[80]

Legend, Genre, and Profit

Jean Bodel, however, was not Peter Cantor. And the term *illicit,* which is used so often in the preceding section, must be understood in the context of a Neoplatonic view of proper sign use, not Jean Bodel's view. More pre-

---

79. A very similar text is "Le Credo à l'userier" (Barbazan, *Fabliaux et contes,* 4:106–14), which devolves into a long list of the loans ("credos" or "credences") that the usurer has granted and that are still outstanding.

80. Faral, *Les jongleurs,* 27. The full text is in *PL* 205.

cisely, *Le Jeu de Saint Nicolas* suggests a familiarity with Neoplatonic semiology and also an explicit engagement with it in both economic and poetic terms. But what Peter Cantor or Augustine might call a theft, a violation of *propertas,* or a regrettable exploitation of the inherent imperfections of the humanly instituted sign, the play presents as the very source of its comic and literary creativity and value. The multiple meanings of the play, its usurious surplus of senses, is the reason why it is to be valued, and this poetic usury is as acceptable as a loan would be for any good proto-capitalist merchant. Money and language are not measures, the play suggests, but commodities, and self-referential, fertile ones at that.

Indeed, many of the poetic high points of the play center on language's tendency to become a reified commodity. Much of the dialogue in the tavern scenes consists of rapid one- or two-line cries and responses on the part of the players, including oaths, cries of delight or despair, and numerous slang terms, in which the referential function of language dissolves away and the words draw our attention to them as pure sound, as play or a game, as a celebration of vocal productivity. I cite one example.

Clikés.	Giete! Dieus te doinst set en deus!
Pincedés.	A defoit! Mais hasart ou seize! Hasart, Dieus!
Rasoirs.	Ains avommes treize! Or te donriemmes nous hasart.
Pincedés.	A deffoy, segneur! Dieus m'en gart! Escapar! de par saint Guillaume!

(vv. 1109–14)

[*Clikés.*	Toss! God grant you seven in two!
Pincedés.	The hell you say! But hasart or sixteen! Hasart! Good God!
Rasoirs.	So we have thirteen! Then we'll give you hasart.
Pincedés.	The hell you will sir! God help me! One got away! By Saint William I swear!]

(Note that "hasart" is cognate with English "hazard" and refers here specifically to the dice game of the same name, in which the object was to throw a specific score determined by previous rolls.)

Even in the context of these few lines in an exchange that continues for nearly fifty verses, words and phrases ("Dieus," "hasart," numbers) are repeated and return over and over in a kind of circular dance going nowhere in particular, and effects of assonance and alliteration ("gart! / Escapar! de par saint Guillaume") dissolve all referentiality. In its performative nature, language becomes not communication but a physical act, a reified sign. The passage is not simply about a game of dice: more fundamentally, it mimics in its poetics the random, repeating patterns and fluctuations of a series of tosses of the dice. The passage is not only about playing dice: it is playing dice—with words. It is a celebration of the pure ludic creativity of the sign. The passage not only draws our attention to the poetics that produces the text but imbricates the practice of that poetics into the dice games, the acts of theft, and the drinking sessions that characterize the play. In the end, despite the crucial relevance of the tavern scenes for the themes of the play, one cannot help admiring at the same time their audacious, aleatory gratuity as the cursing, arguing, and counting go on for hundreds of verses in the middle of the "saint's play."

Bodel often seems simply to revel in his artistic freedom and creativity. Many readers have noted the degree of radical innovation in the play with respect to the traditional legend, which I have already mentioned at the beginning of this chapter.[81] Fittingly enough, Saint Nicolas himself could be seen in the Middle Ages as a kind of patron saint of clerkly artistic production and creativity. A large amount of poetic production was generated concerning Saint Nicolas, including a long vita by Wace.[82] The festival of Saint Nicolas was especially celebrated in episcopal schools and monasteries by the performance of semiliturgical dramas.[83] Nicolas was himself a source of and inspiration for artistic production by the clerk, and in the text "Les deux bourdeors ribauds," one of the ribauds (jongleurs) swears "par saint Nicolas," his patron saint, that the other one is crazy.

---

81. See Vincent, *The "Jeu de St. Nicolas,"* 19ff. See also Dane, *Res/Verba;* Arens, *Untersuchungen zu Jean Bodels Mirakel.*

82. On Nicolas as a patron saint, see in particular del Valle da Paz, *La leggenda di S. Nicola,* 27–28; Jones, *The St. Nicholas Liturgy,* 109–12. For his vita, see Sinclair's edition of Wace, *The Life of Saint Nicholas.* For additional references, see Albert Henry's 1965 edition of *Le Jeu de Saint Nicolas,* 34.

83. Del Valle de Paz, *La leggenda di S. Nicola,* 29.

And Nicolas himself was a precociously clerkly figure, beginning his read-ing of sacred texts at the age of five according to legend.[84]

Of course, many medieval saints were the inspiration for a great deal of literature. But Saint Nicolas was particularly associated with the clerk. An apocryphal legend widely known in the Middle Ages told of his revival of three dead students after they were killed by their master—thus he was cel-ebrated in the episcopal schools.[85] This legend is referred to in verse 1432 of the play. Another version of the legend features Nicolas in the garb of a pilgrim arriving to save three clerks murdered by a treacherous couple who have agreed to lodge them in hopes of profit, evoking the conflict seen in chapter 1 between pilgrim and profit-seeking host, though in this case Nicolas intervenes on the side of the pilgrims.[86] In Bodel's play, Nicolas saves the three thieves from eternal damnation. So that they can return the treasure before their lives become literally "fourfaites" (v. 1283), he wakes them from their sleep (i.e., figurative death): "Or sus! Trop i avés dormi" (Wake up! You've slept too much!) (v. 1275). Yet Saint Nicolas could be seen as privileging not only the clerk and his literary production but the specific poetics of the tavern. Not only does he save the three thieves/poets from "death," but Nicolas appears only to the thieves and only in the tav-ern, and Arnold Arens in particular has noted that Nicolas' language and rhetoric in these appearances is that of the thieves as well—as opposed to the "high" rhetoric used by the angel to deliver other holy messages in the play. Nicolas becomes practically the patron saint of the jongleur thieves. If we accept that the thieves do indeed represent the poet (whether he be clerk or jongleur), then Nicolas, the muse of clerkly literary production, privileges the thief/poet and the tavern as the locus of his presence and of artistic creativity. He is of course the one who is responsible for the cre-ative doubling of the king's treasure as well. And he also further privileges the common, colloquial rhetoric of these thieves through his own speech.

The gratuity and innovation of the tavern scenes seem to force this priv-ileging of creativity to our attention. Attempts by critics to locate a single source for Bodel's text have been unsuccessful precisely because of the large number of major innovations that he introduced to the Saint Nicolas legend. For example, he reverses the pagan invasion of Christian lands at

---

84. "Les Deux bordeors ribauds" is cited in Faral, *Les jongleurs,* 152. For Nicolas' pre-cocity, see Thurston and Attwater, *Butler's Lives of the Saints,* 4:504.

85. Del Valle de Paz, *La leggenda di S. Nicola;* Jones, *The St. Nicholas Liturgy,* 106ff.

86. Orleans MS. 201, "Ludus sancti nicolai de clericis," in Cohen, *Anthologie du drame liturgique,* 249–59.

the opening of the traditional legend, converting this into a Christian invasion of pagan lands. He is the first to introduce the motif of the doubling of the treasure on its return (for obvious thematic reasons, as we have seen), and in his play, the intervention of Saint Nicolas occurs not simply to stop the molestation of a wooden idol by the pagans (as was typically the case) but to save the *preudomme*—thus lending more humanity to the situation, but also diminishing the importance of the idol itself as an immanent sign. It has been argued that the prologue's emphasis on past authorities as a basis for Bodel's work despite the fact that there is no such particular past authority betrays the author's awareness of his very originality and of the problem this might pose for parts of his audience. The same critic concludes that Bodel stands in isolation to all other works on Saint Nicolas, which show a "marked uniformity of subject and . . . continuity to Diaconus."[87]

The poet Bodel thus accomplishes in a larger frame what the poet/thief and usurer accomplish in the play: the sign (the legend as a whole) is destablized and redefined, revalued. The prologue (authentic or not) serves to underline this fact. Not only does it emphasize past authorities, but it tells basically the standard version of the Nicolas legend: Joseph Dane has called it "a record of the audience's expectations."[88] The prologue's authenticity has been questioned in part because it is then immediately contradicted by the rest of the play. The play does not simply revalue the traditional legend but explicitly places that legend at its beginning and then contradicts or alters it at every turn. Bodel no more respects the audience's expectations than the tavern keeper respects those concerning a proper glass of wine. His renewal of the legend is a celebration of poetic creativity in the context of a new, fluid, multigeneric genre—the theater—performed before what was most likely a multiclass audience dominated by a bourgeoisie that was itself more innovating than traditional. Bodel's creation is, no less than Adam de la Halle's *Le Jeu de la Feuillée* (as we will see in chapter 4), a text partially about the writer himself and the act of

---

87. Vincent, *The "Jeu de St. Nicolas,"* 36. See also Dragonetti, "Le *Jeu de St. Nicolas* de Jean Bodel." There has, however, been much discussion of the authenticity of this prologue. See Albert Henry's 1965 edition of *Le Jeu de Saint Nicolas,* for more on this question. A prominent argument for its authenticity is contained in Hunt, "The Authenticity of the Prologue." "Diaconus" refers to the author of the Latin saint's vita that formed the basis for all further medieval versions of the Nicolas legend. Diaconus' version was written in the early eleventh century.

88. Dane, *Res/Verba* 53.

writing—both works are "autobiographies" in that they tell the tale of the subject's creation and working out of the tale.

Having mentioned genre, I would like to add that Bodel's play does to genre exactly what it does to the specific legend of Saint Nicolas. Bodel seems to have had a definite conception of genre and genre expectations. Not only does he make the famous three-part distinction between the "materes" of literature in the opening of his *Chanson des saisnes* (the "matere de Rome," "matere de France," and "matere de Bretagne"), each corresponding to a specific genre or to particular genres as well as to a typical metric form, but in his own works he generally showed a great sense of metric propriety. This makes *Le Jeu de Saint Nicolas* all the more striking, for Bodel clearly undermines medieval expectations for the telling of any saint's life, not just that of Nicolas. In the play, he mixes not only epic, hagiographic, and "realist" thematic elements but also a great number of metric forms, characteristic of a number of genres. He furthermore fails to assign consistently any given metric form to any given locale or set of characters: there are tendencies, but always there are exceptions.[89] The text always slips and slides away from attempts to pin it down.

While I argued at the beginning of this chapter that the prologue and the arguments over prices could be seen as emblems of the text as a whole, an equally fitting emblem in the light of the preceding discussion might be the idol Tervagan. A wooden idol covered in gold, its outer shell has more value than the wood below, to which the shell figuratively refers. This more valuable shell serves only to misrepresent the idol's essence—another example of amplification of reference and commodification of the sign. At the same time, the idol, when interrogated, both laughs and cries, signifying victory and defeat simultaneously for the Saracens and, indirectly, the Christians. Its refusal of a single answer echoes the play itself, which can (and typically has been) read as an orthodox Christian text, but which at the same time depicts a consistent idolatry of the sign.[90] The idol is certainly overthrown in the end, but the surprising false conversion of one of the king's admirals implicitly raises the question of where the newly converted Saracens' loyalties lie.

---

89. He uses both couplets and stanzaic forms, as well as eight-, ten-, and twelve-syllable lines. For an extremely minute working out of the metric relations and correspondences in the play, see Arens, *Untersuchungen zu Jean Bodels Mirakel.*

90. Dragonetti ("Le *Jeu de St. Nicolas* de Jean Bodel") notes that the two idols of Tervagan and Nicolas in the play are always on the verge of equivalence.

Sains Nicolais, c'est maugré mien
Que je vous aoure, et par forche.
De moi n'arés vous fors l'escorche:
Par parole devieng vostre hom,
Mais li creanche est en Mahom.

(vv. 1507–11)

[Saint Nicolas, it is against my wishes
That I adore you, and because of force;
Of me you will have only the bark;
By words I become your servant,
But the belief is in Muhammad.]

The text never resolves this troubling conversion, and it seems reasonable to question the reasons for the king's conversion as well. He is as impressed by his doubled treasure as by any other motive, and his loyalties remain in a sense with the "bark" of the sign, as he exchanges the gilded idol for solid gold. Tervagan is not so much thrown aside as traded in for something better, which is nevertheless more of the same.[91] This conclusion certainly reinforces our sense that the final decision between laughing and crying, orthodoxy and semiotic "heresy," remains to be resolved.

If we can consider the Nicolas legend, and even whole genres, as evoked in the play either formally or thematically, as complex signs, then in this case as well as with simple monetary or linguistic signs, Bodel consistently revalues these complex signs and even undermines them entirely so as to deny their communicative or referential function.[92] Genre, instead of communicating a series of expectations and implicit interpretive signals to the audience, becomes simply a commodity to be played off against other genres or parodied, and the communication is generated internally to the play, in the confrontation of the genres themselves. The theater, like the fabliaux, can from this point of view be seen as a metagenre in that it

---

91. Jean-Charles Payen remarks that Nicolas could be seen as a kind of "gendarme" who is especially effective at guarding property ("Les Eléments idéologiques dans Le *Jeu de Saint Nicolas*").

92. For a precedent on the idea of "complex signs," see Gravdal, *Vilain et Courtois*, 4. Gravdal is discussing stereotyped characters in the fabliaux, but her concept matches mine. Moreover, Per Nykrog *(Les fabliaux),* in his attempt to establish a "grammar" of the fabliaux via a study of the "typical" characters and their functions in the text, implicitly recognizes this same idea.

assimilates many other genres to the single polyvalent genre of the theater, forming a totalizing literary space outside normal generic bounds, where genres communicate not so much to an audience as with each other. The theater, which so often makes use of the tavern in the thirteenth century, here mirrors the economic nature of the tavern—we saw in chapter 1 its tendency to subsume other métiers and blur the distinctions between them. This connection of tavern and theater as metageneric vehicles is not an isolated or accidental occurrence. In chapters 3 and 4, we will see that Bodel is simply the first in a line of authors who use either the tavern alone or the tavern in conjunction with the theater as vehicles for consideration of the nature of genre and quite often as vehicles for undermining the normal communicative functioning of genre.

Thus while the tavern offers a certain thematic unity for the play, the text nevertheless seems aggressively to deny its own generic unity (and interpretative univocity) when compared to other prevailing genres of the time, such as the epic and hagiographic texts. The text, with its intricate series of mirror images between tavern and palace and its pairs of characters—king and tavern keeper, admirals and thieves, the two criers—functions much as Jean de Meun's portion of *The Romance of the Rose*, written several decades later; the dialogic text undermines external reference and becomes a vast game of self-referentiality and self-refutation, as the commodification of the sign is repeated on higher and higher levels.[93] Profit and play are finally one and the same, each made possible by signs whose very mutability (through usury) is not a crisis to be normatively resolved but a source of creation. Both of these concepts serve to refute the notion of the zero-sum game, suggesting instead that there is a space where such constraining equivalencies can be superseded and where not just God but poet and merchant as well can create wealth and value.[94]

---

93. This aspect of *The Romance of the Rose* has recently been discussed by many authors; one of the most succinct example studies is Brownlee, "The Problem of Faux Semblant." Rey-Flaud *(Pour une Dramaturgie)* has proposed that the mirroring of the two images in our text—Saint Nicolas and Tervagan—serves in a similar way to put into question the status of images in general as representation. Here again the question of the idolatry of the sign is raised.

94. For more on usury and language from a postmodern point of view, see Derrida, "White Mythology," in Derrida, *Margins of Philosophy,* 207–71. Derrida plays on two opposing senses of *usura,* one of which corresponds roughly to the surplus of sense—the profit—that is the focus of this chapter. The second sense is the "using up" of a word's sense—most particularly in the effort to efface the original "natural" meaning of a word in order for philosophy to suggest that the meanings it uses (which are all finally metaphorical, Derrida argues) are themselves natural. In my third chapter, the ways in which medieval usurious poetics works to reveal this second process of usury will be explored more fully.

Situating *Le Jeu de Saint Nicolas* in Its Literary Context

To summarize, the tavern is a locus of semiotic superabundance, with this abundance being achieved through the revaluation and commodification of the sign. The revaluation and commodification effectively privatize the sign, and this private superabundance, or profit, refuses the notion of a fixed sum of public *propertas.* I have argued that *Le Jeu de Saint Nicolas* is effectively a valorization of this process. The explicit valorization (as opposed to mere representation) of this process, and more generally of the desire for profit, is not an especially widespread feature of medieval literature when it is considered in its entirety, and its representation in terms of both economics and language simultaneously is more or less limited to a certain number of comico-realist texts, many concerning the tavern. However, a general concern with semiotic superabundance, especially of the linguistic sort, is a common or even dominant feature of several genres of European vernacular literature beginning in the late twelfth century, including the romance. For this reason, I would like to end this chapter by considering the exact status of the tavern, its poetics, and comico-realist texts within the larger confrontation of semiologies in the thirteenth century.

The issue of and propriety of *amplificatio* (to borrow a term—this time from medieval rhetoric—that has important connections to the idea of "superabundance") are discussed and debated explicitly in the rhetorical treatises of the twelfth and thirteenth centuries and indirectly in a number of courtly texts of the period as well. Marie de France's "Prologue," with its mention of the "surplus" involved in poetic production and reproduction, offers one example of the theme of the semiotic surplus.

> Custume fu as ancïens,
> Ceo testimoine Precïens,
> Es livres ke jadis feseient,
> Assez oscurement diseient
> Pur ceus ki a venir esteient
> E ki aprendre les deveient,
> K'i peüssent gloser la lettre
> E de lur sen le surplus mettre.

(vv. 9–16)

> [It was the custom of the ancients,
> According to Priscian,
> In the books that they made then,

To speak rather obscurely
For those who would follow
And who would have to learn these books,
So that they could gloss the letter
And add the surplus to their sense.]

She represents artistic production as an appropriation of existing signs, either simple or complex (a text), and a revaluing of those signs to produce a surplus of meaning. Interestingly enough, here it is the literary tradition that "lends" the text, which the writer then uses as the basis for his or her own surplus production; and the writer then returns the text to the tradition at a profit—the surplus added by the writer constituting the "interest." Marie thus resembles the thieves in Bodel's tavern.[95] Chrétien de Troyes suggests a similar view of artistic production in his opening prologue to *Erec et Enide,* suggesting that the preexisting matter of his romance ("un conte d'avanture"—the plot, roughly) amounts to something far less than the "bele conjointure" that he draws from that material, which will then live on as long as Christianity lasts (vv. 9–26).

Among those who wrote explicitly on *amplificatio* in the narrowly rhetorical sense was the rhetorician Geoffrey of Vinsauf, who joins Matthew of Vendome as the most famous exponents of what has been called the "new rhetoric." These and other writers of the late twelfth and early thirteenth centuries wrote a number of poetic arts, in Latin and addressed primarily to the production of texts in Latin, on the theory and practice of poetry. As the title of Geoffrey's work explicitly reveals *(Poetria nova),* they sought consciously to react against earlier models of *grammatica* and *rhetorica,* favoring an increased emphasis on human art and rhetoric over the normative content of texts. As such, they represent one side of what Robert Sturges refers to as two "competing semiologies" of language and interpretation.[96]

The study of the "semiotic competition" of the twelfth and thirteenth centuries has been one of the most important single themes of recent studies in medieval literature, being either the explicit object or implicit background for a number of important recent studies. The ultimate theoretical roots of this approach can be traced to Julia Kristeva's ideas in *Semei-*

---

95. For more on Marie and usury, see Cowell, "Deadly Letters."
96. Sturges, *Medieval Interpretation,* 23.

otike.[97] Within this scholarly tradition, the first of these two semiologies corresponds broadly to the Augustinian hermeneutics that I have already presented, while the opposing semiology has been formulated in a number of ways. In his *Etymologies and Genealogies,* R. Howard Bloch uses the metaphors of vertical reference to transcendental truths and horizontal emphasis on inter- and intratextual creation of meaning. Stephen Nichol's concept of "theosis" in his *Romanesque Signs* provides a model of licit semiology, while Alexandre Leupin uses the term *barbarolexis* for illicit semiology in his book of the same name. In *Arthurian Fictions,* Jane Burns uses the more widely recognized concept of the conflict between "Scripture" and "Rhetoric." Eugene Vance predicates much of *Mervelous Signals* on the medieval concepts of a prelapsarian and postlapsarian semiotics: medieval semioticians, he notes, were preoccupied, and haunted, by the Fall.[98] Though these formulations are often at variance in their details, they generally share a recognition of the poetics that Alain de Lille attacks,

---

97. Kristeva, *Semeiotike,* especially 113–42. Kristeva's ideas on the transition from symbol to sign, while broadly paralleling those of more recent medieval scholars in claiming a shift away from the transcendental (117), nevertheless are somewhat anachronistic in that the sign/symbol debate was actually an ongoing feature of the eleventh and twelfth centuries themselves, with Augustine and Hugh of Saint Victor representing the "sign," while John Scotus Eriugena and Pseudo-Dionysius the Areopagite represented the "symbol," broadly speaking. See especially Chénu, *Nature, Man, and Society;* Wetherbee, *Platonism and Poetry in the Twelfth Century.* The actual issue, as I suggest in the subsequent discussion, was more in intentions of language use (either signs or symbols) rather than modes of expression.

98. Bloch analyzes the two competing medieval semiologies as characterized by "verticality" and "horizontality." The "vertical" semiotics is essentially Platonic and at least ideally prelapsarian, while the "horizontal" semiotics is resolutely postlapsarian. Vertical semiotics is a semiotics of transcendental reference to realities outside the realm of the signs themselves, to divine "truth," as exemplified in the discourse of the Bible.

Sturges adopts a similar framework: the first of these semiologies, fundamentally Neoplatonic, nevertheless recognized the degraded nature of the sign in the physical world, since it partook of that physicality; but it sought to avoid indeterminacy through the immanence of God in the world and in language, thus guaranteeing correct interpretation and understanding (8, 15). This semiology found its greatest proponent in Saint Augustine, and ultimately Augustine's theory of the sign came to represent the Neoplatonic semiology. He understood the sign as a fundamentally telementational vehicle for transferring ideas from one mind to another, and he believed that all signs were guaranteed a natural relation to their referent.

On a more ambitious level, Stephen Nichols' *Romanesque Signs* is fundamentally an attempt to elucidate the basic unity of all Romanesque discourses in a single "semiology." In this attempt, all elements of society are viewed as "discourses," including the philosophical, economic, legal, and so forth, and all are characterized by the use of signs, whether they be linguistic, monetary, artistic, vestiary, architectural, or other. The sign in fact becomes the unitary and determining element of society, and the entire world can be read as a book.

a poetics that, in the words of Alastair Minnis, "began to suggest that new literary works could legitimately be created with an emphasis on their own surface beauty and the aesthetic pleasure they could give, rather than on any spiritual truths to be discovered through symbolic deep reading."[99] Thus figural and allegorical readings, governed by God's immanence and theoretically univocal or at least not in conflict, were de-emphasized or replaced by literal readings, which were vulnerable to the vagaries of the physical sign and human intentionality. Ultimate truth was replaced by multiple carnal seductions.

The roots and ultimate causes of this shift are of course difficult to isolate. However, the great increase of written literature in the twelfth century and the concurrent rise of vernacular literature could be seen as broad factors in this development. Certainly literacy, as Plato suggests in the *Phaedrus,* to take one very early example, introduces a distance between author and text. Plato represents writing as "a thing outside" the writer that poses the threat that writers "will not remember of themselves and from within" (p. 275 Cooper). Into this gap between authorial intentionality and textual meanings flows the corrupting (from Plato's point of view) desire of the reader. The opening of texts to such vagaries of meaning and the simultaneous divorce of literature from the normative influence of religious inspiration and epic exemplarity are certainly suggestive explanations for the rise of aesthetic and semiotic play. There is a shift from reading and writing for content and communication—figural or literal—to reading and writing for the aesthetic pleasure of the text itself. Much of this aesthetic pleasure was to be generated through multiple expressions of the same meaning *(amplificatio):* "Although the meaning is one, let it not come content with one set of apparel. Let it vary its robes . . ." (Geoffrey of Vinsauf, *Poetria nova,* vv. 220–25). And much was to be generated through a kind of willful inadequacy of the sign and dislocation of linguistic propriety, principally accomplished via metaphor: "An object does not come before us with unveiled face, and accompanied by its natural voice; rather an alien voice attends it, and so it shrouds itself in mist . . ." (*Poetria nova,* vv. 1045–50).

This rhetorical concern with artistic texture over textual communication can be best understood as one of the more radical aspects of a general tendency to read texts, whether sacred or temporal, more attentively at the literal level, with more concern for the intentionality of the human

---

99. See Minnis, *The Medieval Theory of Authorship,* 5ff.

authors, as well as more care in evaluating the specifically literary and rhetorical devices used to express meaning in the texts. Yet though the rhetorical privileging of the sign as artistic object rather than vehicle of truth corresponds to the poetic tendencies of tavern scenes, this rhetoric was not stigmatized per se. As Alastair Minnis has shown, scholastic theologians themselves played an important role in rehabilitating a concern for literal meanings and human authorial intentions, even in sacred texts.[100] Augustine had already recognized the value of a gap (or "mist," as Geoffrey would say) in the language of a text in creating a desire for knowledge and leading the reader toward true understanding (*DDC* II.vi.7).

Indeed, even semiotic superabundance in the form of usury could be acceptable in some forms. In discussing the prohibitions against usury, I noted that in terms of intentionality it was an important step. While this certainly widened the field of possible transgressions (to the chagrin of the merchant), it also allowed a rethinking of the status of literary activity. To take one example, around 1226–27, Guillaume le clerc de Normandie, in his *Le besant de Dieu* (vv. 108–16, 153–58) evokes the parable of the talents to explicitly connect the doubling of money (the vulgate text uses the word *usura*) and amplificatory artistic production—his rewriting and amplification of the parable through his commentary will be his divinely sanctioned method of doubling the "besant" that God has given him—his writing "talent." He employs language in a useful way for the service of God and generates a profit of goodness.[101] This trend toward the literal in medieval exegesis and rhetoric occurred in the latter twelfth and early thirteenth centuries, at the same time that the Catholic Church was itself showing greater and greater interest in the question of human intentionality, culminating in the Fourth Lateran Council of 1215, with its imposition of mandatory confession and its concurrent emphasis on penitence as opposed to mere penance. The concept of intentionality is the key to understanding the transgressive nature (from moralists' point of view) of the specific types of revaluation and *amplificatio* that were performed in the texts of the tavern: it is a concept that has already been raised repeatedly. It is in the conflict of human intentions, leading away from God and divinely sanctioned prescription and toward private profit and abuse of

---

100. Minnis, *Medieval Theory;* see also Chénu, *Nature, Man, and Society,* chap. 7.

101. Another appropriate example would be *Le mariage des sept arts* by Jehan le teinturier d'Arras, a text from Arras that depicts "Rhetoric" employed to aid Christian society, marrying it with "Proiere."

the sign, that the tavern comes to achieve its status as the church of the devil. The more or less simultaneous development of vernacular literacy, a truly monetary economy, and the church's interest in intentionality can be seen as part of the same general development: the rise of abstract means of representation (writing and money) leaves the semiotic system open to many more forms of human manipulation than previously—at least in the eyes of medieval thinkers—and the intentions of the users of those signs become of paramount importance because of the very impossibility of normative external controls on the users.

As was stated earlier, medieval Neoplatonic sign theory was a normative and prescriptive, rather than a descriptive, sign theory. Indeed, the entire body of *grammatica,* of which what we today call "sign theory" was a part in the Middle Ages, functioned in the same fashion. *Grammatica* was a body of learning that provided the codes and context for reading accepted texts within the confines of accepted interpretation.[102] Plato asked in the *Phaedrus* by whose authority one should interpret the silent, written text, since no speaker was present, and who would provide the codes for reading texts that could not respond to one's query. Augustine seeks to provide the answer to this puzzle in the case of the Scriptures. It is clear that Augustine himself recognized the imperfection of the sign in relation to Neoplatonic models. His *De doctrina Christiana* addresses over and over the potential for difficulty in understanding signs, not because of any lie on the part of a writer, but simply because understanding is uncertain in a fallen world. Human good intention, as discussed in the introduction to this book, was the safeguard to ensure that the system stayed as close as possible to the Platonic model for communication. The thirteenth-century rise of semiotic activities motivated by private profit, rather than public utility, wherein the guarantee of rightly oriented intention was destroyed, constituted a true crisis of the sign and of society. The high medieval semiotic or epistemic shift analyzed recently by a number of scholars—from "vertical" to "horizontal" modes of reference, from immanent to human guarantees of language's authority, or from interest in divine authority to interest in human intentionality in language—is less a changing appreciation or redefinition of the way in which signs do or

---

102. For much more on the normative nature of medieval *grammatica* and sign theory, see Martin Irvine's *The Making of Textual Culture.* See also Suzanne Reynolds' recent argument that much medieval glossing was determined by the public setting of school education—a situation that, though very different from that of monastic culture, also included an important normative component (*Medieval Reading,* 18, 29, 31).

should work (though this aspect is certainly present, especially in the later thirteenth-century speculative grammarians) than a shift in intentions as to how to use those signs. New semiology is defined less by new theories of semiosis than by new intentions of semiosis.

Similar statements could be made regarding the economic sign as well. Among moralistic theologians and the early church fathers, there was certainly a condemnation of the gap in the exchange—profit—in economic transactions. Yet as I have stressed, there was in fact no explicit condemnation of profit as such among most medieval economic theorists, especially among the more liberal canonists; they recognized that the objectively established just price of a good might change, so that one could conceivably make a profit: monetary signs, like linguistic ones, were not permanently fixed and unitary, so that metaphor and price shift were equally possible. The canonists also recognized that merchants did often perform some labor meriting them a profit, just as Guillaume le clerc de Normandie's literary labor led to spiritual profit. However, any exchange motivated purely by the desire for such a profit was condemned. The condemnation was not of profit or rhetorical amplification per se but only of the intention purely for profit or the intention of using rhetorical amplification for means other than a drawing of the reader to the truth, especially when it was used for private gain at the public expense.[103]

Of course, the abuse of language might be prevented by divine immanence whatever the intention of the human user. God was the guarantor of correct interpretation, just as his immanence in the judicial duel guaranteed justice. Without this immanence, along with the corresponding human effort to read according to divine will, one was faced with proliferating, surplus, and indeterminate meaning and a turning of language inward on itself, the referential function being sacrificed to the commodification of language and the idolatry of the sign. Thus the thirteenth-century crisis was the loss of normative forces from both above (God) and below (human intention) simultaneously. More broadly still, one could say that the rise of vernacular, secular literature and market, monetary economy made possible the realization of formerly unrealizable semiotic intentions.

Without normative strictures, a kind of "unnatural" rhetoric was pro-

---

103. Thus Alain de Lille quite often speaks of the garments of Nature with their brilliant colors, recalling the well-known medieval concept of the "colors of rhetoric," but accuses humans of "discolouring the colour of beauty by the meretricious dye of desire" *(DPN* 132). He objects not to the colors (of rhetoric) but to their alteration by private desire.

duced, in the words of Alain de Lille;[104] and as the passage quoted earlier from the *Poetria nova* makes clear, the "natural" voice of the thing was to be avoided. Geoffrey of Vinsauf clearly states that "the order of art is more elegant than the natural order" (*Poetria nova*, v. 100). To a certain extent, these terms are merely technical labels for the means of beginning a text. To begin in media res is to begin "artificially," as opposed to starting with the chronologically earliest events of the narrative. Yet as Douglas Kelly has suggested (correctly in my opinion), the artificial beginning is above all a way for the writer both to impose an intention—the writer's own—on the events to follow and to impose a mode of reading on the writer's text, by orienting the reader to certain key focal points and by prefacing the writer's narration.[105] The mark of artifice among medieval rhetoricians is the mark of human intentionality, the mark of individual authority, and the mark of a subjective aesthetic.

Interestingly, the language of rhetoric echoes the discussion of natural versus artificial wealth in the context of usury. In both cases the emphasis on the surface, nontranscendental aspects of the sign as commodity produces "unnatural" excess and dislocation.[106] "Art," "artificial" wealth, and "artificial" (i.e., "unnatural") rhetoric are potentially all conceptually linked in a transgression against Neoplatonic semiology in that they value both the sign over the referent and individual intentionality over public utility. While the epic and hagiographical legend had been characterized by theosis (primarily hagiography) and a single textual community (both genres) that could arrive at a unitary understanding of the text, romance was not.[107] In the absence of divine immanence and human right intentions, willfully dislocative and amplificatory rhetoric could become nothing more than a carnal seduction. Jane Burns' reading of Arthurian fiction provides another example of this conflict between what she terms

---

104. See Bloch, *Etymologies and Genealogies,* 133–36, for a discussion of Alain's concept of natural, or "straight," rhetoric as opposed to unnatural, or "crooked," rhetoric and of his linkage of unnatural rhetoric to unnatural sexual acts, especially homosexuality.

105. Kelly, "La spécialité dans l'invention des topiques."

106. See Bloch, *Etymologies and Genealogies,* 173–74, for a similar discussion of money as a sign, usury, and the ability of "usurious" signs in general to disrupt the natural order—in this particular case, the natural order of lineage and reproduction.

107. On epic and hagiography, see Sturges, *Medieval Interpretation,* 20–22. Here Sturges is principally using the arguments of Stephen Nichols *(Romanesque Signs).* On romance, Sturges uses the particular example of Lancelot and Guinevere, who consistently violate the interpretative norms of the community, setting up their own "antisocial semiology" that defies unitary understanding, so that their behavior is consistently misunderstood.

"Rhetoric" and "Scripture": "The battle between language and Truth is presented in terms of words that deceive and seduce the reader as opposed to words that point toward transcendent meaning."[108] Many Old French comico-realist texts raise these same issues, but as I have suggested, they do so in a celebratory rather than problematizing mode. They glorify an ethic of destabilizing, subjective semiosis.

It is in this light that one must read the famous critique of the jongleur by Thomas Cobham.[109] He divides the jongleurs into three types, the last being the literary and musical type, as opposed to the fool, the juggler, the acrobat, and so forth. He then further divides this third type of jongleur into a category of acceptable literary jongleurs, who are portrayed as performing primarily epic and hagiographic texts, and a category of disreputable jongleurs, who are portrayed as lascivious and—of course—frequenters of taverns. In reality it could be questioned whether there was ever such a strict division of material among jongleurs; the extremely varied production of both Jean Bodel and Rutebeuf certainly argues for a less categorical distinction. Most important, however, is the seeming approval or disapproval of the jongleur based on whether they perform works whose poetics is marked by divine theosis and/or proper human communal intentions or not. The disapproval of certain types of literature is artificially defined by a disapproval of a certain type of jongleur, and most important, Cobham, and likewise Jean le Marchant, places the disapproved poetics in the tavern.

The jongleurs whom Cobham is discussing, particularly those performing epics, quite probably performed them orally for an audience that heard but did not read the text. Many comico-realist texts were probably similarly restricted to aural reception. *Le Jeu de Saint Nicolas* is of course a play and thus was also spoken and heard, not written and read. But in discussing this work in the context of both courtly literature and Latin rhetoric, I wish to emphasize its connections to the literate milieu in which medieval theories of the sign were originally propounded. It is also important to stress that it is sign use that is at stake, in all its forms. For this reason, I will continue to use the terms *reading* and *writing* to discuss comico-realist texts, despite obvious differences in the conditions of receptions

---

108. Burns, *Arthurian Fictions,* 22. For another example of this commonplace idea, see Hugh of Saint Victor's distinction between the "arts" and the "appendages of the arts" in *Didascalicon* III.4.

109. Faral, *Les jongleurs,* 67.

between them and other parts of the larger tradition in which they participated.[110]

It is characteristic of the literature of the tavern and comico-realism that it appropriated the broader debate over *amplificatio* or "superabundance" or *usura* to its own thematic interests. Within this particular textual framework, the "new rhetoric," in its fully transgressive, "atheotic" form, is assimilated to the frequenters of the tavern and more broadly to the bourgeoisie. It is explicitly allied to their economic interests, in contrast with traditional rhetorical and economic models.[111] The tavern could most properly be characterized as the locus of a semiology that operates on the desire for (or intention of) private "profit," where this profit is obtained through the revaluation and commodification of the public sign for private gain. Furthermore, this semiotic activity operates in a world where divine immanence is absent from the sign, so that proper exchange, understanding, and interpretation become incurably problematic.

Though I have outlined here the shared features of the poetics of the tavern and that of the new rhetoric, suggesting links to such writers as Marie de France and the authors of the Vulgate Cycle, it is important to stress that while there is a certain broad unity in the notion of proper semiology in the thirteenth century (going back ultimately to that of Saint Augustine), the forms of anti-Platonic semiology are multiple and varied.[112] Thus it is impossible to read high medieval culture as a battleground between only two competing semiologies. While many cultural and liter-

---

110. I tend to agree with Brian Stock (*The Implications of Literacy,* 3) that the rise of literacy beginning in the eleventh century lies at the origin of the many new assumptions about language and texts that arose in the twelfth and thirteenth centuries. In reference to his claim that the accompanying changes in thought were produced by a "renaissance" in the learned disciplines during this time (455), I suggest that the entry of a whole new class of readers into the literate tradition, via vernacular literature, had a perhaps even greater effect, at least in the case of comico-realism and its resistance to many of these "learned" concepts. See my conclusion.

111. It is in fact common in the Middle Ages to ally the treacherous, the sinful, and the transgressive with the merchant. A classic theatrical example occurs in *La passion du Palatinus.* Like the other dramatic pieces we have discussed, it contains comico-realist scenes within the context of the religious drama, all of which serve to parody the villains of the play. Of these five scenes identified by Grace Frank in her edition of the play, four depict merchant transactions of one sort or another. In the case of Judas in fact, there is a specific case of usury: the Jews are short of cash and tell Judas that if he will take twenty-eight coins now, they will give him four later rather than the two needed to reach thirty. Of course the anti-Semitic element is apparent, but neither in this play nor elsewhere is the conflict of merchant/villain versus church/Truth confined to Jewish merchants.

112. This broad cultural unity corresponds in general extent to the sign theories that Stephen Nichols shows to be operating in Romanesque sculpture, illumination, history, and

ary confrontations may be framed as binary oppositions, the two binary terms do not remain constant in any useful sense. For example, while many thirteenth-century texts and glosses make use of the conventional and imperfect nature of language to play with metaphor and other rhetorical devices, only certain among these profess or imply an overriding intention to undermine or even destroy any essentialist referentiality. This feature of intention separates the professed rhetorical aims of Geoffrey of Vinsauf and Matthew of Vendome, for example, from those implicit in *Le Jeu de Saint Nicolas* or in much troubadour poetry, to take another example. Geoffrey may urge that the "robes" of poetry be varied, but he admits that "the meaning is one" below these robes; and Matthew of Vendome notes that "the conceptual realization of meaning comes first," to be followed by the poetic ordering of the text, evoking the classical division of rhetoric into invention and arrangement, but also echoing the privileging of meaning that lay behind such an ordering of poetic activity.[113] To take another example, Chrétien de Troyes often explores the problematic nature of interpreting signs in his courtly romance, but the multiplicity (or impossibility) of interpretation is typically a problem, even a tragic problem—as in *Perceval* and Perceval's attempt to understand the meaning of the Grail ceremony—whereas Jean Bodel's play seems to celebrate this feature of interpretation.

Among other examples, we could consider the increasing indeterminacy featured in both Marie de France's "Prologue" and *The Romance of the Rose,* with its multiple, unresolved discursive confrontations. These texts, to one extent or another, could be broadly read as implicitly valorizing indeterminacy of interpretation and privileging a phenomenological hermeneutics—that is, the value of varying private interpretations by each reader who encounters a text. Yet none of these texts allies this valorization of a private profit in the gloss to any positive view of monetary profit in the sense that many tavern texts do. While the tavern shares broad poetic features with some aristocratic literature, its economics is funda-

---

literature, for example *(Romanesque Signs),* and to what Jesse Gellrich seems to mean when he refers to the "single cultural language" that characterized the Middle Ages (*The Idea of the Book,* 30–31). Alastair Minnis, in *The Medieval Theory of Authorship,* likewise speaks of an overarching cultural consistency in the Middle Ages. Clearly, I am arguing that this single cultural language of the eleventh and twelfth centuries began to break down into multiple cultural languages of change or resistance in the later twelfth and thirteenth centuries and that one of those languages is the discourse of the tavern. If there is a unity to be found here, it is in the multiple responses to the same Neoplatonic target of resistance.

113. *Poetria nova,* 26. For Matthew, see *The Art of Versification,* pt. III, no. 52.

mentally opposed to that of the aristocracy. The particular alliance of poetics and economics in the tavern, and more broadly in comico-realism, makes its semiology unique among the constellation of high medieval anti-Platonic responses to proper and consecrated semiology.

As so often in the Middle Ages, it is in the literature of the turn of the thirteenth century that such combinations are first carried out, antedating the explicit formulation of these matters in rhetorical and theological texts by several years or, in some cases, even decades.[114] Having seen how poetry takes as its subject the economic gap of illicit profit in exchange and then appropriates this theme to use it as the locus for broader questions of class and economics (in chapter 1) and then allies economics and poetics to consider the broader question of semiotic gaps and imperfections (in chapter 2), we will see in chapter 3 how comico-realist "bourgeois" literature locates its very source in this semiotic gap—and most particularly in the tavern, which is the most potently representative locus of both the new rhetoric and the new economics.

---

114. For a related argument, see Gellrich, *The Idea of the Book,* 50. He pinpoints "Fiction" as the starting point for important changes in ideas on signification that later spread to philosophy and other domains.

Chapter 3

The Moral Economy of the Tavern

The Corporeal Economy and Natural Desire

The short narrative text "La devise au lecheor" is one of a number of Old French *devises,* creeds, and paternosters that apparently were often declaimed by jongleurs as comic monologues.[1] It features a lecher comparable to the one in Jean le Marchant's miracle. The particular transgression of this lecher, from the standpoint of a medieval moralist, is excessive desire. Specifically, he violates the laws of what could be termed the proper "corporeal economy" as it was conceived in the Middle Ages—an economy that saw the body as the earthly home of the soul, to be sustained until no longer necessary, and as the vehicle for the production of new bodies. This lecher's desires surpass the needs of the body for sustenance and reproduction, with the result that his acts become not necessary but gratuitous, sources of pleasure. His desire is "unnatural" rather than natural.

The most typical pleasures of the lecher in question are wine, women, and dice, three leitmotivs of the tavern. True to form, the lecher admits, "taverne ai moult aimée" (I have greatly loved the tavern) (v. 81), and he concedes that he has drunk and gambled to excess. Vice virtually always leads to poverty in medieval texts,[2] and the lecher admits, "bon morsel / m'ont la borse vuidée" (tasty morsels have emptied my purse) (vv. 132–33). The poem is a tale of excess desire consummated and money spent.

Much of "La devise au lecheor" is in fact nothing more or less than a

---

1. Méon, *Nouveau recueil de fabliaux et contes,* 301–8.
2. One traditional proverb states, "Par vin, par feme et par dez si vient toust homme a povretez" (Morawski, *Proverbes français,* no. 1603).

listing of the ways in which these desires are consummated, a catalog of transgressions.

> Taverne ai moult aimée
> N'est pas droit que la hée,
> Tote ai m'amor donée
> A savor destranpée
> De garingal
> De citoal..

(vv. 81–86)

> [I have greatly loved the tavern;
> It is not right that I should hate it.
> I have given it all my love,
> With the unbridled taste
> Of garingal
> Of citoal . . .]

Garingal and citoal are aromatic spices.

There follows a long list of foods and drinks that the lecher has enjoyed, as corporeal gratuity is mirrored by poetic gratuity. The living out of these moral transgressions against proper corporeal economy becomes coterminous with the structure of the poem itself and its creation. While in a certain sense this is true of any narrative work, the particular gratuitous nature of medieval "listing poems"—of which there are many—points to their status as a celebration of the pure commodity of word and object. Fittingly, many of the lists involved are of commercial commodities or activities.[3]

Yet the lecher's desires are not only unnatural in their excess but also potentially limitless. Aquinas, speaking specifically of the desire for wealth, writes:

> Appetitus naturalium divitiarum non est infinitus, quia secundum certam mensuram naturae sufficiunt. Sed appetitus divitiarum artificialium est infinitus, quia deservit concupiscentiae inordinatae, quae non modificatur.

---

3. See "Le dit des marcheans," "Les vins d'Ouan," "Les crieries de Paris," and "Le dit des paintres," all in Barbazon, *Fabliaux et contes.*

[The appetite for natural wealth is not infinite, for after a certain point nature is satisfied. But the appetite for artificial wealth is infinite, for it is a slave to concupiscence without order, which is without regulation.][4]

The Old French proverb "Quand plus boit len, plus veult len boivre" (The more one drinks, the more one wants to drink) seems even more apropos in this case.[5] Unnatural economic profit (as discussed in chap. 2) and the unnatural desire of the lecher can clearly be allied in their "artificiality": Aquinas' preceding discussion of desire immediately follows his remarks on natural and artificial wealth quoted in chapter 2: the illicit economic profit is really just the realization of morally illicit desires. Indeed, much medieval resistance to the merchant's activities was due to the belief that the search for profit would produce an unquenchable cupidity.[6] There was no natural way to arrive at a "sufficient" profit. The usurer was the classic example of someone who profited unnaturally and thus of the merchant or financier whose desire could not be sated.

Ja uns useriers
N'aura tant deniers
Con ses cuers voldroit
Ce dist Salemons.

[Never will a usurer
Have as many deniers
As his heart would desire—
Thus says Solomon.][7]

Yet unnatural desire and unnatural economic profit arising from usury may conceptually be allied to the "unnatural" and "artificial" rhetoric exemplified in the quotations from the *Poetria nova* in chapter 2, since all

---

4. Aquinas *Summa Theologica* Ia, IIae, q. 2, art. 1.

5. Morawski, *Proverbes français,* no. 1755.

6. For more details, see Baldwin, *Masters, Princes, and Merchants,* 262. In fact, this idea can be found in the passage from Plato's *Laws* that was discussed in the first chapter (II.xi.918). Plato cites the tendency to desire "without limit" as the reason for the "violent abuse" of inn keeping, as well as retail trade and commerce. Thus in a larger sense the lecher who is the victim of the tavern keeper in this text is also closely allied to him in his desires.

7. "De Marco et de Salemons," in Méon, *Nouveau recueil de fabliaux et contes,* 416. See also "La Patenostre a l'userier" (Barbazon, *Fabliaux et contes,* 4:99–106), vv. 171–72: "Li Useriers qui jamès n'iert / Saoulez d'amasser deniers."

four move beyond natural utility and into gratuity. The lecher could easily be seen as a poet—particularly the type of transgressive poet that Thomas of Cobham criticizes, as seen in chapter 2. The lecher in Jean le Marchant's miracle is also a "janglior" and "menestrel." Thus the generalized medieval lecher not only engages in an idolatry of the body but, like the usurer, idolatrizes the "body" of the monetary sign and, like the rhetorician, does likewise with the "body" of the linguistic sign. Metaphorically, the desire of the lecher, in its excess, is avarice, and its fulfillment, in its gratuity, is gluttony.[8] In the *devise,* consummation of desire is at once the poetic creation of the poem and an exhausting of the contents of the "borse," leading to poverty and thus the forced end of the poem. Language, money, and bodily indulgence become consumptive commodities that ultimately consume each other, as the key utilities of human existence and reproduction turn on themselves in a gratuitous bout of self-destruction.

This, at least, is the way the moral status of the corporeal economy might be seen by a preacher from the circle of Peter Cantor or the Mendicants. But these ideas had a much broader general resonance in the Middle Ages as well. The notion of pleasure—whether of the body, the text, or the merchant's wealth—was a central problem of medieval thought, and whether this notion was defined more narrowly in terms of profit, game, gratuity, or artifice, it never enjoyed complete approval from church thinkers.[9] Yet the connection of gratuity, pleasure, and artifice as located in the body could also be seen in a more favorable light. In several texts in this chapter, literary creation will be figured in terms of a series of corporeally transgressive activities typical of the tavern, including drinking, dicing, and prostitution. Thus, as a medieval moralist might say, the idolatry

---

8. I will discuss extensively in chapter 4 the deeper connections between the sins of avarice and gluttony. For the moment, I will simply note that among the seven deadly sins, these are the two that are by far the most intimately associated with the tavern. Thus the association in this poem is entirely typical. It is important to note that avarice does indeed indicate specifically excess desire. In the *Tabula Exemplorum,* we find under "Avarice" the example of the "avare" who fails to keep only what he truly needs from his income. He should ideally give all the excess away to the poor, but specifically because he keeps the excess, he is like a pig (Welter, *La Tabula Exemplorum,* no. 14). As another example, the text "Triacle et Venin" (Barabazan, *Nouveau recueil,* 360–71) links gluttony and usury closely (vv. 365, 366), as does a text in the *Chansons et Dits Artesiens* (ed. Jeanroy, no. 6) that accuses the merchant of being both usurer (v. 34) and pig (v. 37). For more on the connection between usury and excess, see Langholm's discussion of Robert of Courson's *Summa* on usury (*Economics in the Medieval Schools,* 40–42). "Superfluentia" is also an important concept in Peter Cantor's *Verbum abbreviatum* (*PL* 205).

9. See in particular Verdon, *Le plaisir au Moyen Age,* pt. 2.

of the body is linked to the idolatry of the body of the text, or from the opposite point of view, the pleasure of the text and body are one.

When the subject of the body arises in the Middle Ages, special attention is called to the most problematic of medieval bodies, that of the woman. I have already mentioned prostitution and brothels in passing and have noted their connection to the tavern, and it is perhaps not surprising that issues of gender should occur in tavern texts.[10] One particular focus of interest in this chapter will be to examine more closely these issues. The play *Courtois d'Arras* and certain fabliaux in particular are crucial to this question, because they—like the preceding *devise*—locate a specifically masculine textual authority in the male "purse"—both the change purse and the testicles. The ways in which a specifically feminine-gendered poetics of the tavern, the brothel, and prostitution threatens to dislocate and emasculate this textual authority will be of central interest. But first, I will begin with the Latin roots of the comico-realist tradition.

The Goliards

The poetry of the goliards, dating primarily from the late eleventh, twelfth, and early thirteenth centuries, is celebrated for its depictions of drinking, gambling, and taverns, most famously in the *Carmina Burana*. Emblematic of these themes is "Potatores exquisiti" (*CB* 644–46). This poem does not explicitly occur in a tavern, but it deals entirely with drinking, and by implication the tavern is the most common site of this activity. Like many goliard poems, it features a shifting of normal order and propriety. The shifting in this poem is linguistic—the poem is a farcical parody of the sequenced hymn "Peccatores exquisiti." Such farcical rewritings were common in the Middle Ages in both Latin and French, but more interestingly, a large number of hymns are rewritten based on themes of gambling, theft, and usury,[11] which, as we have seen, imply a shifting and revaluation of signs. Here, the shift is in vocabulary, as "peccatores" becomes "potatores," and drink is the agent of slippage, as the drinker himself often "slips" in his speech.

---

10. An additional source on the connection between taverns, prostitution, and brothels is Karras, *Common Women,* 71–72.

11. See "Le Credo au ribaud" (Barbazan, *Fabliaux et contes,* 4:445–52), "Le Credo à l'usurier" (Barbazan, op. cit., 4:106–14), and "Le Patenostre a l'usurier" (Barbazon, op. cit., 4:99–106). For an interesting and convenient comparison of the original and the parodic, Jeanroy and Langfors, *Chansons Satiriques et Bachiques* contains an original Latin hymn, the medieval French translation, and the farcical French version.

ita bibas absque pare
ut non possis pede stare
neque recta verba dare.

(vv. 26–28)

[you drink without ever getting enough
so that you cannot remain on your feet
nor correctly speak.]

The words "recta verba" foreshadow the terminology of such critics of rhetoric as Alain de Lille, as well as recalling the medieval definition of grammar as the art of *recte loquendo.*[12] The reference to "pede stare" like-wise recalls the proper practice of Latin meter. The playful revaluing of the religious "relic" of the original poem is thus linked not just to drunken stammering and babbling but implicitly to the undermining of proper grammar and rhetoric—as exemplified in the original Latin hymn.

The link of drink to linguistic dislocation is likewise found in "Denudata veritate" (*CB* 616–20), mentioned already in chapter 1. Water says to wine:

Tu scis linguas impedire,
titubando solet ire
tua sumens basia,
verba recte non discernens,
centum putat esse cernens
duo luminaria.

(vv. 49–54)

[You know how to impede the tongue,
and you customarily stumble forth
to gather drink's kisses.
Unable to speak or hear straightly,
you believe that you see a hundred candle lights
where there are only two.]

Yet drink is linked not only to the commonplace linguistic dislocation of the babbling drunk who again fails to use the "verba recte" but to creativity. Wine proclaims:

---

12. See Bloch, *Etymologies and Genealogies,* 133–36, for a more extensive analysis of the concept of "rectitude" in both grammar and nature in the work of Alain de Lille.

Per me senex iuvenescit,
per me ruit et senescit
iuveneum lascivia.
per me mundus reparatur;
per te nunquam generatur
filius vel filia.

(vv. 97–102)

[By me is the old man made young,
By me is lascivious youth
toppled and made old.
By me is the world made good again;
By you has there never been generated
A son or a daughter.]

The last line of this poem is particularly interesting in that wine generates not only life in the form of sons and daughters but declensions as well. It is possible to find several instances in the Middle Ages where grammatical declension and conjugation are linked to poetic creation. In the *Poetria nova,* Geoffrey of Vinsauf remarks that declinable forms are preferable to undeclinables in poetry: "The unchanging array of words which do not admit of inflection, although permissible in discourse, are well set aside" (p. 77, v. 1710). The play of syntactical relations and functions within the phrase seems more interesting than any transcendental referentiality on the part of the root forms. Alain de Lille, in *De planctu Naturae,* similarly notes that nouns and adjectives come together in grammatical declensions that are also sexually fertile relationships.[13] Thus, as Howard Bloch notes, "nouns and adjectives copulate according to the rules of heterosexual combination."[14] Declension equals sexual reproduction.[15] Not only may nouns and verbs copulate, but Alain suggests that the deviant and incorrect grammar may be linked to deviant sexual practice, and more broadly, he offers in *De planctu Naturae* a list of the causes of the debasement of grammar and sexuality that reads like an attack on the tavern: he cites lust, idleness, drink, and gluttony (*DPN* 165–74). In fact, he goes on to suggest

13. Cited in Bloch, *Etymologies and Genealogies,* 257.
14. Bloch, *Etymologies and Genealogies,* 133
15. For more on Alain de Lille and the link between grammar and poetics, see Bloch, *Etymologies and Genealogies,* especially 133–36. The use of grammar to portray moral degradation is in fact quite general in the Middle Ages (see Hélin, *Medieval Latin Literature,* 93, for example) and argues for the primacy of the sign in medieval thought.

that these "pests" form "a bridge over which the brothel of lust is reached." In the goliard text, wine produces both masculine and feminine declension, suggesting an unnatural androgyny that violates "natural" law much as usury violates the natural law of the infertility of signs.[16] The creativity implicit in the medieval practice of *amplificatio* is ironically deviated from the "recte" path (see my introduction) toward an "unnatural" poetics that celebrates disorder and disruption of proper grammatical conjugation and proper bodily sustenance through the act of drink.

The disordering of the world is the central theme of "Denudata veritate," as old becomes young and young old, but it is in this disordering that re-creation occurs. Water replies that it, too, is productive, but this occurs in a "natural" way, as opposed to the artificial and lascivious desires and reproduction generated by wine. Water, the drink of the pilgrim, is the natural generator of "surplus," as in the rhetoric used in the service of God, while wine is the artificial generator of "surplus." This artificial generation depends on a semiotic dislocation and disordering equivalent to that which we have seen in chapter 2 occurs in usury and metaphor. In verses 105–7 the same "declining" procedure is used: "malus, peior, pessimus: / facis verba semiplana / balbutire . . ." (bad, worse, the worst: you make weakened words stammer . . .), says water—poetry and conjugation are a degradation in the eyes of "correct" rhetoric. Thus

Aqua surgit; se defendit
atque vinum reprehendit
de turpi colloquio.

(vv. 139–41)

[Water springs forth and defends herself
and reproaches wine
for his filthy speech.]

The theme of dice functions in a similar manner and, like drinking, locates itself most commonly in the tavern. In "Si quis deciorum" (*CB* 620–28) we read,

---

16. Another example of this fascination with the androgynous explicitly thematized in terms of grammar is Heldris de Cornouaille's thirteenth-century *Le roman de Silence.* Here, a woman (Silencia) is raised as a man (Silencius), and the violations of the natural sexual, grammatical, and poetic orders are simultaneously considered.

Si quis Deciorum dives officio
gaudes in Vagorum esse consortio,
vina nunquam spernas,
diligas tabernas.

(vv. 1–4)

[If you want to share in the pleasures of dice
and enjoy the company of uncertainty,
never spurn wine,
and love the tavern.]

Dice poems often feature the loss of a cloak, usually as part of a general rearrangement of normal order, both by the dice themselves as servants of Fortune and by the cheating that characterizes the games.

Perdentis tedia
sunt illi gaudium,
qui tenet pallium
per fraudis vitium.

("Si quis deciorum," vv. 25–28)

In taberna
fraus eterna
semper est in ludo.

(vv. 40–42)

[The trouble of the loser
is joy to those,
who possess the cloak
through the vice of fraud.]

[In the tavern
eternal fraud
is always in play.]

Howard Bloch in particular has suggested the importance of the garment as a representation of the sign in medieval literature. In particular he has stressed the use of the ill-fitting garment (of the poet) as a kind of representation of representation itself and, above all, due to its ill-fitting nature, a representation of the failure of representation.[17] The shifting, ill-fitting garment of the jongleur was widely noted: to take just one example, in the *Vita Saint Beraldi,* we read of those who "mixtis coloribus vestmenta variabant, quod proprie joculatorium est."[18] The cloak as sign is typically reassigned in the tavern through the mediums of drink, dice, and outright theft. It comes to mirror the linguistic sign as it is inappropriately assigned to someone other than its rightful owner, its proper signified. This is not surprising since the Middle Ages featured an often elaborate series of rules for dress, requiring both prostitutes and fools, for example, to wear identifying garments or at least identifying signs on these garments. Thus proper clothing was easily associated to general semiotic propriety, as we will see in *Courtois d'Arras* as well. We will also see an excellent example of this phenomenon in the vernacular later in this chapter, where a play on the word *robe* as meaning both "cloak" and "theft" (accomplished via cheating at dice) will thematize this issue.

A great number of poetic texts that concern drinking and dicing can be considered under the aegis of the tavern even when they do not explicitly locate themselves there. These texts are unified by a poetics and thematics that implicitly always find their home in the tavern, whose poetics further elucidates the individual texts. The tavern thus constitutes a kind of structuralist topos, whose realization in any given text may not be complete, but whose overall thematics are present at a deeper structural level in all individual, partial actualizations. The tavern in this sense functions similarly to such poetic genres as the *pastourelle* or *aube,* where partial reference to certain thematic elements evokes the others and creates a series of expectations on the part of the reader with regard to form, theme, or plot.[19] The "tavern piece" as such is never named as a genre or type of poetry in the Middle Ages as far as I know. Yet if we accept H. R. Jauss' description of genre as a "series of works that are bound by a structure forming a continuity and that appear historically," then certainly the tavern poem could be seen as an independent genre within the corpus of the goliards. The tavern within the dramas of Arras, however, does not constitute such an independent genre, since the tavern alone never serves to

---

17. Bloch, *Scandal of the Fabliaux,* 28–44.

18. Cited in Faral, *Les jongleurs,* app. III, no. 32.

19. For more on genre concepts, see Jauss, *Towards an Aesthetic of Reception,* 76–110; Bec, *La lyrique française au Moyen Age,* 33–44.

"independently . . . constitute texts."[20] Yet it clearly serves a strong "accompanying" function, to again use Jauss' words, and its thematics show evidence of a strong historical continuity from the goliard texts on through the theater of Adam de la Halle, even as they are constantly altered and remodeled, as is the case with any living, productive genre or subgenre.[21]

The tavern piece, as defined by the goliard poets, could be defined as a thematic genre that features action occurring at least implicitly in or near a tavern, with the characteristic actions including drinking and playing at dice. The resultant behaviors typically result in the loss or threatened loss of the cloak of some character, either due to gambling and drinking debts or via an outright theft, and they more generally lead to poverty and nakedness. Both economic and ludic transactions are characterized by fraud (false bills, cheating at dice, watered-down wine), as are linguistic transactions. Sexual desire and prostitution are sometimes, but not necessarily, present. The scenes involve a gratuitous fulfillment of excessive or "unnatural" desires. And finally, the scenes almost always explicitly thematize the idea of poetic production, representing their own illicit, "usurious" poetics in terms of either economic usury or morally illicit drinking, gambling, and theft—and once again we recall the representation of usury itself in terms of gambling and its prohibition as a form of theft. More generally, the poems underline the amoral nature of the tavern, often via oppositions to the church.

This is admittedly an excessively long definition of a genre, especially without a formal component. (One could also note that virtually all tavern scenes occur in either satiric and/or moralizing poems, the theater, or the fabliaux.) Yet I choose to use the word *genre* rather than *mode* or *topos* because the tavern, in the hands of the goliards and elsewhere, does in fact generate its own texts. Consider the following complete text (*CB* 694).

Ego sum abbas Cucaniensis,
et consilium meum est cum bibulis,
et in secta Decii voluntas mea est,

---

20. Jauss, *Towards an Aesthetic of Reception,* 80, 81.

21. Clearly, the tavern scene must be considered a strongly "thematic" genre, to use Pierre Bec's distinction between the thematic and the formal (*La lyrique française au Moyen Age,* 37). Yet I am also obviously arguing in this book for a poetics that is, if not specific to the tavern, at least strongly identified with it, so that there are also formal elements involved in the tavern scene's identity as genre or subgenre.

et qui mane me quesierit in taberna,
post vesperam nudus egredietur,
et sic denudatus veste clamabit:
"wafna, wafna!"
quid fecisti, Sors turpissima?
nostrae vitae gaudia
abstulisti omnia.

[I am the abbot of Cocagne,
and my counsel is with the thirsty,
while my will lies with the sect of Dice,
and he who should seek me in the tavern in the morning
will leave naked in the evening,
and thus quit of his clothes will cry out:
"Alas, alas!"
What have you done, most foul Fate?
All the joys of our life
you have taken away.]

The poem, from the *Carmina Burana,* contains every element of my definition of the genre except the thematization of poetic production, if we accept "Sors turpissima" as being equivalent to fraudulence, or at least irregularity, in exchange or transaction.

Thus the goliard poets had already provided a model of the tavern as a locus of linguistic and/or semiotic dislocation, effected via both drinking and gambling, and often symbolized by the random reassignment of the cloak. The very activities of drinking, gambling, and theft had themselves been assimilated to the production of poetry, which then likewise can be seen in terms of this linguistic dislocation. This disordering is represented as a creative function, as the source of poetry.

I would now like to look more closely at what I will term the "moral economy" of one of the most famous medieval Latin tavern poems, "In taberna quando sumus." Not only is this poem representative of the goliard corpus in its framing of ethics and morality in terms of a particular (morally illicit) economic model, but it reveals key differences with the moral status of the tavern in later vernacular texts, differences that are important for understanding the evolution of the genre.

"In taberna quando sumus" is found in the *Carmina Burana* (*CB* 628–32). There are five key themes in this poem. First is a lack of concern for the outside world, so that the tavern serves as a kind of lyric interlude in existence: "non curamus quid sit humus, / sed ad ludum properamus" (we care not for the world, but hurry to gaming) (vv. 2–3). Second is the primacy of drinking and dicing over all other activities: "Quidam ludunt, quidam bibunt, / quidam indiscrete vivunt" (Some gamble, some drink, some live quite disgracefully) (vv. 9–10). The idea of the *ludo* is insisted on over and over, further establishing a disjunction between the outer world of work and the ludic world of the tavern. Third is the rupture of normal rules of buying, selling, and economic exchange, underlined via the dice games, which can convert one small coin to a limitless source of wealth providing all the drinks—that is, "ubi nummus est pincerna" (where a penny is worth a pitcher) (v. 6). Fourth is the reassignment of debts, especially in a random manner: where once consumption resulted in concomitant debt on both a financial and a moral level (i.e., sin), now these debts are ignored or randomly redistributed, so that the individual is freed of his accountability: "primo pro nummata vini / ex hac bibunt libertini" (first they drink to whomever will pay, to sate the thirst of all and sundry) (vv. 17–18). I argue that the individual monetary debt (as well as the ethical debt of sins against God) constitutes a signifier for the individual. The monetary debt should be removable only via labor; the ethical debt, only via the grace of God. Thus the treatment of these debts in this tavern parallels the treatment of other more conventional signs. The tavern, with its lack of moral and economic debts, comes to represent a space similar to that of tavern poetry (in the broadest sense)—where univocal reference ends and the "proper" rules of language and meaning are broken, meanings being shifted, negated, or ignored. Fifth is the tendency to shift garments as well as debts, in particular to lose one's garments at dice.

> Sed in ludo qui morantur,
> ex his quidam denudantur,
> quidam ibi vestiuntur,
> quidam saccis induuntur.
>
> (vv. 11–14)

> [But those who stay in the game,
> certain among them will be left naked,
> certain ones are well clothed,
> others wear only sackcloth.]

This particular poem represents the tavern as a self-centered ludic world, where normal rules of economics and morality, as well as language, are suspended or broken in favor of random shifting and reassignment of debt, sin, money, purchasing power, and clothing. This emphasis on disorder (i.e., the shifting of *propertas*) is further increased when the round of drinks begins. One drinks "pro fratribus perversis . . . pro monachis dispersis . . . pro discordantibus" (for evil friars . . . for shiftless monks . . . for bringers of discord) (vv. 25–28). The idea of the breaking or suspending of normal rules in favor of gratuity is also furthered by the fact that the drinking occurs "sine lege" (without rule) (v. 32) and "sine meta" (without purpose) (v. 51). Normal moral and economic order is replaced by an orgiastic effusion of desire to be satiated at any (or ostensibly no) cost. Here, as in "La devise au lecheor," desire is unnatural in that no "natural" limits can be placed on it.

The act of drinking becomes the equivalent of the production of the poem, as in "La devise au lecheor." Each new line of "In taberna quando sumus" becomes the equivalent of another round of drinks—they drink

> decies pro navigantibus,
> undecies pro discordantibus,
> duodecies pro penitentibus,
> tredecies pro iter agentibus.
>
> (vv. 27–30)

> [tenth for sailors,
> eleventh for sowers of discord,
> twelfth for those doing penance,
> thirteenth for the wayfarer.]

Finally each new line becomes nothing more than the act of drinking.

> bibit pauper et egrotus,
> bibit exul et ignotus,
> bibit puer, bibit canus.
>
> (vv. 41–43)

> [The poor man drinks and the sick,
> the stranger drinks and the fool,
> the young boy drinks and the old man.]

The poem continues thus, each line of the fifth and sixth stanzas beginning with "bibit," culminating in the plural "bibunt" of the last line of stanza six—"bibunt centum, bibunt mille" (a hundred drink, a thousand drink) (v. 48)—figuratively suggesting the totalizing nature of the poem, as it expands without limits. All of society drinks—"soror . . . frater . . . anus . . . mater . . . clerus . . . decanus . . . miles . . . presul" (vv. 33–48). Here no one escapes the world of the tavern, as the ludic realm, initially so carefully distinguished from the outer world, expands to swallow or drink up its exterior in a ludic totality. "Bibit" in fact echoes the verb *vivit* and the tavern represents the theater of life itself. While "La devise au lecheor" swallows up itself and ends in a centripetal movement of linguistic and economic exhaustion, "In taberna quando sumus" swallows up the world outside it in a movement of centrifugal expansion to infinity.

The tavern here represents a world without natural limits, where gain is not equivalent to labor, where debts come and go as Fortune wishes, where the amount one eventually purchases or consumes has no relation to the value of the coins in one's purse, where the ethically questionable or sinful act bears with it no guilt, no moral debt, and no penance to be performed. This is a world of pure idolatrous gratuity, a world not far removed from that evoked by the gambling scenes of *Le Jeu de Saint Nicolas,* where the drunken, gambling thieves play out their game of "hasard."

This world is typical of the goliards.[22] The tavern is not framed within a miracle play, a moralizing voyage to hell, or a sermon. It instead occupies its entire frame, as independent genre, expanding to engulf the world of carnal existence. These expansions of the tavern are also repeated in the works of Rutebeuf and Adam de la Halle in chapter 4. The tension between unlimited expansion and constraining frame is one of the interesting features of the tavern piece from one text to the next. More generally, the tension evokes a particularly medieval vision of limitless desire and infinite creation of value, of a crossing of Aquinas' liminal space between the natural and artificial. Is the space beyond the limits of nature a space of freedom or only of delusion? This is the question implicitly posed by many thirteenth-century texts. The answer they offer depends on their differing responses to the question of where literary meaning inheres.

---

22. "Potatores exquisiti" also includes many of the elements of such a moral economy: there is gratuitous desire without measure ("licet sitis sine siti," v. 2) and a neglect of the larger world ("et bibatis expediti / et scyphorum inobliti," vv. 3–4). The dice poem cited also echoes the themes of the tavern and drink poems: the release from normal moral laws and constraints ("curarum que tedium / solvit, et dat gaudium," vv. 9–10) and the neglect of eventual consequences of the "lyric interlude" ("terminum nullum teneat nostra concio," v. 11).

Courtois d'Arras attempts to establish a homology between meaning and nature (as embodied in the male reproductive organs), while the fabliaux locate meaning in encounters of artificial (textual, monetary, and corporeal) desire.

Courtois d'Arras and the Female Body

By placing the tavern within at least ostensibly "moralizing" frameworks, *Le Jeu de Saint Nicolas* and *Courtois d'Arras* altered its import, fundamentally remodeling the genre even as it passed formally from genre to subgenre within the metageneric space of drama. It was this remodeling as subgenre, with the oppositional possibilities that the term subgenre implies, that allowed the tavern to become such a rich poetic device. In more theoretical terms, the tavern in *Courtois d'Arras* loses its status as a locus for the ecstatic celebration of disorder and dissemination and as a means of affirming the tendency of such dissemination to engulf all textuality (the world). It is drawn into a much more logocentrically founded debate and placed in the position of expressing semiotic dualities in such a way that its most important meanings lie in the "absences" that it connotes, both of morality and of signification. This generic tradition then lies at the base of the numerous shorter tavern texts of the thirteenth and fourteenth centuries, such as "Le jeu des dez," "La devise au lecheor" (discussed earlier in this chapter), "Les fames, les dez et la taverne," "Le credo au ribaut," and "Le clerc Golias."[23]

In *Courtois d'Arras,* the economics of the tavern involves usury even more explicitly than in Jean Bodel's play, revealing the important generic links between the two. Yet its moral message is quite different. A dramatization of the parable of the prodigal son, the play can also be read as the story of the prodigal merchant, who abandons a traditional economic system to engage in the seductive new world of usury and speculative investment as found in the tavern, only to be victimized by the system he tries to exploit before finally returning to the fold of tradition. But more interestingly, the play takes the important step of gendering the economics and rhetoric of the tavern/brothel specifically in terms of the feminine and, more exactly still, in terms of prostitution. The debate of *Le Jeu de Saint Nicolas* is reformulated in terms of the opposition between feminine semi-

---

23. Respectively, Jubinal, *Nouveau receuil,* 1:229–34; Méon, *Nouveau recueil,* 301–8; Barbazon, *Fabliaux et contes,* 4:485–88; ibid., 445–51; Méon, op. cit., 447–51.

otics and masculine desires, and proper "reading" becomes a specifically male prerogative.

The prodigal son of *Courtois d'Arras,* Courtois, after abandoning his father's country estate, is enticed into the tavern by a "garçon" at the door. This medieval salesman promises all the drinks one could want and says, "ne l'estuet fors conter la dete" (all you have to do is put it on your account) (v. 109). Everything is on credit, and payment can apparently be delayed indefinitely. Courtois, after entering the tavern, meets two prostitutes named Pourette and Manchevaire. After some conversation to lower Courtois' guard, they offer him a proposition: if he will loan them all his money, then without having to raise a finger ("sans oeuvre faire") (v. 171), he will make a handsome profit when they return it to him after using it for their own ends. In other words, Courtois should loan them some cash at interest—engage in usury.

In addition, the crier trumpets the fact that payment is on credit—a form of usury in the Middle Ages.[24] And Courtois himself hopes to make a living by playing dice in the tavern (vv. 74–78). Recall that dice were also closely associated with usury: Phillipe de Beaumanoir explicitly connects the two in his *coutumier,* noting, "autres convenances y a encore qui ne sunt pas a tenir, si comme se je convenance a paier detes du jeu des des ou d'usure" (there are other contracts that need not be respected, as when I agree to pay debts from dicing or from usury).[25] Seduced into the tavern by an initial offer of usury by the crier and hoping to engage in games of chance and usury, it is hardly surprising that Courtois should fall for the prostitutes' proposition of usury.

Yet the prostitutes' proposition itself is proposed in a slippery language replete with double entendres and "fertile" with meaning.

Ciertes vilains ne sanblés mie;
ains croi bien en mon cuer et pens
q'an vous ait cortoisie et sens.

. . . .

Par un convent, ne rois ne quens
n'orent onques tant de lor boens
com vous ariés sans oevre faire.

(vv. 164–71)

---

24. Baldwin, *Masters, Princes, and Merchants,* 274–75.
25. Cited in Semrau, *Würfel und Würfelspiel im alten Frankreich,* 19.

je vous creant et aseür
que vous avés trové eür,
biele dame mignote et cointe,
bien gaagnant et bien repointe,
si ne vous ainme mie a gap.

(vv. 191–95)

[Certainly you scarcely seem a villain;
Rather I believe in my heart and consider
that in you there is *courtoisie* and sense.

. . . .

With this agreement, neither king nor count
will ever possess such a treasure
as you will have with no engagement at all.]

[I promise and assure you
that you have found happiness.
A lovely lady appealing and charming,
profitable and clever,
and I love you entirely sincerely.]

With "croi" (v. 165) and "je vous creant et aseür" (v. 191), they play on the meanings of the word *croire,* meaning both "to believe" and "to lend" in Old French—Courtois is asked simultaneously to believe their words and to lend them his money. The words "bien gaagnant" (v. 194) are used to describe Pourette, in which case they mean "industrious" and "an honest worker"; but they also carry the more general sense of *gaaigne,* which could refer to any profit, including the dishonest type—in particular that from prostitution in this case.[26] Other words, such as "repointe" (v. 194) likewise have the sense both of "clever" and of "tricky." Thus the usurious monetary surplus to be gained by Courtois from his "crediting" the prostitutes is echoed in the usurious linguistic surplus and profit generated by the prostitutes.

　　Their language not only revalues signs and produces excess meaning but also commodifies these signs for their private gain. Courtois fails to see the problems in such utterances as "ains croi bien en mon cuer et pens / q'an vous ait cortoisie et sens" (vv. 165–66), wherein his name is altered

---

26. There are numerous other oblique references to prostitution. Jean Dufournet ("*Courtois d'Arras* ou le triple héritage") suggests vv. 168–69, 173, 176–77, 191–92, and 214ff., for example.

from signifier for the person to nominal commodity, since *courtois* is literally in *co[u]rtoisie*. Likewise "sens" refers here to the money in his *bourse*, soon to be gone, though it will ironically be replaced by "sens" as he himself initially understands the utterance. Usurious economics and usurious poetics are thus explicitly allied in the persons of the prostitutes.

The two prostitutes, as the primary producers of the text and as controllers of the action and plot, can in fact be considered the inscribed poets, or jongleurs, of the scene. Indeed, jongleurs and prostitutes were closely associated in the Middle Ages; both were seen, for example, as sinful in that they distorted their bodies—which were in theory "naturally" given to them in the image of God—either through their actions (theatrical or sexual) or through adornment.[27] This violation of nature is echoed by Gratian, whose criticism of prostitution in his *Decretum* is based not on its monetary aspects but on its promiscuity (excess desire, beyond the needs for natural procreation). He considers any woman who takes many lovers to be a prostitute. Prostitutes and professional entertainers were also subject to many of the same legal penalties.[28] Peter Cantor noted that only the jongleur, among all professions, had no utility in the world (see chap. 2). However, a more astute author of a thirteenth-century penitential connected jongleurs and prostitutes, noting, "Quaedam officia sunt quae ex toto peccata sunt, ut meretricum et histrionum . . . non est danda eis poenitentia" (There are certain offices that are entirely sinful, such as prostitutes and histrions . . . penance should not be granted them).[29] This Latin pronouncement finds its vernacular equivalent in the fabliau "Les Putains est les lecheors," where the author notes that God originally created three classes of people—clerics, knights, and workers. The fabliau goes on to reveal that the two groups left out of this divine world order were the prostitutes and the *lecheors* (jongleurs). Without any inherent utility or place in the established order, they must be assigned to another, established group to be supported—the jongleurs to knights and the prostitutes to clerics in this case.[30] The parallel inutility of jongleur and prostitute is again explicit.

---

27. For details on prostitution and its relation to the body and adornment, see Baldwin, *Masters, Princes, and Merchants,* 134; Brundage, *Law, Sex, and Christian Society;* and especially Otis, *Prostitution in Medieval Society.* For the jongleur and especially the association between the jongleur and the prostitute due to bodily distortion, see Baldwin, op. cit., 199–203; Faral, *Les jongleurs.*

28. Brundage, *Law, Sex, and Christian Society,* 248; Baldwin, *Masters, Princes, and Merchants,* 199.

29. Cited in Faral, *Les jongleurs,* app. III, 102.

30. Montaiglon, *Receuil général,* 3:175–77.

The jongleur of course also does the same thing with language that both he and the prostitute do with their bodies, taking a community property and distorting and adorning it in producing literature, turning it away from its proper, utilitarian function of reference to "truth." He was seen as a tool of the devil, and someone who seduced honest men with his language—it was said that jongleurs "libentius ponunt linguam ad stercora mundi quam ad lapides pretiosos coeli" (more willingly apply their tongues to the filth of the world than to the precious gems of heaven), and they were often called ministers or tools of the devil.[31] As "lascivious" figures who commonly frequented taverns, jongleurs obviously had much in common with our two prostitutes. Thomas of Cobham, in his early twelfth-century penitential, notes that among *histrionum,* "Quidam transformant et transfigurant corpora sua per turpes saltus et per turpes gestus, vel denudando se turpiter, vel induendo horribiles larvas" (Certain ones transform and transfigure their bodies through obscene leaping about and obscene gestures, sometimes going about shamefully naked, other times putting on horrible masks), others "sequuntur curias magnatum et dicunt opprobria et ignominias" (follow the courts of nobles and proffer abuse and ignominy), and others "habent instrumenta musica ad delectandum homines . . . et cantant . . . diversas cantilenas ut moveant homines ad lasciviam" (have musical instruments for amusing men . . . and sing . . . various tales that inspire men to lewdness).[32] With his emphasis on the "turpes" gestures and movements, the delectation offered by the jongleurs, and the "lasciviam" that results, Thomas portrays the jongleur as virtually a sexual seducer.

Likewise, in a critique of illicit rhetoric and those who used it, Alain de Lille gives the debate an interesting twist. He writes in his *De planctu Naturae* that "man . . . tries to denature the natural things of nature and arms a lawless and solecistic Venus to fight against me" (*DPN* 131), as the desire for the sign, figured in the desire for Venus and the female body, turns men

---

31. "They more willingly use their tongue to speak of the filth of the world than of the precious gems of the heavens" (*Guillaume de Bar,* B.N. MS Lat. 16476, fol. 131, cited in Faral, *Les jongleurs,* app. III, no. 255). Honorius d'Autun says of jongleurs that "intentione ministri sunt Satanae" (*Elucidarium* MII.58, in Kleinhans, *Lucidere*). Peter Cantor notes that only the jongleurs have no useful function whatsoever on the earth (Faral, *Les jongleurs,* 26–28).

32. Cited in Faral, *Les jongleurs,* 67. See also Etienne de Bourbon's 1260 comment attacking old women who "paint and adorn themselves like idols, so that they give the impression of being masked, just like these jongleurs who have painted faces, which are called 'artifices' in French" (cited in Rousse, "Le théâtre et les jongleurs"; my translation).

away from reference to higher truths. This passage is part of Alain's long attack on improper grammarians (130–42), who are essentially the practitioners of the "New Rhetoric." These poets are accused of producing "shadowy figments" (recalling Geoffrey's "mists" [*Poetria nova*, vv. 1045–50, cited in chap. 2]) as well as "falsehood," itself often "cover[ed] . . . with a kind of imitation of probability" (139–40), as Alain again emphasizes the veiling nature of the poetry. Indeed, the perfectly fitting garment of Nature, representing proper reference, is reduced by improper grammar and rhetoric to inadequate rags that both improperly cover and at the same time seduce.

> Many men . . . in their violence . . . tear my clothes in shreds . . . and compel me, whom they should clothe in honor and reverence, to be stripped of my clothes and to go like a harlot to a brothel.[33]

Alain thus makes the prostitute emblematic of imperfect reference and associates her with his attack on unnatural grammarians and lying poets— those who are opposed to "nature."[34]

The idea of the lying poet is fundamental to medieval (and indeed Western) cultural history, finding its origins in Plato. Perhaps less obvious is how deep the medieval connection between this lie and the shredded and improper clothing of Alain's prostitutes can be pursued. As noted in chapter 2, Jane Burns has observed that "only God has the power to create, whereas the artist using words can merely represent."[35] The poet should thus always be implicated in an act of reference when using language. Language is not "free" and without referentiality, just as value production cannot come without the requisite labor. And neither language nor money should create something entirely new "out of the void," as God did at the time of the Creation: they should only refer to what already exists. Indeed, the only "surplus" allowed is assigned to God as well by medieval moral-

---

33. *DPN* 142. Similarly, Truth wears "garments . . . joined to . . . [her] body by a bond so close that no separation by removal could [take the clothes]," while Falsehood sports "a countless assemblage of rags . . . [which] disgraced by deformity whatever Truth graced by conformity" (217).

34. Alain also draws a parallel between clothing and cosmetics. Cosmetics obviously function in a similar manner to clothing—both increasing value and veiling reality, while drawing attention to the physical body and to the cosmetics themselves. See *DPN* 199 and *Anticlaudianus*, 57.

35. Burns, *Arthurian Fictions*, 21–22.

ists: the Creation itself was seen as a "surplus," and God's saving grace was also often interpreted as a "surplus" unearned by humanity.[36] Faced with illicit human creativity, traditional thought had no option but to claim that such creativity did not in fact exist but was rather a theft of someone else's goods. Thus, earning one's keep through literature was theft in the form of a lie; so Rutebeuf noted, "j'ai toz jors engressie ma pance d'autrui chatel, d'autrui substance" (I've filled my belly with others' wealth and others' goods).[37]

But the poet's or grammarian's adorned and improperly referring (lying) language can further be associated with the prostitute's adornment of her body, since both misrepresented the natural form and natural "truth" of the body. A short passage from Alain de Lille speaking of the art of painting, quoted in chapter 2, may be cited again.

> What can have no real existence comes into being and painting, aping reality and diverting itself with a strange art, turns the shadows of things into things and changes every lie to truth.[38]

Alain begins discussing poetry in exactly the same terms just after this passage and then goes on to critique yet a third form of lying misrepresentation, women's use of cosmetics and adornment in general—a practice closely akin to the painting that he critiques in the preceding passage.[39] The prostitute was in fact guilty of theft and lying to the extent that her adornment falsified her "natural" appearance and thus increased her income. She was obliged by canon law to return the surplus profit earned by means of the overproduction of the sign—her adornment.[40] The prostitute is the perfect example of one who "does not come before us with unveiled face" (or body), to refer back to the words of Geoffrey of Vinsauf quoted in chapter 2 (*Poetria nova*, vv. 1045–50). Her use of the signs of clothing and cosmetics parallels the use of signs by the poet.

This concept of the "lie" is crucial to the moral economics of medieval poetry and prostitution. Unlike some theologians and moralists, such as

---

36. On the creation as surplus, see Langlois, *La vie française au Moyen Age*, 3:154–55, where the author cites a text known as "L'Image du monde." On the surplus of grace, see James Simpson's discussion and references in *Piers Plowman*, 75ff.

37. "La repentance Rutebeuf," vv. 19–20, in *OC* 1:297–303.

38. *Anticlaudianus*, 49. See also *DPN* 138–41.

39. *Anticlaudianus*, 57, 97; *DPN* 199.

40. Baldwin, *Masters, Princes, and Merchants*, 134.

Alain de Lille and Peter Cantor, more liberal thinkers, especially canonists, did not consider sex evil even when practiced for profit, and prostitutes could keep the earnings they made without the advantage of adornment.[41] Nor was writing and the production of literature per se to be
condemned, since many clerics engaged in this activity; and even Thomas
of Cobham allowed that some jongleurs, specifically those who performed
hagiographic or epic works, were acceptable.[42] But the use of "artifice" to
produce a profit, through an artificial enhancement of value, certainly was
considered illicit by all canonists, moralists, and theologians. When
"empty" signs increased the value of a referent that itself remained
unchanged, income from this increase was considered to be theft.[43] The
fault was all the greater because of the public commodity at stake; not only
was language a type of public property, but as Ruth Karras has suggested,
in the Middle Ages the "public and indiscriminate availability of a
woman's body" was the "defining feature" of prostitution.[44] The prostitute's body and the jongleur's signs were all part of the same public economy; neither the possessor of the body from whom the linguistic signs
issued forth nor the prostitute whose body was so often publicly "possessed" was allowed any private manipulation of their bodies, which were
to remain always at the service of the public. The fundamental connection
between the lying bodies of jongleur and prostitute is perhaps most deeply
revealed in the parallel between the "lie of literature" mentioned earlier
and the fact that prostitutes—both ancient and medieval—were considered unworthy to give valid testimony in legal proceedings.[45]

Yet we have seen already, in chapter 2, that Rutebeuf and others found
the merchant also guilty of chronic lying for the sake of profit. The excess

---

41. See Brundage, *Law, Sex, and Christian Society,* 393. See also Rossiaud, *Medieval
Prostitution,* chap. 6.

42. Cobham wrote: "Sunt autem alii . . . qui cantant gesta principum et vitam sanctorum,
et faciunt solacia hominibus. . . . Bene possunt sustinere tales, sicut ait Alexander papa"
(cited in Faral, *Les jongleurs,* 67). Though Cobham distinguishes different individuals as performing different works, I argue that in reality he is speaking of distinctive types of literature,
prescribing "Platonic" genres—the epic and hagiography—and proscribing anti-Platonic
ones.

43. In fact, this concern with the manipulation of signs and theft extended even to teachers and lawyers, who also merely "spoke" and did not "create." Those teachers and lawyers
whose fees were not commensurate with any actual work that they did were often also considered thieves. See Baldwin, *Masters, Princes, and Merchants,* 125.

44. See Karras, *Common Women,* 10.

45. For the medieval era, see Karras, *Common Women,* 98–99.

produced by the artifice of the sign parallels the excess "unnatural" profit earned from usury. And in shifting money from sign to commodity, the usurer idolatrized the sign just as jongleurs and prostitutes idolatrized the body, clothing, and language. The usurer was a thief distorting "nature" just as the jongleur and prostitute supposedly did.[46] Though most thirteenth-century medieval canonists had no objection to profit per se (even for merchants), the usurer was condemned *secundam se* (by his very nature), and he was obliged to return any profit earned by means of usury as stolen goods,[47] just as the prostitutes' gain from adornment and cosmetics and the jongleurs gain from the lie of literature were ill-gotten wealth. Where reference was altered or ceased—be it to economic value, the body, or ideas and objects—theft began. Exchange, whether literary, sexual, or economic, was allowable, but any attempt at private manipulation, commodification, and revaluation of the sign was not. This is, however, exactly what the two jongleurs/prostitutes/usurers are doing in the *Courtois d'Arras*.

Courtois is thus faced with a text replete with slippery meanings and outright denials of reference to any value or commodity outside the text itself. Unfortunately for him, he consistently reads with reference to his own presence as subject, external to the text, and imposes that presence on the language of Manchevaire and Pourette. Yet the two prostitutes, by means of the pun on *courtois,* explicitly decenter the subject. Courtois is converted to a nominal commodity, becoming purely the verbal content of *courtoisie,* thus revealing the illusion of his presence (or of the presence of unique meaning in language). While Courtois believes that he can "possess" the word *sens,* both as money and as a single, present and determined signification, the two prostitutes take away *sens* in all senses of the word: Courtois loses his cash; the word loses any unitary meaning; and to the extent that Courtois defines the word in relation to his own objective self, a part of that self is dissolved as well. Finally, since reference to the *bourse* and *sens* is a common medieval pun on the male testicles and semen, the prostitutes also take away his masculinity in the scene, creating a nexus of absences—of money, of presence in language, of the masculine, and of meaning—and this nexus occurs precisely at the point where Courtois is

---

46. For discussion of the "natural law" case against usury, see Gordon, *Economic Analysis,* 170–71; Noonan, *Usury,* chap. 3.

47. On usury as a sin *secundam se,* see Le Goff, *Your Money or Your Life,* 50. On the return of goods, see Noonan, *Usury,* 32.

located in the text.[48] Courtois ironically underlines his own status when he notes as he assures the prostitutes that they can trust his word, "je tieng por fole ki cuide / que je parole a borse vuide" (I hold him a fool who thinks I speak with an empty purse) (vv. 183–84). He does indeed speak with a "borse" that will soon be literally empty and that is already figuratively so, and it is he who plays the fool.

The prostitutes demonstrate a keen awareness of the tricky, slippery, disseminating nature of language in their summation of their poetics.

> Ki bien vieut boire et bien mangier,
> querre l'estuet et engignier
> et par sens traire le meriele.

(vv. 307–9)

> [Who wishes to drink and eat well
> must seek this and engineer it
> and by his wits play the game well.]

"Engignier" could mean both "to create through artifice" and "to trick." "Traire" could of course mean "to write a literary text" or "to invent a tale," and it is clear that this literary invention will be of a highly tricky (and profitable) nature. In addition, "traire le meriele" was itself a fixed expression that most commonly meant "to play a good game of dice." In one usuriously "artificial" and fertile phrase, the prostitutes nicely assimilate illicit poetic and economic profit. Indeed, in a poetics that denies a transcendental, essentialist or logocentric function to language, the game of dice is a perfect metaphor. Where language becomes open to the vagaries of vocal and textual homophonies and homographies, of slippery contextual meanings, of confusion of reference, "reading" comes to resemble a toss of the dice, just as the writing of poetry is also a toss of the dice—a scrambling and disordering of language. The inventor of dice, according

---

48. This passage raises interesting correspondences with Jean-Joseph Goux' suggestions (*Freud, Marx,* especially 173–201) that the phallus and the coin are both abstract symbols that share in a tendency to reduce or even render absent their material status, denying the real in favor of a fetishized ideal. The prostitutes in this case suggest that, contrary to Goux' suggestion (116–17, 130), this abstraction is not a mystification that hides the material reality of the signs but rather one that seeks to hide the very emptiness that underlies these abstracting gestures. In this case, Saussure (Goux, op. cit., 116) and Derrida, rather than Marx, were right after all.

to the Middle Ages, was the Greek hero Palamedes, who was held to have invented not only dice playing but also letters and numbers.[49] Writing, counting, and gambling are therefore attributed to the same source, and the figure of Palamedes becomes a convenient focal point for the linking of rhetoric (letters), economics (numbers and counting), and gambling, all having a common origin in the gambler, the disseminator of disorder.

Even more appropriately, dice were representative of the goddess Fortuna in the Middle Ages, and Fortuna herself was often represented as a shape-shifter, as a frequent changer of face and dress, and as a showy, gaudy dresser, drawing attention to her garments.[50] Fortuna bears more than a passing resemblance to both the ill-clad jongleur and—even more so—the prostitute as described earlier. The poetic "credo" of Pourette and Manchevaire turns out to be a masterful imbrication of prostitution, poetry, dice playing, and usury, all operating under the aegis of desire ("qui vieult bien boire et manger"): it not only expresses but exemplifies this poetics. All the activities merely represent different aspects of a more general illicit, private manipulation of the sign for the sake of "semiotic profit," earned by means of an idolatrous commodification of the sign.

Faced with this anti-Platonic semiology, Courtois persists in believing that some immanent presence in language can guarantee its validity and univocity, in the manner that God's immanence supposedly guaranteed the just result in the case of the judicial oath and judicial combat in the earlier Middle Ages. In this case, Courtois associates the validity of his words with the fullness of his purse, so that signs are backed up by semen—he does not speak "a bourse vide" (with an empty purse). Thus the "immanence" of the masculine presence guarantees language's validity, in a parody of the immanence of God. Courtois genders Platonic, logocentric discourse as masculine.[51]

Of course the purse really is empty, and as a result, Courtois' reading must inevitably fail. In a larger sense, Courtois' empty purse continues the parody of divine presence or immanence, since it signals the entire loss of that immanence in the tavern of Arras. There is no free verbal credit any-

---

49. Tauber, *Das Würfelspiel im Mittelalter*, 9.

50. Patch, *The Goddess Fortuna*, chap. 2. See also Siciliano, *François Villon*, 281ff.

51. It is interesting to compare the role of the prostitutes in this case with that of Iseut in the famous judicial scene of *Tristan et Iseut*. In both cases, women are profoundly implicated with the absence of immanence or controlling presence in language. From a religious point of view, Courtois is a good representative of the proverb "Qui croit mechine et dez quarrez, ja ne morra sanz povreté" (Morawski, *Proverbes français*, no. 1878), which seems written especially for him.

more, just as there is no longer any free lending or economic credit, despite the Bible's injunction to lend freely, "nihil inde sperantes" (Luke 6:35), and to have faith in language. This same lack of credit—belief—is criticized in Jean le Marchant's miracle, where the tavern-frequenting jongleur needs to have the efficacy of the saint proved to him before he will believe.

Ironically, his own desire for monetary signs leads Courtois to read and "credit" so eagerly the prostitutes' initial text offering him a profit through usury. Courtois' own semiology is therefore inconsistent. While his method of reading exemplifies a Platonic and essentialist view of language, his own economic ideas are part and parcel of a very anti-Platonic semiology; we have seen that he hopes to make his living at dice, as a usurer. Courtois' idolatrous desire for the monetary sign creates an idolatrous desire for the textual sign.

The act of reading is thus itself an idolatrous act in the text, both motivated by a desire for the sign and conducted (despite Courtois' wishes) at the level of the sign, with its multiple possibilities of meaning. By reading, Courtois entraps himself in a quite literally disseminatory process where crediting means simultaneously believing and lending; the word *credit* resists any reduction to univocity, for to believe the prostitutes' offer is to lend to them, and to lend is to believe. The single imposition of either of the two meanings to the sign precipitates misreading and debt, as it does in so many places in the text for Courtois. Yet reading, at least according to his understanding, always involves such an imposition of meaning. Thus there is no way for him to read successfully a text of this anti-Platonic semiology.

It is entirely appropriate that the desired text should be authored by the characters in the play who are the most desired from the masculine point of view—the prostitutes. In fact, these two prostitutes in many ways exemplify typical medieval misogynistic ideas regarding all women. Howard Bloch, among others, has discussed in detail how all medieval women were seen as potentially dangerous objects of desire.[52] Furthermore they were always veiled, by clothes and by cosmetic adornment. While proper and adequate reference in the Middle Ages was typically gendered as masculine, the female body, as text and as producer of text, typically escaped adequate male reading because it supposedly lacked proper and adequate reference.[53] The nature of this feminine poetics as veiling and as theft is nicely captured by the prostitute's promise that they will deliver to Cour-

---

52. Bloch, *Medieval Misogyny,* chap. 1.
53. Bloch, *Medieval Misogyny,* chap. 2.

tois, in exchange for his loan, "reubes et ronchis" (v. 175). "Reubes" plays on both the meaning "robe"—a robe being a cloaking and veiling device in so many cases—and on the verb *dérober,* meaning "to steal." The robe is also typically used as a sign for the sign itself in medieval poetics,[54] so that the promise is really a promise of veiling, shifting, deceiving, and thieving signs. "Ronchis" carries the sense of both "horse" and "thorns," producing further "usurious" poetic surplus in value and profit. And where there is profit, there must be loss: Courtois in fact loses his cloak to the tavern keeper, to pay the prostitutes' bills, and departs destitute and without his own proper sign—his cloak—from the tavern.

Thus in an explicit conjunction perhaps unique in the Middle Ages, the tavern frames an illicit series of semiotic practices, including usury, theft, and poetry, in the body of the woman and the practices of feminine adornment and prostitution. The medieval prostitute, and the medieval woman in general, is both writer and text, while the reader—the desirer of the body and/or the text—is gendered as masculine. But the text finally genders as masculine not only the reader but also a particular, fittingly "phallogocentric" mode of reading. The male's desire precipitates the reading of the anti-Platonic text, and the male, Platonic reader is both victimized and more specifically emasculated, for through desiring and reading he loses all that is "masculine" in the Middle Ages—proper reference, *sens,* metaphysical presence, and his own proper clothing, his cloak. In this case, Courtois suffers a fate similar to the courtly poet who also desires the woman. Howard Bloch speaks of the "self-inflicted annihilation of the self implicit to courtly love," wherein the poet is "disembodied . . . seized . . . or dispossessed," because of his desire for the woman.[55] Courtois' fall, featuring the same consequences, reveals this text to be yet another example of the more general medieval fear of the desire for the woman. It represents the economic and linguistic encounter with the prostitutes as an element of a more archetypal medieval fear of the decentering and emasculation of the male reader resulting from his desire for the female body and the text identified with it. In this sense, *Courtois d'Arras* is one of the multiple enactments at all levels of medieval literature and society of the male's misogynistic fear of the female body that he so ardently desires.

The most important difference between the tavern of this play and the taverns of the goliards is that here the tavern is entered by someone who

---

54. See Bloch, *Scandal of the Fabliaux,* chap. 1. See also Alain de Lille's extensive discussion of Nature's cloak in *DPN* 85ff. and of that of Concord in *Anticlaudianus* 73ff.

55. Bloch, *Medieval Misogyny,* 150.

brings with him the linguistic and moral (though not economic) rules of the Augustinian Christian world. It is in the contrast between these two sets of rules, enacted via the victimization of Courtois, that the author gains an entrée to this other world of the tavern, thus allowing him to critique it. The critique is framed from outside the tavern so that the poet can leave again with Courtois to return to the "proper" world of the framing, moralizing parable.

The motif of the stranger entering the tavern (and typically being victimized) is quite common. We saw this same phenomenon in *Le Jeu de Saint Nicolas,* and it will be repeated in the person of the monk in *Le Jeu de la Feuillée.* In all cases, the stranger represents a world with different semiotic rules, and the tavern is the locus for a confrontation of these rules, with the stranger's victimization usually due to his unfamiliarity with the rules of this alien locale. On another level, the visitors typically come from another genre as well—epic, romance, or hagiography—and the confrontation serves to illustrate the conflicting poetics of the respective genres;[56] word definitions, language function, and behavior are all genre-specific. Apparent here is the nature of the tavern as a metagenre, where the status of other genres is considered, and where these genres are typically undermined. The audience expectations and rules of interpretation that the other genres provide to their own exemplars—the strangers—fail these exemplars.

The full moral implications of this tavern scene extend well beyond the sins of usury and prostitution, however. The scene implicitly elaborates a complete moral economy of sin and debt that can be read as both hell and a parodic Eden. Money, for example, in addition to being paralleled to words and masculine immanence in language, also becomes a symbol of life itself in the play. "A la borse me reconois" (I am known by my purse) (v. 88), says Courtois, equating his person with his cash. "Sa borse emporte bien enflée / qu'il a si grant et si huvée: / ja ne cuide veoir ke faille" (His purse he carries all swollen, so big and full that he believes never to see it lacking) (vv. 93–95), notes the author in one of the narrative interpolations. Here the connection between money and life could not be more explicit—the figure of the "borse" expressing Courtois' belief in the endless creativity of money as well as the endlessness of life itself. Courtois' remarks might be read as a particularly male dream of a particularly male vision of both economic and sexually re-creative plenitude—another

56. See *Gautier d'Aupais,* where a knight returning from a tournament enters a tavern precipitating a series of economic and generic confrontations and crises.

vision of infinite desire. Neither death nor impotence will ever arrive. Nor apparently will the day of reckoning, for the actions that Courtois plans to engage in, and that the tavern keeper encourages, are clearly actions that have a moral as well as a sexual and economic cost. Courtois believes that he will face neither monetary nor sexual nor moral "debts": the crier at the tavern door has already promised that one can virtually drink for free, that all is on credit. This idea of credit is important because it holds within it the larger sense of a postponement of not only the time of monetary repayment but all forms of repayment of "debts," including the sins that Courtois will have to "pay for" on the day of reckoning. The image of the limitless *bourse* neatly circumscribes the economic and moral corruption of this consumption without paying in either money or accumulation of sin. The endless potency of the purse promises endless re-creation and endless life itself. The tavern then becomes a representation of earthly existence with all its carnal pleasures, the locus of desire and its consummation, and a place of endless "fertility."

> Çaiens sont trestout li delit . . .
>
> (v. 133)

> Çaiens boivent tote la gent,
> Çaiens boivent et fol et sage.
>
> (vv. 106–7)

[Herein are all the delights . . .]

[Herein everybody drinks,
The foolish drink with the wise.]

If money is life, then spending money is the equivalent of the passage of time, or the spending of one's life, and wine becomes another symbol of the vices on which one spends that life. We have already seen that usury was considered to be theft of time from God, and here the tavern has been presented as the place where one engages in actual usury. Yet the tavern crier has proposed that time can also be directly stolen from God, since the inevitable progression of life toward the day of judgment can be postponed in the tavern—one can live without passing time, without spending any money, without acquiring any moral debts. The tavern is a place characterized by a sort of "moral usury"—since one both consumes without paying and sins without apparently accruing any spiritual cost. Behavior, like money, becomes a floating signifier that can be endlessly revalued, with no inherent connection to any system of signified values, whether they be economic commodities and utility or Christian moral codes.

In the meantime, not only Courtois but everyone else as well is in the tavern engaging in carnal existence—wine, food, drink, games, and sex.

> E se n'i laisse nus son gaje!
> Ne l'estuet fors conter la dete...
> . . . .
> qui çaiens mangüent et boivent
> et s'acroeint quanqu'eles doivent,
> n'en paient vaillant un festu.

(vv. 108–13)

> [And no one leaves a deposit!
> All you have to do is add it to your account . . .
> . . . .
> whoever eats and drinks in here
> and puts on credit whatever they owe
> won't pay a single penny.]

The tavern is a world of credit, like the new economic world of the times. Yet the tavern seems to be at the same time a prelapsarian world, ignoring the eschatological reality of the times. For if credit may seem timeless, paradise truly is timeless. The tavern is not only a "hellish" world, explicitly opposed to the church, but also a kind of parody of heaven—heaven on earth, or the Garden of Eden perhaps. Time, life, and money pass by, and the "borse" is emptied, but no one notices. It seems as if men (and specifically men, not women) are immortal, without original sin that will one day consign them to death and retribution. This at least is the deceptive, seductive offer of the "garçon" (vv. 103–13).[57]

Courtois' dream of endless fertility includes specifically the concept of "plantet" (v. 116) and "si grant plenté" (v. 120)—again evoking the phantasmic plenitude of the prelapsarian Garden of Eden suggested by the tav-

---

57. The entrance to the tavern is clearly marked by a seductive rhetoric of excessive promises that cannot be delivered. This is in fact the function of the *hucier* in all tavern scenes—to incite desire and to offer the tavern as the locus of its consummation. Most important, rhetoric incites desire.

ern: "Que quanc'on veut i trueve l'on" (Whatever one wants, one finds here) (v. 143). "Plenté" is in fact a key concept for the medieval tavern scene. In *Le Jeu de Saint Nicolas,* the crier Raoules advertises the tavern's product as "Le vin aforé de nouvel, / A plain lot et a plain tonnel, / Sade, bevant, et plain et gros" (Wine newly opened in its cask, glassesful and barrelsful, smooth, tasty, full and strong . . .) (vv. 642–44); quantity seems limitless. One of the tavern fabliau is entitled "La plantez." There is no scarcity in the tavern and therefore no need for an economy that might regulate the distribution of scarce resources. (It is interesting to compare this phantasm of plenitude to its aristocratic equivalent as seen in Marc Shell's "The Horn of Plenty" in *Money, Language, and Thought.* The aristocratic vision is born of economic decline and fundamentally escapist, positing God as the source of unlimited wealth [through the mechanism of the Grail]. The bourgeois vision, in contrast, posits the illicit semiology itself as the source of unlimited production and, rather than seeking escapes, seeks to apply that semiology fully and without hindrance to actual economic practice.) This economy of the tavern recalls the illicit corporeal economy that we saw at the beginning of this chapter: there is no limit to desire once the natural need is satisfied, and thus desire spins wildly toward plenitude and totality. It is noted of the jongleur in "Les deux bordeors ribauds":

Tout son gaainz i despendoit,
Toz jors voloit il estre en boule,
En la taverne ou en houle.
Un vert chaplelet en sa teste,
Toz jors vousist que il fust feste.[58]
(Emphasis added)

[All his earnings he spent there,
Every day he wanted to be debauching
In the tavern or in the brothel,
A green cap on his head.
Every day he wished that it was a feast.]

In postponing debts of time, life, penance, retribution, and money indefinitely, the very regularity of the flow of time is broken. The totality

---

58. Faral, *Mimes français,* vv. 28–32.

of "tout" both in the preceding passage and in vv. 106 and 133 of *Courtois d'Arras* dissolves the variegated moments that make up the differences of countable time, replacing them with a single, perfect, everlasting, plenitudinal moment. Time is literally stolen from God, through the mechanism of generalized credit.[59] But as the play reveals, the tavern is all too Eden-like, for in the medieval misogynistic tradition, it has its own Eves, the prostitutes, and it is their semiology—their bodies and the carnal bodies they make of signs—that leads to man's downfall. Once again, the woman is the agent of the Fall from this (illusory) paradise.

In the most general sense, sin can be considered as a debt equivalent to money in this play. But more importantly, both forms of debt (money and sin) function as signs within their respective moral and economic semiotic systems. In particular, the debt of sin is a sign that refers to the individual who is responsible for such sin. An example of such a system can be found in a sermon of the popular preacher of the time, Maurice de Sully, involving a sinful debtor who refuses to forgive those indebted to him monetarily, even though God has the grace to forgive those indebted to God in a spiritual sense. The sermon ends with the remark, "la dete senefie pecie . . . quar lors s'endete cascuns envers Dieu; quant il mesfait e il peche" (Debt signifies sin . . . for each of us goes into debt with God at some time, when he does wrongly and sins).[60] In a short text entitled "Le Vergier de Paradis," the acts of *aumonier* and *desdetter* are likewise paralleled; the alms are really an explicitly calculated payment for sin.[61]

Such an identity between debt and sin is not at all surprising: it has been argued that the high medieval invention of purgatory was in fact a response to the evolving possibility of quantifying sin and penance in exact terms equivalent to monetary debt. Jacques Le Goff has in fact linked the rise of the concept of purgatory specifically to the rise of bourgeois capitalism in the High Middle Ages.[62] This economic activity and the necessary "sins" that it involved forced the church to come to terms with issues such as usury so that the conundrum seen in chapter 2, where virtually

---

59. This breaking of time mirrors that which occurs when the instantaneous exchange of the barter economy is replaced by the credit sale of the new economics. This is exactly why the credit sale was considered usury, since it was a "theft of time."

60. Robson, *Maurice de Sully,* 165.

61. Jubinal, *Nouveau recueil,* 2:291–96.

62. See Vance, *Mervelous Signals,* chap. 5; and see especially Le Goff, *Your Money or Your Life* and *La Naissance du Purgatoire.*

every merchant was a usurer and sinner, would not result in universal damnation.[63] A key development of this period was, in the words of one scholar, that "values of time, space and service could be precisely measured and exchanged."[64] Once this was the case, it became possible to institute a "moral economy" that allowed not just for the simple opposition of heaven and hell, saved and damned, but for a middle ground, where the tainted but uncondemned sinner could pass some specific time in penance, "paying for" his sins. Thus purgatory was a kind of heaven on the layaway plan—on credit, ironically enough, as the economic mechanisms that got men into purgatory in the first place (i.e., moral "debt") became the ones that then allowed them to escape it. Of course, this moral economy became an economy in the most literal sense with the gradual rise in the sale of indulgences and so forth.

In fact, this moral economy was elaborated in quite explicitly economic terms at times. Peter Cantor, the great opponent of usury, quotes Augustine: "Usura enim est cum plus exigitur in poena, quam commissum sit in culpa" (Usury is moreover when more is demanded in penance than was committed in sin). He thus frames moral reckoning in economic terms, and he speaks often of the "talentum peccati" (talents—or wages—of sin) in glossing the parable of the talents.[65] Of course, as Peter makes clear here, in the moral as well as the monetary economy, an exact equivalence was required in all exchanges—there should be no profit or loss in a proper economy. Despite the problems with the sale of indulgences, the moral economy elucidated by Peter Cantor and others was still predicated on normal rules of buying, selling, and exchange. Thus the concept of the zero-sum game used in chapter 2 is applicable here as well. (These ideas could be related more specifically to the Pelagian idea that one's reward from God was strictly correlated to one's "work" on earth—a source of great debate in the Middle Ages.) According to this point of view, Courtois and his companions in the tavern have to pay up for their moral and economic consumption at some point.

Yet in *Courtois d'Arras* the tavern seemingly becomes a great irregularity in the ordered calculus of sin, wealth, and language. The illicit semiotics of the tavern and brothel, incarnated in the feminine body of the prosti-

---

63. For an examination of the ways in which canonists gradually found ways to make usury licet as the century progressed, see Baldwin, *Masters, Princes, and Merchants;* Noonan, *Usury.*

64. Vance, *Mervelous Signals,* 116.

65. Peter Cantor *Verbum abbreviatum,* in *PL* 30.156–57.

tute, results in this worst-case scenario in a complete commodification of the sign. In the case of the sign of moral debt, its referential quality is entirely severed. Put another way, a given action does not "refer" in any way to a given sin: the semiotics of Christian morality, which assigns moral judgments to actions via the rules of Christian ethics, is shattered. In their illicit gratuity, actions mirror language and money in their illicit commodification. There is an entire refusal of the utilitarian in favor of an idolatry of the commodified sign, body, action, and pleasure. Indeed, the sign is a body, and the body is a sign: we saw that Courtois himself is reduced to the status of a nominal signifier by the prostitutes' plays on his name and *courtoisie*. This commodification and resultant idolatry of the sign— the "lechery" of so many *lecheors*—is the fundamental reason that the semiology of the tavern must be presented by all "licit" texts as morally damnable. The tavern of *Courtois d'Arras* is in this sense reflective of the general moral status of the tavern in thirteenth-century religious literature. Like Jean le Marchant's miracle, it frames the hellish tavern in a context of religious condemnation.

The status of the tavern's moral economy as both hellish and a parody of prelapsarian Eden, a utopia ("Cocagne" in medieval terminology), is particularly fascinating. We have already seen earlier in this chapter that the high priest of the tavern among the goliards is the "abbot of Cocagne" (*CB* 694), and there is in fact a short text entitled "Li fabliaus de Coquainge" that I believe can help elucidate this delicate balance. The tale is told by an old and foolish narrator, who claims to have been unwise enough to leave Utopia and is now unable to find his way back. In "Li fabliaus de Coquaigne,"[66] the utopian world of "Coquaigne" is depicted as a world without scarcity, without uneven distribution of commodities, without the need for exchange, and thus without markets: "Nus n'i achate ne ne vent" (No one either buys or sells) (v. 106). Since there is no need of exchange, there is likewise no need for a mediator of value in these exchanges. Thus money is also absent or useless: it lays about on the streets unheeded (vv. 101–5).

Ne ja n'i paieront escot,
N'apres mengier n'i conteront
Ausi come en cest païs font.

(vv. 54–56)

---

66. Barbazon, *Fabliaux et contes,* 4:185–91.

[They will never pay a bill,
Nor will they figure the charges after eating
As we do in this land.]

("Cest païs" is here the everyday world, not Cocagne, as the tale is
being told on return from Cocagne.) One thinks immediately of the
tavern in *Courtois d'Arras* on reading this passage. Unlike the closed,
zero-sum economy that was the ideal of the medieval moralist position,
where all consumption leads to debt that must be paid, and where all
ethical misconduct leads to a debt of sin likewise to be repaid at some
time (and all use of language should likewise implicate the speaker in
an act of reference, so that language is never used gratuitously as a
commodity), the world of Cocagne is characterized by an open, prelapsarian economy.

Si puet l'en boivre et mangier
Tuit cel qui vuelent sanz dangier;
Sanz contredit et sanz deffense
Prent chascuns quanque son cuer pense.

(vv. 45–48)

[You can drink and eat
All that you want without worry;
Without denial and without refusal
Each takes however much his heart desires.]

This motif of the immediate gratification of one's thoughts and desires, of
the absolute identity between internal being and external commodity, is
emphasized over and over in the text.

Ainz en prent tout a son voloir.

(v. 100)

Et si en fet a son plesir
Tant come il vuet et par lesir.

(vv. 111–12)

[They all take as much as they wish]

[And each man does his pleasure
As much as he wishes and all at his leisure.]

The identity between the individual's desire and the commodity available in the external world mirrors the Augustinian depiction of communication before the Fall: thoughts might be perfectly shared by all in a single community, so that there was no need for physical language as a medium of exchange. The Bible implicitly shares this conception of the superfluity of the sign provided that other means of communication are available.[67] In Cocagne also, there is no need for mediation between individual desire and its outer reified form. In fact, no one speaks in Cocagne as far as the author reports.

According to Augustine, true desire only enters the world of language after the Fall, when the imperfections in the physical nature of human language lead to a gap between thought and its expression or understanding; this gap leads to desire. Likewise the gap between physical want and available external commodity creates economic desire. Before the Fall, there was no shortage, no scarcity, and thus no enduring desire. Shortage and scarcity enter only afterward. Of course, economics as it is understood today is simply "a method of allocating scarce resources."[68] It is thus dependent on scarcity and desire. In a world of plenitude, where all material desires of all people were met, there would be no need for exchange and redistribution of these goods. The very concept of utilitarian exchange, and thus the concept of economics, rests on and is identifiable with desire resulting from scarcity after the Fall. Thus exchange and economics in general are postlapsarian phenomena in medieval thought. And since the Middle Ages blamed Eve for the Fall, exchange, economics, language, and clothing—indeed all socially "mediatory" phenomena—could potentially be linked to the category of the feminine. This was commonly done in the case of language, clothing, and cosmetics. Medieval misogynist texts abound with "garrulous" and "adorned" women leading men to damnation. As stated earlier, the uniqueness of *Courtois d'Arras* is in its extension of this blame across the full spectrum of exchange—monetary, linguistic, and moral—and thus in its realization of an implicit tendency of medieval misogyny.

---

67. For more on this concept of "surrogationalism" in the Bible, see Harris and Taylor, *Landmarks in Western Linguistic Thought*, 38–39.

68. By "economics" I mean here the process of exchange and distribution of goods and services.

The gratuity of commodities in this open economy of Cocagne is mirrored by the gratuity of ethical behavior that existed before the original sin. The absence of rules and restraints on behavior is mentioned several times (see v. 47 quoted earlier).

> Et boivre par mi et par tout
> Sanz contredit et sanz redout,
> Ne ja n'i paiera denier.
>
> (vv. 73–75)

> [Drink a little or a lot
> Without refusal and without worry,
> And you will never pay a penny.]

Here again we see the assimilation of ethical to monetary debt. In the previous example (vv. 111–12), the poet also notes that pleasures can be engaged at one's "lesir," thus evoking the rupture of the movement of time in this eternal locale.

> Six semaines a en un mois
> Et quatre Pasques a en l'an.
>
> (vv. 78–79)

> [There are six weeks in a month
> And four Easter seasons in a year.]

Like usurers, the citizens of Cocagne operate outside the ordained framework of time.

The similarities of this world to that of the tavern scenes of both the goliards and *Courtois d'Arras* are of course evident. In fact, given the designation of this work as a "fabliaus," a term that normally carries the connotation of narrative invention and fantasy, it seems legitimate to suggest not only that the tavern scenes are themselves a parody of (the desire for) Cocagne but that the fabliau itself might also be a parody of this world. There is clearly no "labor theory of value" in Cocagne—in fact, the inhabitants sound suspiciously like the classic bourgeois usurer.

> Qui plus i dort, plus i gaigne:
> Cil qui dort jusqu'a miedi,

Gaaigne cinc sols et demi.

(vv. 26–28)

[Whoever sleeps the most gains the most:
He who sleeps until noon
Gains five sous and a half.]

Both the self-productivity of monetary signs and the general mobility of signs are emphasized.

Diverses robes i a tant
Dont chascuns prent a sa devise.

(vv. 134–35)

[There are many diverse robes
Among which each one chooses according to his desires.]

Rather than constituting appropriate dress, signs can be shifted and reassigned at one's desire. Thus Cocagne is above all else perhaps a paradise for the scandalous poet, as well as for the usurious merchant.

The poem is at the same time itself a seemingly illicit creation of just such a poet. The speaker notes that he should be honored by his listeners "com vostre pere" (v. 3), but he then goes on to claim that "en grant barbe n'a pas savoir" (v. 10). He thus undermines his own authority, and he then continues:

Se li barbé le sens séussent,
Bous et chievres molt en éussent.
A la barbe ne baez mie,
Tels la grant qui n'a sens demie.

(vv. 11–14)

[If bearded ones had good sense,
They would have many oxen and goats.
Don't judge anyone by their beard;
Many have a large one who have no sense at all.]

He himself is in fact poor and lacks any form of natural wealth, specifically cattle, the very synonym of such wealth. As in the case of "La devise au lecheor," the source of the poem is implicitly posited in the poverty and necessity of the poet: lacking in money, he weaves his tale of Cocagne, the land of infinite wealth, not only to seduce his listener but to convert the tale of Cocagne's wealth into his own actual wealth in the form of the pay he receives as a jongleur for telling the tale.

The teller also reveals that he ran across Cocagne on the way to Rome, where he was going to seek penance, thus marking himself as a sinner (vv. 16–17). Jean-Charles Payen has also noted that tales such as this were often told at the feasts of fools that were so common in the Middle Ages and that such tales were in fact often the province of the king of the fools.[69] The narrator then ends by telling us that he foolishly left the land and was unable to ever find his way back. Thus the lack of authority of the old but not necessarily wise poet in the beginning is mirrored by the unlocalizable, irretrievable referent of the text in the conclusion. The entire work is thus ironically no more than a description of the open-ended rhetoric and semiotics (of Cocagne) that made possible the production of the work itself. The poem, in describing Cocagne—a utopia thereby marked for nonexistence—does no more than describe the conditions of its own genesis out of thin air, ex nihilo. Even more paradoxically, given the nonexistence of Cocagne, one could say that the text actually not only describes but generates the conditions of its own generation. It is a self-(re)producing circularity whose value is based on nothing at all but its own recognition of its lack of value. It is something from nothing—the ultimate utopian dream.

Why have I spent so much time on this text that does not ever mention or even evoke the tavern explicitly? I believe it is one of the few medieval texts that represents an ethically gratuitous utopia in uncommonly clear economic terms and thus represents a model that is referred to in less complete fashion by many of the tavern texts. Other examples of the same line of economic reasoning can be found in medieval literature. The depiction of the "Golden Age" in *The Romance of the Rose* features many of the same themes: there is no exchange ("l'uns ne demandoit riens a l'autre," v. 9527), there is no private property, and there are no coins. The "Fall" from the Golden Age occurs with the entry of "Baraz," representing both commercial exchange and its concomitant trickery and deceit, and this is concomitant with Poverty, scarcity, and the stamping of coins.[70] Yet this cel-

---

69. Payen, "Fabliaux et Cocagne."

70. Baraz appears at v. 9528, Poverty at v. 9535; and the coin is stamped at vv. 9640–41. For another very clear example of this line of thought, see Bernard of Cluny, *De contemptu mundi*. The "Golden Age" is depicted on pages 77ff., and here again artificial forms of wealth

ebrated text does not extend its analysis to the level of detail of "Li fabliaus de Coquainge," which, while purporting to represent heaven, actually thematizes the supposed dangers of the open economy (with its open, fertile rhetorical and ethical economies as corollaries) when such an economy is posited in a fallen world whose economy is by necessity "closed." Once again, the concept of the zero-sum game can be used. Truth, wealth, and the ethical debt of sin came in a fixed, finite amount that could only be represented or exchanged in the High Middle Ages. There could be no new creation, or abrogation, of any of these. The concept of the zero-sum game, or the "conservation of value," as applied to multiple spheres of medieval theory by many thinkers of the time is a crucial concept for understanding medieval attitudes toward commerce, art, and the poet, as both an artistic and an economic actor in medieval society.

While *The Romance of the Rose* writes a history of economic and ethical decline in sequential ages, "Li fabliaus de Coquainge" and *Courtois d'Arras* offer a more detailed synchronic confrontation of open and closed economies. And in a similar vein, "Li fabliaus de Coquainge" is ultimately a satire of the bourgeois merchant's idea of an economic "paradise" of usury and "unnatural" monetary wealth, which, like the fool's tale of this fabliau of Cocagne, told by a narrator unable to rediscover the actual location or reality of the land he describes, is really just a collection of empty signs.[71] In this sense, it functions in the same way as *Courtois d'Arras* to point out the traps of a break between poetics and economics—the idolatry of the economic sign cannot be allied to a vertical, referential reading of the linguistic sign. The tavern scenes of the play, to the extent that they present an open economy resembling that of Cocagne, must be read with an understanding of an open rhetorical system, by both the modern reader and the inscribed visitor/reader. Or even better, *Courtois d'Arras* suggests, one should not read the new poetry at all. If women are seducers, then this play is a call for chastity from secular literature.[72]

---

are either absent or, in the case of gold, considered to be a vice, while buying is considered shameful and goods are held in common, so that property and exchange are virtually absent. The modern race, however, lusts after artificial wealth (81).

71. Payen, "Fabliaux et Cocagne." Payen has noted the elements of "bourgeois mentality" in the text. For an example of Arthur's court as an aristocratic "cocagne," see Kellogg, *Medieval Artistry and Exchange,* 77.

72. One thus sees more clearly the need for the written legal restrictions and statutes applied to economic dealings within the tavern, which were discussed in chapter 1. The fundamental difference between ritual/traditional law and modern civil law is in fact the assumed immanence and absence, respectively, of God as guarantor of truth. The victimization of Courtois in the tavern thus is a parallel to the parodic ordeal scene in Thomas' *Tristan*—in

But Courtois does read, and he reads the tavern as if it were a Neoplatonic text, whereas its poetics is in reality that of the *Poetria nova,* taken even a step further by the loss of divine presence in language. Courtois has assimilated the lessons of the new economics, being a kind of "prodigal merchant," but he has clearly failed to assimilate the larger lesson of the fabliau about Cocagne and of this study—that economic and literary semiotics are realizations of the same basic semiology, characterized by a desire for (semiotic) profit.[73] Language, economics, and ethics mirror each other in their "atheosis." The moral economy of this tavern scene is inseparable from the deeper semiology of a desire for the sign.

But though Courtois is prodigal, he is not entirely subsumed into the world of the tavern and may still be saved. The text is, no less than Dante's story of Paolo and Francesca (*Inferno,* canto V), a lesson on the dangers of reading, especially the dangers posed by the reading of a text whose signs fail to refer beyond the text but rather incite an illicit desire for the signs and the text itself. In Dante's story this illicit desire is figured in the physical desires of the young couple, while here we see the victimization of the "innocent" reader who fails to understand the true nature of the signs he is reading. Courtois' desire for cash is really the figuration of the desire for the sign in general, including the desire for the text. Having been victimized by the two prostitutes, Courtois realizes at least partially the error of his ways. Thus chastened, he nevertheless falls victim to another bourgeois, characteristically avaricious and failing to keep his word in a mirror of the tavern scene. This is the famous scene where the prodigal son is reduced to taking care of the bourgeois' pigs and eventually to eating the slop that he is supposed to be feeding them. That Courtois may be interpreted as a lecherous and gluttonous desirer of signs is made clearer by two medieval citations regarding this particular scene in the parable. Earlier I quoted Gautier's *Les épopées françaises:*

---

both cases, the "losers" in the scene fail to recognize divine absence and the concomitant loss of guaranteed truth.

73. Jean Dufournet has argued that Courtois is a "paysan parvenu" who believes he is entering a courtly world as he enters the tavern. Again, this seems acceptable from a linguistic standpoint—Courtois certainly falls for the prostitutes' compliments on his "courtoisie"—but his economic tendencies are anything but courtly. Courtois' confusion about what the tavern actually represents and about what he actually wants are particularly disastrous for him. One could argue that as a poor reader, he is unable to correctly sort out the generic status of the tavern. See Dufournet, "*Courtois d'Arras* ou le triple héritage." See also Goux, *Marx, Freud,* 173–80, where the author discusses the possibility of temporary contradictions or "decalages" between economic modes of symbolization and other modes of symbolization in a society. Courtois is the incarnation of such a disjunction.

Verba lasciviae sunt in joculatoribus, qui similes sunt porcis . . . aut libentius ponunt linguam ad stercora mundi quam ad lapides pretiosos coeli.[74]

[In jongleurs there are lascivious words, and they are like pigs . . . more willingly putting their tongues to the filth of the world than the precious gems of heaven.]

We read elsewhere, in the "Miserere":[75]

Mais au fol cui je voi joglant,
Et qui va de bourdes jenglant,
A chelui est li pains destrois.
Ordement vi en fabloiant:
Pors est, manjut faine et glant.
De pain gouster n'est pas ses drois.

[But to the fool who I see *joglant*
And who goes about telling his tattle,
To him is bread denied.
Filthily he lives in telling tales:
He is a pig, and eats hay and acorns.
He has no right to taste bread.]

These two citations, especially the second, seem to be references to the parable of the prodigal son, and they both link the gluttonous desire for the sign to the medieval symbol of gluttony par excellence, the pig. They also point to the appropriateness of Courtois' position in *Courtois d'Arras* and to a broader medieval interpretative tradition of the gluttonous lechery of the jongleur, traces of which we have already seen several times.

Only when his desires finally return to their natural place, to the utilitarian need for food, is Courtois ready to return home (vv. 500–510). He has come full circle from the moment when he refused "del pain et des pois" (bread and peas) which his father offered him on his departure (v. 50).[76] His final rehabilitation from the world of the tavern is marked by a

---

74. Faral, *Les jongleurs*, app. III, no. 255.

75. Faral, *Les jongleurs*, app. III, no. 146.

76. Since peas were a medieval symbol of folly (figuring prominently in the speeches of the *dervés* in *Le Jeu de la Feuillée,* for example), the father's offer was perhaps already an ironic comment on his son's future fate, since Courtois himself ends up "fole," and his father tells him in v. 51 to "lai ester ta fole entente!"

great feast arranged for him by his father and by his regaining of proper clothing. Upon his return, his father tells him:

> Afuble toi, que trop ies nus
> ja mais ne te reconeüsse.

(vv. 614–15)

> [Clothe yourself, for you are almost naked.
> I would never have recognized you.]

As we have seen, his remaining clothing, after the visit to the tavern, constitutes an improper sign that fails to refer properly to the bearer; he has lost his own cloak, as well as his own recognizability, his own name, and his own "presence." The reinstitution of the correct sign marks his recentering in the masculine, agrarian world of his father.[77]

This interpretation allows for a consistency in the ending of the play. Jean Dufournet has noted that the ending seems ambiguous since Courtois returns home not out of moral contrition, as does the prodigal son in the Bible, but rather simply out of hunger, suggesting that his conversion to good is incomplete.[78] While this may be true on a moral level, on an economic level his conversion seems legitimate. I might add that in addition to the reinvestiture with the cloak, the sacrificial "gift" of the feast mirrors the gift economy that I discussed in chapter 1, in contrast to the profit-oriented economy of the tavern. Semiotic propriety is mirrored in the profitless transfer of commodity. Contrary to the goliard texts, there is an "outside" to the tavern—a place where the rules do still hold—and through the grace of God, the reader is rescued. Thus the world inside the tavern, which seems to parallel the Edenic world of plenitude, can safely be seen as illusory by the edified medieval audience.

Or maybe the world inside the tavern is not so illusory. As with *Le Jeu de Saint Nicolas,* the prostitutes end up unpunished and with a profit as well. *Courtois d'Arras* could be read in a fashion similar to *Le Jeu de Saint Nicolas,* though I have not done so simply because it would closely repeat the previous reading and also because the semiotic confrontation between

---

77. This same theme of the restoration of proper clothing corresponding to a general reinvestiture of propriety can be found in many forms. Howard Bloch has noted (*Scandal of the Fabliaux,* 29) that the "Joie de la court" at the end of *Erec et Enide* likewise uses the "robing" of Erec as a representation of the restoration of "propriety," and in particular it would be the ultimate symbol of his fully rewinning his reputation in the world and thus fully revalorizing his own "sign"—his proper name.

78. Dufournet, "Variations sur un motif."

Courtois and the figures in the tavern, as well as his own semiotic disjunction between reading and economy, seems more distinctive to this play. But divorced from its frame, *Courtois d'Arras* closely resembles nothing so much as a fabliau, with the prostitutes as "heroic" author figures.

Desire Fulfilled: The Fabliaux

Though the inn, tavern, or brothel could not be considered the single dominant locale of the fabliaux, it is still interesting to consider the number of works that contain one of these places.[79] One could also enlarge the list by noting the number of tales that generally concern the topoi associated with the tavern, such as problems of lodging. And finally, one of the most common personages of the fabliaux is the bourgeois merchant.

Historically, a number of attempts have been made to link the genre of the fabliaux to a specific social class, and in the majority of cases, that class has been the urban merchant class—the bourgeoisie. Joseph Bédier laid the groundwork of this type of approach, linking the fabliaux to a bourgeois audience on the basis of style, vocabulary, and subject matter, among other reasons.[80] In addition, he locates the texts geographically in the north of France, in the exact regions that were witnessing the greatest economic expansion and revolution at the time.[81] More recently, critics have tried to establish an "ethos" of the fabliau, and they have seen in this ethos a reflection of the new urban economic life of the thirteenth century—a valuing of cleverness, ingenuity, and flexibility within a dynamic world, for example.[82]

79. A complete list would include, at least, "Boivin de Provins," "Les trois aveugles de Compiegne," "La plantez," "Estormi," "Le prestre qu'on porte" (and its three variant versions), "Le villain de Farbu," "Les trois dames de Paris," and "Constant du Hamel,"; indirectly, "Le prestre et les deux ribauds," "St. Pierre et le jongleur," and "Le prestre teint"; and finally, as we have seen in chapter 1, "Le prestre et le chevalier."

80. See Joseph Bédier, *Les fabliaux,* especially chap. 13. Bédier goes so far as to claim that the fabliaux were born with the constitution of the bourgeois class: "le genre naquit le jour où se fut vraiment constituée une classe bourgeoise" (371). Nevertheless, it should also be noted that Bédier is actually far less didactic on this point than has generally been supposed: he follows the preceding statement with a long series of concessive analyses and ends with an admission of the "confusion des genres et promiscuité des publics" that prevailed at the time.

81. Bédier, *Les fabliaux,* 38. More precisely, he locates the origin of most of the texts in Picardie. This localization convinced Bédier to adopt the Picard dialect form "fabliaux" rather than Gaston Paris' standard French "fableaux" to name the genre.

82. Charles Muscatine sees the fabliau as representing a particular social subclass; in particular he claims that "The flourishing of the fabliaux, the rise of the cities, and the emergence of an urban middle class are equally visible symptoms of the same social and spiritual climate" (*The Old French Fabliaux,* 28–29). Muscatine sees the fabliau not as a direct product of the other elements mentioned but rather as a concurrent "symptom" of the social subculture

Such questions are, however, fraught with difficulty. Bédier himself admits that the fabliaux could have had a mixed audience (see my note 80 to this chapter). Jean Rychner has tried to link different fabliaux to different audiences via stylistic and aesthetic judgments, but this rests on a sometimes tautological assumption as to what those stylistic tastes may have been.[83] Per Nykrog's claim for the essentially aristocratic nature of the fabliaux seems overly simplistic since it must assume that so-called courtly literature always had only a courtly audience and that noncourtly audiences could not appreciate parodies of courtly genres with which they must have had at least some familiarity.[84]

More recently, Howard Bloch's *Scandal of the Fabliaux* turns away from such socioeconomic approaches to analyze the texts in terms of the problematics of the sign, reading, writing, and interpretation. But unlike earlier formalistic readings, Bloch's analysis locates this series of issues in a specifically medieval intellectual framework while at the same time suggesting that the texts defy attempts at straightforward identity with certain authors, audiences, and so forth.[85]

In fact, the two approaches can be combined. The unique feature of the fabliaux that will be examined here is that their historically specific hermeneutics is framed in terms of an equally historically specific eco-

---

to which he refers, and which cuts across traditional medieval classes to include a certain group that values ingenuity, wit, and the power of words to deceive (93–98). Jurgen Beyer, through his conception of the "Schwank" element, takes a similar approach. He sees "Schwank" as a general human "pressure-release" tendency that seeks to show "all humanity without transcendence." This reductive process supposedly precedes any specific literary genre, being theoretically possible at all times. The tendency appears at the surface, in the form of certain specific genres, at historically propitious moments, of which the increasingly liberal and innovative twelfth century would be one such moment (Beyer, "The Morality of the Amoral," 22–23).

83. Rychner, *Contribution à l'étude des fabliaux.* See also Howard Bloch's short critique of this approach (*Scandal of the Fabliaux,* 13).

84. Nykrog, *Les fabliaux.* It is clear that many of the fabliaux do not rely on any external subtext for their humor, and Benjamin Honeycutt ("The Knight and His World as an Instrument of Humor in the Fabliaux") has argued that virtually all the fabliaux rely fundamentally on mechanisms internal to the texts to achieve their comic effect. This argument, however, seems to go to the opposite extreme, and in my approach to the fabliaux as metagenre, I tend to agree with Knut Togeby ("The Nature of the Fabliaux") that much fabliaux humor is attached to the oblique repetition of a model genre and especially to the distance from the model. In the case of the "tavern fabliaux" however, the oblique model is that of medieval discourse on the sign, rather than any specific other genre.

85. Bloch, *Scandal of the Fabliaux.* For formalistic readings, see especially Thomas Cooke's *The Old French and Chaucerian Fabliaux,* where Cooke explicitly denies their historicism (21).

nomic metaphor, that of the newly originated market.[86] We can begin with "Les trois aveugles de Compiegne" and "Boivin de Provins," which locate the source of literary production in an initial gap in language and linguistic exchange. These gaps are figured in terms of monetary gaps of profit and loss in economic exchange, occasioned in these two instances by false coins. This gap then becomes literally fertile and productive within the tavern: the (false) coins elicit desires that can only be realized in the space of the tavern, and in the realization of these desires, a text is produced. The theme of the semiotic gaps suggests the mechanism for the creation of desire and text.

This production, however, is a function not only of readerly, textual desire but of an encounter with the producers of texts—the tavern-frequenting jongleur. Just as the tavern could function as an economic marketplace (see chap. 1), it functions here as a literary "market" where textual and corporeal desires can encounter the texts and bodies that they seek. Capitalist market theory insists that commodities have no essential value outside of that which is determined by the market. A meeting of productive and consumptive desires determines the value of a given commodity at each market exchange, and that value may vary from moment to moment. In addition, before it enters the market, a commodity has in a sense no value at all—only potential value to be realized in the act of exchange. And indeed, in medieval moral texts, it is typically money, and implicitly the market, that characteristically disorders medieval social values, turning rich into poor, wise into foolish, and ugly into beautiful. Money refuses essential value or identity, filling the hands of the sinner as willingly as those of the saint.[87] This section will examine how this economic model of the source and determination of value is used to represent the acts of writing, reading, and interpreting literature in many fabliaux, which themselves take place in market settings. The tavern is the place where buyer/reader meets seller/writer and where literary value is determined in the contexts of the exchanges that occur there. If the fabliaux can in any way be considered "bourgeois," it is in their participation in a liter-

---

86. Although my use of the model of the market here may recall the language of Bourdieu (see *Language and Symbolic Power,* pt. 1), the market here functions in a manner diametrically opposed to that which he elaborates. Here it increases possible meaning, as opposed to delimiting it.

87. See especially the minor genre of the "poem of the coin," including such texts as "Du denier et de la brébis" (Jubinal, *Nouveau receuil,* 2:264–72) and "De Dan Denier" and "De la maaille" (Jubinal, *Jongleurs et trouvères,* 94–100, 101–6). See also Little, *Religious Poverty,* chaps. 2 and 3; Le Goff, *Your Money or Your Life,* chaps. 1 and 2.

ary economy based on market principles, with all that this will entail. These texts question the nature of textual meaning in ways quite different from other Old French genres and traditions.

In "Boivin de Provins,"[88] Boivin, a merchant returning from a fair, takes a seat before a brothel and proceeds to count out his money. He has only twelve deniers, but as he counts and recounts the same twelve deniers (in a parody of runaway usury), he seems to the prostitutes in the brothel to have a fortune, and his action whets their desire for this "artificial" wealth, itself a product of art or "artifice." Indeed, the entire episode plays on the verb *mesconter* in both senses of the word: unnatural linguistic and economic profit are paralleled, arising from the false word and false coin. By also playing on such words as "créance" (v. 57) and "oes" (v. 88), meaning both "use" and "profit or interest," the tale further evokes the connections of money and language.

In addition, Howard Bloch notes that Boivin is shabbily dressed, his ill-fitting garments further emphasizing his role as personification of the inadequate sign and inadequate representation.[89] Matthew of Vendome insists that words must "bear the markings of the sense that creates them, not . . . that [which] they create," and he disparages the "stitcher of patches" who fails to produce the artistic conjunction that marks the author's ordering intention on the text.[90] Yet Boivin's new name that he invents for himself ("Fouchier de la Brouce") is polyvalent in its connotations, including "trickster" and "swindler." As Bloch notes, "self-creating economic and literary value coincide in Boivin's imaginary purse,"[91] or more precisely, in the gap or empty space in his purse where the imaginary coins might lie, itself replicating the gap between sign and referent in his speech.

But the value in question is not entirely self-creating. It is fundamentally a function of the listeners' desire to "buy into" the account that has been offered, to credit Boivin's words. The empty space in his purse remains just that until readers can be found who are eager for his "(mis)counting" in both senses of the word. Boivin's choice of the brothel, the emblematic site of desire, is thus quite fitting, as is the initial juxtaposition of fair and brothel as locales of exchange.

---

88. Noomen, *Nouveau recueil*, II:77–106.

89. Bloch, *Scandal of the Fabliaux*, 96.

90. Matthew of Vendôme, *The Art of Versification*, pt. I, no. 115; prologue, no. 7. Alain de Lille and Bernardus Silvestris both used images of the whole, well-fitting garment as metaphors for human poetic ordering of textual meaning as well. See especially Wetherbee, *Platonism and Poetry in the Twelfth Century*, 158–86 (on Bernardus), 187–219 (on Alain).

91. Bloch, *Scandal of the Fabliaux*, 98 (see this source on the name as well).

The poet and the prostitute can both be seen as merchants engaged in a negotiation. Both Boivin and Mabile, the madam of the brothel, are described as knowing much about "barat," which could refer to either trickery and deceit or negotiation in general, especially commercial. Boivin "mout de barat sot" (knew much about *barat*) (v. 12), and Mabile "plus savoit de barat et de guile / que fame nule qui i fust" (knew more about *barat* and guile than any other woman there) (vv. 22–23). The negotiation turns ultimately around the concept of *croire* (belief and loan). The meaning of this word is being negotiated. Boivin's verbal and economic usury, his loaning to the prostitutes, is matched by their belief in both his words and his coins and by their eager desire for both. And in a larger sense, the meaning of the tale turns around the multiple senses of the word *croire* as well.

Though the prostitutes hope to lull Boivin into inattention and then to seize his *bourse,* he is finally able to trick them and escape with his twelve deniers as well as with memories of an evening of sexual and culinary indulgence. He is able to read enough of the prostitutes' intentions to confuse them into thinking they have succeeded in their task, and he is long gone when they discover otherwise. Boivin comes out ahead in that he gets the literal bodies (and food and drink) that he wants, whereas the prostitutes get only words. But once again, the corporeal is united with the economic and linguistic in a three-way semiotic exchange.

This feature underlines the fact that Boivin's victory is not the result of any moralistic superiority based on a lack of "artificial" or textual desire. Indeed, the entire fabliau and all in it are placed under the aegis of bodily and textual desire. Boivin is described in the first line as "mout bons lechierres" evoking that bounteous desire. Though the word "lechierres" normally indicates a desire for some physical indulgence, by the end of the fabliau it becomes apparent that the lecher desires signs—a story—as well. Even at the beginning of the tale, Boivin "porpenssa . . . que . . . si fera de lui parler" (thought that he would make himself a topic of talk) (vv. 2–4).

Once again, in fact, the analogy between merchant, prostitute, and jongleur is played out to the full. The fabliau is not just an economic negotiation fueled by corporeal desires but a version of the poetic "jeu parti," where two jongleurs vie for dominance. And the poetic contest is itself a bodily contest. We have seen that both jongleur and prostitute were stigmatized for their deformation of the sign and the image, including that of God himself, after which the human body is formed. In this tale, one sees a battle fought in terms of just such deformations. The prostitutes continually use awkward gestures and particularly facial contortions both to communicate with each other as their conspiracy evolves and to deceive Boivin, just as he deforms words to trick them.

> Vers aus se retorne .i. petit,
> Et tret la langue et tuert la joe,
> Et li houlier refont la moe.
>
> (vv. 152–54)

> Adonc font au vilain le lorgne.
>
> (v. 209)

> A Ysane cluingne de l'ueil,
> Que la borse li soit copee.
>
> (vv. 258–59)

> [He turned toward them a bit,
> And stuck out his tongue and wrenched his cheek,
> And the whores did the same in return.]

> [They pretended as if the fellow could not see.]

> [She winked her eye at Ysane,
> To signal that she should cut off his purse.]

The prostitutes echo the performing jongleur in their physical contortions. The body, as much as language, becomes the site of negotiation and the determination of value. More fundamentally, just as usury involved illicit commodification of money, language in this text is less a referential vehicle than a commodity that is to be valued and that produces excess value, and bodies are up for sale. The all-encompassing market of the tavern and brothel commodifies everything, and everything can thus be exchanged for everything else.

In this world of commodities whose values are always open to the negotiation of competing desires, why does Boivin really win? Boivin proves to be the better reader and writer and avoids the prostitutes' stratagems, not because he can successfully interpret the specifics of their signs, but because he knows that such signs have no essential meaning within this literary marketplace, where the contingent meeting of particular desires determines values. The prostitutes, like Courtois d'Arras, mistakenly try to read in relation to their own essentialist presence and believe that Boivin, with his purse, possesses an equivalent authority of presence in the text. But while Courtois tries to locate the source of textual authority in the masculine "borse," this fabliau suggests that there is in the end no *bourse* of full textual authority. It is ironically Boivin's nearly empty purse that becomes valued, if only in the context of this particular market transaction. And as in the case of Courtois, the readers who have shown too much confidence in the stable, essentialist meaning of the sign ironically lose their own outer "sign"—their clothes. Mabile ends up naked in the riot that ensues after Boivin successfully escapes with his money and without paying for their hospitality, and the other occupants of the brothel have their clothes torn and shredded.

> Lors veïssiez cheveus tirer,
> Tisons voler, dras deschirer,
>
> . . . .
>
> Teus i entra a robe vaire
> Qui la trest rouge et a refaire.

(vv. 359–68)

> [Then you would have seen [if you were there]
> Hair torn, rags flying, and clothing shredded,
>
> . . . .
>
> Some entered with cloaks of fine fur
> Only to come out with them all red and torn.]

As so often happens in the fabliaux, the figural implications of the tale are made literally real in the ending—the implied poetics is rendered explicit in the shredded clothes of the rioters, themselves echoing Boivin's initial shabby appearance. The fabliaux in general implacably reduce the figural and allegorical to the literal, just as the usurer implacably reduces money as sign and abstract unit of measure to money as physical commodity.[92]

The story ends with Boivin telling his own tale to the local provost, "qui mout ama la lecherie" (who greatly enjoyed lechery) (v. 373). Here the "lecherie" of the tale's opening is clearly redefined as a desire for the sign and for narration. Lechery's desire for the body achieves its natural exten-

---

92. Another example of this process is "Brunain, la vache au prestre" and "La Plantez."

sion as a lecherous desire for the body of the text. And Boivin has succeeded in a classic usurious venture—his initial twelve deniers generate ten sous from the provost, as payment for the tale, which was itself also generated from the deniers. It is ironically in the very emptiness of the purse that fertile poetics and economics are found—in the susceptibility of the sign to revaluation and commodification.

While I have concentrated on the metaphor of the market in this fabliau, especially as that metaphor turns around the word *croire* and its cognates, the term *bourse,* which functions as the second key negotiable term in the tale, opens up important issues of sexuality and gender. Boivin's equivocation over the contents of his "bourse" after sleeping with one of the prostitutes is the key to the tale's ending. He claims that the prostitute has gotten the contents of his "bourse," and Mabile reads this remark in relation to her own desires—her own horizon of expectations, one might say. She reads money where she should read masculine sexuality, making the same mistake as Courtois d'Arras.

Despite the differences between "Boivin de Provins" and *Courtois d'Arras,* both do refer to the message that the masculine reader should resist the seductive rhetoric of prostitution, which threatens to emasculate him by stealing his purse. In the case of *Courtois d'Arras,* such a reading recalls Michel Foucault's definition of the author as "the ideological figure by which one marks the manner in which we fear the proliferation of meaning" and attempt to delimit it.[93] In *Courtois d'Arras,* the masculine purse occupies this ideological figure. The prostitute and the brothel become, to paraphrase Foucault, the ideological figure and locus by which one marks the agency of the proliferation of meaning. In comparison, the emptiness of the purse in "Boivin de Provins" not only explicitly and ironically reveals the cultural attempt to gender proper rhetoric as masculine but also underlines the emptiness both of this gesture and potentially of all rhetoric. Boivin is saved from emasculation because there is really nothing—or almost nothing—actually there to be removed. Where there is no essential value or contents, the threat to this value is meaningless. Indeed, specifically the empty gap produces the fundamental value in the tale.

The empty purse has additional important resonances in relation to Abelard's remark in the *Historia calamitatum* that only the loss of his own "borse" through his castration allowed him to become a proper reader.[94]

---

93. Foucault, "What Is an Author?"
94. See Dinshaw, "Eunuch Hermeneutics."

Abelard clearly concurs with the author of *Courtois d'Arras* in his insistence on the need for a lack of desire in order to avoid falling into the trap of misreading, specifically for a lack of masculine sexual desire. His position is conservative in the sense that, like the author of *Courtois d'Arras*, he foresees the possibility of proper reading as long as improper textual desires (incarnated in the bodies of Pourette, Manchevaire, and Héloise) are avoided. Yet he, like the authors of the texts I am discussing, locates linguistic anxieties in the interplay between male testicles and female bodies.[95] It is therefore only appropriate that the texts of the tavern and brothel should lend themselves particularly well to the consideration of such medieval anxieties. Indeed, the deep connections between tavern and brothel, between the menacing female figure and the menace of dice and wine, were perhaps most clearly evoked by the medieval author of "Le blasme des fames,"[96] who wrote:

Fame est taverne qui ne faut
Qui qui i viegne ne qui aut.
Fame est taverne deseur voie,
Qui tout reçoit, et tout avoie.
Fame est enfers qui tout reçoit,
Toz dis a soif et toz dis boit.

[Woman is a tavern always open
No matter who comes or who goes.
Woman is a tavern along the road,
Who receives all, and sends all on their way.
Woman is hell who receives all;
She is always thirsty and always drinking.]

It would be hard to top such a frankly Freudian vision of the supposed threat to the male "purse" from this limitless, emptying, all-absorbing and all-consuming tavern and brothel. In this light, the de-essentialization of meaning that occurs in "Boivin de Provins" through the figure of the market offers an avenue to the satisfaction of sexual desire (on Boivin's part at

---

95. This last idea is borrowed from Carolyn Dinshaw, whose reading of Chaucer's "Pardoner's Tale" suggests how widespread this image of problematic reading was in the Middle Ages. See "Eunuch Hermeneutics."

96. Jubinal, *Jongleurs et trouvères*, 80–84. Another text that offers a very similar image is "Des Femmes" in Jubinal, *Nouveau recueil*, II:330–33.

least) in the recognition of the relative emptiness of this emasculating threat due to the emptiness of the purse. The sexual—and economic and textual—encounter no longer threatens to "take away" something that the male brings to the affair but becomes rather a creator—indeed the only creator—of value. Pleasure can only be had when one finally realizes that there is no nature to be preserved and when artifice is embraced and desired.[97] In this context, the fabliau also works to de-essentialize the categories of gender elaborated by *Courtois d'Arras.* The gender of the various competing merchants/jongleurs in this text is only important as a reference to the gender categories that it destabilizes.[98]

In "Les trois aveugles de Compiegne,"[99] the false coin—the empty sign—is again introduced into a tale, this time in the form of a gift from a traveling clerk to three blind men. Meeting the men on the road and noting that they have no sighted companion, he decides to have a little fun. He offers them a gold coin, a *besant,* but in reality there is no coin, though each of the three blind men believes that one of the other two has really received a *besant.* In fact, a gold *besant* was an extremely uncommon coin for most of the thirteenth century, and in this case, the particular identity of the coin virtually signals the fraudulent nature of the offer—or at least it would do so if the receivers were not "blind" with desire. The "aveugles" then decide to return to town and indulge themselves. Again, the "readers"—the three (doubly) blind men—misread the sign, "buying" the words of the clerk (his announcement of the gift) and thus accepting the value both of the words and the coin, though both are false.[100]

Yet the gap between the real and imagined value of the sign does not actuate the tale until the three men arrive back in town at the tavern to consummate their desires. The tavern is, characteristically, a place of limitless desire. A crier at the door echoes the seductive promises of previous taverns that we have seen.

---

97. See Goux, *Marx, Freud,* 81, where the author discusses the way in which castration can lead not to the end of desire, as Abelard claims, but rather to the liberation of desire, as "Boivin de Provins" suggests. His own ideological stance, like that of the medieval church, is opposed to this potential, however.

98. See Gaunt, *Gender and Genre in Medieval French Literature,* where the author makes a similar argument about gender categories throughout the fabliaux (235–36). Gaunt locates his argument within the larger context of social mobility, however, rather than in that of mobile economic values (267).

99. Noomen, *Nouveau recueil,* II:151–84.

100. Howard Bloch's reading in *Scandal of the Fabliaux* (94–96) provides the starting point for my analysis in this paragraph.

Chi a boin vin fres et nouvel!
Cha d'Auchoire! Cha de Soissons!
Pain et char, oissons[101] et poissons!
Chaiens fait boin despendre argent:
Ostel i a a toute gent!
Ci puet on aise herbregier!

(vv. 72–77)

[Here we have good wine, fresh and new!
Wine of Auxerre! Wine of Soissons!
Bread and meat, drink and fish!
Here's a good place to spend your money:
There's a place for everyone!
Here you can lodge in comfort!]

The guests are offered unlimited consumption—the phantasm of the open economy: "En la ville n'a boin morsel / Que vous n'aiés, se vous volés" (There's no tasty morsel in the city / that you won't have if you so desire) (vv. 93–94). (In reality, the open economy functions only for words in this case—they can be used without implication in truthful acts of reference, so the clerk will succeed in getting something [food and lodging] for nothing.) It is at this point that the blind men mirror the behavior of Boivin de Provins, speaking of their money and promising to pay well for hospitality, and in exchange, the second reader—the tavern keeper—likewise misreads their words and provides them with food, drink, and entertainment. As in the case of the three blind men, the tavern keeper's desire for a profit, for the material sign of wealth, motivates his reading—and thus inevitable misreading. As in "Boivin de Provins," the victim also willfully ignores the warning of the clothing of the guests, which in its shabbiness is an indication of the potential inadequacy of the signs—monetary and linguistic—of these guests: of the three blind men, the narrator has already informed us that "Moult povre estoient lor drapel, / Car vestu furent povrement" (Their clothing was very poor, for they were poorly attired) (vv. 18–19). (The narrator himself has even informed the attentive reader of the untrustworthy nature of the poetic sign through his use of the word "mesconter" in v. 8; as in "Boivin de Provins," the double sense of the

---

101. This word must certainly be *boissons.* Montaiglon *(Recueil général)* gives "et vin." Note also that once again both food and lodging ("herbregier") are available at the same place—this is another inn/tavern combination.

word is key.) Though reader and innkeeper are both forewarned, they both plunge ahead in their readings: as Howard Bloch says, the tale "reveals a desire for narrative that is thematized throughout."[102] I would add again, as in the previous case, that this desire for narrative is paralleled by the desire for economic profit and that both of these desires are really one form of a desire for the sign itself, be it monetary or linguistic—not for its use or utility, but simply for its value as a commodity. The pleasure of the text is no different from the possession of the coin.

Of course, when the tavern keeper demands his payment, the three blind men discover that they have no money. The clerk, however, who has followed along to watch what may happen, gives a whole new meaning to the term "authorial intervention" by assuring the tavern keeper that he can put the men's bill on the clerk's account: "Anchois les metés sur mon conte" (Put it on my tab) (v. 189), he says, again playing on the word "conte."[103] He then informs the tavern keeper that the local priest owes him a debt and that if the tavern keeper wants all the money, he should go to the church and ask the priest for his money. Of course, he also manages to tell the priest that the tavern keeper is crazy, assuring that the request will be met with refusal. The debt is indeed added to his tale ("conte") but not to his bill ("conte"). The excess of meaning contained in his words is further amplified and underlined by the use of the verb *croire,* with its typical suggestion of usury, three times in the next forty lines, during the scenes in the church.

Thus the initial gap in the semiotics precipitates a cascade of writings, readings, and rewritings. The initial tale of the clerk produces the initial misreading of the "aveugles," leading to their monetary difficulties, which then produce the need for additional narration on their behalf (the clerk's intervention). The misreading of the tavern keeper—and his monetary shortfall—then forces him into a second misreading (of the clerk's second story) in an attempt to recoup the first misreading. Once in debt from reading and writing, the only way out is seemingly more reading and writing, in an attempt to recoup the debt. Poetic profit and loss lead to monetary

---

102. Bloch, *Scandal of the Fabliaux,* 84.

103. The passage also has implications for the concept of "authority" and linguistic dissemination: even the clerk himself has not been sure where the tale that he has initiated will lead. Once a proverb, an expression, a coin, a body ("Le segretain moine"), or any other sign of questionable validity has been released, it has a tendency of either getting out of control or coming back to haunt the author, as in "La Plantez," "Brunain et la vache au prestre," "Le prestre, le chevalier et la dame," "Estormi," and other fabliaux, especially if it is taken purely at face value.

profit and loss, which lead to poetic profit and loss, in a vicious cycle.[104]
The fabliau, like "Boivins de Provins," ultimately presents the founding
moment of a textual tradition, in the which the false coin leads to a cas-
cading realization of desire. Writing, reading, and rewriting can in theory
continue ad infinitum, each act of imperfect exchange producing surplus
and debt, which create anew a desire for the sign and for texts. It seems
appropriate to point out the similarity of this comico-realist poetics to that
of courtly literature. The obscurities of the ancients mentioned by Marie
de France in her "Prologue," which lie at the origin of a series of textual
interpretations and rewritings and of a long textual tradition, are in a certain sense simply another version of the missing coins and linguistic gaps
of the fabliaux. The final ironic twist of the tale is that the tavern keeper's
desire for the sign, which is initially figured in his desire for money, is
finally realized and made explicit when he ironically receives a "text" in the
end from the priest—the Bible, which the priest has read to him to cure
him of his madness.

As both *Courtois d'Arras* and these two fabliaux suggest, the sign can
never be read "properly" as long as there is a desire for profit—for signs
themselves. This very desire leads to the literary market exchanges that
produce values that escape writer, reader, or sometimes both. Each literary market transaction produces its own unique values, which refuse the
notion of essential *propertas* represented by the idea of "just price." As in
"Boivins de Provins," the "author's" false coin in "Les trois aveugles de
Compiegne" does in fact have value in terms of the desire of some readers.
And on the basis of the false coins and a subsequent series of "mis"-read-
ings, the comic value of the tale is produced and the various figures attain
their various texts. *Courtois d'Arras* laments this loss of *propertas,* while
the goliards and the fabliaux see it as the very source of poetic creativity
and celebrate it. For these last two, in fact, linguistic propriety and literature (as an aesthetic practice of play and linguistic surplus) are mutually
incompatible. But despite these differences, all of the texts mentioned
share a certain representation of the foolishness of those who are ignorant
of the dangerous, glorious ambivalence of language. Reading at the literal
level in particular is a matter of chance, error, and confusion. Since language is open to the vagaries of individual intentionality, of vocal and textual homophonies and homographies, of slippery contextual meanings,
and of confusion of reference, as well as of all the other features that mark

---

104. This could be compared to Goux' ideas on the endless concatenation of merchandise
that is produced through the process of exchange (see *Freud, Marx,* 96).

textual exchanges and interactions, "reading" comes to resemble a toss of the dice, a risky investment, a "Jeu de Hasart," just as the writing of poetry is a toss of the dice—a scrambling and disordering of language.[105] That the three blind men of "Les trois aveugles de Compiegne" come out ahead in the end is a key index of the fabliau's fundamental opposition to the semiotics of Jean le Marchant's miracle, where the jongleur, described as "aveugle," loses out in the end. In the miracle, where immanence prevails, blindness becomes a symbol of the impossibility of benefiting from the immanent divine light. But where communication really is a matter of chance, ruled by the goddess Fortuna—who was typically depicted in the Middle Ages as being blind—then the sightless reader has as good a chance as any other.[106]

Another slightly different example of "chance reading" occurs in "Le credo au ribaut."[107] A thieving dice player in a tavern boasts of how he robs each of his innocent victims.

Par deniers, par chevaus, par robe,
Par le geu des dez qui tout robe:
Tout li toli, tout li juai.

[His money, his horses, his clothing,
By the game of dice that steals all:
I have taken it all, I have won it all from him.]

The poet rhymes the "robe" (theft) accomplished by the dice with the "robe" (cloak) that is unjustly reassigned to a new owner by means of the dice. This simply mirrors the linguistic reassigning of the sign (symbolized by the cloak ["robe"]) to new reference in the metaphorical scrambling or "robbery" of linguistic propriety that is poetry. Yet this occurs not only in these few lines but in this entire text, since the Christian creed is contextu-

---

105. Reading as a toss of the dice, where pure chance determines who "wins" and who "loses" in the game of reading, is also thematized in a number of nontavern fabliaux, perhaps most famously in "Estula," where purely by chance a robber named "Estula" gets involved in a midnight exchange with a shepherd who calls out over and over, "Es tu la?" See also "La male honte."

106. Fortune was classically represented as being blind (see Patch, *The Goddess Fortuna,* 11–12; Siciliano, *François Villon,* 293–94), and of course dice and Fortune are intimately related. Thus the use of dice to represent the "blind" nature of reading is even more appropriate. Likewise the three "aveugles" of Compiegne discussed earlier, through their blindness, underline the same point.

107. Barbazan, *Fabliaux et contes,* 4:455–51.

ally redefined, word by word, and the reference of each sign is shifted: "Dominum nostrum apelons le tavernier . . . ," we read, and so forth. The entire poem becomes not only a revaluation of formerly vertically referring signs but an overproduction, since the creed is expanded via the surrounding interpolated text, acquires a new meaning, yet still carries the echo of its original reference as well. This is thus a "usurious" text par excellence, underlined by the title "Credo," which recalls both belief and the credit and lending of the usurer.

This creed bears consideration because it does suggest a limitation to the concept of the literary speculative marketplace. Here, as in "Boivins de Provins" and "Les trois aveugles de Compiegne," at least one participant in the game does succeed in controlling the encounter to his profit, and apparently his success is not due to chance alone. Both fabliaux, especially "Boivins de Provins," offer an image of the poet as a powerful figure who successfully manipulates signs, just as the bourgeois banker did in most cases. These signs are inherently open to manipulation, and final outcomes are not guaranteed, but an awareness of this very fact seems to offer the astute poet an advantage that is often not shared by his more credulous readers. Language and poetry may come down to a game of dice, but the dice are clearly loaded in the writer's favor in many of the fabliaux.

Implicit in the metaphor of poetry as dice playing however is the suggestion that the haphazard nature of the poetic scrambling can lead to the loss of authorial control on the part of the poet as well. Another fabliaux that thematizes the problems of literal (as opposed to figurative) reading and also the loss of intentionality that can occur when signs escape the control of the writer is "La plantez."[108] In this tale, a customer in a tavern pays for a glass of wine, but the tavern keeper spills a good portion of the wine in giving it to the customer, who is irritated at the loss of so much of his purchase. The tavern keeper responds by citing the proverb that spilled wine brings good luck. Unfortunately, the customer is once again a literal reader and takes the words to their logical conclusion—if a little spilled wine brings a little luck, a lot of wine should bring a lot of luck—and he opens all the taps, flooding the tavern with wine to bring the tavern keeper much good luck. The overproduction of meaning produced by this literal reading is mirrored in the overflowing wine, and the way in which the literal meaning of words can escape the intentionality of the speaker (as opposed to the supposedly controllable figurative meanings) is parodied.

---

108. Noomen, *Nouveau recueil,* VII:203–14.

In a world of immanence, unitary interpretations and readings are guaranteed by the textual community for the higher figural levels, while this is not so at the literal level. Even the tale's title serves ironically to evoke the absence of immanence, just as this key word is used in the Arras comedies simultaneously to evoke the vision of the tavern as a prelapsarian paradise and to mock such a false vision.

The tavern, already characterized by a poetics of idolatry of the sign, here becomes the locus for a meditation on the nature of authority and intentionality in such a poetics. Helsinger has in fact noted that the fabliaux are often a "parody of allegory and higher reading" marking the "unexpected success of literal-mindedness." They function in a kind of anti-Pauline or anti-Platonic sense, often playing on the "making real" of words at the cost of the destruction of higher figural meanings.[109] Similarly, in the fabliau "Brunain, la vache au prestre" a priest promises that he who gives to the Lord will receive twice his gift in return: "il fesoit bon doner . . . Que Dieus au double li rendoit" (It is good to give to God . . . for God returns the gift doubled) (vv. 6–8).[110] Brunain, suitably inspired, gives his cow to the priest for the church. But the cow soon wanders home to Brunain, trailed by the priest's own animal as well. The spiritual doubling so often found in medieval miracle literature, which I referred to in discussing *Le Jeu de Saint Nicolas,* is here ironically reduced to a very secular doubling. The "chancy" nature of reading on this literal level is underlined by the chance arrival of the second cow at Brunain's farm, literally doubling the wealth of the giver as the priest's proverb has promised.

A final fabliaux that dramatizes excess value, beyond expectation of either reader or writer, is "Estormi."[111] A "preudomme" (v. 4) with three dead priests on his hands sends his niece to the tavern, has his cash-poor nephew brought home, and offers him a text about a dead priest that turns out to be more than either the man or the nephew bargained for. He tells his nephew he has one priest to get rid of; then, in order to get the nephew to carry away the second priest, he insists that the first priest has risen from the dead; and so forth. All goes well until the nephew runs into a fourth priest on the road (vv. 514ff.) and kills him too, as the tale of resuscitation

---

109. Helsinger, "Pearls in the Swill." Jurgen Beyer sees the same phenomena on an ethical level, noting that the fabliaux reveal "a non-moral view of the world that ironically reduces all . . . to the real" ("The Morality of the Amoral," 22).

110. Noomen, *Nouveau receuil,* V:39–48.

111. Noomen, *Nouveau receuil,* I:13–28.

produces an unexpected excess of "desuscitation." This fabliau is again marked by monetary, corporeal, and textual desires. It opens with the *preudomme* and his wife impoverished (vv. 4–7), perhaps by the same market forces that were impinging generally on aristocratic prosperity at the time. The wife tells her husband:

Or feroit bon croire conseil
Par quoi nous en[de povreté] fussons geté!
Li prestre sont riche renté,
S'ont trop dont nous avons petit.
Se vous volez croire mon dit,
De povreté vous geterai.

(vv. 56–61)

[Now it would be good to heed counsel
On how we might be released from poverty;
Priests are richly endowed;
They have too much of what we lack.
If you will trust my word,
I will release you from poverty.]

The desire for money is here represented more specifically as a desire for money to be obtained through textual production, suggesting ultimately a desire for those texts themselves. The success of both textual and economic strategies are intimately related in the double sense of "croire mon dit." Subsequently, the three priests' desire for the woman's body results in their "crediting" of a text that she offers them about her willingness to sleep with them, a crediting made literal by their willingness to pay her for the pleasure. Here, however, in a reversal of "Boivins de Provins," the money is real but the sex is not. The woman's husband takes the priests' money and kills them before they can fulfill their desires.

At this point, the tale has produced a profit for the *preudomme* and his wife, but it has hardly done so for the reader, as it would be entirely pointless if it were to end here. The final literary value is dependent on the meeting of the *preudomme*'s tale of a single priest and his repeated resuscitations with his nephew's willing reading of such a tale. The nephew, in the tavern, is indebted and eager for both money and the story that comes with it. The *preudomme* assures him, "Je te conterai, biaus amis . . . tout le voir" (Good friend, I'll tell you the whole truth) (vv. 318–19)—in other words, that he will pay *(conter)* his debt—which he does—and offer him *(conter)* a tale. The tale is far from being the "truth" as it exists outside the tavern. But with the nephew's acceptance of the payment (credit) comes belief (credit) in the text and the subsequent actualization of its potential value. While the tavern is not the only place to find willing readers, it is certainly one of the best. The meeting in the tavern and the literary exchange that follows set in motion the events leading to the comic climax. The tale's humor lies in the surplus of priests and meaning that neither "writer" nor "reader" anticipated.

These fabliaux all finally insist on the status of literature as a product of momentary conventions established between two parties to meet momentary needs, and they ultimately insist on the conventional, as opposed to "natural," status of textual meaning. The text becomes a contract, whose existence as a vehicle of meaning depends on the accession of both parties to the agreement. But it is a contract that governs not simply a commercial exchange but a speculative investment (a form of usury in the Middle Ages) whose outcome is unknown to either party.

As in my earlier readings of the comico-realist drama, I have used the terms *reader* and *writer* when talking of these tales, which were in reality probably performed orally. Despite this oral status, the texts seem to be replete with a semiotic awareness typically associated with the highest levels of medieval literacy. These tales seem to suggest a penetration of semiotic concerns throughout medieval literature and culture, from Aquinas to the most obscene fabliau.[112] As a result, comico-realist literature must be read with many of the same concerns in mind as when one reads the Vulgate Cycle or troubadour lyric. This is not entirely surprising for the drama, since Jean Bodel and Adam de la Halle both wrote in a wide variety of "high" and "low" forms, but it has until recently rarely been done with the fabliau and even less often with the many short *dits,* creeds, and *devises* that I have periodically discussed. Certainly I do not argue that the thematic and ideological content of the typical fabliau is equivalent to that of a courtly narrative. Yet a true understanding of the tavern strongly suggests that there is far more thematic unity throughout medieval literature, at least as far as semiotic issues are concerned, than has often been recognized. If we accept Eugene Vance's contention (see my introduction) that meditation on the nature and functioning of the sign is not only a charac-

---

112. Roy J. Pearcy ("Modes of Signification and the Humor of Obscene Diction") has in fact provided an extremely interesting reading of the obscene diction of the fabliaux as ultimately concerning a rivalry between Platonic and Aristotelian semiotics and epistemology.

teristic of the learned superstructure of medieval society but a fundamental structural component, then this unity is hardly surprising; I believe that the texts of the tavern provide strong support for this contention. Indeed, I hope that I have shown that these texts are not really about reading and writing at all in the narrowest sense but rather about the tension between semiotic stability, on the one hand, and productive creativity, on the other, whether oral, written, monetary, or ethical. Readers and writers are, in the broadest sense, users, consumers, and producers of signs. Yet at the same time, it is no longer the linguistic sign, the *vox significativa* of Latin grammar, that offers the basic model for sign use. Rather the economic sign— the coin used in the exchanges of the market—becomes the master narrative of comico-realism and of the medieval urban, secular society.

A final tavern fabliau that combines a concern with reading and interpretation (as well as a love of the "real") with the goliard representation of poetry as equivalent to drinking is "Les trois dames de Paris."[113] Here poetry is again presented as arising from the disordering yet creative activity of drink, and the tale also finally assimilates poetry to the merchant's taking of his inventory, so that poetry merges literally with economic commodity. In the tale, three women decide to enjoy a "girls' night out" at the local tavern. What follows is an orgy of drinking and eating that leaves the women in a state of drunken stupor. They are found the next morning naked and seemingly lifeless and are subsequently buried in the cemetery. They eventually awaken, disinter themselves, frighten the townspeople to death, and are beaten to a pulp since they are mistaken for devils. Thomas Cooke has noted the extreme concern of this fabliaux with proper names: the names of the women are carefully given, as are the different varieties of wine that they drink, as well as the names of the various taverns they visit.[114]

> . . . la fame Adam de Gonnesse
> Et sa niece Maroie Clippe
> Distrent que chascune a la trippe
> Iroient .ii. deniers despendre,
> S'en alerent, sans plus atendre,
> Entre elles .ii. a la taverne,
> En la maison Perrin du Terne.
> . . . .

---

113. Montaiglon, *Recueil général*, 3:145–56.
114. Cooke, *The Old French and Chaucerian Fabliaux*, 32.

Atant se metent a la voie
Vers la taverne des Maillez.
La vint[115] li filz Druins Baillez.

(vv. 18–48)

[. . . and the wife of Adam of Gonnesse
And her niece Maroie Clippe
Said that they were each going
To spend a little on some fun.
Away they went, without delay,
The two of them to the tavern,
At the house of Perrin of Terne.

.   .   .   .

Then they set out on their way
To the tavern of the Maillez
Where the son of Druin Baillez plys his trade.]

This concern is unusual in a genre most often noted for its stock characters and formulaic plots, where names are usually confined to designations of class. Both naming and a general listing of the women's consumption eventually runs riot as the tale revels in the realistic details of the scene. The fabliau becomes in fact an inventorying of their consumption—poem as purchase receipt—detailing the precise cost and amount of this consumption.

. . . va nous aporter
Pour nos testes reconforter
De la garnache .ii. chopines,
Et de tot revenir ne fines.
S'aporte gauffres et oublées,
Fromage et amandes pelées,
Poires, espices et des nois,
Tant, pour florins et gros tornois,
Que nous en aions a plenté.

(vv. 83–91)

---

115. I take "vint" here to be the verb *vendre*—thus the sentence translates literally "There sells the son (subject) . . ."

[. . . go bring us
Two glasses of *garnache*
To soothe our heads,
And stay alert to keep our glasses full.
And bring us some honey cakes and pastries,
Cheese and shelled almonds,
Pears, spices and nuts,
Enough that, for gold florins and *gros tournois*
We'll have all we could want.]

(Note the use of the word "plenté"—once more, the tavern is an escapist locale offering the phantasm of plenitude.) In addition, the poem devolves into a chronicle of drinking, thus echoing the goliard poems in which a line of poetry becomes the equivalent of a drink, line after line.

Commere, or en bevons assez.

(v. 100)

Lors but chacune, mais, ancois,
C'on eust tornées ses mains,
C'une plus que li autres mains,
Fu tous lapez et engloutis.

(vv. 104–7)

Druins, raportes en .iii. quartes,
Car, avant que de ci departes,
Seront butes . . .

(vv. 115–17)

Manjue .i. morsel, puis si bois.

(v. 121)

Je le boif trop plus volentiers.

(v. 125)

[Ladies, let's drink our fill.]

[Then they all drank, but before
You could get a breath,

Or cross one hand over the other,
The wine was all drunk up and swallowed down.]

[Druin, bring us three quarts,
For before we leave here,
We're going to be good and drunk . . .]

[They ate and bit, then drank some more.]

[I drink this stuff quite willingly.]

As the tale continues, the women, who started out as clearly individu-ated "signs" complete with proper names, gradually lose their clothing (their proper signification) piece by piece in great detail, then their con-sciousness, and eventually their very life (in a figurative sense) as they end up lying in the street covered with mud: "Gisant, nues et desrobées, / Comme merdes en mi la voie" (Lying, naked and unclothed, like shit in the middle of the road) (vv. 208–9). They are no longer recognizable—no name can be assigned to them—so that they have lost both proper name and proper clothes through the semiotically disordering activity of drink. Found in the street, they are thus "misread" by the townspeople as being dead and are taken to be buried. The women finally are lost both to the townspeople, to whom they are unidentifiable, and to themselves, since they are literally unconscious of their own existence. Intentionality and even identity are destroyed by the disordering semiotic activity of the tav-ern. The tavern and its most characteristic activity of drinking are thus a filter through which the sign is passed, and that filter gradually shifts and disorders the original semiotics that existed outside the tavern. The initial emphasis on precise proper naming in the fabliau can be seen in this light as a necessary prelude to the disordering that follows. This disordering process (drink by drink, line by line) is assimilated to the process of poetry, in a fashion similar to the way in which the disordering activity of dice is also assimilated to poetry.

As the tale concludes, the women eventually disinter themselves and stumble back down the street, only to collapse in a drunken heap again, covered with mud and worms from the cemetery, as they have been trans-formed by drink and the tavern into not only a semiotic chaos but also a parody of a moralizing vision of death and hell itself.

Elles ont les deables es cors.
Voies les, a chascun des cors,
Comme elles sont de vers chargiés,
Enterrees et demengiés,
Les cors noirs et delapidés.

(vv. 279–83)

[They look like they're possessed by the devil.
Look at them, at each of their bodies,
How they're all covered with worms,
Covered in dirt and all gnawed at,
Their bodies black and wretched.]

Excess has led to comic disaster. And verbal excess, in the form of a concentration on the most concrete and literal elements of language, such as the proper name, and in the form of nominal inventorying, has ironically lead to a verbal failure where even fundamental names and identities are lost.

The tale invites a series of readings. It could be taken in a moral context. There is a certain redemption in the tale in that the individual "signs" of the tale's beginning—the three women—have been converted to universal signifiers of a potential moral lesson on reading. Thus their gratuity is converted into productive wisdom.

But the loss of clothing and essential identity again points to a proto-capitalist literary economy, where the "value" of the initial buyers and sellers is subsumed by the meaning of the tale. The market must always seize and reassign clothes. This is perhaps the deepest sense of the tale's refusal to grant privileged status to nominal identity of either people or things. The disordering of drinking, and poetry, is finally an economic disordering and revaluing.

The three women's gratuity could also be read in a more heroic light, and their figurative death can even be seen in the context of the notion of "sacrifice" as elaborated by Georges Bataille. Their minutely detailed "non-productive expenditure," to use another term from Bataille, is part of a larger literary endeavor that seeks to pass beyond the utilitarian, the socially productive, the zero-sum game of medieval life and into the realm of an open, plenitudinal literary economy. This is the usurious economy that has been the centerpiece of the last two chapters. Bataille himself invokes the idea of usury as a model for the transgressive and sacrificial acts of which he speaks.[116] Yet whereas Bataille argues that the bourgeoisie acts as the repressive agent opposing such acts, Jean Bodel and many of the fabliaux suggest that at this early point in their social history, the urban middle classes were in fact intimately linked to such acts by the threatened social powers of the time, the church and the aristocracy. While these classes would not join the "powers that be" until the fourteenth century, at least within the context of literary representations such as the tavern scene in *Piers Plowman*,[117] the need for the "sacrifice" of "Les trois dames de Paris" suggests a step in that transformation. Already there is perhaps pressure from this new rising power for another version of the closed economy, whose barriers must be broken by the orgiastic potlatch of the night in the tavern. Like Pourette, Manchevaire, and, to a lesser extent, Mabile of "Boivins de Provins," the "trois dames" are the heroines of a poetics whose practitioners recognize the tenuousness of their prestige and the constant pressure toward the margins that their literary practice inspires. This pressure is expressed here in terms of the sexual politics of gendering, and in chapter 4 it will be expressed in the connection of poetry to the psychopathology of folly. In other words, feminine gendering could be read as a marker that indicates a desire to marginalize the poetic practice in question (as in *Courtois d'Arras*). But it could also be read as the marker of awareness of this potential marginalization and of the creative potential that lies at this marginal, liminal space. The drunken celebration across the boundaries links "Les trois dames de Paris" to "In taberna quando sumus" and makes both poems such strong emblems of a medieval poetics that sought to move beyond the limitations of Neoplatonic semiology and nature, beyond the adequate and the essentialist, to a new vision of the sources of poetic value.

Suitably, the tavern scene attains full generic status in the fabliaux, as it did previously in the goliard poems. This is consistent with the fact that the fabliaux, like the goliard works, often present their particular semiology as creative and dynamic and in many cases present the practitioners as transgressive "heros." Thus there is no need to locate the tavern within the morally recuperative framework of a broader text. It has in fact been suggested that both the fabliaux and the goliard poems may share the same authors to at least some extent.[118] A distinction, however, is that the

---

116. Bataille, "The Notion of Expenditure."
117. See Simpson, *Piers Plowman,* chap. 2.
118. See especially Wailes, "Vagrantes and the Fabliaux." Wailes notes the similarities of the use of taverns and dice between the two traditions.

goliards often present the open moral economy of their texts as a phantasm—the figures in the poems often end up penniless and naked despite the poetics. The fabliaux, however, often present the semiological "transgressor" as the one who profits—the inscribed literary figures of the fabliaux "get away with it" in many cases. The rise of the tavern scene to full generic status in the fabliaux is intimately linked to the triumph of the anti-Platonic semiology in this larger genre.[119]

The independence of the tavern scene as a genre in the fabliaux is further emphasized by the fact that the tavern is rarely used as a metageneric locale, even though the fabliaux themselves are often quite metageneric: unlike several other fabliaux, few of those using taverns can be seen as parodies or underminings of other genres. In this sense, my readings of the tavern fabliaux do not tend to support Nykrog's well-known general contention that the fabliaux as a whole constitute a secondary aristocratic genre that parodies primary aristocratic genres. Rather than commenting obliquely on other genres, the tavern fabliaux comment on signs and poetics as a whole. Far from being a genre that depends on the existence of other genres for its function, the tavern fabliaux quite consistently meditate on the sources of texts. And in many cases, the tavern itself serves as the sourcing mechanism for the tale. This function is most explicitly thematized in the fabliaux, yet the function exists in virtually all of the tavern texts that I have considered and will consider.

---

119. My reading clearly conflicts with several recent readings, however, that have suggested that the fabliaux are socially and morally conservative. I agree that this is true in many cases in terms of the surface content of the texts—in other words, the lecherous priest is often punished; the villain is typically the victim of the bourgeois. But the artistic sense of the fabliaux—the true literary "meaning" of the tales—argues strongly for the contrary point of view. The heros of the tales, with whom we almost inevitably identify, are typically excellent users of "transgressive" forms of rhetoric, to take one example, and the fabliaux in general show an insistent pleasure in the use of metaphor for the purpose of sexual conquest and pleasure.

Chapter 4

Autobiography and Folly

Rutebeuf and the Call to Silence

The previous chapter revealed how the dramatists of Arras and the authors of the fabliaux identify the desire for money with a desire for the sign in general, especially in its linguistic manifestation: poverty constitutes a desire for the text, and poverty and linguistic desire are both products of the tavern. It so happens that the tavern is also the favored locale of the (at least ostensibly) poverty-stricken Parisian poet Rutebeuf, who often presents his personal penury as a poverty of linguistic capability. Rutebeuf is usually considered not only the greatest "realist" poet of thirteenth-century France but also one of the first poets of the city—the home of the tavern.[1] While recent readers have moved away from the traditional autobiographical approach to his poems toward a deeper appreciation of his exemplary status and the tradition-dependent context of his poetry, much remains to be said about his exact relation to the thirteenth-century literature of the tavern and about his larger place in the comico-realist tradition.[2]

In a series of texts often called the "poems of misfortune," Rutebeuf meditates on the status of language and its role as mediator between self and society, couching this meditation in the form of dice playing in the tavern. His exploration of the linguistic sources of poetic creativity in these poems leads him to adopt two intertwined emblems for the poet—poverty and *folie*. Traditionally, Rutebeuf's "personal poetry" has been read as a

---

1. See especially Regalado, "Poets of the Early City."
2. See especially Arié Serper, *Rutebeuf,* for an important survey of Rutebeuf's place in the satiric tradition of the thirteenth century.

confession of poverty and personal failure.[3] In this light, he is a socially and economically marginal poor fool, or in moral terms the poor fool punished for his foolish vices. A second dominant reading has sought to find more "positive" aspects in Rutebeuf's poems, considering his poetic enterprise as finally redemptive, as a precursor to Dante in a certain sense. These readings have typically focused on the Christian virtues represented by the poor, but pure and wise, fool and, secondarily, the secular "teller of truths."[4] Both of the readings are correct to the extent that they engage with the differing connotations of poverty (and folly) in high medieval urban France. However, the context of the tavern, the poetics of dice, and the larger moral issues that this poetics often evokes (replicated here by the figure of the fool) offer a fuller appreciation of the ambiguous position of Rutebeuf between these two readings.

In particular, the multiple and even contradictory implications of poverty and folly in thirteenth-century France will eventually reveal the compromising nature of poetic practice in the context of medieval models of authority and intentionality. And most important, the two emblems engage with more general high medieval ideas on language to bring into question the possibility of successfully knowing or reading the self. As such titles as "La repentance Rutebeuf" suggest, Rutebeuf's poetry ultimately addresses some of the central moral, religious, and linguistic issues of thirteenth-century France—guilt, confession, repentance, and the relation between self and God. Ironically, given the traditional autobiographical bent in much Rutebeuf scholarship, the representation of language as fundamentally ambiguous and polyvalent that emerges from his poetry suggests that this language is not only the source of poetic creativity but also the reason for the impossibility of full self-knowledge and of medieval autobiography. Rutebeuf's "poetry of misfortune" may be seen as an exploration of the limits of subjectivity in the Middle Ages. Due to the fundamentally conservative nature of his religious and linguistic philosophy, these limits are more strict than has often been supposed. Poetic redemption in Rutebeuf lies finally in the conscious realization of the impossibility of full self-expression or repentance.

---

3. This is the reading of those who take his poetry in a more or less straightforwardly autobiographical manner. See, for an exemplary instance, Pesce, "Le Portrait de Rutebeuf." See also Frappier, "Rutebeuf, poète du jeu."

4. This is essentially the reading of Jean Dufournet (*Rutebeuf,* introduction), Jacqueline Cerquiglini ("Le Clerc et le louche"); and Paul Zumthor ("'Roman' et 'Gothique'"). Though they certainly differ on many points, they do share a vision of Rutebeuf's successful disengagement from tradition.

Rutebeuf is perhaps most famous as the poet of poverty and "misfortune." In many of his "autobiographical" poems ("Li mariages Rutebeuf," "La griesche d'yver," "La griesche d'esté," "La complainte," "La povretei"),[5] he insists on this poverty, and it becomes an emblem of his poetic persona in his works. He continually presents an ironic image of himself (and his tavern-frequenting companions) as shabbily dressed or naked, penniless, and flea-bitten in summer and tormented by cold in winter (see "Li diz des ribaux de Grève," *OC* 1:199–201). This ironic detachment recalls a similar posture adopted by a number of late medieval poets. Jacqueline Cerquiglini has shown that such a posture is often signaled by a series of physical handicaps, particularly one-eyedness or blindness (for Rutebeuf, see "La complainte," especially vv. 23–25, and "Li mariages Rutebeuf," v. 125) and impotence (the empty purse of Rutebeuf's poverty can certainly be read in conjunction with the sexual connotations of this figure seen in previous chapters).[6] Such features, she argues, shift the focus of the text from the events themselves, as if they were seen by God (to use her image), to the particular angle of vision of the particular individual poet. They function to mark the poet as an individual and marginal figure and to authorize this outsider's satirical vision of society. They are thus perverse marks of individual poetic consciousness—even pride—on the part of the poet.[7]

Of course, such marks could also be read as translations of a negative social or moral evaluation of the poet by society at large. Rutebeuf's poverty is a similar marker of this poetic status, a marker that plays on the evolving status of poverty in this time period.[8] Such poverty carries a number of negative connotations. The most important are of a religious nature and connote the poverty that traditionally results from vice in the Middle Ages. The secular connotations are of the poverty of social marginality and economic failure in the urban precapitalist milieu. In the two "Griesche" poems, his dice playing has impoverished him, while in "La com-

---

5. All citations are from *OC.* Translations into English are my own.

6. See in particular Cerquiglini, "Le Clerc et le louche."

7. Michel Zink argues in *La subjectivité littéraire* (67) that these features, and those associated with the tavern more generally, serve also to dissuade the appropriation of the "je" in these works by the public, as compared to what occurs in the courtly lyric. Again, the emphasis is on distance and subjectivity. Likewise, in light of Evelyn Vitz' analysis of Abelard in terms of quantitative, as opposed to qualitative, distinctions in his persona ("Type et individu dans 'l'autobiographie' médiévale"), these markers constitute an important shift toward qualitative distinctions.

8. See Little, *Religious Poverty.* On Rutebeuf specifically, see Regalado, *Poetic Patterns,* 16–19.

plainte" (*OC* 1:285–95) and "Li mariages Rutebeuf" (*OC* 1:243–51) he presents himself as a generally hard-luck ne'er-do-well who is nevertheless also probably responsible for his present situation.

> Or n'ai je pas quanque je aing:
> C'est mes damaiges.
> Ne sai ce s'a fait a mes outrages.
> Or devanrrai sobres et sages
> Aprés le fait
> Et me garderai de forfait.
>
> ("La complainte," vv. 39–44)

> [Nothing goes as I would like:
> To my great misfortune.
> I don't know if its because of my faulty behavior.
> From now on I'll become sober and wise
> (After the fact)
> And I'll avoid my past errors.]

His poverty thus represents a social or even divine judgment against him.

In "Les plaies du monde" (on The Wounds of the World, *OC* 1:67–75), a satirical poem critical of avarice, he again presents a picture of the impoverished, marginalized figure.

> Qui auques at, se est ameiz,
> Et qui n'at riens c'est fox clameiz.
> . . . .
> N'est mais nuns qui reveste nu,
> Ansois est partout la coustume
> Qu'au dezouz est, chacuns le plume
> Et le gietë en la longaigne.
> Por ce est fox qui ne gaaigne
> Et qui ne garde son gahaing,
> Qu'en povretei a grant mahaing.
>
> (vv. 21–32)

> [Whoever has a little wealth is liked,
> And whoever has none is called a fool.
> . . . .

There's no longer anyone who clothes the naked one;
Rather its everywhere the custom
That whomever is down and out, everyone abuses him
And tosses him into filth.
Therefore whoever does not make a profit is a fool
And whoever doesn't keep what he earns,
For poverty is a grave ill.]

Here, however, Rutebeuf is satirizing not himself, but the avaricious, the people who hold the view of poverty expressed in the poem. In this light, the poor fool has positive rather than negative connotations. From a religious standpoint, he is the charitable individual, the one who has given (alms?) (v. 31), and more generally the one is the more free from sin because of his lack of avarice. From a secular standpoint, he is the "teller of truths" about society, for Rutebeuf notes elsewhere that one is paid primarily for lies (see vv. 79ff. of "L'estat du monde" [*OC* I:77–87], for example, where he attacks lawyers and clerks, and vv. 121ff., where he attacks merchants who lie for profits).[9] Rutebeuf thus presents poverty as a positive emblem that validates his poetic practice and satirical project.

More generally, he is playing on the multiple and often contradictory implications of poverty in the High Middle Ages. Poverty is not just alternately positive or negative in his poetry, but each type of poverty can turn into the other. If, for example, the impoverishment that results from his vices, such as dice playing, is a negative factor, by learning from it and seeing the error of his ways while remaining in poverty, he can convert a negative Christian poverty to positive Christian poverty. Jean Dufournet, for example, reads Rutebeuf's poverty, his nakedness, his "Descent aux enfers" via the representation of personal suffering, as a process of "dépouillement" that strips away the accoutrements of the world—wealth, clothing, money, and so on—that vitiate the attempt to speak "truthfully."[10] Nakedness and poverty seem to point out the poet as one who dares to speak the truth.

Such a descent into the "enfers" of vice—particularly the drinking and gambling that find their most favorable home in the tavern—poses a special danger to the poet, however. He must be sure to escape. In this light, the fact that "La griesche d'esté" (*OC* 1:109–97) opens with the act of "recordant ma grant folie" (v. 1) is highly significant. Rutebeuf's "poetry

---

9. For more on this as a general topos, see Regalado, *Poetic Patterns*, 283.
10. Dufournet, *Rutebeuf: Poèmes de l'Infortune*, préface, esp. 10–11.

of misfortune" often reveals separation between the present (characterized by wisdom but also by poverty due to his past sins), the time of his becoming impoverished (the past time of his "folie" in the tavern), and the future, with its promise of better times. He says in "Li mariages Rutebeuf": "Saveiz coumant je me demaing? / L'esperance de l'andemain" (Do you know how I get by? The hope of the morrow") (vv. 113–14). He is typically outside the tavern looking back or looking forward, unlike the goliard poets of the ecstatic lyric moment (in, e.g., "In taberna quando sumus").[11] In the entirety of the three clear-cut tavern poems, he is never still wealthy, he is always already poor, and the only time we glimpse him actually engaged in dicing is in the past.

> Li enviauz que je savoie
> M'ont avoie quanque j'avoie
> Et fors voiie,
> Et fors de voie desvoiie.
> Foux enviaus ai envoiie,
> Or m'en souvient.
> Or voi ge bien tot va tot vient . . .
>
> ("La griesche d'yver," vv. 43–49)

> [The eager gamers whom I met
> Have had from me all my wealth
> And led me astray,
> And turned me from my path.
> Foolish gamers I've tricked as well,
> Now I do remember.
> Now I see well that everything goes, everything comes . . .]

His poetry seems always to flee the present moment. "La griesche d'yver" is in a present-time mode, but the choice of season—winter—and the suffering implied suffuses the poem with a nostalgia for the past summer of warmth, as well as with hope for the coming summer.[12] "La griesche d'esté" is initially in the past as the author laments his folly, but then it

---

11. In "Le Dit des ribauds de greve" (*OC* 1:200), the critique is framed in the form of an address from outside the tavern to those inside: "Ribauds, vous voila . . ."

12. Winter is typically the season of Rutebeuf's wisdom, but at the same time, it represents the continuing folly of those whom he satirizes. See "L'Estat du monde," v. 4, for example.

moves into the present as it mockingly describes not Rutebeuf but other, nonreformed gamblers. Rutebeuf is looking not only back at himself but in on the tavern from outside.

This fracturing of time and place via the narrative/historical and the descriptive, as opposed to the lyric present and the personal confession of the courtly "I," has been discussed by Paul Zumthor. He distinguishes between the "romane" aesthetic of Thibaut de Champagne and the "gothique" aesthetic of Rutebeuf via a comparison of Thibaut's "Contre le tens qui devise" and Rutebeuf's "La griesche d'esté." He notes that "la chanson s'oppose à la durée vécue, à l'expérience, à la memoire [of "La griesche d"esté"]" and that the "je" of Thibaut is the "sujet d'actions typiques . . . de caractère abstraite" while that of Rutebeuf's is the "object d'actions particulières" in situations "dépourvues d'ambiguité."[13] He concludes that the "je" of the chanson is a "je exemplaire, a-historique" while that of Rutebeuf evidences a break between the "je" and the "extérieur" so that "cette séparation . . . rend possible une séparation du poète et du poème."

A critique of the tavern in terms of an apparently autobiographical experience where the subjective "I" writes the story of the objective "me" of the past is a new phenomenon in the comico-realist literary tradition. Rutebeuf's poems also constitute the first such critique that functions not as subgenre but as an independent genre: the critique is not "framed" by a larger, encompassing form, such as a miracle play, biblical parable, or sermon. The elements of (apparent) autobiography and generic independence characterize the works of two authors whose treatment of the tavern constitutes both its chronological and its thematic culmination—Rutebeuf and Adam de la Halle.

Like Rutebeuf's poems, Adam's *Le Jeu de la Feuillée* has often been read in an autobiographical fashion by literary scholars. As stated earlier, such approaches have fallen into disfavor—an attitude with which I agree.[14] However, these two writers do have important implications for the question of writing about the self. Both certainly make use of what I will call an "autobiographical mode of presentation," in which the "I" of

---

13. Zumthor, "'Roman' et 'Gothique,'" 1231–33. We have already seen an example of this in a passage from "La griesche d'yver" cited earlier (vv. 52–57).

14. More generally, autobiographical approaches to reading the High Middle Ages, such as Colin Morris' *The Discovery of the Individual, 1050–1200* or Georg Misch's earlier *A History of Autobiography in Antiquity,* have been supplanted by a general agreement on the absence of true autobiography in the Middle Ages. Philippe Lejeune, for example, places its origins in the eighteenth century *(Le pacte autobiographique).* See also Zumthor, "Autobiographie au Moyen Age?" in *Langue, texte, énigme,* 165–80.

a given text is represented as corresponding to the author of that text, but where the "I" is exemplary of a general poetic tradition. This mode of presentation will also be understood as including a temporal/narrative component.[15] Rutebeuf and Adam's use of this mode does not serve to reveal the life or personality of the individual author, however. Rather it allows both writers to establish a critical distance from the tavern. We saw that earlier critiques, such as sermons and the two other Arras dramas, tend to use the tavern at a subgeneric level in order to allow an "escape" from this locale: the larger generic space offers the framework for the critique. Here, however, the autobiographical split between the writing, subjective "I" and the objective "me" being described by the "autobiographer" allow for the presentation of a "me" inside the tavern—and the language of poetry—and an "I" at least potentially on the outside.[16]

The autobiographical mode of presentation can be seen in this light as closely connected to the concept of the poetic emblem elaborated by Cerquiglini. It operates with respect to the poem the way the poetic markers of one-eyedness or poverty operate with respect to the poem's imagined audience—as indicators of self-consciousness and critical distance. Both constitute representations of a fundamental separation of the poet

---

15. This is essentially the distinction established by Paul Zumthor between the "je" of the "romane" aesthetic and that of the "gothique." See Zumthor, " 'Roman' et 'Gothique' " and *Langue, texte, énigme.* For a discussion of the exemplarity of the medieval "je" (as opposed to the "personal" nature of the "je" found in true autobiography), the classic work is Spitzer, "Note on the Poetical and Empirical 'I.' "

16. The changing generic status of the tavern in the twelfth and thirteenth centuries actually reflects the process of appropriation of this locus into a broad spectrum of vernacular literature. The tavern piece in the hands of the goliards is an independent genre, but at the same time, it is a relatively marginal genre, whose rhetorical space offers an escape from the normal rules governing literary and economic exchange; this escapist quality in fact is intimately linked to the socially marginal character of the genre, practiced primarily by clerics in a non-vernacular tongue (Latin) usually reserved for less profane purposes. The assimilation of the tavern piece into vernacular literature, and into more central literary genres and a more central literary function, is marked by its demotion to a subgenre. The theater exploits the transgressive character of the existing marginal genre to produce a vision of an illicit rhetorical, economical, and ethical space that can be framed in a larger generic depiction of the miraculous triumph (either real or, in the case of Jean Bodel, only ostensible) of virtue and semiotic rectitude. The same process also occurs in exempla and other pieces of vernacular didactic literature of a religious nature. Rutebeuf, by opening personal poetry to the possibility of historicity and a separation between poet and poem, allows the tavern piece to again assume full generic status in some cases, so that the critique of the tavern space, which in the theater and the exempla was "generically framed," can now become an all-encompassing vision once again, framed within the personal consciousness of the (exemplary) poet. Thus Rutebeuf could be read as Courtois d'Arras, returned from the tavern having realized the errors of his ways, writing his own story.

from his or her social milieu and tradition. Both Cerquiglini and Zumthor, while rejecting straightforward autobiographical readings, therefore still locate in Rutebeuf an important moment in the rise of poetic consciousness and individual identity in western Europe. Poverty and autobiographical presentation turn out to be intimately related in Rutebeuf's case. To the extent that these breaks are seen as effective and that the emblems are read as true signs of critical distance, Rutebeuf may be seen as a "redemptive" figure, a moralist and "teller of truths."

A third and final break is needed, however, for the poet to finally speak the truth about himself and society. Not only wealth and clothing or unreflective engagement in vice inhibit the speaking of the truth in thirteenth-century poetic tradition. Poetic language and the practice of poetry itself can do so as well. One could argue that in choosing to write, the medieval poet places himself under the aegis of a poetic tradition whose form and content often decisively dominate the production of meaning. Such a circumstance could be read, in modern terms, as representing a crisis of intentionality in (poetic) language. In more medieval terms, one could say that to speak with a poetic voice was often seen as a vitiation of the ability to speak the truth. Precisely for this reason, discourses that sought to mark themselves as "true" turned to the use of prose in the early thirteenth century. By Rutebeuf's time, both historical writing and romance had moved largely to prose, in part due to a generalized suspicion of the truthfulness of verse. One translation of this attitude in Rutebeuf is his consistent rejection of the "courtly" mode, which was typically allied to the courtly love lyric and versified courtly romance, culminating in Guillaume de Lorris' portion of *The Romance of the Rose*.

"La griesche d'yver" (*OC* 1:184–89) opens in an anticourtly mode, opposed to the normal springtime motif of the courtly exordium, and this anticourtly motif is specifically linked to the poet's poverty.

> Contre le tenz qu'aubres deffuelle,
> Qu'il ne remaint en branche fuelle
> Qui n'aut a terre,
> Por povretei qui moi aterre,
> Qui de toute part me muet guerre,
> Contre l'yver,
> Dont mout me sont changié li ver,
> Mon dit commence . . .

(vv. 1–8)

[At the time when the trees shed their foliage,
So that no leaf remains on any branch
Which does not descend to earth,
Because of poverty that brings me down,
And attacks me from every angle,
In the wintertime,
When my verses tell a whole new tale,
I begin my story . . .]

Is specifically the rhetoric of courtly literature impoverished in this instance? Or does Rutebeuf's own poverty suggest a rejection of the false promise of poetic richness offered by the worn-out genres of courtly poetry? "Li mariages Rutebeuf" can offer a clearer answer to these questions. This poem presents an "autobiographical" portrait of the author and his woes—in this case the woes of marriage. Michel Rousse has noted that Rutebeuf places the date of his marriage as the first of January. He points out that such a date not only was unlikely in the Middle Ages but also was the traditional date of the widely practiced Fête des Fous. This burlesque ceremony typically featured the singing of farcical versions of Latin hymns; men, especially clerics, disguising themselves as women or jongleurs; and general revelry concentrating on "l'inversion de l'ordre normal." Appropriately, Rutebeuf proceeds to invert the normal opening found in courtly poetry, as in "La griesche d'yver": the woman is changed from beauty to hag in what Rousse describes as "une véritable désacralisation de la femme dans un univers bétourné à l'invers, qui est celui de la folie" (a veritable desacralization of the woman in a universe turned upside down, a universe of madness).[17]

En l'an soixante,
Qu'abres ne fuelle, oizel ne chante,
Fis je toute la riens dolante
Qui de cuer m'aimme.

("Li mariages Rutebeuf," vv. 4–7)

Et si n'est pas jone ne bele:
Cinquante anz a en son escuele,
C'est maigre et seche.

---

17. Rousse, "Le Mariage de Rutebeuf et la fête des Fous," 439.

N'ai mais poaour qu'ele me treche!

(vv. 35–38)

[In the year sixty,
When the trees were leafless, and the birds were silent,
I accomplished the sorrow of the one
Who loves me with all her heart.]

[She's not at all young or pretty:
She's got fifty years under her belt,
And she's thin and dry.
I'm not worried that she'll betray me!]

Punning on Jaufre Rudel's famous "amor de lonh," the poet notes that because of the wife he has gotten, "Je cuit que Dex le debonaires / M'aimme de loing" (I believe that our good Lord loves me from afar) (vv. 54–55). Rousse also locates a number of typical Rutebeuf puns and instances of wordplay, such as "N'ai pas buche de chesne encemble: / Quant g'i suis, si a fou et tremble" (There is no shrub of oak together: But when I'm there, doesn't flame and shake) (vv. 68–69), wherein "fou" can mean either "fol" (foolish), a hedge, or "feu" (fire). "Tremble" could be regarded either as a form of the verb *trembler* or as a reference to the aspen tree, and "buche" could refer to both a fire and a bush. Language is destabilized and genre subverted in this complicated series of double and triple references. Noting that, as in the poetics of dice, "chaque phrase risque de se muer en son contraire" (each phrase threatens to turn into its opposite), Rousse argues that the poem is in large part about nothing but linguistic jokes and the undermining of genres.

The inversionary quality of Rutebeuf's poetry has received attention from several readers, especially but not exclusively in its anticourtly expression.[18] This is typical of Rutebeuf, whose "rude" language—he writes of "Rutebuez qui rudement huevre" (Rutebeuf who works "rudedly") in "Li mariages Rutebeuf" (v. 45)[19]—seems to especially resist and seek to disengage from the courtly poetic tradition. While Rousse suggests that the "autobiographical" content of the poem is simply the

---

18. See Berthelot, "Anti-Miracle et Anti-Fabliaux"; Zink, "Bonheurs de l'inconséquence" (Zink stresses the "esthétique de la rupture" that predominates in Rutebeuf); Dufournet, "A la recherche de Rutebeuf" (Dufournet stresses his opposition to courtliness).

19. For other occurrences of this formula in Rutebeuf, see *OC* 1:3.

difficulty of the act of writing itself, the difficulty of mimetic reference for the poet, it seems that the language of the courtly tradition is a particular target here. It is not clear whether Rousse understands this "autobiographical content" (his phrase) to be truly a statement by Rutebeuf about his personal relation to language and poetic tradition, so that an indirect personal reading is possible, or whether he considers this relation to be exemplary of that of all poets to language. My own reading leans to the latter interpretation, since I am considering Rutebeuf as an exemplary high medieval urban poet.

The inversion of, and disengagement from, the poetic language of courtliness is thus linked by Rutebeuf both to his poverty and nakedness and to *folie*. The two figures of poverty and folly are in fact generally connected in Rutebeuf's poetry. He evokes his alter ego the "fou" on many occasions,[20] and we will see in the remainder of the discussion of Rutebeuf that the fool and folly are even more revealing emblems than poverty and nakedness for understanding Rutebeuf's relation to his culture, himself, the practice of poetry, and language in general. The opening line of "La griesche d'esté"—"En recordant ma grant folie"—serves to encapsulate virtually Rutebeuf's entire poetic essence, linking as it does the subjective distance of autobiographical presentation, the social and moral concept of the fool (an "être à part," as Philippe Ménard calls him),[21] and the poverty that results through folly—the three marks that authorize Rutebeuf's representation of self, intention, and society. Even more important, however, the medieval connotations of *folie* combine to suggest the final failure of Rutebeuf's project of speaking the naked truth, about either society or self.

As was the case with poverty, folly had multiple and contradictory connotations in the Middle Ages, though many of them overlap with those of poverty.[22] From a religious standpoint, medieval folly is the folly of vice but also the wisdom of the biblical "wise fool." From a secular point of view, it is akin to the social failure connoted by poverty, yet the court fool is, like the poor urban poet, the privileged teller of truths—the only person who can insult the king. With its competing senses in both the secular and religious realms, folly approximates poverty as an enigmatic emblem for

---

20. See "Les plaies du monde," v. 69; "Li mariages Rutebeuf," vv. 21, 42; "La complainte," v. 83; "La griesche d'esté," v. 1.

21. Ménard, "Les Fous."

22. See Fritz, *Le discours du fou;* Ménard, "Les Fous"; Ménard, "Les Emblèmes de la folie dans la littérature and dans l'art"; Billington, *A Social History of the Fool;* Santucci, "Le Fou dans les lettres françaises médiévales."

the poet. As with poverty, the choice of which connotation is to be emphasized—social or religious, negative or positive—is a critical determinant in reading Rutebeuf's poems. Thus Rutebeuf's escape from the past folly invoked in "La griesche d'esté" proceeds into the renewing and demystifying folly of the Feast of Fools, which Rutebeuf adopts implicitly elsewhere in his critique of the mendicant orders, hypocrisy, and so forth. An extended reading of folly would largely replicate that already done with poverty. Instead, I would like to examine an important linguistic connotation of *folie* that has received less attention.

In the mid–thirteenth century, the French theologian Guilelmus Peraldus produced a tract on the seven deadly sins that was one of the three most widely read of all works on this topic in this century.[23] For him, as for many medieval moralists, the greatest of sins is pride. As with the other sins he treats, he divides pride into outer and inner manifestations. The first outer manifestation is adornment. He interprets this as a form of exhibitionism of the human body, an exhibitionism that to Peraldus seems ridiculous given the imperfect, mortal nature of the body.[24]

We have already seen that adornment of the body was often used as a metaphor for the use of signs in the Middle Ages. The body was viewed as the natural object, the referent, and adornment was equivalent to the "representation" of the body, the sign that evoked the referent. This representation was furthermore often viewed as inadequate to its task, as the garment was frequently ill fitting. A further failure of representation, in church moralists' eyes, occurred when the garment did not simply cover the body, for the sake of warmth or protection, but rather drew attention to itself. This was most often the case with the prostitute; with the jongleur, who was noted for wearing baggy and ill-fitting rags on many occasions; and most important for our purposes here, with the fool, who either sported a colorful, bicolored hat with bells and baubles on top, as well as bicolored garments of the same sort, or was dressed in tatters and rags much like the jongleur.[25] The jongleur, the prostitute, and the fool (along with the wealthy with their luxurious garments) were therefore emblematic of the sin of pride in the mortal body (as well as their supposed misuse of

---

23. *Summa seu tractatus de virtutibus et vitiis* (1236 and 1249). The other two works were *Summa casuum poenitentiae* by Pennaforte (1220s and 1230s) and *Somme le roy* by Friar Laurent (1279). See Bloomfield, *The Seven Deadly Sins*, 123–24.

24. See Billington, *A Social History of the Fool*, 20. Peraldus is generally considered important for his association of the fool with the devil in especially explicit terms.

25. Billington, *A Social History of the Fool*, 1–4; Ménard, "Les Fous."

this body for the sake of profit), due to their tendency to misrepresent that body and to draw attention to the act of representation itself.

The real sin of these prideful sinners, however, was not simply the prideful misrepresentation of the imperfect and mortal human body. It was rather the use of signs—themselves contaminated in church eyes (due to their physical nature) by the imperfections and mortality of earthly existence—as a profession and for private profit.[26] While even the church fathers recognized the degraded and imperfect nature of the sign in the physical world, they also recognized the necessity of using the signs as best as possible. The use of signs per se was not a sin (though it reflected, and was a result of, the original sin). Rather a pride in the sign, as object itself rather than as representer, was at the heart of the sin of adornment. In church eyes the sin of the prostitute, the jongleur, and the fool was that they adorned rather than simply covering and clothing. The pride is really in the presumption of appropriating God's instrument of representation for their own idolatrous purposes and thus to a certain extent in establishing themselves as rivals to God as definers of the use and meaning of signs.

Several instances of the conjoining of the fool and the poet can be found in medieval French literature, in addition to those in Rutebeuf (and Adam de la Halle). (Recall that the Feast of Fools often involved otherwise upstanding citizens dressing up as jongleurs, among other possibilities.) Not only did jongleurs often "play the fool" according to the literature, but in Wace's *Brut* we find an example of a character who disguises himself as a jongleur, only to be described as appearing to be a "lecheor ou fol."[27] The qualification of "lecheor" serves to clearly underline the fool's (and the jongleur's) fascination with the body, just as Peraldus suggests. And, as we saw in chapter 3, this word connotes their fascination with the body of the text as well. In this light, the tavern is a key feature in the geography of folly. It is the locus of the jongleur, of the prostitute, and most generally of the adorned and the adorner, the player with signs. As source of comico-realist literature, the tavern is the place where people are fascinated by the body and/or the text—where people engage in *folie*. (The association of pride with the tavern may come as a surprise since typically gluttony is the classic sin located in the tavern. But gluttony is just an

---

26. Interestingly, Eugene Vance locates a similar conjunction of carnal lust and the use of signs in Augustine, and there as well, both transgressions are figured as products of pride. See Vance, "The Functions and Limits of Autobiography," 403.

27. For more on these and other examples of the "jongleur fou," see Fritz, *Le discours du fou,* 329. The quote is from v. 9110 of *Wace* (ed. Ivor Arnold).

excess desire for the physical, while the pride in question here is specifically a pride in the physical and mortal. Indeed, we have seen that the real gluttonous transgression of the tavern is the desire for the sign itself, whether linguistic or monetary. Pride in the sign and gluttonous desire for the sign are the marks of all of the works we have considered. In all cases, the public instrument of communication is subverted and transformed into physical commodity for private profit.)

In this light, folly is an emblem of not only social and moral but linguistic transgression against proper ecclesiastical models. This would then be the folly of poetic practice that Rutebeuf seems to locate in the courtly tradition. Since this linguistically negative sense of folly can be allied to its socially and religiously negative senses, it seems reasonable to search for an equivalent positive sense to the fool—a naked rather than an adorned fool. Such a representation of the fool does in fact exist. But its implications, rather than supporting an authorization of "naked truth," instead go to the heart of the reasons for the impossibility of Rutebeuf's poetic project and reveal an ambiguity centered on the question of the status of language in the thirteenth century, an ambiguity that probes far more deeply into the questions of sin, guilt, repentance, and confession than does the figure of poverty.

One can return, in fact, to Peraldus. For it turns out that the second outer manifestation of pride is precisely nakedness—the twin of adornment. How could this also be seen as a manifestation of pride? Nakedness would seem to be emblematic of the absence of an attempt to represent in any way. On the contrary, from an ecclesiastical standpoint, nakedness really represents the presumption of the possibility of perfect representation, of access to the "truth" in its purest form. Thus no clothing was needed in the Garden of Eden, but after the Fall, humanity was forced to adopt the use of the sign—clothing, which symbolically represents the loss of nakedness and perfect reference. Nakedness is the presumption that perfect representation, meaning no "representation" at all, is possible in the fallen, degraded world of the high medieval sign. Since clothes are used as a metaphor for the sign, dispensing with clothes becomes symbolic of the attempt to dispense with the imperfections inherent in the use of all worldly signs. The best one could do with signs was to try to limit the imperfection, to use the signs with goodwill and good intention. While the abuse of these signs through ill will and misrepresentation was clearly a sin, the presumption that one could attain a perfection of representation, symbolized by nakedness, was equally a sin of pride, since one then presumed an ability to represent and communicate that could be attained only by God. (He also implicitly denied the reality of the Fall and original sin: Adam and Eve were the last properly naked humans, before the fateful taste of the apple that Adam de la Halle evokes at the end of *Le Jeu de la Feuillée*.) The naked man rivaled God as did the adorned man.[28]

The concept of pride in the naked letter recalls the common medieval condemnation of devotion to the letter, as opposed to the sense of the letter. Idolatry of the sign and the prideful belief in the naked truth of the sign are intimately related concepts. The linking of the nakedly literal with pride is an important medieval idea, crystallized in the tale of Croesus and Phanie in *The Romance of the Rose*. Croesus, who was fittingly the king who instituted the monetary sign—the coin—and who was proverbially devoted to wealth, has a dream wherein he is bathed and dried by Jupiter and Phoebus. Quite pleased by the image of two such gods bathing him, "il come fos s'enorguilli" (Like a fool he became filled with pride) (v. 6512), and he proceeds to misinterpret the dream as a positive augur. Phanie mocks his pride and tells him that the dream really foretells his death by hanging. But Croesus, "Touz pleins d'orgueil e de folie" (All full of pride and folly) (v. 6598), responds that "Cist nobles songes, / Ou fausse glose voulez metre, / deit estre entenduz a la letre" (This noble dream, which you wish to falsely gloss, must be understood literally) (vv. 6608–10). Pride, folly, and a belief in the "naked" perfection of the literal sign are embodied in Croesus, the devotee of the coin, who is bathed—no doubt in a naked state—by the gods. The true folly of his position is revealed by his subsequent demise.

The sin of pride, in both its outer manifestations as depicted by Peraldus, is the sin of pride in representation. It involves pride not only in the mortal, imperfect body but in physical, imperfect signs—either in abusing them through adornment or in assuming one's access to the perfect, naked Word. This dual nature of pride is also captured by Alain de Lille in *De planctu Naturae*. He writes that excessive outer adornment is an indication of the pride of the mind within (*DPN* 185), but he then notes that outward

---

28. See Hunt, "Rhetoric and Poetics in Twelfth-Century France," 169, for the medieval insistence on the need for the *integumentum,* from Augustine through the Neoplatonists. Poets went so far as to say that the failure to use the *integumenta* was a profanation of nature; thus came about the scandal of the "naked truth." See also Spence, *Texts and the Self in the Twelfth Century,* chap. 1, on the patristic association of the naked body and sin.

See Baumgartner, "The Play of Temporalities," especially 35, for more on the concept of medieval literary endeavor as a search for the "nakedness of the Word." Clearly, the Word must indeed be naked to God, but words, as corporeal signs, by their very nature veil such nakedness. In another standard example of the dangers of the temptation of perfection, Rutebeuf's *La vie de Sainte Marie l'Egyptienne* (*OC* 1:397–469) features a monk named Zozimas whose greatest fear is that he may be overcome by pride in his own virtue.

silence (a seeming lack of representation, we could say) can also be a sign of inward pride (186). More important, he portrays the dual nature of the poet's sin in the same work. Nature demands:

> Do you not know how the poets present falsehood, naked and without protection of a covering, to their audiences so that . . . they may . . . intoxicate the bewitched ears of their hearers? Or how they cover false-hood with a kind of imitation of probability? (140)

This linking of pride to representation helps to suggest the deeper significance of the common medieval topos of the author's insistence on his lack of pride. Alain uses this same topos in the introduction to his *Anti-claudianus:* "It was no congestion of inward pride . . . that drove me to compose this work" (p. 42).[29] We have also seen in several cases that those who have confidence in the absolute trustworthiness of language and the sign often end up ironically naked, losing their cloak, as in *Courtois d'Ar-ras* or "Boivin de Provins." While these two texts approach the question of language from opposite points of view, one denouncing and one celebrat-ing the potential of its imperfection, both agree on the need for an aware-ness of the complex, nontransparent nature of texts and mock as naked fools those who lack such awareness.

Fittingly, the medieval figure of the fool was often represented not just as colorfully clothed but sometimes as naked, at least in the period prior to 1350.[30] The two states are even combined in the anonymous thirteenth-century romance *Amadas et Idoine.* Amadas, temporarily insane, is wit-nessed by another character, who sees

> Amadas trestout nu venir,
> Tous déguisés, en crins tondus,
> Com cil qui a le sens perdus.
>
> (vv. 2722–24)

---

29. For yet another linking of the concepts of nakedness and adornment, specifically in the person of the jongleur, see Thomas of Cobham's remarks in a twelfth-century penitential. Speaking of "histrionum," he relates: "Quidam transformant et transfigurant corpora sua per turpes saltus et per turpes gestus, vel denudando se turpiter, vel induendo horribiles lar-vas" (cited in Faral, *Les jongleurs,* 67). This quote also clearly anticipates the fool and his activities in *Le Jeu de la Feuillée.*

30. Billington, *A Social History of the Fool,* 4–5; Ménard, "Les Fous," 436.

[Amadas quite naked proceeding,
All disguised, wearing shorn horsehair,
Like one who has lost his senses.]

The paradox of simultaneous nakedness and disguise suggests a paradox of language in which Rutebeuf, we will see, finds himself trapped, and it also underlines the transgressive natures of both disguising adornment and nakedness as prideful abuses of the sign. By using nakedness and adornment as the two manifestations of pride, Peraldus allies the fool to these two outer manifestations of pride and to pride in general, just as the story of Croesus has already suggested. The fool is unaware of the Fall, of the necessity of clothing and representation, and also ignores the need for adequate, useful, unadorned clothing. He is the incarnation of pride in representation. The fool is thus the perfect emblem for the professional "representer"—the poet.

The linguistic sense of folly elaborated here can help clarify the equivalent linguistic sense of poverty in Rutebeuf. We have seen that "La griesche d'yver" opens with an image of Rutebeuf's poverty (see vv. 1–8, quoted earlier in this chapter). The poverty of his purse is then paralleled by an insistence on the poverty of his language.

Mon dit commence trop diver
De povre estoire.
Povre sens et povre memoire
M'a Diex donei . . .

(vv. 8–11)

[I begin my story all wrong
From a poor history.
Poor sense and poor memory
Has God given me . . .]

Yet ironically, Rutebeuf, as much as any French medieval poet, uses a language characterized by an extreme surplus of sense—his language is not so much "poor" as overflowing with polyvalent and often ironically contradictory meanings. Thus in verses 19–21, he writes, as regards the effect of the "griesche" (dice and dice games):

Bien me paie, bien me delivre,
Contre le sout me rent la livre
De grand poverte.

[I am well paid, well acquitted;
For a sou I receive a pound
Of great poverty.]

"Delivre" means simultaneously that he is acquitted of his debts and also, literally, that he is separated from "la livre," his money. "La livre" itself only briefly means money and wealth and is redefined by the following phrase into "a wealth of poverty." This use of an ambiguous term at a syntactic nexus is characteristic of the style of Rutebeuf. Even more characteristically, not only does the meaning slip from one signification to another, but the two meanings are contradictory. The use of "la livre"—with its monetary connotation—to evoke his poverty also resonates ironically with his earlier lament about his "povre sens": his claim of linguistic poverty is subverted by the wealth of meanings contained in his statement of that claim. Similarly, poverty becomes a great burden: "Et ge que fais, / Qui de povretei sent le fais?" (And what can I do, who so feels the burden of poverty?) (vv. 66–67). Literally the weight of "nothing"—no possessions—weighs upon him. Debt is similarly a burden: "De sa dete pas ne s'aquite, / Ansois s'encombre" (From his debt he gains no relief, but rather is more burdened) (vv. 77–78). The word "s'aquite" initially takes a financial sense due to the word "dete," but in the light of its opposition to "s'encombre," it takes on the physical sense of relief from an actual burden as well. Rutebeuf ironically "acquires" poverty and debt through a process of "dépouillement" (see "despoille" in v. 38), or stripping away, that reduces him to nakedness.

Griesche li at corru seure,
Desnuei l'at en petit d'eure.

(vv. 85–86)

[Unlucky gaming had the best of him,
And unclothed him in no time at all.]

Thus he possesses a lack of possessions and acquires this possession through a depossessing.

To complicate matters further, the image of the dice turning a "sout" into a "livre" is a classic figure for usury, seen in both of the dramas of Arras. In using this figure, Rutebeuf evokes what a medieval moralist might call the "usuriously" overproductive nature of his poetics.[31] Just as dice have the potential to revalue the money wagered with every toss, each succeeding line of Rutebeuf's poem destabilizes, revalues, and amplifies the meanings of that which precedes. The poem's language becomes richer and richer as it narrates the poet's progressive monetary impoverishment. The process of creating poetry becomes a dice game with language, a game where the poet keeps on winning right to the end, as the dice/poetic process enriches the "sout" into "la livre," which is so tantalizingly close to "le livre"—the book, or the text.

It should also be noted that the sou and the livre existed in circulation as actual coins in northern France at the time of Rutebeuf but were also widely used as "money of account"—theoretical accounting aids having no actual physical presence in a transaction. Thus the "sou . . . livre" phrase suggests that what is really going on here is simply a playing with signs (just as the usurer through a loan, and similarly the dice player through dice playing, "plays" with money to make more money rather than using it to buy or sell a commodity). The whole game of the poem is all about nothing at all except the poem itself in a very real sense. This same conundrum is suggested in verses 29–30 with the words "De mon avoir ne sai la soume, / Qu'il n'i at point" (Of my wealth I do not know the extent, for there is none at all). Since he has already established that his "avoir" or lack of it is to be reckoned in linguistic terms (vv. 4–10), it is hard not to read the word "soume" with its medieval connotation of the "sense" of language, the deeper meaning behind the surface denotation of the words.[32] Thus "il n'i at point [de soume]" in his "ver . . . [et] estoire" (vv. 7, 9). In this light, the poem recalls the circularity and involution of

---

31. This act of specifically thematizing his poetics as illicit is particularly important for Rutebeuf, since he uses basically the same poetics in his devotional and polemic texts. Indeed, his intricate plays with *annominatio* and other rhetorical devices derive in many cases from the Latin liturgical tradition, where their use was quite "proper" (see Regalado, *Poetic Patterns,* 222ff.). Thus, key here is not the poetics but rather its thematization via illicit economics and overproduction.

32. We find, for example, in Greimas *(Dictionnaire de l'ancien français)* the definition "Ce qu'il y a de plus important, l'essentiel, le capital," as in Marie de France's "de ceo vus dirai ja la summe" ("Lanval," v. 146). A related definition is that given by Greimas as "résumé," as in Marie de France's "Ceo fu la summe de l'escrit" ("Chievrefoil," v. 61), suggesting the fundamental narrative or logical content, as opposed to the artistic elaboration of that content (often termed the *escorce).*

William IX's famous troubadour chanson "Sur dreit ren" (On nothing at all).

In the end, Rutebeuf turns out to be at least partly correct about his poverty of "sens." Poetry has produced a wealth of linguistic senses or significations but no deeper "soume" or referential sense behind the various senses of the words, except perhaps for the message that there is no such sense. He suggests that he has bought poetry at the expense of sense, so the poetic dice game has indeed left him poor of "sens." The "soume" or "sens" of his language corresponds to the coins in his purse: both have been exhausted in exchange for a wealth of poetic senses.

The poet's victimization by the dice is emphasized in part by the fact that he is most often object while the dice are subject.

> Li dei que li decier ont fait
> M'ont de ma robe tot desfait,
> Li dei m'ocient,
> Li dei m'agaitent et espient,
> Li dei m'assaillent et desfient,
> Ce poize moi.
>
> (vv. 52–57)

> [The dice that the dice maker made
> Have robbed me of my robe,
> The dice are killing me,
> They lie in wait and spy on me,
> The assault me and defy me,
> And I am greatly aggrieved.]

The "hazardous" poetics of the tavern write the poet, rather than the reverse. From another point of view, the poet has written the text that now writes the poet, and he has imbricated himself in a cycle of loss of sense and authority that he cannot escape. Here, then, is the same linguistic trap that was discussed earlier. But in this case, the poetics of *folie*—the inversionary, destabilizing poetics of "Li mariages Rutebeuf"—constitutes the trap. This is a new poetic language and practice that undermines the poet's authority and "sens."

In the poem, there is at least a crisis of confidence in the words of the poet, or more precisely in the value of both the "soume" of his words and the sum in his coin purse. As the poem ends, he is sent away with the advice to try and buy himself a new cloak on credit (vv. 91–93). However, though he has produced plenty of verbal senses, he seems lacking in both money and the ability to have his words "credited": he is told that if the cloth merchant will not lend to him, he will have to go to the bankers at the fair (vv. 94–96), which he does. "Or ai ma paie," he concludes (v. 105), though the pay seems more moral than financial here, as he is in even more debt than before. He who attempts to be usurer (with language and dice) is ironically himself the victim of usury, as the cycle of debt and desire reiterates itself.

Given this ending to "La griesche d'yver," it seems reasonable to read Rutebeuf as a fundamentally moralist poet. Michel Zink, perhaps the poet's most perspicacious recent reader and editor, has seen in not only the overtly religious poems but also those of "misfortune" a "courant poétique [qui] relève d'une inspiration religieuse, morale et satirique." At the same time, however, he sees an essential "inquiétude" in Rutebeuf regarding the act of writing.[33] Because of the irony with which Rutebeuf treats his own inquietude, and because of the dazzling fashion by which he expresses his disquiet by making use of the very poetic processes that so disquiet him, the "griesche" poems suggest a poetic self-consciousness, as well as a detachment from the tradition in which he operates, that rarely characterizes the strictly moralizing versifiers who are so common in the Middle Ages. In Rutebeuf's case, this is more than a critical distance from either society or self, which is typical of most moralists; it is an awareness of a disjunction between language and "pure truth." "La griesche d'yver" suggests a need to disengage not just from courtly discourse but from the discourse that operates against it as well. His poetry will finally suggest a need to disengage from all language. This critical awareness of the insufficiency of the language of his morality will ironically undermine the possibility of a distance from—an ability to "read"—either self or society fully.

Rutebeuf's poverty, in this light, can be seen as part of a critique of the moral and especially linguistic status of his poetic practice. Writing poetry means selling out referential sense, exhausting his purse, and becoming figuratively impotent, even as he produces his dazzling wealth of verbal senses. In its ambiguity, "La griesche d'yver" stands at the crossroads between a text such as *Courtois d'Arras,* which presents a stern critique of the poetics, economics, and ethics of the tavern and of

---

33. *OC* 1:23, 25.

secular literary practice in general, and fabliaux such as "Boivin de Provins," which offers a celebration of the nearly infinite multivalent potential of language.

"La griesche d'este" echoes many of the themes of the first poem. Rutebeuf explicitly establishes an identity between "joueur" and "jongleur."

> Or vos dirai de lor [les joueurs] couvainne:
> G'en sai asseiz;
> Sovent an ai estei lasseiz.
> Mei mars que li froiz est passeiz,
> Notent et chantent.
> Li un et li autre se vantent
> Que, se dui dei ne les enchantent,
> Il auront robe.
>
> (vv. 47–54)

> [Now I will tell you of the gamer's ways:
> I know plenty about it;
> I have often been taken in by it.
> In mid-March when the cold is gone,
> They play and sing.
> Each and every one boasts
> That if the two dice don't bewitch them,
> They'll be clothed well enough.]

The playing and singing at the beginning of spring evoke the traditional exordium of the courtly chanson and, more generally, the practice of composing poetry. Rutebeuf also uses the notion of bewitchment ("enchantent," rhymed with "chantent") to link the effects of dice and those of poetry or song. In either case, the result of the enchantment is poverty, and even when one has money,

> Ne s'en vont pas longue chargent:
> Por ce que li argens art gent,
> N'en ont que faire,
> Ainz entendent a autre afaire:
> Au tavernier font dou vin traire.
>
> (vv. 73–77)

[They don't go about long weighed down:
Because money burns people,
They've got nothing to do with it,
But think about other pastimes:
They have the tavern keeper pour some wine.]

Dice and poetry are even more intimately connected here than in the first poem, and the poetics of the tavern is once again a poetics of poverty.

Given this poverty, Rutebeuf's opening his poem on dice playing with an invocation of *folie* thus serves to underline the theme of disjunction and absence that Rutebeuf develops so strongly throughout his poetry. *Folie* is the figure not only of pride but of absence—the figural distance between the adorning or naked sign and its desired referent. R. A. Shoaf refers to Aristotle's claim that money represents a kind of "folly" since it reduces everything to itself—assigning vastly different commodities a given value that can always be expressed in terms of money. Language can be seen in the same way and, according to Shoaf, it was so seen by both Chaucer and Dante: the multiplicity of experience is reduced to a finite series of linguistic signs, and the attempt by human language to represent human experience is itself "folly."[34] Thus the inadequacies of the sign, whether linguistic or monetary, are represented by the gap between "sense" or "value" and its representation—some "sense" is literally lacking in the representation, and the act of representation risks becoming "folly." The gap between sign and referent are portrayed not as a surplus, an amplification of sense on the part of the sign, as in the fabliaux or *Le Jeu de Saint Nicolas,* but as a lack, a reductivity of sense by the sign—a poverty of the sign, which cannot fully signify. And this is in fact exactly the economy of Rutebeuf's "griesche" poems: the poetic process features a wealth of significations internally to the poem and also, according to Rutebeuf, a reduction of "sens" or "soume." Aristotle's "folly of the sign" in its reductivity and absence of sense is simply the other side of an unwarranted pride in representation. Thus from the church's moral point of view, the poet can be seen as the poverty-stricken fool. The poet as a figure of lacking is perhaps best captured by Isidore of Seville, who in his *Etymologies* derives "carmen" from "carere mente."[35] Poets are lacking in sense.

The opening invocation of *folie* also leads to a more general question-

---

34. Shoaf, *Dante, Chaucer, and the Currency of the Word,* esp. pp. 7–12 on Aristotle.
35. *Etymologiae* I.39.4, cited in Fritz, *Le discours du fou,* 367.

ing of the value of the poet's endeavor, for his "ouevre" (v. 10) has gone to naught.

> Ai si ouvrei
> Et en ouvrant moi aouvrei
> Qu'en ouvrant n'ai riens recouvrei
> Dont je me cuevre.
> Ci at fol ovrier et fole oeuvre
> Qui par ourveir riens ne recuevre.

(vv. 9–14)

> [I have worked so much
> And in working I worked myself out
> For in working I have recovered nothing
> With which I can cover myself.
> It is a foolish worker doing foolish work
> Who in working recovers nothing.]

There is the suggestion that no true labor has been done. Or at least the "oeuvre" has not been considered worthy of any tangible reward; and this "oeuvre" is poetry itself. Language, or at least language as used by this poet, seems to have failed Rutebeuf. Not just poetic language is at issue here, however. The poem's vocabulary suggests a particularly medieval Neoplatonic view of language (see chap. 2), a view that enlarges the scope of consideration to language in general. The rhymes with "recouvrei" (recover) and "cuevre" (cover) function here to evoke the cloak as the traditional reward of the poet and also as a symbol for representation in general, as the sign of the sign. As already seen in previous chapters, the sign both covers (negatively) and recovers (positively) its referent in medieval sign theory. Language use becomes a trap, in which the attempt at reference (recovery) automatically implicates the writer in inadequate representation (covering of the referent). The trap is nicely paralleled by the trap of dice, for as seen in chapter 3, as soon as one plays, one begins to lose and thus is obliged to continue playing in order to try and recoup one's losses, which leads further and further into debt. (Recall, however, that even as the dice lead further and further into debt of sense or reference, they lead to more and more wealth of significations.) In the title, the word "griesche" itself contains the two senses of gambling and the ill fortune that gambling inevitably brings.[36] The only solution, in terms of adequate reference or "sense," is not to play, or not to speak.

The thematic of work and the lack thereof is another indicator of a larger linguistic engagement. As seen in chapter 2, "working" with signs, whether monetary or linguistic, is not truly work at all, since it produces not a "natural" but an "artificial" profit, according to Aquinas and others. Unlike the "natural" profits from agricultural fields and farm animals, any profits Rutebeuf makes are the result of the manipulation of the "artificial" sign, which "can bear no fruit," to recall Innocent III's words. Rutebeuf is in effect accusing himself here of what church moralists would call a misuse of signs and in fact of theft (see chap. 3), since any money earned is not the result of true "production." This theme of the illegitimacy of his poetic practice recurs several times in his works.[37] Its appearance, even in his purely religious texts, is one more argument for his (and the Middle Ages') general disquiet about writing, not just a concern limited to the poetics of the tavern.

I will end my treatment of Rutebeuf with a discussion of the "La repentance Rutebeuf" (OC 1:297–303). Here again, the issue of labor is raised. Rutebeuf has never truly "earned" his living.

> J'ai touz jors engraissé ma pance
> D'autrui chateil, d'autrui sustance:
> Ci a boen clerc, a miex mentir!
>
> (vv. 19–21)

> [I've spent all my days filling my belly
> With other people's wealth and others' goods:
> What a good clerk am I, only fit for lying!]

Rutebeuf's dicey poetics may provide a wealth of signification, but there seems to be a poverty of real value or "truth." Here the moral issues raised by the tavern come clearly to the forefront. Rutebeuf establishes an elaborate series of parallels and oppositions between God and good deeds, on

---

36. OC 1:182.

37. It is often expressed in such phrases as "Since I can't work, I'll work at poetry." See "Li diz de la mensonge," vv. 1–11. See also "La vie de Sainte Elyzabel," vv. 1–15; "De Sainte Esglise," vv. 1–4. For more on this topos, see OC 1:24; Regalado, Poetic Patterns, 120; Serper, Rutebeuf, 50–53.

the one hand, and the tavern and poetry, on the other. The rhetorical opposition is expressed via the terms "rimoier" (to write rhymes) (v. 1) and "saumoier" (to make psalms) (v. 9), with the former to be abandoned in favor of the latter. He contrasts the term "geu" (v. 8) with that of "servir (Deu)" (v. 6).

> . . . onques ne me soi amoier
> A Deu servir parfaitement,
> Ainz ai mis mon entendement
> En geu et en esbatement.
>
> (vv. 5–8)

> [. . . Never have I gotten myself
> To serve God as I should;
> Rather I've put all my concentration
> Into games and amusement.]

The word "geu" is particularly rich in meaning here since it suggests at once games and amusement in general (often to be found in the tavern), dice and gambling in a more restrictive sense (clearly linked to the tavern), and, one might suppose, the "geu" of poetry, since this is the specific item that he is giving up in this poem.

He then goes on to establish the corporeal and devilish nature of "rimoier" in a following stanza.

> J'ai fait au cors sa volentei,
> J'ai fait rimes et s'ai chantei
> Sus les uns pour aux autres plaire,
> Dont Anemis m'a enchantei.
>
> (vv. 37–40)

> [I've done the will of my body,
> I've composed rhymes and sung poetry
> About some to please others,
> And the devil has enchanted me with it all.]

The link between poetry and "enchantment" not only echoes that found in "La griesche d'esté" but is all the more interesting since Adam de la Halle echoes it very closely in *Le Jeu de la Feuillée* to evoke a similar negative connotation for the poet.

Rutebeuf also notes that God "me dona sen et savoir" (gave me sense and knowledge) (v. 27), and he reiterates that God "sens me dona" (gave me sense) (v. 31). This is perhaps the same "sens" that Rutebeuf has used up (according to "La griesche d'yver") to procure the many verbal senses of his poetry. In this case, it is indeed "others'" wealth (of sense) that he has used up to earn his living through poetry.

Having established the sinful nature of his previous poetic pursuits, he ends with the lines

> Por cest siecle qui se depart
> Me couvient partir d'autre part.
> Qui que l'envie, je le las.

> (vv. 82–84)

> [From this world that is going away
> I must now go to another place.
> Whoever wants this place, he can have it.]

Verse 84 has been more loosely translated by Michel Zink as "Double la mise qui voudra, je quitte le jeu" (Whoever wants can raise the stakes; I'm quitting the game).[38] He notes that "envier" meant to continue a game by raising the stakes and that "laier" meant to quit the game. Thus the poet assimilates the practice of poetry, and carnal existence in general ("cest siecle"), to a game of dice, quite likely played in a tavern. The (implicit) tavern here echoes that of *Courtois d'Arras* in its metonymical representation of the life of the flesh, and the poetics of "rimoier" likewise echoes the poetics of the tavern of Arras. The poet notes, "Je cuidai engignier Renart: / Or n'i vallent enging ne art" (I thought I could trick Renard: now trickery and art aren't worth a thing) (vv. 79–80). The linking of "Renart" and "art," with their literary connotations, to the verb "engignier" clearly implicates the poet in the practice of a tricky and deceitful poetics parallel to that of the tavern of Arras. For Rutebeuf, the escape from the devil must be an escape from the art of "rimoier," and this constitutes no less than an escape from the tavern. Yet the space of the tavern has been

---

38. In *OC* 1:302.

expanded to cover carnal existence in general ("cest siecle"). The fact that the poem is a "repentance" and the fact that he asks, "que puis je fors la mort atendre?" (what can I do other than wait for death?) (v. 66), further emphasize the global sense of the "siecle" and game that he is leaving. But in equating the end of the poem with the end of a game of dice, Rutebeuf frames the entire poetic enterprise of the poem, including the mode of repentance, as part of the poetics that he seeks to escape; that is, he must repent in the language of which he repents. Since the poem ends with the ending of the dice game, he implies that all language, even the repentant, is ultimately engaged in the same imperfections. All language must end in order for him to be fully redeemed. In the divinely immanent world of Chartres as depicted in Jean le Marchant's miracle tale discussed in chapter 1, redemption brings speech to the formerly mute believer, but when the space of the tavern expands to include all rhetoric and earthly existence, the only escape from the space or from the genre is silence.

It should be stressed that the way in which the previously cited passages from the two "griesche" poems and "La repentance Rutebeuf" are read is central to understanding Rutebeuf's view of his poetic practice. To the extent that they are to be read as referring only to the language of dice—to poetry—then there remains a locus of linguistic redemption for him. Recent work on the chronology of Rutebeuf's poetry has placed "La repentance Rutebeuf" at a decisive moment for him—the years 1261–62, when he abandons the excessively "worldly" polemic of the struggles regarding the University of Paris.[39] This chronology places the poem at the end of Rutebeuf's personal, misfortune cycle and suggests a narrower reading of verses 37–42 wherein these verses would refer specifically to his polemical poetry. From this point of view, "psaumoier" (v. 9) offers a locus of poetic redemption.[40] However, as noted earlier, this chronology tends to rely excessively on the features of the autobiographical mode of presentation that are as much exemplary as factual, such as the supposed

---

39. See Michel-Marie Dufeil, "L'oeuvre d'une vie rhythmée." While many of Dufeil's dates, based on topical references, are convincing, Dufeil is in my opinion far too willing to accept the poems of misfortune in a strict autobiographical manner, which may compromise some of the dating.

40. Thus Jean Dufournet remarks: "la vraie douleur du ménestrel se manifeste dans la dissolution du poème courtois et du langage, par les formes les plus obscures de celui-ci qui échappent à la raison et donne à l'absence une présence. . . . A mesure que le sens se vide pour ne signifier que le néant, le langage prend de l'épaisseur et de la lourdeur . . . pour signifier la faiblesse de l'homme devant le monde" ("A la recherche de Rutebeuf" and "Un sobriquet ambigu," 110). My reading of Rutebeuf in the remainder of this chapter will closely agree with these words, with the exception that the specification of "courtly" language be removed.

date of his marriage. Rutebeuf's use of the figure of *folie,* the way in which his various texts undermine each others' differing poetics of redemption, and his vocabulary's engagement with general Neoplatonic common-places on sign theory lead to the interpretation that language in general is a trap of imperfection from which the poet cannot escape. The figure of poverty, for example, is used by him throughout his work. Michel Zink's mention of Rutebeuf's "inquiétude" regarding writing could then be extended throughout his works. Jean Dufournet raises this question in the end of his 1986 preface to the "poems of misfortune," noting that one of Rutebeuf's "religious" poems actually brings into question the true solici-tude of God. He notes that "La paix de Rutebeuf" (*OC* 2:413–17) is "tout entière construite sur une opposition significative, entre un appel et une absence de réponse."[41] Rutebeuf seems to be suggesting that God does not necessarily answer the degraded language of men. And in a similar vein, the degraded fool of "Les plaies du monde," who is discussed early in this chapter, and who was rehabilitated in the light of Rutebeuf's critique of avarice, occupies a much more ambiguous position. To the extent that the moralizing but also destabilized rhetoric of the "griesche" poems is the language of poverty and folly, it is the language of this first fool as well. While Rutebeuf may have overcome these doubts at a later point, as wit-nessed by the large amount of religious poetry written after the supposed date of "La repentance Rutebeuf," the moment of crisis seems to be not just about certain uses of language for certain ends but about language itself. In his most self-reflexive poems, those of the tavern and its after-math,[42] Rutebeuf seems to offer either an amused smile or disturbed uncertainty at his own moralistic pretensions to the "naked truth" of satire. His only truly effective target may be himself, and this effectiveness may be dependent on his failure to be in a position to effectively critique even this target.

If Rutebeuf is to be read as fundamentally a moralist, then it is dis-turbed uncertainty that he offers the reader in the "griesche" poems. But

---

41. Dufournet, *Rutebeuf,* 27.

42. Though some critics have argued against the division of Rutebeuf's poetry into cate-gories, in particular the "misfortune" category, as is done in the edition by Faral and Bastin (see *OC* 1:19), these poems do seem to share a certain heightened degree of reflexivity about poetic practice and the language that is its vehicle. As in earlier texts, this reflexivity is located in the tavern—the privileged locus of poetic meditation in high medieval France. Since auto-biography functions here as a second means of meditation on the status of the sign and the self, it is appropriate that the tavern should also become, in Michel Zink's words, the "lieu privilégié de l'exhibition du moi" (*OC* 1:28).

the indulgently ironic tone of his depiction of himself and the bravado of his turning the "sou" into a "livre de povretei" suggest that at least in these self-reflexive poems of the tavern and the self, he may be seen as more akin to the fool of the Feast of Fools. To be a fool is not the problem, nor is, perhaps, to write poetry of even the diciest type. (After all, Rutebeuf himself, in "Renart le bestournei" [*OC* 1:253–63], criticizes King Louis for closing his court to the jongleurs.) It is only the naked fool who is at fault—the one who pretends to a naked truth. Is the emblem of blindness or one-eyedness finally not only a mark of the poet's fundamental linguistic blindness—a disenabling of the gaze at the self—but also a mark of his very lack of blindness about his own at least partially blind status? Rutebeuf's medieval redemption of poetry lies in the conscious vision of one's blindness. The objectionable fool is the naked fool who is blind to the status of the poetic practice in which he engages, who believes in the naked truth of the sign, who is unaware of the distance between intention and language—the very distance that obviates full critical distance between self and world, or "I" and "me." In this sense, Rutebeuf falls squarely in the tradition of the fabliaux. As he writes in "Charlot le juif" (*OC* 2:263–71):

> Qui menestreil wet engignier
> Mout en porroit mieulz bargignier;
> Car mout soventes fois avient
> Que cil por engignié se tient
> Qui menestreil engignier cuide,
> Et s'en trueve sa bource vuide.
>
> (vv. 1–6)

> [Whoever desires to trick a minstrel
> Could do better at other endeavors;
> For many times it happens
> That he himself is tricked
> Who thinks he'll be the trickster,
> And finds his purse empty for his effort.]

Though the fool of the Feast of Fools may be masked and adorned (like Rutebeuf's own showy poetry), he is fundamentally a conscious unmasker of pretensions and emptier of purses—in Rutebeuf's case, not only the pretensions and purses of the hypocrite, the false Mendicant, and the avaricious townsman but also those of language and, in his lighter moments, of himself.

Despite the levity evoked in the preceding quotation, one aspect of Rutebeuf's final rehabilitation of poetic practice in terms of the self-conscious, self-ironic figure of the "feasting fool" involves the suggestive unmasking of a pretension of signal importance for the thirteenth century. The people of the Middle Ages firmly believed that humanity's relationship to God was mediated via the sign and most concretely by language. Paul Zumthor has spoken of the "high degree of semioticity" of the Middle Ages—a culture that "thought of itself as an immense network of signs."[43] In the ninth century, John Scotus Eriugena formulated what Robert Sturges has called a "transhistorical medieval phenomenon"—the idea that the entire world is a series of signs that refer back to God and his divine plan.[44] The Romanesque doctrine of the sign—fundamentally similar to that of Augustine, with its basis in *caritas*—theoretically guaranteed the possibility for man to read these signs correctly and thus to know God. The semiological revolution of the twelfth and thirteenth centuries, however, included a turning toward the literal level of the sign—the level where human intentionality could come into play and with it the dangers (from a religious standpoint) of multivocity or even a failure of communication.[45] Yet this interest in the human intentionality of the text, biblical or otherwise, was simply part of a larger interest in intentionality as it affected man's relation to God. It is a commonplace of medieval studies that this era witnessed a transformation from a "shame culture" of external judgments to a "guilt culture" of interiority, for example, with its concomitantly greater emphasis on reading one's own intentions in order to determine guilt rather than being judged by one's peers as in *The Song of Roland*.[46] The decision of the Fourth Lateran Council in 1215 that confession would henceforth be mandatory is a classic example of the new emphasis on "interiority" and self-examination. The penitentials of the time were necessary in part due to the great complexity of sin when intentionality was taken into account. The result of this turning inward was that the greater "textual community" of Christianity could no longer simply read actions as sins and shameful. The moral relation of man to God was to a certain extent determined by the individual's relation to himself and was dependant on self-examination for the first time. The individual was forced to read himself to determine his intention.

---

43. Zumthor, *Speaking of the Middle Ages,* 30.

44. Sturges, *Medieval Interpretation,* 10. See also Gellrich, *The Idea of the Book.*

45. See Minnis, *The Medieval Theory of Authorship;* Wetherbee, *Platonism and Poetry in the Twelfth Century;* Chénu, *Nature, Man, and Society.*

46. See especially Payen, *Le motif du repentir;* Le Goff, *La naissance du Purgatoire;* Gurevich, *Categories of Medieval Culture.*

It would seem that the concurrent rise in the "autobiographical mode of presentation" in literature must owe something to this larger trend.[47] Though it is not truly about autobiography in the modern sense of the word, this mode does enact moments of reading and representing the self. Rutebeuf and Adam de la Halle are exemplars of the act of reading the self—the "me"—and then interpreting and writing that self (as the "I"). This reading is by definition a reading of "intentionality"; yet this very intentionality may make the reading of the sign difficult or impossible, since it tends to alter the public, stable sign for private profit. Part of the transgression of "naked pride" in the sign was what R. A. Shoaf has called "erasing the difference between the sign and its referent." In his words, it is the temptation of the poet "to be tempted by the illusion of permanent identity between the sign and his meaning."[48] The poet is tempted to corrupt signs to himself, to his own personal meaning, so that the public sign becomes no more than a personal reflection of his own inner meaning. This is one sense of Narcissus' gaze into the fountain at his own reflection, for example. This phenomenon could only have been encouraged by the new emphasis in the High Middle Ages on the literal meanings of signs and the intentions of human authors discussed earlier. Thus, in a classic paradox, a shift in the paradigm of reading both makes the reading of self and the world more important than ever and, at the same time, produces an interpretive model that makes that reading harder than ever to accomplish.

Rutebeuf's representation of a failure to establish a stable locus of "sens" in language from which to fully authorize his own satirical and moral critiques can be read in the light of the question of intentionality, sin, and guilt. As noted earlier, his failure to disengage linguistically from the poetics of the tavern (except through silence) is in a larger sense a failure of the subjective "I" to disengage from the objective "me." The two sides of the poet are equally engaged in "la folie"—the imperfections that inhibit complete intentionality and authority. In refusing the possibility of a fully productive separation between the "je" and the "moi," Rutebeuf can finally be seen as refusing the possibility of the notion of autobiography, because there is no way for the "je" to fully read the "moi," and

---

47. See Zink, *La subjectivité littéraire*, 202ff., for example, where the author discusses the links between confession and the rise of literary subjectivity in general.

48. Shoaf, *Dante, Chaucer, and the Currency of the Word*, 32.

because there is no linguistic tool that will allow the "je" to preserve its intentionality in order to successfully write the "moi."[49]

In this failure of objective distance, Rutebeuf recalls the similar nature of Abelard's position in his *Historia calamitatum*. As Evelyn Vitz has shown, he lacks the "retrospective distance" from himself that is so characteristic of autobiography.[50] She has located a similar lack of distance in the narration of *The Romance of the Rose* and has argued convincingly for the general decentered nature of the subject in medieval narrative. She furthermore has suggested (correctly in my opinion) that there are broadly religious bases for this characteristic—specifically the devaluation of the individual, who is typically a desiring "outsider," and the centrality of God (*Medieval Narrative and Modern Narratology*, 87–91). Rutebeuf, as a subjectively decentered, cloakless, impoverished figure looking in on, or back to, the tavern, corresponds in many ways to this position. He does, however, mark a progression in relation to the narratives in question. While Vitz warns against the "typically modern temptation to see irony everywhere" (60), Rutebeuf's uniqueness lies in his evocation of the ironic distance between language and self that precludes the distance—necessary for "autobiographical" irony—between self as subject and self as object. Rutebeuf's own brand of irony and consciousness does thus fundamentally distinguish him from his autobiographical predecessors.[51]

In fact, such an ironic critique is in one sense the logical outcome of medieval Neoplatonic sign theory. Its stress on the imperfections of the sign and the resultant importance of intention on the part of reader and writer lead inevitably into Rutebeuf's trap when the focus is turned to reading and writing the very intentions that should guarantee proper intention. The question Rutebeuf seems to pose at certain moments is, How can one read and write the self when the language available for doing so is inadequate and infected with potentially misleading intentions? His implication is that one cannot or at least cannot fully. In this context, the

---

49. Rutebeuf would thus stand at a midpoint between Augustine and Dante within the analysis of Sarah Spence (*Texts and Self in the Twelfth Century*, 7–9). She notes that while Augustine "moves beyond the body" (7), Dante "incorporates it into his hermeneutics" (7). Rutebeuf, like Dante, incorporates the body into his hermeneutics but never suggests the possibility of any purification. For him, there is no getting out of purgatory—or the tavern.

50. Vitz, *Medieval Narrative and Modern Narratology*, 39.

51. See Zink, *La subjectivité littéraire*, 171ff., for a discussion of this same necessity of reading the self, and in particular for the example of Guibert de Nogent's lack of problematizing of this process in comparison to Rutebeuf.

notions of confession and penitence, based ultimately on a reading of the self and of intention, are themselves problematized. The "povre estoire," "povre sens," and "povre memoire" with which Rutebeuf begins his "La griesche d'yver" seem to echo ironically in their meagerness the bountiful words of Augustine as he begins his *De doctrina Christiana.*

> The Lord has granted those things necessary to the beginning of this work, and when they begin to be given out they will be multiplied by his inspiration, so that in this task of mine I not only shall suffer no poverty of ideas but shall rejoice in wonderful abundance. (*DDC* I.i.1)

Despite the contrast here between Augustine and Rutebeuf, they do share a basic conception of self-knowledge as "an epistemological rather than an autobiographical problem," to use Eugene Vance's words.[52] And the problem, at least in Rutebeuf's case, is expressed in terms of a *folie* that is a matter less of individual psychology than of universal semiotics. (As Evelyn Vitz says of the High Middle Ages, "psychology is not conceived of as individual at all," since the experience of the "I" is always of transindividual interest.)[53] Folly is thus a problem of language, not of the self. The question posed is, What is the status of humanity's relation both to itself and to God in the circumstances of Rutebeuf, exemplified in the poet's relation to language, self, and God in "La repentance Rutebeuf"? Must the universal book of the divine plan be replaced by either silence or a continuing rhetoric that constitutes only *folie*? If Rutebeuf cautiously poses this question, Adam de la Halle seems to answer it.

The Triumph of Folly: *Le Jeu de la Feuillée*

We now turn to our second principal text of this chapter, Adam de la Halle's *Le Jeu de la Feuillée.* Like Rutebeuf, Adam uses the autobiographical mode of presentation as a means to explore the larger relation between the writer, his literary and social tradition and milieu, and language itself. And as in Rutebeuf's works, the concept of folly, allied with the tavern, plays a dual role in his poetics, serving to pose important metapoetic and metalinguistic questions.

The tavern is the location for a series of vices, or "blindnesses," that Adam critiques in terms comparable to those Rutebeuf uses to critique

---

52. Vance, "The Functions and Limits of Autobiography," 408.
53. Vitz, *Medieval Narrative and Modern Narratology,* 85.

"blind folly." Adam is interested less in narrowly moralistic critiques of traditional vices, however, than in underlining the true "sociosemiotic" status of Arras. Adam suggests, for example, that any rhetoric and genre offering hope of "successful" communication in the narrowly moral terms proposed by ordained church sign theory, such as the epic and hagiography, are conclusively dead: the work begun by Jean Bodel in *Le Jeu de Saint Nicolas* is concluded. Instead, the language and literature of the city, as well as its economy and morality, are represented as versions of the semiology of the tavern.

What Adam seems to mock so insistently in the play is not so much this fact, however, as the blindness—willful or otherwise—of the citizens of the town toward their own semiotic practice. But in addition, Adam makes use of the very rhetoric of the tavern, and of folly, to invert and undermine genre and language and fully reveal their true status, in a fashion similar to Rutebeuf's unmasking fool of the Feast of Fools, as conscious folly unmasks blind folly. Though this process seems quite similar to that of Rutebeuf, Adam finally suggests a quite different and more positive standing for the tavern and folly than that offered by Rutebeuf. The Feast of Fools, or the "Play of Folly," are no longer marginal locations outside quotidian reality but the most truthful and "real" locations of all, while the quotidian itself comes to resemble the Feast of Fools.

Le Jeu de la Feuillée, or *Le Jeu d'Adam,* as the work is called in two of the three manuscripts, was most likely composed sometime soon after 1270. It consists of a series of scenes involving the author, Adam de la Halle, and various other citizens of the town of Arras. As the play opens, Adam is on the verge of leaving for Paris to pursue his fortune as a clerk—a pursuit interrupted by marriage and an attempted literary career in Arras. Successive scenes include an anticourtly depiction of his wife, disputes with his father, the arrival of a doctor who runs through the list of local citizens sick with hypocrisy and avarice, the arrival of a monk bearing relics meant to cure the mentally ill, a debate over clerkly bigamy, the appearance of the local fool and his father, the arrival of three fairies and the "wheel of fortune," and finally a scene in a tavern where the monk is tricked into paying the bill for everyone.

Much of my analysis of the tavern in *Le Jeu de la Feuillée* and its characterization via "folly" will rest on the affinities (and in some cases identities) between Adam and the fool (the "dervés"). The suggestions by the author of an affinity between Adam (as character in the play) and the *dervés* have been noted by several critics.[54] Adam opens the play with a proverbial quotation that refers to pots and pottery—"Encore pert il bien as tès queus li pos fu" (Whoever owned this pot has really taken a loss) (v. 11)—representing himself as a breaker of pots or as a broken pot of which only shards exist. It turns out that the father of the *dervés* is also a potter (vv. 531–35), so the motif of pottery and the breaking of pottery links Adam and the fool. Indeed the very presence of Adam's father links the two characters—they are the only ones in the play to have a father (or mother), and each set of relations is characterized by difficulty and implicit rivalry and struggle. This struggle, we shall see, mimics the greatest struggle of all—that between the writer and his "patrimony" of rhetoric and genre. Although D. R. Sutherland has argued that the pottery motif is simply based on the contemporary expression "mad as a potter,"[55] in fact the image of the pot is more fundamental to the play than this, and even if we accept Sutherland's reading, Adam and the fool are still clearly linked in their suggested mental instability and even madness. The connection between Adam and the *dervés* goes much deeper, however. Gordon McGregor has linked the shattering of the pots to the shattering of literary tradition that is undertaken by Adam in the play and particularly to the shattering of the epic tradition.[56] This idea recalls Rutebeuf's shattering of both courtly discourse and his own discourse as well, and indeed in "Li mariages Rutebeuf" he notes, "Mes poz est briziez et quasseiz / Et j'ai tous mes bons jors passeiz" (My pot is broken and cracked and I've passed all my best days) (vv. 71–72). Such "tradition shattering" plays an important role in Adam's text. The opening description of Adam's wife, Maroie, clearly shatters the tradition of courtly love, for example.

> Adont me vint avisions
> De cheli ke j'ai a feme ore,
> Ki or me sanle pale et sore;
> Adont estoit blanke et vermeille,
> Rians, amoureuse et deugie,
> Or le voi crasse et mautaillie,
> Triste et tenchant.
>
> (vv. 68–74)

---

54. See especially Adler, *Sens et composition du "Jeu de la Feulliée"*; MacGregor, *The Broken Pot Restored.*

55. Sutherland, "Fact and Fiction in the *Jeu de la Feullée.*"

56. MacGregor, *The Broken Pot Restored,* 38, 41.

[Then came to me a vision
Of she who is now my wife,
Who now seems to me pale and wilted;
Then she was white and crimson,
Laughing, loving and graceful,
Now I see her fat and ill formed,
Sad and quarrelsome.]

The opening moments of the play also recall the *congé,* a genre peculiar to Arras in which a poet departing the city—usually due to impending death or leprosy—tenderly takes leave of all his friends and relatives and sums up his life. A form of the word *congé* itself is used in a scene in *Le Jeu de la Feuillée:* "Mais je voeil a vous tous avant prendre congiét" (But I wish to say good-bye to you all before leaving) (v. 4). But unlike the *congé* of Jean Bodel and that of Baude Fastoul—though exactly like Adam's own *congé,*[57] this particular scene presents not tender leave-taking but rather rancor, bitterness, and a father who refuses to give his son the money necessary for the trip to Paris, though it is clearly implied that the father has this money (v. 189). To take another example of the recall and subsequent shattering of genre, the scene involving the three fairies who suddenly appear out of nowhere to give gifts to the poet and his friends recalls the phantasmatic visions of such texts as Marie de France's "Lanval," wherein the failure of the feudal gift economy and the impoverishment of the lower nobility are recouped by the magical savior in the person of the fairy/woman. Unfortunately, in *Le Jeu de la Feuillée,* because the table is incorrectly set for the three women's dinner (a knife is missing), the scene ends with Adam being cursed by an angry fairy. The scene parodies the *roman d'aventure* in another fashion as well, since the intended lover of the fairies' queen turns out to be an inept coward and fraud rather than a noble knight.[58]

The arrival of the monk is not specifically a literary event, but it does feature a *boniment* of a type that must have been very common in medieval

---

57. Ruelle, *Les congés d'Arras.* See also Dane, "Parody and Satire in the Literature of Thirteenth-Century Arras," for more on the status of the *congé.* Dane notes that unlike the previous works of the genre, in this case Adam is healthy and the society is sick (15). I suggest that the differentiation is of vision rather than health, however.

58. This particular detail reminds one of the parodic fabliau "Berengier au long cul," which features a similar fraudulent hero.

Arras.[59] Likewise, the appearance of the "wheel of fortune" recalls many medieval didactic texts, but after a suitable number of edifying examples of the folly of devotion to carnal existence, the women involved go off to help plot how to get "Dame Douche" into bed with "Uns hom ke [elle] voeil maniier" (A man whom she wants to get a hold of) (v. 860), and they even sing a frivolous little tune, "Par chi va la mignotise" (v. 874), clearly undermining the lessons of the wheel.

Though it is the author who "shatters" many of the literary traditions through the composition of his text, it is the *dervés* who immediately attacks the monk and ruins his *boniment*. It is also the *dervés* who proclaims the shattering of the epic tradition (vv. 536ff.), so that the author and "dervès" seem accomplices in their destruction of tradition. Gordon McGregor further notes that the fool and Adam seem to share a similar perspective on the matter of clerical bigamy, as both withdraw from the center of the protestations and ultimately take the side of the pope.[60] Indeed, to the extent that the play can be read as a critique of Adam's milieu and of Arras in general, it is often the fool who serves as the mouthpiece of Adam. He is the one who remarks of the monk, "Creés vous la ches ypocrites?" (Do you believe these hypocrites?) (v. 394). Adam himself rarely overtly criticizes this milieu, yet the entire tone and structure of the play constitute just such a critique, and the single most effective critical voice is that of the fool.

Given the nature of the pairing between Adam and the "dervés,"[61] concentrating as it does on their shared literary, authorial functions, it is tempting to see the fool as a "poet" in the play and, more precisely, an inscription of the poet that becomes an alternative inscription of Adam himself. McGregor notes "the extravagant verbal flights that are [the fool's] trademark in the *Feuillée*."[62] He links the formal techniques and images employed in these flights to the characteristic Arras genre of the *fatrasie*.

---

59. We have already seen such *boniments* by the criers at the doors of the taverns in both *Le Jeu de Saint Nicolas* and *Courtois d'Arras,* and other literary works—for example, "Les crieries de Paris" (Barbazan, *Fabliaux et contes,* 2:276–86)—consist primarily or entirely of such cries. Thus the *boniment* itself formed virtually a literary genre, at the boundaries between poetry and commerce. The most famous example of a medieval literary *boniment* is Rutebeuf's parodic "Le dit de l'herberie."

60. MacGregor, *The Broken Pot Restored,* 72.

61. Jean Dufournet (*Adam de la Halle à la recherche de lui-même,* 336–37) establishes an elaborate series of correspondences between the two, down to the level of individual vocabulary items.

62. MacGregor, *The Broken Pot Restored,* 72.

Even the hastiest reading of the fatrasies in the light of the *Feuillée* reveals an extraordinary commonality of references. Allusions which in the play appear utterly casual or even obscure are invariably paralleled in the fatrasies. Fatrasie 24, for example, features several objects or actions which figure prominently in the *Feuillée:* the paying of the tab, the wise fool crowned in feathers, and most notably, the pot. . . . The rest of the Fatrasie corpus anticipates or echoes the *Feuillée* at every turn. (McGregor, *The Broken Pot*, 73–74)

Though these "fatrasies" are not the exclusive product of the *dervés,* McGregor notes that "it is the dervés and his antics that most strikingly represent [the *fatrasie's*] style and substance" in the play.[63] The fool can indeed be seen as an inscribed author for much of the play, doubling the role of Adam, and as an author whose specialty is the Arras nonsense genre of the *fatrasie.*

The *fatrasie* is characterized by McGregor as containing

a rapid series of vividly anti-thetical images or propositions, mostly involving the juxtaposition of places, objects, creatures, and qualities not found altogether in reality, and the performance by them of utterly impossible actions, with a predilection for violent and obscene ones, ones involving drastic displacement and disruption or vehement utterance . . . a string of outright improbabilities and self-contradictions. (73)

Certainly the language of the *dervés* distinctively illustrates the aleatory and improbable nature of the dialogue, as it often depends on phonetic correspondences at the level of the signifier rather than on mental correspondences at the level of the signified.

Li Peres.   Or cha, levés vous sus, biaus fieus,
            Si venés le saint aourer.

Le Dervés.   Ke ch'est? Me volés vous tuer?

                                        (vv. 390–92)

---

63. For more on the *fatrasie* and the *fatras,* see Garapon, *Le fantaisie verbale et le comique;* and see especially Lambert Porter, *La fatrasie et le fatras.* The complete "Fatrasies d'Arras" can be found in Porter. Jean Dufournet has also noted the resemblance of the play to the *fatrasie* (*Adam de la Halle à la recherche de lui-même,* 398–401).

| *Li Moines.* | Quant un peu il ara dormi, |
| | Aussi ne fait il fors rabaches. |

| *Li Dervés.* | Dit chieus moines ke tu me baches? |

(vv. 550–52)

| [*The Father.* | Come on now, get up, my good son, |
| | And come praise the saint. |

| *The Fool.* | What is all this? Do you want to kill me?] |

| [*The Monk.* | When he has slept a little, |
| | He'll only torment us the worse. |

| *The Fool.* | Is this monk telling you to beat me?] |

In verses 1029–30, the *dervés* uses a similar procedure. After the host of the tavern notes of a parodic religious recitation, "onques mais si bien dit ne fu" (never has it been better said), the *dervés* responds, "Ahors! Le fu! Le fu! Le fu! / Aussi bien cante jou k'il font" (Hey! Fire! Fire! Fire! I can sing as well as they do). The connotation of "fou" seems certainly intended, and it is also interesting to remember that Rutebeuf makes a similar play on the same words *(feu/fu)* in his "Li mariages Rutebeuf." The repetition of the syllable also is a good example of the "centrifugal" nature of the *dervés'* speech: phonetic correspondence sets off a flight into total nonsense, and the "referential center" of the discourse is rapidly shifted or even abandoned. When the father of the *dervés* notes of Adam, "Biaus fius, ch'est uns [clers] parisiens" (Good son, this is a clerk from Paris), the *dervés* responds with a deformation of phonetics and meaning: "Che sanle mieus uns pois baiens. / Bau!" (He seems more like a mushy pea. Ha!) (vv. 423–25). The effect of the deformation is again heightened by the specific reference of "pois baiens," since peas connoted insanity in the Middle Ages. Following this twist, the *dervés* then brings up the question of bigamy, apparently based purely on the random correspondence with the word "clers," and the play lurches on to an entirely new topic (vv. 426–27). The segment of the play concerning bigamy then itself ends when one of Adam's friends, Rikeche Auris, becomes too frustrated with the continual non sequiturs of the *dervés*—"K'est chou? Seront hui mais riotes? / N'arons hui mais fors sos et sotes?" (What is this? Are there going to be more disturbances today? Are we going to have nothing but madmen and madwomen today?) (vv. 557–58)—and switches to the topic of the imminent arrival of three fairies. Thus the centrifugal dialogue of the fool impels the play from one apparently random scene to the next,[64] dramatizing his role as shatterer of language, dramatic structure, and genre. It is entirely appropriate that his model should be the "shattering" parodic and anticommunicative genre of the *fatrasie.*

Though the poetics of the fool may clearly be that of the *fatrasie,* it was noted earlier that this poetics is not unique to the fool in the play. McGregor's description of the *fatrasie* closely matches that offered by Eugene Vance of the dialogue structure of the play in general in many respects: Vance characterizes the dialogue as not circular or linear but rather "aleatory" and centrifugal. The motivating forces of the dialogue are never reason, he argues, but rather chance, theft, drink, avarice, and sexual desire.[65] I certainly agree with this characterization: indeed, the play in general seems governed by the poetics of the *fatrasie* in many cases. The dialogue seems often to operate under the spell of drink, for example.[66]

Maistres Henri.	Las! Dolans! Ou seroit il pris?
	Je n'ai mais ke vint et nuef livres!
Hane li Merchiers.	Pour le cul Dieu! estes vous ivres?
	(vv. 188–90)

[*Maistres Henri.*	Alas! Oh my! Where will we get the money?
	I've got no more than twenty-nine pounds!
Hane le Merchiers.	By God's ass! Are you drunk?]

The preceding passage combines phonetic confusion with the suggestion of drunken confusion, and the reduction of the "livres" to "ivres" recalls a similar operation in Rutebeuf's "La griesche d'yver," though involving

---

64. The analogies to modern surrealist theory, especially in the emphasis on chance, are obviously intriguing. In addition, the medieval fool was typically depicted as a very unstable personality (Ménard, "Les Fous," 443). Adam himself is likewise described as being of "muavle kief" (*Le Jeu de la Feuillée,* v. 21).

65. Vance, *Mervelous Signals,* 214, 221.

66. Claude Mauron has spoken of the "ivresse triomphale" that reigns over the play (*Le Jeu de la Feuillée,* 60), while Norman Cartier has noted the "ebriatas inspirée" that seem to lie at the heart of its poetics (*Le bossu désenchanté,* 145).

dice rather than drink in that case. The accusation of drunkenness appears elsewhere, and it is often noted that different characters drink too much.[67] The intentionality of speakers, especially Adam, is often undermined by the redefining of a given word by a subsequent speaker. One example is verses 17–18, where Adam's use of "livre" to indicate books and book learning is twisted to mean a "livre" of money: "boins clers et soutieus en sen livre? / Oïl; pour deus deniers le livre" (a good clerk and clever in reading? Truly; for two pennies a pound). This example is particularly interesting since it is even closer to one of Rutebeuf's puns. At other points, phonetic correspondence threatens to send the dialogue into a centrifugal flight from communication, as we have already seen with the fool. "Honnis soit ki le me loa!" (Shame on whoever advised me to do this!), cries Adam's father at one point, and Adam responds: "K'i a? K'i a? K'i a? K'i a" (What? What? What? What?) (vv. 193–94). The echo of the verb *kier* (*chier*, "to shit") only heightens the effect, and the similarity to the quote of the fool is another example of the parallels between the fool and the character of Adam. These are simply a few examples of the way the dialogue of the play often departs from vertical reference and depends on the physical sound of the sign rather than on the referents. To the extent that reference does occur, it is in relation to other signs in the text and never to outside "reality." Robert Garapon has noted the number of "propos sans suite" in the play, and he points out that the "propos" themselves are not funny and rather that the lack of logic between the "propos" produces the comic effect.[68] Comedy lies not in the reference of the sign to the external world but in the relation, or lack thereof, between signs in the text. Language is freed from all communicative function and becomes purely a source of pleasure.

This poetics recalls that of the tavern. Many scenes recall especially the gambling scenes in the tavern of Jean Bodel's play. As the preceding citations of the *dervés* and others suggest, "reading" and language use come to resemble a toss of the dice, as in *Courtois d'Arras*. An aleatory and drunken poetics, as seen in so much of *Le Jeu de la Feuillée*, is entirely characteristic of the tavern throughout medieval French realist literature. Though the tavern may not be omnipresent in the play, the individual motivating forces of the dialogue—avarice, chance, drink, sexual desire, and theft—certainly represent a classic list of the vices of the tavern. The

---

67. See vv. 276–82 for another accusation of drunkenness, and see vv. 234–35, where the "fisiciens" notes a number of excess drinkers.

68. Garapon, *La fantaisie verbale et comique,* 27.

tavern is also the spot where most of the speakers will end up. The poetics of the *fatrasie,* of the fool, and of the play in general in many instances are really the expression of the poetics of the tavern—full of multiple meaning, centering as much on the phonetic material of the sign as on its referents, refusing straightforward "vertical" reference. In this play, the tavern's particular poetics is simply taken to its logical conclusion—nonsense and on occasion an absolute refusal of communication, or an absolute poverty of "sens," as Rutebeuf might say. The play's poetics works centrifugally on meaning, structure, and genre and in the fashion that Aristotle feared as well, as the fool's runaway metonymical and metaphorical tendencies reduce all meaning and sense to the folly of the fool himself, allowing him to impose his own representational "nakedness" on the rest of the world as he reinterprets it in his own insane image. On several occasions, the fool's responses are entirely physical in nature—he is described as being like a trumpet, a dog, or an ass (vv. 398–401, 556, 524–26), and he uses farts, physical blows, and other types of behavior to resist attempts at verbal communication. In so doing, he evokes the medieval suspicion of the gesture which Jacques Le Goff has noted. Not only are these physical acts essentially communicative nonsense, but in their reduction of communicative signs to the purely physical, they ironically comment on the logical conclusion of the rhetorical practice in question.[69]

In summary, we can say that Adam and the *dervés* are both poets who use a poetics that not only undermines that of the epic and other genres but corresponds in its "idolatrous" and aleatory nature to the poetics of the tavern. As such, the tavern and its particular language are a kind of tool in the hands of Adam and the fool for the inversion of all of the play's other economies, genres, and rhetorical practices that might presume to escape the fundamentally imperfect nature of language.

Yet, as noted earlier, this poetics characterizes the play in general in many instances, including those not specifically involving Adam and the *dervés.* The connection between the world of the play and the (implicit) tavern thus serves to emphasize the fundamentally imperfect nature of language in the play (and Arras) in a general sense. The semiology of the tavern seems to characterize all of Arras.

Thus the play alternates between scenes of the "idolatry" of Arras that

---

69. The use of the dog barking is particularly interesting since the great medieval debate over the nature of meaning and intentionality in signs other than spoken language was most often treated in terms of the barking dog. See Eco, *On the Medieval Theory of Signs,* 8. On the gesture, see Le Goff, *The Medieval Imagination,* 86.

present various literary genres and rhetorics with pretensions to adequate expression, on the one hand, and the unmasking of the true status of these discourses, on the other—an unmasking accomplished using the poetics of the tavern to invert and undermine the new arrivals. These two different functions of the tavern—as locus of blind or "naked" folly and as a tool of an inverting folly that marks its own self-consciousness—can be difficult to sort out. They must be sorted out, however, to appreciate the way in which they reveal not the confusion of the play but the fundamental linguistic trap in which all authors in Arras find themselves. Adam and the *dervés,* the key figures in the play, are finally doubly fools, first in their participation in the world of Arras (including as writers), and second in the specifically "foolish" and inverting nature of their relation to that world.

Jean Dufournet has rightly noted of verses 31–32 ("Puis ke Dieus m'a donne engien, / Tans est ke je l'atour a bien") that Adam seems to implicitly critique his anterior productions,[70] and this particular "topos" has already been seen in "moralizing" works of Rutebeuf. But Adam also poses a more interesting question—in particular, whether literary language is the place to engage in such a critique. The ending of the play will question whether any particular moralizing "bien" can be accomplished in this context.

Having established this at least partial identity between Adam and the *dervés* based on folly and poetry, we are now in a better position to appreciate certain fundamental unities that exist in *Le Jeu de la Feuillée* as a whole and that will be made more explicit via the final use of the tavern. These unities will reveal the crux of the trap mentioned earlier. The question of the unity of Adam de la Halle's *Le Jeu de la Feuillée* has vexed critics and scholars of the Middle Ages for well over a century, in much the same manner as has the same question when asked of *Le Jeu de Saint Nicolas.* Throughout the nineteenth-century, the play was seen as a kind of "revue" that almost by definition lacked any degree of unity.[71] A large group of scholars in the first half of the twentieth century chose to read the work as primarily biographical—as a depiction of the life of Adam de la

---

70. Dufournet, "Adam de la Halle et *Le Jeu de la Feuillée,*" 224.

71. See Juleville, *Histoire du théâtre en France—les mystères.* This approach is also taken by Grace Frank in *The Medieval French Drama* and by Henri Roussel in "Notes sur la littérature arrageoise du XIIIe siècle." For a general review of the various theories and explications of the play, see Cartier, *Le bossu désenchanté.* More recently, see Ménard, "Le Sens du *Jeu de la Feuillée.*"

Halle.[72] Alternately, the play has been read as a satire of Adam and his milieu.[73] Here the central theme of the play is simply Adam himself, and his existence provides the only unity in what is otherwise still a "revue," but a biographical revue in this case. However, as early as 1891, the idea of "la folie" was proposed as the "fil conducteur" of the play by Marius Sepet. He proposed that the play was in fact composed for a Fête des Fous of the type that were so common in medieval France, and which we have already discussed in connection with Rutebeuf. Virtually all of the episodes depicted in the play could be broadly viewed as examples of folly, according to Sepet, and each one reflected a vice, such as avarice, pride, or concupiscence.[74]

H. Roussel likewise sees *folie* as the central idea of the play,[75] though he again sees the play purely as a "revue d'étudiant," so that folly is less a central idea in a certain sense than a thematic that explains the very lack of any real unity. The evidence for the theme of folly as the central "fil conducteur" that unifies the play is ultimately the lack of any other sign of unity.

In reality, we have already seen in the pairing of Adam and the *dervés* the suggestion of a broader link in the play between a state of *folie* and the act of poetic creation: poet and fool mirror each other. Specifically, each subverts language and genre, turning them upside down in a grand Fête des Fous.

At the same time, both poet and fool present an unmasking of the society of Arras. This critique is especially framed in terms of avarice and hypocrisy. Hypocrisy was of course one of the bêtes noires of Rutebeuf, constituting as it did one more example of the failure of the sign—outer appearance—to faithfully represent "the truth." And as we saw in chapter 2, Arras was the virtual European capital of avarice in the eyes of contemporary moralists. The question of bigamy in Arras, for example, was really a matter of avarice: typically middle-class merchants took the clerical oaths simply to be exempt from taxes, while of course remaining married.

The hypocrisy and avarice of Arras can, however, be seen as fundamentally semiotic issues and as issues of folly. The connections between

---

72. See Guy, *Essai sur la vie et les oeuvres littéraires;* Adler, *Sens et composition du "Jeu de la Feuillée";* Sutherland, "Fact and Fiction in the *Jeu de la Feuillée*"; and Jean Dufournet, *Adam de la Halle à la recherche de lui-même.*

73. Marie Ungureanu *(La Bourgeoisie naissante)* even goes so far as to deny any autobiographical import.

74. Cited in Cartier, *Le bossu desenchanté,* 5.

75. Roussel, "Notes sur la littérature arrageoise du XIIIe siècle."

the avaricious desire for money and a more general desire for the sign have already been discussed in chapter 3. And as we have seen, Aristotle considered money a kind of madness or nonsense because of its dependence on convention and its imperfection. He also himself compared money and language on this basis, considering both a kind of nonsense in their reduction of infinite experience and value to a few conventional and wholly inadequate signs.[76] The relevant passages by Aristotle, originally translated by Boethius, were widely read in the Middle Ages and provide an example of the theoretical basis that existed for a general representation of the desire for the sign as folly, in either its literary or economic manifestations. It is only a short step from this desire to a generalized (unjustified) pride in the sign—the essence of folly as discussed earlier.

Likewise, hypocrisy plays on, and attempts to seduce people toward, a belief in the naked, adequate truth of the sign, blinding them to the problematic status of representation. Understanding folly and the fool to represent a pride in the sign (and in representation), the concept of folly includes not only the specifically literary and parodic elements of the play, and not only the scenes involving the *dervés,* but also the social critique aimed at the bourgeoisie of Arras. Unlike Adam, however, they are blindly avaricious, and their hypocrisy seeks to blind others.

Folly thus can be associated not only with pride (in representation) but also with desire for the monetary sign, and it therefore becomes the link— and emblem—for the two great vices of the thirteenth century, pride and avarice. Not only is the poetics of the entire play characterized by a poetics of folly, but the entire world of Arras can be likewise characterized. Avarice and pride in representation are elements of a more general blind idolatry of the sign.

The critique of trust and pride in the sign is played out in many ways in the play. One example is the reading of urine and palms by the "physicien" (vv. 200–275), with its clear overtones of parody recalling Rutebeuf's "Le dit de l'herberie." Reading seems generally to be a fraud, and interpretation seems purely the whim of the reader. Another example is the treatment of the monk and the relics. The relics, of Saint Acaire, can supposedly cure mental instability. However, the play clearly suggests that the monk and his relics are a fraud.[77] In case there is any doubt on this point,

---

76. Shoaf, *Dante, Chaucer, and the Currency of the Word,* 7, 12.

77. The very fact that the relics are carried from town to town would have strongly suggested fraudulence at the time—true relics were usually closely guarded (see Dufournet, *Adam de la Halle à la recherche de lui-même,* 326). The monk is thus yet another example of the usurer who abuses signs (or invents fake ones) for his personal profit.

the *dervés* effectively undermines the efficacy of the relics by triumphing over the monk, much as he undermines language and genre in other instances in the play.[78] Indeed, in this degraded, avaricious world turned upside down by folly, instead of pilgrims going to see relics and staying at church hospices, as in the case of Jean le Marchant's miracle of Notre Dame, the relics go on pilgrimages and end up at the tavern, all for the sake of turning a nice "profit" in offerings. The miracles no longer work in a degraded, imperfect world, unlike the world of Jean's Chartres, because speech no longer serves to allow man to communicate with God, and because God is himself no longer immanent in language.

To sum up my argument to this point, the tavern is the emblem of a general complex of pride and folly—foolish pride—that exists in the play. One fundamental form of this foolish pride consists in a blind devotion to the commodified and/or degraded sign, in either its rhetorical, monetary, religious, or other manifestations. Both the result of this devotion and the poetics that this devotion produces are expressed in the figures of excessive drink, excessive sexual desire, lying and fraudulent behavior, avarice, and aleatory types of communication. The second fundamental form of folly in the play, to continue the summation, is in the use of the tavern poetics as a tool for inversion by Adam and the *dervés,* thus recalling the inversion associated with the Fête des Fous.

These then are the forms of folly in *Le Jeu de la Feuillée.* I have already suggested that the poetics of the play is equivalent to that of the tavern, and it appears that the economic and ethical worlds of the play strongly resemble those of the tavern as well. In fact, the forms of folly in our text correspond in large measure to the characteristics of the tavern genre. Though there is no explicit geography in the majority of the play, these thematics, poetics, ethics, and economics clearly correspond to the geography of the tavern. The actual scene in the tavern may not occur until the end, but all the other scenes in the play can best be visualized as occurring in some open, public space, such as a market area or central town meeting place—the kind of place that is virtually an extension of the tavern in many respects, and a locale that might well have a tavern nearby, as we saw in chapter 1. Jean Dufournet has proposed that the action was likely set in Arras' "Petit markiet."[79] Among his reasons is that this area is

---

78. This treatment of sacred relics certainly recalls the similar treatment found in Bodel's *Le Jeu de Saint Nicolas* and illustrates another point of continuity between Adam de la Halle and his predecessors of Arras. The reading of the palms and the urine likewise recall the interpretation of the idol Tervagant by a Saracen wise man in the same play.

79. Dufournet, *Adam de la Halle à la recherche de lui-même,* 218–20.

referred to in some Arrageois texts as "La foillie." At least two brothels were located in the vicinity of this market area, and he believes that certain references in the text (vv. 304–5) concern these brothels. Whatever we might imagine the actual setting of the play to be, it seems quite probable to me that any audience member who was well versed in the literature of the mid–thirteenth century in general and in the literature of Arras (especially the entirety of Arras' dramatic production that we know of) could not fail to feel the broad association of most or all of the scenes of the play with other, related literary productions that occur in or near the tavern. It would not be surprising if this were the case for virtually the entire audience. The majority of scholars have considered that the play, if it was performed at all, was most likely performed before the *puy* of Arras or for some other small group of "initiates." Certainly the highly allusive nature of the play and the subtle parodies of multiple genres, some of which—the *congé* and the *fatrasie*—were specialties of Arras, argue for this type of audience. Such an audience would most likely have grasped many of the references to the earlier plays or at least caught the general echoes of these works and their use of the tavern. Not only is the tavern the only explicit geographical location given in the entire play (except for the "pré" where the fairies go after the "wheel of fortune" scene), but the title itself, in the word "Feuillée," carries connotations not only of folly but also of foliage. This foliage has been associated with the scene involving the fairies, but it happens that the common sign of the inn and tavern, in both Roman and medieval times, was a branch of foliage attached to a pole outside the building.[80] It should also be noted that in *Le Jeu de Saint Nicolas,* the first visitor to the tavern in that play is invited by the innkeeper, "Seés vous cha en ceste achinte," with "achinte" being a foliated arbor (v. 261). In the same light, the title (of one manuscript at least) of Adam de la Halle's play could be translated as *The Play of the Tavern.*

The claim that a large part of *Le Jeu de la Feuillée* is really a tavern piece, an example of the tavern "genre" as I defined it in chapter 3, with the tavern an overarching implicit presence throughout, may seem forced. However, it is far more clear that if we broaden the scope of this genre's "geography" to include inn, tavern, marketplace, and trade route, then the connections between our play and the literature associated with the geography of the tavern are quite strong. The very structure of the play seems to echo the chance meetings and interactions that must have characterized

---

80. Coulet, "Inns and Taverns."

this geography. Certainly, if we sum up the play as being all about fraud, avarice, theft, dice, Fortune, drink, sex, lies, verbal misunderstandings, failed communication, inefficacious signs and *folie,* the combined weight of the entire assemblage of themes certainly reminds one strongly of the tavern and the new literature and economics that I have argued that the tavern comes to symbolize. Only the tavern combines this particular nexus of themes so completely.

This reading of *Le Jeu de la Feuillée* as another work that is in large part about what a medieval moralist would call the "semiotic sin" fits well with other, more traditionally autobiographical or psychological readings of the play. For example, Claude Mauron associates the *dervés* in the play with the ideas of desire and the pleasure principle. The tavern is the locus where one is freed from social control and allowed to engage in pleasures and desires.[81] Pleasure and desire contrast with the utilitarian world dominated by the reality principle. The bases of Mauron's reading are quite different from mine, since her approach is more ahistorical and seeks elements of a general psychology of comedy. Yet the concepts of desire and the pleasure principle correspond to my discussion of the usurer/poet's transgression of the public, utilitarian sign via a private reification for the sake of profit, and the tavern as the world of the pleasure principle, free of social control, likewise corresponds to my reading of the tavern as presented by the goliard poets and others. Thus in both this reading as well as in my presentation, the tavern is characterized by desire for physical commodities and a valorization of the private and pleasurable over the public and utilitarian.[82]

Seen in this light, the "universality" of the play lies not just in its comic psychology, as Mauron suggests, but even more so in its use of the long tradition of the tavern and its associated thematics (as well as so many other literary genres and subgenres). The psychological and/or "autobiographical" elements of the play constitute its particularity; *Le Jeu de la Feuillée* uses the autobiographical mode of presentation to examine the same semiotic acts that are treated elsewhere in terms of poetics, economics, and morality. Here, the treatment is unique in supplying a psychology of (semiotic) desire that corresponds to the poetics, economics, and morality seen in earlier chapters.

---

81. Mauron, *Le Jeu de la Feuillée,* 56, 68.

82. Mauron actually reaches a conclusion quite similar to mine in defining the role of the tavern as the locus of both *folie* and illicit desire, though his reading is more Freudian and traditionally "psychological" (Mauron, *Le Jeu de la Feuillée,* 68).

Another unique feature of the autobiographical presentation is the way in which the personal relation of Adam to individuals within the play is assimilated to his personal relation to literary tradition and to rhetoric. Clearly the play is about the shattering of genre, literary tradition, and language and about the failure of these traditions and of literature in general. Yet it is also at least ostensibly about Adam's relationships with those around him in Arras. The two best examples are his relationships with his wife and his father, but virtually everyone in the play is an acquaintance. Invariably, these personal relationships are destructive failures—his wife is now ugly and unbearable (like Rutebeuf's wife as well), and his father (like Rutebeuf's patrons) refuses to help or support him. Eugene Vance has called the play "a study of failed relationships." He then goes on to note that "the twins rhetoric and money are the principle forces of subversion."[83] I hope my analyses of the texts have demonstrated why this pairing of rhetoric and money is hardly a surprising fact. We have seen that this pairing occurs because the "pair" are fundamentally one and the same on a semiotic level. In fact, we could enlarge Vance's statement to say that it is really the sign in all its manifestations that is inadequate and subverts potential relationships. To take the example of Adam's relationship with his father, this pairing is characterized primarily by Adam's requests for money and his father's pleas of poverty in response. Adam's monetary poverty echoes his implicit rhetorical poverty, since he is attempting to leave Arras because of his failure as a poet. This dual use of poverty recalls again the self-representation of Rutebeuf. (And both poets are poor due to engagement with the tavern and its poetics.) Each writer is failed by the sign, and it is folly to have any confidence in the sign. For each, rhetorical poverty is equated with monetary poverty.

It is important to notice that the personal relationships of Adam in the play are paralleled in several cases by relationships to specific literary genres. I have associated the opening attempt at departure, where Adam asks for his father's help, with the *congé*. His relationship with his wife can be associated with the courtly chanson. Adam's relation to the fairies is in another sense his relation to the *roman d'aventure*. The failed personal relationship corresponds to a failed literary relationship with the genre— neither have been productive for him. The play presents the disaggregation of Adam from all around him—from personal relations and from literary tradition, certainly, but also from himself. We have seen that the

---

83. Vance, *Mervelous Signals*, 225.

poetics of the play is highly aleatory, and the intentionality of all speakers, especially Adam, seems always to be at risk of being lost. If Jean Bodel presents the first step in the breakdown of traditional textual community in his tavern scene, then Adam de la Halle presents the culmination of this breakdown, as the individual is fundamentally separated from every single other element of society—and even from himself—due to the inadequacies of the sign. Philippe Ménard has written of the *dervés* that he reveals "la conduite paradoxale et la psychose profonde des schizophrènes" (the paradoxical conduct and the profound psychosis of the schizophrenic), that "il a perdu tout contact vital avec la réalité. Son langage témoigne d'une grave désagrégation du moi . . . [et] une hypertrophie pathologique du moi" (He has lost all real contact with reality. His language suggests a serious disintegration of the ego . . . and a pathological hypertrophy of the ego).[84] While one need not agree with the precise medical diagnosis offered, the fundamental elements of the fool's personality do seem to correspond to his poetics and to those of the play in general in many instances. Yet the play is the "Jeu d'Adam," and the fool and Adam are intimately paired: their psychic conditions are not so very far apart.

Fittingly, the play comes to an end in a tavern. The tavern scene (vv. 899–1099) is in many ways a classic example of the type we have already seen. The various characters are welcomed by the tavern keeper, who praises the quality of his wine and hospitality in typical (exaggerated) fashion (vv. 907–10). There are then the usual intimations by some customers in the know that the wine is watered down (vv. 940–44) and that the herrings are left over from days before (vv. 928–30): the tavern keeper is cheating his customers. There are the usual disputes among the customers and exchanges of insults; a friend mocks Adam for using his money here rather than to go to Paris.[85] When the customers see the monk asleep, they agree among themselves to say that one of them has rolled the dice for him to see who pays the bill and that he has lost. The sleeping monk is interesting since we saw in discussing Jean Bodel's play that the thieves were also asleep in the tavern and that this recalled the legend of Saint Nicolas, the savior of the clerks. It is tempting to see an echo of this here, especially since the parting words of the monk (vv. 1097–99) include a reference to

---

84. Ménard, "Les Fous," 446–47.
85. Aimi! Dieus! Con fait escolier!
   Chi sont bien emploiét denier!
   Font ensi li autre a Paris?

(vv. 960–62)

Saint Nicolas. Unfortunately for him, however, Saint Nicolas is no more efficacious than the monk's own relics in saving him from being deceived and cheated: there is no rescue from the tavern. Certainly the dice and the cheating both clearly echo *Le Jeu de Saint Nicolas*. There are the typical uses of the verbs *croire* (v. 984) and *prester* (v. 981) with double meanings. The monk is threatened with the loss of his cloak if he does not pay the debt (vv. 991–93), and when he leaves his relics instead, the tavern keeper jokes about the need for solemnity (vv. 1021–24). The function of the tavern, I would argue, is to make explicit what has been only implicit in the rest of the text—that Arras is characterized by a semiology represented by the thematics of chance, drink, inadequate or usurious language, deception, unstable signs, fraud, theft, and the absence of "theosis" in language—the semiology of the tavern.[86] Indeed, given the totalizing nature of the play, especially in its presentation of virtually every literary genre of the thirteenth century, it is not hard to see the semiology of Arras as representing the semiology of humanity in general, of which Arras is simply the most convenient and clear example.

At this point in the scene, the *dervés* suddenly arrives and immediately interrupts the proceedings with a misunderstanding that leads to him crying out, "Le fu! Le fu! Le fu!," a citation I discussed earlier. In verse 1041, the *dervés* states that he is almost dead from starvation—"Par le mort Dieu, je muir de fain" (By the death of God, I'm starving to death)—subtly evoking via his use of the commonplace expression "le mort Dieu" the "transgressive" desire that is emblematic of the tavern. His father then tosses him an apple: "Tenés, mengiés dont cheste pume" (Here, then eat this apple) (v. 1042). Certainly for any medieval spectator, the apple must evoke the memory of Adam and Eve, of the Fall occasioned by humanity's (gluttonous) desire to rival God in knowledge and wisdom. The folly of pride condemns humanity.

The *dervés* implicitly recognizes this fact, replying that the apple is rather a scholar's quill: "Vous i mentés, ch'est une plume" (You're lying, its a feather) (v. 1043). The *dervés* assimilates a symbol of representation, of writing and literary production, to the sign of humanity's pride and its Fall. Here we see again the expansion of the play's field of critique to

---

86. Jean Dufournet, in a quite similar vein, notes of this last scene that in its display of "la goinfrerie et l'ivrognerie, la débauche et la vulgarité, la sottise et la folie," it presents a final summation of Arras (and the play) as "un monde irrationnel, régi par la fortune" ("Adam de la Halle et *Le Jeu de la Feuillée*," 243–44). I would simply note that the tavern and "irrational fortune" are virtually inseparable.

humanity in general. And here, quite clearly, folly, pride, and rhetoric are one (as Peraldus suggested) and are united in the tavern (as I have suggested they should be). The quill is also the instrument both of Adam's failure in Arras as a writer and of his hoped-for future success in Paris. The *dervés* apparently tosses the quill to Adam: "Alés, ele est ore a Paris" (Go on, the quill is now [should be] in Paris) (v. 1044). Alternately, it could be understood that he tosses the quill back to his father and that Adam has already left for Paris, but in either case, he clearly associates the quill and himself with Adam.

Having established the folly of rhetoric, the fool then proceeds to begin drinking everyone's wine (v. 1054)—a fitting symbol of his drunken poetics—and causes such general commotion that the revelers are obliged to abandon the tavern.

> *Gillos.*   Pour l'amour de Dieu, ostons tout,
> Car se chieus sos la nous keurt seure,
> .   .   .   [line missing].   .   .   .   .   .
> Pren le nape, et tu, le pot tien.
>
> *Rikeche.*   Foi ke doi Dieu, je le lo bien,
> Tout avant ke il nous meskieche.
> Cascuns de nous prengne se pieche.
> Aussi avons nous trop veilliét.
>
> (vv. 1055–62)

> [*Gillos.*   For the love of God, grab everything,
> For if this fool gets hold of us,
>
> .   .   .   .
> Grab the tablecloth, and you, the pitcher.
>
> *Rikeche.*   By my faith in God, I seriously advise it,
> Before we come to regret it:
> Everybody grab what he can.
> We've stayed here too long.]

The fool, the breaker of pots, has already shattered all the other genres and traditions in the play, and now, in threatening to shatter the tavern scene, he threatens to ironically shatter the genre that itself represents the rhetoric of inversion. He in fact succeeds in doing so, since the scene and, with it, the play (since they are now in a sense coterminus) now end. The fool alone refuses to leave the tavern in the end, though he is finally dragged away by his father (v. 1093).

This second half of the tavern scene, after the arrival of the fool, again makes explicit a fact that has heretofore been only implicit in the play: the poetics of inversion, undermining, and folly—the other until now implicit use of the tavern in the play—are explicitly the poetics of this tavern. Once again, a member of the Adam/fool pair uses this poetics as a tool for inversion, as has been done so often before. Now, however, the emblem of the inverter is itself inverted. The tavern is turned on itself. Appropriately enough, the inversion is accomplished via a kind of *fatrasie* performed by the fool.

Conclusion

By framing his play as a journey to the tavern, Adam makes this tavern the locus of self-reflection not only on his own relationships to language and literature in general (or rather those of the "je" to language and literature) but also on the form of the play itself and on the theater. McGregor has noted that the tavern scene is "both the effective termination of the dramatic action and the true goal of the poetic pilgrimage the play carries out."[87] That this scene does indeed serve as a type of framing device, with a metafunction, was implicitly noted even in the nineteenth century, by Henry Guy, to take one example. He divides the play into exordium, main body (a satire of Arras and its vices), and the tavern conclusion.[88] If we accept Guy's division of the play, then the central problem that the tavern scene addresses may be said to be that the unmasking of the semiology of Arras is carried out in a poetics that participates in that same semiology— Adam and the fool use inverting folly to critique folly, the only difference being that they mark their own consciousness of their folly, while the rest of Arras seems engaged in a blind folly that purports to be the naked truth.

On a psychological level, the reading and writing (and critique) of the self must be done using this same semiology as well, as Rutebeuf suggests. Adam seems to pose even more clearly than Rutebeuf the question, How could one critique illicit desire and sin, even in the self, when the only semiology available to mediate the relation between "je" and "moi" not only is imbued with the same illicit characteristics of desire but is itself the source

---

87. MacGregor, *The Broken Pot Restored,* 92.
88. Guy, *Essai sur la vie et les oeuvres littéraires,* 359ff.

of this desire? The play finally confronts what Roger Dragonetti calls the "folie de l'impossible"—the impossibility of language and identity itself.[89]

Such a question is fundamental to the entire edifice of sin, guilt, confession, and penitence that the church sought to establish in the thirteenth century, particularly after the Fourth Lateran Council of 1215. As in the case of Rutebeuf, the individual's salvation depends on the reading and knowledge of the self. But the combination of pride and the inadequacy of representation at the individual's disposure combine to allow, and even encourage, a self-interested misreading of the individual and the world. Pride and desire so contaminate the semiology employed in representing the self that one reads only one's own desires, in what David Hult calls a "self-fulfilling prophecy" in his book on *The Romance of the Rose*.[90] The centrality of pride as an obstacle to correctly reading the self, and ultimately to salvation, is best illustrated by Dante's treatment of the theme in the *Purgatorio* a few decades later. The specific torment of the prideful in their work is to bear a heavy burden on their backs so that they are bent over and unable to see the divine light that shines above them and toward which they strive. Pride thus becomes in Dante a problem of vision, more specifically a downward, earthbound vision. It could also be considered a literal and individual vision according to our discussion, as opposed to an allegorical and collective one. In the *Purgatorio* passage, Dante specifically warns his own readers: "Non attender la forma del martire: / pensa la succession" (Pay no attention to the form of their suffering: consider only where it leads) (canto X, 110–11). The line evokes the commodification of the sign that is so dangerous to the Christian reader—the devotion to the literal. And Dante later speaks of the confused vision that pride causes in the Christian: "O superbi cristian, miseri lassi, / che, della vista della menta infermi, / fidanza avete ne' retrosi passi" (Oh prideful Christians, miserable and weary, who are sick in the vision of the mind, who place your trust in backward steps) (canto X, 121–23). Pride is so fundamental a problem that it is the first of the seven deadly sins to be worked off in Dante's purgatory. No progress is possible until this fundamental problem of vision is removed. Yet while Dante's *Purgatorio* offers the means to finally reach the divine light and shed the burden, *Le Jeu de la Feuillée* never seems able to—or even to want to—escape the "backward steps," the reflexive, inverting steps that turn the play back onto itself.

I have repeatedly distinguished between the dual natures of folly in the

89. Dragonetti, "Le Dervé-Roi."
90. Hult, *Self-Fulfilling Prophecies.*

play and the dual roles of the tavern. The distinction is crucial because this duality reveals the fundamental trap in which Adam finds himself. I have suggested that the tavern implicitly dominates the entire play and that the final scene serves to make this domination explicit by presenting the tavern as a kind of frame for the play. The poet's depiction of the tavern turning on itself reveals his awareness of the dilemma he finds himself in as writer and as individual in general, concerned with interiority and intentionality: there is no escape from either the self, the tavern, or Arras, no discourse that offers the exteriority of the divine view. Appropriately, Adam is still stuck in Arras as the play ends, and in fact he is still "hanging out" in the tavern (and being mocked for doing so). As noted earlier, it is unclear whether he in fact escapes Arras or not—one suspects that he is still present to receive the scholar's quill tossed by the fool, for there is at least thematically no real escape from the tavern.[91]

It seems appropriate to point out here that the literary pairing between Adam and the *dervés* that I established earlier and that is rendered entirely explicit here in the tavern (along with so many other things) itself serves to illustrate the trap of the poet. Not only are Adam and the fool paired, but in fact the two represent a split of the writer in the same way that Rutebeuf represents a split between the "je" and the "moi" in his "autobiographical" texts. I have already noted that the fool is often the mouthpiece for Adam and is more generally the most dynamic "agent" in the play, the one who often impels the text forward and determines where it will proceed next.[92] As such, he is the inscribed author, or the subjective "je," in the play, while Adam is more typically the objective "moi," the victim. The fool consistently victimizes his father ("Chertes, il m'a ja tant cousté / K'il me couvient querre men pain," says the father [vv. 1039–40]), while Adam is victimized by his father.[93] Adam is also the victim of his wife, of the fairies who curse him, of the bourgeois who reject his poetry, and of Robert Sommeillon, his rival in the poetic *puy*. In the final tavern scene, Adam has only four, passive lines (vv. 953–54, 957–58): the first two are a defense

---

91. Roger Dragonetti ("Le Dervé-Roi") has noted the "trap" element of the play as well: "le piège de la littérature étant que le poison de sa 'fiole' contient une promesse de guérison" (115). The promise, he suggests, is illusory.

92. This is entirely appropriate, since the fool is typically represented in medieval literature as behaving with an "aggressivité perpetuelle" (Ménard, "Les Fous," 443).

93. Roger Dragonetti ("Le Dervé-Roi") writes that "le poète . . . se [sert] de la loi interdictive . . . du père . . . pour y faire triompher . . . contre lui . . . ce chant souverain" (121). This admirably captures the fool's ability to resist his father, but Adam seems to be the exact contrary of a "souverain."

against a mocking attack, while the second two are another request directed to his father. The fool meanwhile dominates the scene and takes the role of active inverter. The fool in fact criticizes Adam himself at one point, calling him a "pois baiens" and mocking his pretensions of going to Paris. (Adam's response in vv. 953–54 is to this very remark, so the end of the play marks the first moment of active engagement between the two sides of Adam. Fittingly, the engagement is an argument that figures the fractured nature of Adam himself.) To the extent that inversion and undermining occur from "within" the text (by one of the characters in the play) it is the fool, and never Adam, who is responsible, except for on the one occasion where he describes his victimization and "enchantment" by love. Thus, in contrast to Rutebeuf, there is a split of the writer but no "escape" from the text, since both "je" and "moi" are literally inscribed into it together and trapped there. The final irony is that Adam's other half turns on him in the end, not only critiquing him but disrupting his carefully crafted tavern scene and abruptly ending the play in an illustration of the failure of intentionality and of the possibility of the "je" to write and read itself—the "moi."

The nature of the tavern as trap allows us finally to appreciate the full significance of the pot mentioned in the opening lines of the play. Not only does the pot represent folly via the proverb "mad as a potter," and not only does its shattering denote a shattering of literary genre, but the pot has philosophical and theological overtones as well that suggest a shattering of language itself and human intentionality. Alfred Adler has noted that the metaphor of the pot is used by Saint Paul and adopted by Saint Augustine to represent the very coherence of man's reason and personality.[94] This too is shattered in the play, figuratively. And the primary means of this shattering is the centrifugal destruction of the intentionality of language that I noted earlier: phonetic accident displaces the referential center of speech over and over. Language as a tool given to man by God, and guaranteed by God via his immanent, or "theotic," presence in the world, is no more. Univocal speech has been replaced by a "toss of the dice" in a world where God is absent. The great care that Adam takes to establish a highly coherent tavern scene allows him not only to explicitly expand the realm of the tavern to cover the entire play and the world of Arras but also to recall the other great taverns of Arras, the traditional literary locus from which God is absent. The tavern is the "devil's church," center of a

---

94. Adler, *Sens et composition du "Jeu de la Feuillée,"* 20ff.

fallen world. Jean Dufournet notes that the scene is virtually a parody of a church service, with the tavern keeper as priest, the wine as holy water, and so forth.[95] We have already seen such a parallel in an exemplum cited in chapter 1, and I have also noted the explicit opposition of church and tavern in other works, so the scene is effectively a culmination of this tradition and serves to emphasize the absence of God from this semiotic universe.

Yet unlike Jean le Marchant's miracle, or *Courtois d'Arras,* this play does not seem to consider the status of worldly signs as a "tragedy" to be redeemed somehow in the end by a reestablishment of "theosis." The play's final reconnection with the medieval moralizing tavern, the church of the devil, serves more as an ironic comment on that particular discourse than an attempt to return to it. In fact, the play as a whole unmasks the discourse of morality and intentionality and reveals its final impossibility as a complete perfection. In a world of imperfect signs, this discourse itself—this "pot" of Paul and Augustine—can never be fully whole and must always reveal its partially shattered status.

While the play unmasks the status of this discourse of moral intention, its true target seems to be less the discourse itself than the citizens of Arras. In the scene in which the monk sells the relics, for example, the central target is the monk, not the ultimate status and efficacity of relics or faith. Adam targets two general pretensions: first, that of adopting the religious discourse (along with a number of others on the part of many other characters) for oneself alone; second, the claiming of a falsely "unfractured" "whole" status for the discourses adopted. The hypocrisy of these intentions lies, first, in the will to mask what is really a "blindly avaricious" desire for the sign and, second, in the attempt to claim an impossible, unfractured authority for oneself. In both cases, the "Arrageois" are only fooling themselves.

Once such hypocritical pretensions are unmasked, the knowing, reflexive pleasure of the sign seems to be less problematic for Adam than for Rutebeuf. In Adam's text there is always an "intermittence," an "edge," a "tear" in discourse, to use three words from Barthes.[96] But it is in these gaps in language that Adam locates a poetics of the tavern that emerges, in a certain sense, triumphant at the end of the play. While the inverting folly of the fool undermines the tavern scene, this act is a mark of

---

95. Dufournet, *Adam de la Halle à la recherche de lui-même,* 325. See also Fritz, *Le discours du fou,* 332.

96. Barthes, *The Pleasure of the Text,* 10.

the triumph of this inversion over even itself.[97] After all, the pot reappears—whole—in the final tavern scene. The poetic language of the tavern and of folly, which accepts the sign in its full unstable potential, represents the only "wholeness" in the play. It is fittingly the fool who drinks wine from the pot. Not only is wine the characteristic drink of the tavern and of gluttony, but it also represents one general vision of the source of poetic production. We have seen the pervasiveness of the vision of the poet and jongleur drinking wine in the tavern—the elements are virtually inseparable. More importantly, we have seen that drinking wine and drunkenness produce the same disordering of language (and deverticalizing) that are characteristic of the *fatrasie* and the poetics of the tavern, as was best exemplified by the goliard poets discussed in chapter 3—drunken poets writing drunken rhetoric. The fool gluttonously seizes on an idolatrous mode of rhetorical production, to slake his desire. The fool's desire (for the sign) finds its fulfillment in a rhetoric that reifies the sign. Poetry, gluttony, and the tavern become one. The fool fully represents the only remaining intact rhetoric; as Eugene Vance says, he "remains true to himself and immovable in his nonsense."[98] The only "wholeness" is in an undermining folly (of which the fool is the "roi" [v. 395]), which of necessity must finally undermine itself and thus bring the play to an end consistent with its own inexorable poetic and rhetorical logic.

Adam's play suggests that folly is finally the truest expression of the psychology and epistemology of its time. Mikhail Bakhtin has argued in his discussion of this play that folly is a "gay festive wisdom, free from all laws and restrictions."[99] But it appears that folly is actually the embracing of the fullest implications of such laws and restrictions as they apply to the sign and the self. Those who seek freedom from these restrictions are either blind or hypocritical, according to Adam, and only in fully appreciating the limitations that the sign places on reading and representing the world and the self does one arrive at a higher level of creative freedom. Far from

---

97. In this sense, Roger Dragonetti ("Le Dervé-Roi") is correct in writing that the play "inclut son propre geste critique" (126). But at the same time, the critique is the necessary precondition to the play's final triumph. Dragonetti argues essentially that the play involves a destruction of previous literary tradition in order to renew ("reveiller," 121) the tradition. I am suggesting that the destruction is rather the destruction of a mask of pretensions to authority, in order to reveal the true sources of poetic creativity in the linguistic imperfections that refuse such authority.

98. Vance, *Mervelous Signals,* 221.

99. Bakhtin, *Rabelais and His World,* 260.

"mak[ing] no pretense of being a problem play,"[100] the play addresses—and then celebrates—the "problem" of language as the central enabler of literary production. As Alexandre Leupin has said (speaking of another text), the fall of language is finally the redemption of the poet.[101] In other words, not only is this problematic language represented as preventing the achievement of complete subjectivity and personal textual authority in the Middle Ages, but it serves to replace these categories in the role of textual creator, "fictor," and pottery maker.

---

100. Bakhtin, *Rabelais and His World,* 262.
101. Leupin, *Barbarolexis,* 29; see also 67, where he speaks of the defects of language as being the "jubilant font" of creativity.

Conclusion

Tavern and Theater

Though the tavern occupies proportionately less of *Le Jeu de la Feuillée* (about 20 percent) than it does of *Le Jeu de Saint Nicolas* (nearly half) or *Courtois d'Arras* (over half), I argue that the identity between theater and tavern is carried farthest in Adam's play. In fact, though the word "Feuillée" in the title of one manuscript of the play could refer to the tavern, it is also true that the theater was connected, in medieval iconography, to the idea of the *feuillée,* so that in this last play at least, the tavern and theater may be explicitly linked through this term. Servius, in his widely read, fourth-century commentary on Virgil, notes that "apud antiquos enim theatralis scaena parietem non habuit, sed de frondibus umbracula quaerebant" (among the ancients, moreover, the stage of the theater had no walls but was shaded by leafy boughs).[1] The connection between the "scaena" as a place of natural, leafy shade and the "scaena" as an element of the theater was a commonplace throughout the Middle Ages. In the *Magnae derivationes* of Ugaccione of Pisa, composed between 1197 and 1201, and considered perhaps the most authoritative of all high medieval dictionaries, we find "scena" defined as follows: "id est umbraculum, scilicet locus adumbratus in theatro et cortinis coopertus similis tabernis mercennariorum" (this is the shade, that is to say, the shady spot in the theater, covered with curtains similarly to the booths of the merchants).[2] Here, the word "tabernis" most properly refers to the booths of merchants selling their wares, not to a tavern, but in any case the notation of "feuillée" serves to evoke simultaneously the iconography of the tavern and that

---

1. Quoted in Marshall, "Theater in the Middle Ages," 6.
2. Cited in Marshall, "Theater in the Middle Ages," 25.

of the theater and its "scena," as well as the idea of "la folie."[3] Thus when Richard of Devizes warns a young twelfth-century traveler on his way to London, "vita thalum et tesseram, theatrum et tabernam" (avoid dice and gambling, the theater and the tavern), he links these vices not only for the sake of alliteration but for much deeper thematic reasons as well.[4]

Similarly, the theater as well as the tavern has been linked to the Fête des Fous. It has been claimed that "il faut attribuer, dans la genèse du théâtre comique, un rôle prépondérant à certaines réjouissances popu-laires . . . particulièrement à la Fête des Fous ou Fête des Sots."[5] Whether these once-a-year events played the dominant or preponderant role in the establishment of comic theater might be questioned, and this popular source of inspiration was closely coupled with more learned concerns, as suggested in the chapters of this book. Nevertheless, high medieval French theater does seem to engage in many of the same practices of creative destabilization that characterize the tavern piece in its nondramatic appearances.[6]

The moral status of the theater in Christian thought was, appropriately enough, similar to that of the tavern. Saint Augustine and the early church fathers, as well as classical Roman writers, left to the Middle Ages a view of the theater as a locus of the secular and unholy, as a rival to the church. Augustine was fond of contrasting the Roman *spectacula* to the divine, Christian spectacle.[7] "In theatris labes morum, discere turpia, audire inhonesta, videre perniciosa" (In the theaters morals go to pieces, obscen-ities are learned, lies are heard, and evils are seen), he wrote, "sed adju-vante Domino ea ex cordibus vestris firmiter repellamus" (but with the help of God let these things be firmly repelled from your hearts) (*PL* 36.639). One could easily extend the list of examples of the condemnation

---

3. To push this identity even further, we could recall Dufournet's speculation that the play was performed in the public marketplace known as the "Petit Marchié." This is significant because the broadest definition of *theatrum* in the Middle Ages was simply any open public space or marketplace, which may have itself been shaded. Thus tavern, theater, and urban marketplace are all intimately linked in a geography quite similar to that seen in chapter 1.

4. Richard of Devizes, *Cronicon Richardi Divisensis,* 65.

5. Paul Thiry, cited in Cartier, *Le bossu désenchanté,* 103. See also Mannoni, *Clefs pour l'imaginaire ou l'autre scene,* 301–14, where the author argues for further medieval thematic links between "la folie" and the theater; and see Fritz, *Le discours du fou,* 328–31.

6. Among other dramatic productions of the thirteenth century, Rutebeuf's *Miracle de Théophile* parallels *Courtois d'Arras* in enacting a negative example of transgressive, "bour-geois" economics, as discussed in chapter 1. The anonymous "Le garçon et l'aveugle" cer-tainly conforms to our model of the theater, while Adam's *Le jeu de Robin et Marion* also contains elements of generic destabilization.

7. See *PL* 35.1440, 40.638–39, 36.439–40.

of theater and spectacle, and these reprobations are repeated countless times in medieval moralizing texts, in both Latin and the vernacular, in the form of more general attacks on the jongleur, the "scurri et histrionae," of the Middle Ages.[8] Furthermore, the particular target of the inverting parody of the Fêtes des Fous, one probable source of medieval theater, was most typically the liturgy.[9]

The Decline of Semiotic Authority

Fundamentally, the theater and the tavern were both locations for meditation on, and contestation of, normative doctrines of sign use, most particularly those of the medieval church. The high medieval church's understanding of the sign began with two axioms. The first was that perfect communalism had been lost at the time of the Fall, with the result that exchanges (linguistic and economic, for example) were necessary for the maintenance of human community—exchanges mediated by signs. With the Fall came humanly instituted language, clothing, and private property (and eventually money). The second axiom was that the sign was fundamentally part of the imperfect, temporal world and thus was inherently open to inadequacy as a referential vehicle—it was carnal. Thus only by the application of normative constraints on the users of these signs (charitable intentions guaranteed by faith and divine immanence, the just price, or an education in *grammatica,* for example), could semiotic stability supposedly be insured. This in turn would insure the continuance of community, whether religious, social, economic, or textual.

From this ultimately religious point of view, deviation from correct use of signs was understood as an orientation of desire toward the temporal and individual (the tavern) and away from the spiritual and communal (the noble home, the church, or the monastery and its *hospitalium*). It

---

8. See Faral, *Les jongleurs,* and also Reyval, *L'église et le théâtre.* A more postmodern perspective on the issue of church and theater is in Leupin, *Barbarolexis,* 80–87. The most famous patristic text, beyond Augustine, is Tertullian's *De spectacula.* But see Hugh of Saint Victor, *Didascalicon,* 76, for a contrast between theater and "public houses," with the latter being the negative site.

9. See especially Fritz, *Le discours du fou,* 330ff. Thus the theater, like the tavern, becomes another locus that parodies the church. Indeed, the final tavern scene of Adam's play has been read by Jean Dufournet as such a parody, with the tavern keeper as priest, the wine as holy water, and so forth. Though Dufournet draws a parallel between the scene and certain passages of the *Le roman de Renart* (*Adam de la Halle à la recherche de lui-même,* 325), it could equally well be read in light of the exempla that I cited in my introduction and first chapter, which establish the tavern as the church of the devil.

could also be understood as a crossing of the threshold between the natural and utilitarian—the legitimate source for the creation of additional wealth—and the artificial and gratuitous. In this "illicit" situation, the value of linguistic signs or of economic commodities was no longer a fixed function of community but was determined through the interaction of individual desires. In other words, market replaced community, and the value of a text or a commodity was re-created and redetermined with each interaction of artificial desires—desires oriented toward the temporal sign itself rather than the spiritual community.

This then resulted in the impossibility of semiotic authority, because that authority was founded, within the original axiomatic framework, on community and the status of the individual as member of that community. (In other words, to take the most obvious example, the Bible's authority comes from God, not the human authors.) Individual manipulation of signs offered no basis for such authority and furthermore contaminated the original semiotic system, thus undermining community.

This is the message of the tavern as it appears in the hands of monastic culture, conservative medieval theologians (Peter Cantor, Alain de Lille), and preachers and mendicant friars. Of course, from a more pragmatic standpoint, it could be suggested that the real reason that such "contamination of community" did not occur in a sweeping way in the earlier Middle Ages (a few heresies excepted) was because there were effectively few signs at anyone's disposal: money was rare enough that a true, broadscale market economy, with its resultant qualitative shifts in the way values are determined, was not strongly established; and relatively few individuals had access to the written sign. Those that did achieved this access after passing through the normative constraint of a religious and grammatical education.

Cultural Transformation

For various socioeconomic and intellectual reasons, the sign did in fact become available to far more use—and abuse, in the church's eyes—in the twelfth and thirteenth centuries. Economic growth, an increase in the money supply, the rise of the profit motive, and vernacular literature that rose to a prominence where it was considered worthy of written recording were some symptoms of this development. Concurrent with this growing involvement in intellectual and economic life by many individuals less bound by the constraints of normative influences on sign use came a more general valuing of the particularities of the individual. Evidence of this includes the rise of confession, penitence, and a guilt culture; an interest in reading even sacred texts more closely at the literal level, with a consequent concern with the intentions of their human authors; and an increasing openness to behaviors more oriented toward individual rather than communal benefit.

This particular complex of concerns was broadly interrelated, and comico-realism is one revelation of the era's awareness of this fact. The specific thematic nexus centered on the tavern is a classic example of one "phase of an integrated cultural transformation happening at the same time," to use Brian Stock's words.[10] Though the creation of such emblems or nexuses is culturally ubiquitous, the specifics of the representational strategies employed in elaborating the emblem of the tavern are unique. Fundamentally trained to see the world and its transformations in terms of the sign, high medieval France elaborated a model of cultural evolution and confrontation with the tavern and its semiology as one of the terms of debate. That certain of the individual discourses that were accreted to the emblem of the tavern were distorted in the process is evident. In addition, as each of the discourses continued to evolve independently and as historical conditions changed, the parallels and unities established around the emblem of the tavern were forced to change as well (though Donald Maddox' work on *La farce de maître Pathelin* suggests a relatively strong degree of continuity even until the Renaissance).[11] As early as 1966, Paul Zumthor spoke of the history of the Middle Ages as a series of structures always aggregating and disaggregating in unstable combinations, and he recognized that these structures have no true autonomy.[12] I have tried to seize on one of these combinations, specifically the high medieval tavern, and to disentangle the discourses involved. To do so, it is crucial to appreciate the extent to which medieval learned ideas on the sign came to penetrate all levels and areas of medieval thought. Martin Irvine has noted that

---

10. Stock, *The Implications of Literacy,* 5.

11. See Maddox, *The Semiotics of Deceit,* especially 144–45, where he elaborates a series of overlapping oppositions that are similar to the ones I have located in this book. In particular, his socioeconomic model features an axis of city/town versus manor that closely corresponds to that of the tavern versus the farm in *Courtois d'Arras* and *Le Jeu de Saint Nicolas.* The military model also suggests the axis of the (essentially pagan) tavern versus epic crusaders in *Le Jeu de Saint Nicolas,* and the ecclesiological model's axis of heaven versus hell closely replicates my discussion in chapter 1.

12. Zumthor, "'Roman' et 'Gothique,'" 1223–27. See also Vance, *Mervelous Signals,* 119, on culture as a "configuration of semiotic systems" that feature a continual "displacement" of terms from one discourse to another.

"the political conflicts of the [Middle Ages] were frequently expressed as problems of interpreting cultural and religious scripture, conflicts which masked the deeper ideological oppositions,"[13] and the political sphere could be extended to include the social, economic, ethical, and psychological, at the least. The two-part difficulty for the modern reader of medieval texts—especially of texts as deceptively transparent as some fabliaux and *dits* or as confoundingly opaque as some scenes of Jean Bodel and Adam de la Halle—is to see the semiology that underlies the social, religious, and political elements of the texts and, alternately, to see the social, religious, and political aspects of medieval concerns with signs.

Embracing Profit and Play

The crucial feature of the twelfth and thirteenth centuries that this book has sought to illuminate (through an understanding of the tavern and its role in comico-realism) is a representation of cultural contestation and evolution in terms of an embrace of semiotic "inadequacy" and indeterminacy. This emblematic embrace of the unstable sign by certain elements of society had significant implications for the representation of literary, economic, and ethical practice. The embrace finds its expression in *Le Jeu de Saint Nicolas,* in the goliardic poems, in many fabliaux, and, albeit more ambiguously, in the work of Rutebeuf and in *Le Jeu de la Feuillée.* More generally, it finds its expression in the two concepts of play and profit.

The term *play* has been used in this book in reference to the concepts of the "artificial" and gratuitous. While a medieval moralist would have used a much harsher word than *play* to characterize involvement with this realm, in the hands of the authors central to this study, this is what literature becomes. As suggested by my remarks on *Le Jeu de Saint Nicolas'* double levels of meaning and on the ambiguity of Rutebeuf's linguistic stance, these texts offer multiple possibilities of meaning to the reader. Perhaps as important, they direct the reader not from the literal to religiously figural truths but in the opposite direction. While numerous medieval allegorical exegeses moved from the apparently illicit to the religiously licit, these texts in many cases move from the apparently licit to the allegorically illicit. While "Romanesque" hermeneutics could produce infinite "readings," they all led to a stable system of truths. Conversely, comico-realist texts gratuitously play with language for the sake of play and the creation

---

13. Irvine, *The Making of Textual Culture,* 169.

of a "surplus" of meaning—a creation of semiotic superabundance or profit, rather than a redistribution of a fixed sum of Truth. Of course, virtually all literature does this. Far more interestingly, these texts also represent within their confines their own creation, specifically in terms of play (dice, gambling), gratuity (vast eating and drinking, sexual pleasure), and profit. They explicitly point to the creative possibilities offered by language as a semiotic system open to manipulation and "hasard." They in fact suggest that the gaps that mark the sign's inadequacies are the essential spaces that allow for both gratuitous play and profit. Without these gaps, "Les trois aveugles de Compiegne" suggests, there would be no tale. The texts thus embrace the very aspect of the sign that represented a crisis for medieval religious and aristocratic communities. And they express this embrace most profoundly in their use of these groups' emblem of semiotic crisis (the tavern, inn, and brothel) as the emblem of semiotic creativity in their own discourse.

These texts not only make use of semiotic inadequacies, however, but also insistently underline their existence throughout society. Even more profoundly, they unmask the "inadequacy" not only of the sign but of attempts to overcome or disguise that inadequacy. The texts represent the emptiness of gestures of "authority" that attempt to establish a stability for the sign in either divine immanence, "nature" (and its most (im)potent emblem, the testicles), or a pretension to the naked truth through the adequacy of the sign. This is the deeper sense of the tavern's and theater's shared function as metaliterary, metalinguistic, and metasocial locales and also of their place in opposition to the church, the most powerful source of institutional authority in medieval culture.

These unmaskings have important consequences for the texts' status as "play." While at first glance they seem to "play" with signs outside the normative constraints that society attempts to impose, they far surpass Huizenga's and Caillois' classic definitions of play and the game.[14] Rather than "stepping out of real life" (Huizenga), bringing it to a "standstill" (Huizenga), or being "fictive" (Caillois),[15] the playful literature of comico-realism, in its act of play, is the truest revealer of the real conditions of exchange. As such, rather than being secluded and limited (Huizenga) or "séparée" (Caillois),[16] it engulfs its supposedly limiting frame. And rather

---

14. Caillois, *Les jeux et les hommes;* Huizenga, *Homo Ludens.*

15. See, respectively, Huizenga, *Homo Ludens,* 8 and 22; Caillois, *Les jeux et les hommes,* 43.

16. See, respectively, Huizenga, *Homo Ludens,* 9; Caillois, *Les jeux et les hommes,* 42.

than being unproductive (Caillois) and even "devastating" (Caillois) in its combination of chance (alea) and vertigo (ilinx),[17] it is fertile in finding creativity in the semiotic imperfections that are feared by other institutions of society. Thus while at first the tavern seems to be a world of gratuitous play and semiotic indeterminacy, comico-realism suggests that the whole world is finally a tavern. Literary play reveals the truth about signs, and this truth is that they are all open to play and to profit.

The Limits of Contestation, and New Forms of Authority and Community

In important senses, however, comico-realism does not break with the dominant ideology of the sign. It does accept the basic dichotomy of a possible adequacy and actual inadequacy in semiotic systems. And it furthermore accepts the idea that individual desires do revalue, commodify, and "contaminate" the system of signs. Value and interpretation are functions of individual desire and market transactions. This leads to two interesting consequences. First, the category of the feminine, while still clearly a product of a masculine textual tradition, has an unusual valuation in certain texts. If all language is imperfect and adorned and properly the object of desire, then the prostitute in particular becomes potentially a heroic author figure similar to the jongleur or the fool in their colorful, ill-fitting cloaks. Second, Rutebeuf and Adam de la Halle in particular suggest the possibility of a new foundation of authority outside that of the community. This authority lies specifically in their own vision of their fundamental semiotic blindness, of their inescapable position of being trapped in the tavern. In other words, if all their world is a tavern, then there is no stepping out of the tavern in their world, unlike in the world of *Courtois d'Arras,* where an exit from the tavern is proposed. Augustine noted that one has knowledge only of signs, not of things. And if signs are indeterminate, knowledge is indeterminate. Both Rutebeuf and Adam locate their authority in their superior awareness of this fact. In this context, the authority of the text lies in the authority of the tavern/market, but this authority ceases to be stable and shifts with each new textual and economic interaction.

This then means that even knowledge of the self is finally not fully possible. Everyone is always entangled in a system of signs "contaminated" by

---

17. See, respectively, Caillois, *Les jeux et les hommes,* 43 and 158.

everyone else in the process of exchange, including oneself. Thus there is neither the semiotic stability nor the possibility of disengagement from the system that would allow a fundamentally modern (postmedieval) representation of authority. This is perhaps the most important reason for the extreme passivity that characterizes both Rutebeuf and Adam as figures in their own works—far more often object than subject. Their truest subjectivity comes as the writers of their own entangled position as object. For this reason, the creativity that simultaneously reveals and undermines institutional pretensions of authority is far more socially entangled, self-conscious, and self-critical than the "play" of Bakhtin's "carnival," since the literary texts often do the same thing to themselves as they do to their more obvious targets.

The texts of Adam de la Halle and Rutebeuf thus mediate between play as an oppositional stance, opposed to the natural and utilitarian, and play as a self-reflexive stance, recognizing the limits to which this opposition may be taken due to play's entangling nature. This is the deeper expression of the entangled form of "dissent" that was discussed in the introduction. As that discussion implied, and as this concluding one hopefully demonstrates, medieval writers finally represented the impossibility of breaking entirely free of the discourses that had originally given birth to the tavern itself as a discursive emblem. Each discourse—nature and artifice, utility and profit—consistently informs the other, and dissent itself, like play, can never fully escape its own self-determinations in the medieval world. Within the context of comico-realism at least, play is a form of dissent, but dissent in general could be read as a larger form of play.[18]

This tension between the desire for an independent critical stance and the recognition of its unattainability due to the compromised nature of the sign points to one additional interesting result. If there is a true "rise of the individual" in the High Middle Ages, it is in the rise of play and profit rather than in full subjective authority. This is because in their opposition to Neoplatonic signs, play and profit lie in the space beyond nature, divinely oriented *caritas,* and normative community. They are thus the first representatives of an extracommunal, individual space. (And they are to be distinguished from the more socially sanctioned, "unproductive" play that is closer to the definitions of Huizenga and Caillois.) However, this space ultimately serves a second function: to reveal the inadequacies of the general high medieval model of community based on the linguistic

18. See Patterson, *Negotiating the Past,* especially 49–74, for a reading of these same issues within the context of medieval studies itself (and criticism in general).

sign. It suggests that for the urban, mercantile class, with their vernacular culture and profit economy, more open-ended models of community— such as the semiotic "market"—are needed, models that can account for play, profit, and the individual within a new form of urban community. The semiotic market suggests that both literary and economic value and profit can in fact be legitimately created by the poet and the merchant/investor—that usury is licit in all its forms. It refuses the notion of the zero-sum game of loss, theft, and the lie of literature, and with it the concept of fixed community value and semiotic stability. As such, it points to the eventual decline of the linguistic sign as a single, dominant, master signifier in medieval culture. The monetary sign both enlarges the semiotic domain of medieval culture and delimits that domain in a more dynamic and creative manner, as a community of profit and play.

Bibliography

Abbreviations used in the text or bibliography:

CB	*Carmina Burana,* ed. Vollman
CFMA	Les Classiques français du Moyen Age
DDC	Augustine, *De doctrina Christiana*
DPN	Alain de Lille, *De planctu Naturae*
OC	Rutebeuf, *Oeuvres complètes,* ed. Zink
PL	Migne, ed., *Patrologia Latina*
PUF	Presses Universitaires de France

Adam de la Halle. *Die der trouvère Adam de la Hale Zugeschriebenen Dramen.* Ed. A. Rambeau. Marburg: N. G. Elwertsche, 1886.

——. *Le Jeu de la Feuillée.* Ed. Ernest Langlois. 2d rev. ed. CFMA 6. Paris: Honoré Champion, 1923.

Adler, A. *Sens et composition du "Jeu de la Feuillée."* Ann Arbor: University of Michigan Press, 1956.

——. *"Le Jeu de Saint Nicolas:* Edifiant, mais dans quel sens?" *Romania* 81 (1960): 112–20.

Aers, David. *Community, Gender, and Individual Identity.* London: Routledge, 1988.

Alain de Lille. *Anticlaudianus; or the Good and Perfect Man.* Trans. James J. Sheridan. Toronto: Pontifical Institute of Medieval Studies, 1973.

——. *The Plaint of Nature.* Trans. James J. Sheridan. Toronto: Pontifical Institute of Medieval Studies, 1980.

Alter, Jean. *Les origines de la satire anti-bourgeoise en France.* Geneva: Droz, 1966–70.

Amadas et Idoine. Ed. John Reinhard. CFMA 51. Paris: Honoré Champion, 1926.

Aquinas, Saint Thomas. *Summa Theologica.* New York: Blackfriars and McGraw-Hill, 1963.

Arens, Arnold. *Untersuchungen zu Jean Bodels Mirakel "Le Jeu de Saint Nicolas."* Stuttgart: F. Steiner, 1986.

Aristotle. *The Politics.* Ed. and trans. Stephen Everson. Cambridge: Cambridge University Press, 1988.

Aubailly, Jean-Claude. *Le théâtre médiéval profane et comique.* Paris: Larousse, 1975.

Augustine, Saint. *De doctrina Christiana.* Ed. and trans. D. W. Robertson, Jr. Indianapolis: Bobbs-Merrill, 1958.

Bakhtin, Mikhail. *Rabelais and His World.* Trans. Helene Islowsky. Bloomington: Indiana University Press, 1984.

Baldwin, John W. *Medieval Theories of Just Price.* Transactions of the American Philosophical Society, n.s., vol. 49, no. 4. Philadelphia: American Philosophical Society, 1959.

———. *Masters, Princes, and Merchants: The Social Views of Peter the Chanter and His Circle.* Princeton: Princeton University Press, 1970.

Barbazan, Etienne, ed. *Fabliaux et contes des poëtes françois.* New edition, revised and augmented by Dominique Méon. 4 vols. Paris: B. Warée, 1808. Reprint (4 vols. in 2), Geneva: Slatkine Reprints, 1976.

Barthes, Roland. *The Pleasure of the Text.* Trans. Richard Miller. New York: Hill and Wang, 1975.

Bataille, Georges. "The Notion of Expenditure." In *Visions of Excess. Selected Writings, 1927–1939,* 116–29. Trans. Allan Stoehl with Carl R. Lovitt and Donald M. Leslie, Jr. Minneapolis: University of Minnesota Press, 1985.

Baumgartner, Emmanuelle. "The Play of Temporalities; or the Reported Dream of Guillaume de Lorris." In *Rethinking the Romance of the Rose: Text, Image, Reception,* ed. Kevin Brownlee and Sylvia Huot, 22–38. Philadelphia: University of Pennsylvania Press, 1992.

Bec, Pierre. *La lyrique française au Moyen Age.* Paris: Editions A. and J. Picard, 1977.

Bédier, Joseph. *Les fabliaux.* Paris: E. Bouillon, 1893.

Benedicti Regula. Ed. Rudolf Hanslick. Corpus Scriptorum Ecclesiasticorum Latinorum, vol. 75. Vienna: Hoelder-Pichler-Tempsky, 1955.

Benton, John W. *Self and Society in Medieval France.* Toronto: University of Toronto Press, 1984.

Berger, Roger. *Littérature et société arrageoises au XIIIe siècle: Les Chansons et Dits artésiens.* Arras: Comité départemental des monuments historiques du Pas-de-Calais, 1981.

Bernard of Cluny. *De contemptu mundi.* Ed. Ronald Pepin. East Lansing: Colleagues Press, 1991.

Berthelot, Anne. "Anti-Miracle et Anti-Fabliaux: la subversion des genres." *Romania* 106 (1985): 399–419.

Beyer, Jurgen. "The Morality of the Amoral." In *The Humor of the Fabliaux,* ed. Cooke and Honeycutt, 15–42.

Bianciotto, Gabriel, and Michel Salvat, eds. *Epopée animale fable fabliau.* Actes du IVe Colloque de la Société Renardienne, 7–11 Sept. 1981. Paris: PUF, 1984.

Bibliorum Sacrorum, Nova Vulgata editio. Iussu Pauli PP. VI recognita. Rome: Libreria Editrice Vaticana, 1986.

Billington, Sandra. *A Social History of the Fool.* New York: St. Martin's Press, 1984.

Bitsch, Imgard, ed. *Essen und Trinken im Mittelalter und Neuzeit: Vortrage eines interdisziplinaren Symposiums von 10.–13. Juni 1987 an der Justus-Liebig-Universitat Giessen.* Sigmaringen, Germany: Jan Thorbecke, 1987.

Bloch, R. Howard. *Medieval French Literature and Law.* Berkeley: University of California Press, 1977.

———. *Etymologies and Genealogies: A Literary Anthropology of the Middle Ages.* Chicago: University of Chicago Press, 1983.

———. *The Scandal of the Fabliaux.* Chicago: University of Chicago Press, 1986.

———. *Medieval Misogyny and the Invention of Western Romantic Love.* Chicago: University of Chicago Press, 1991.

Bloomfield, Morton W. *The Seven Deadly Sins.* East Lansing: Michigan State College Press, 1952.

Bodel, Jean [Jehan]. *Le Jeu de Saint Nicolas.* Ed. F. J. Warne. Oxford: Basil Blackwell, 1951.

———. *Le Jeu de St. Nicolas.* Ed. Albert Henry. Brussels: Presses Universitaires de Bruxelles, 1965.

———. *Le Jeu de Saint Nicolas de Jehan Bodel.* Ed. Albert Henry. 3d rev. ed. Brussels: Académie Royale de Belgique, 1981.

Bordier, Jean-Pierre. "*Le Jeu de St. Nicolas*—ou le miracle de l'image." *Revue des Langues Romanes* 95, no. 1 (1991): 59–74.

Bouchard, Constance. *Holy Entrepreneurs: Cistercians, Knights, and Economic Exchange in Twelfth-Century Burgundy.* Ithaca: Cornell University Press, 1991.

Bourdieu, Pierre. *Language and Symbolic Power.* Edited and introduced by John B. Thompson; trans. Gino Raymond and Matthew Adamson. Cambridge: Harvard University Press, 1991.

Bremond, Claude, and Jacques Le Goff. *L'exemplum.* Brepols: Turnhout, Belgium, 1982.

Brownlee, Kevin. "The Problem of Faux Semblant: Language, History, and Truth in the *Romance of the Rose.*" In *The New Medievalism,* ed. Marina Brownlee, Kevin Brownlee, and Stephen Nichols, 253–67. Baltimore: Johns Hopkins University Press, 1991.

Bruckner, Matilda. *Narrative Invention in Twelfth-Century French Romance: The Convention of Hospitality, 1160–1200.* Lexington, Ky.: French Forum, 1980.

Brundage, James A. *Law, Sex, and Christian Society.* Chicago: University of Chicago Press, 1987.

Burns, E. Jane. *Arthurian Fictions: Rereading the Vulgate Cycle.* Columbus: Ohio State University Press, 1985.

Bynum, Caroline Walker. *Jesus as Mother: Studies in the Spirituality of the High Middle Ages.* Berkeley: University of California Press, 1982.

Caillois, Roger. *Les jeux et les hommes: le masque et le vertige.* Paris: Gallimard, 1958.

Carmina Burana: Texte und Ubersetzungen. Ed. Benedikt K. Vollmann. Frankfurt: Deutsche Klassiker Verlag, 1987.

Cartier, Norman. *Le bossu désenchanté.* Geneva: Droz, 1971.

Cave, Terence. *The Cornucopian Text: Problems of Writing in the French Renaissance.* New York: Oxford University Press, 1979.

Cerquiglini, Jacqueline. "'Le clerc et le louche': Sociology of an Aesthetic." *Poetics Today* 5, no. 3 (1984): 479–91.

Chartres, John. "The English Inn and Road Transport before 1700." In *Gastfreundschaft, Taverne und Gasthaus,* ed. Peyer, 153–77.

Chénu, Marie Dominique. *Nature, Man, and Society in the Twelfth Century: Essays on New Theological Perspectives in the Latin West.* Edited, selected, and translated by Jerome Taylor and Lester K. Little. Chicago: University of Chicago Press, 1968.

Chrétien de Troyes. *Lancelot, or The Knight of the Cart (Le Chevalier de la Charrete).* Ed. and trans. William Kibler. Garland Library of Medieval Literature, vol. 1, ser. A. New York: Garland, 1981.

———. *The Knight with the Lion, or Yvain (Le Chevalier au Lion).* Ed. and trans. William Kibler. Garland Library of Medieval Literature, vol. 48, ser. A. New York: Garland, 1985.

———. *Erec et Enide.* Ed. and trans. Charleton W. Carroll. Garland Library of Medieval Literature, vol. 25, ser. A. New York: Garland, 1987.

Clanchy, M. T. *From Memory to Written Record: England, 1066–1307.* 2d ed. Oxford: Basil Blackwell, 1993.

Clark, Peter. *The English Alehouse: A Social History.* London: Longman, 1983.

Cohen, E. "Roads and Pilgrimage: A Study in Economic Interaction." *Studi Medievali* 21 (1980): 321–44.

Cohen, Gustave, ed. *Anthologie du drame liturgique en France au Moyen Age.* Paris: Les Editions du Cerf, 1955.

Cooke, Thomas. *The Old French and Chaucerian Fabliaux: A Study of Their Comic Climax.* Columbia: University of Missouri Press, 1978.

Cooke, Thomas, and Benjamin Honeycutt, eds. *The Humor of the Fabliaux: A Collection of Critical Essays.* Columbia: University of Missouri Press, 1974.

Copeland, Rita, ed. *Criticism and Dissent in the Middle Ages.* Cambridge: Cambridge University Press, 1996.

Coulet, Noel. "Les Hôtelleries en France et en Italie au Bas Moyen Age." In *L'Homme et la route occidentale au Moyen Age et aux temps modernes,* ed. Charles Higounet, Deuxième Tournées Internationales d'histoire, 20–22 Sept. 1980, 181–205. Auch: Centre Culturel de l'abbaye de Flaran, 1982.

———. "Propriétaires et exploitants d'auberges dans la France du Midi au bas Moyen Age." In *Gastfreundschaft, Taverne und Gasthaus,* ed. Peyer, 119–37.

———. "Inns and Taverns." In *Dictionary of the Middle Ages,* ed. Joseph R. Strayer, 6:468–77. New York: Charles Scribner's Sons, 1989.

Courtois d'Arras. Ed. Edmond Faral. CFMA 3. Paris: Honoré Champion, 1922.

Cousins, M. E. "Deux Parties de dés dans *Le Jeu de St. Nicolas.*" *Romania* 57 (1931): 436–37.

Cowell, Andrew. "The Fall of the Oral Economy: Writing Economics on the Dead Body." *Exemplaria* 8, no. 1 (1996): 145–68.

———. "Feminine Semiotics and Masculine Desires: *Courtois d'Arras* and the Proper Male Reader in the Middle Ages." *Symposium* 50, no. 1 (1996): 16–27.

———. "Deadly Letters: 'Deus Amanz,' Marie's 'Prologue' to *Lais,* and the Dangerous Nature of the Gloss." *Romanic Review* 88, no. 3 (1997): 337–56.

Dane, Joseph. "Parody and Satire in the Literature of Thirteenth-Century Arras." *Studies in Philology* 81, no. 1 (1984): 1–27.

———. *Res/Verba: A Study in Medieval French Drama.* Leiden: E. J. Brill, 1985.

Dante Alighieri. *Le opere di Dante.* Ed. Michele Barbi et al. 2d ed. Florence: La Società Dantesca Italiana, 1960.

del Valle da Paz, Ida. *La leggenda di S. Nicola nella tradizione poetica medioevale in Francia.* Florence: Stabilimento Pisa e Lampronti, 1921.

Derrida, Jacques. *Margins of Philosophy.* Trans. Alan Bass. Chicago: University of Chicago Press, 1982.

Dinshaw, Carolyn. "Dice Games and Other Games in *Le Jeu de Saint Nicolas.*" *PMLA* 95 (1980): 802–11.

———. "Eunuch Hermeneutics." *English Literary History* 55, no. 1 (1986): 27–51.

Dragonetti, Roger. *Le gai savoir dans la rhétorique courtoise: Flamenca et Joufroi de Poitiers.* Paris: Editions du Seuil, 1982.

———. "Le *Jeu de St. Nicolas* de Jean Bodel." In *The Craft of Fiction,* ed. Leigh A. Arathoon, 369–91. Rochester, Minn.: Solaris Press, 1984.

———. "Le Dervé-Roi dans le *Jeu de la Feuillée* d'Adam de la Halle." *Revue des Langue Romanes* 95, no. 1 (1991): 115–35.

Dubois, Michel. "Sur un passage obscur du *Jeu de St. Nicolas.*" *Romania* 55 (1929): 256–58.

Duby, Georges. *La société aux XIe et XIIe siècles dans la région maconnaise.* Paris: Armand Colin, 1953.

———. *The Early Growth of the European Economy: Warriors and Peasants from the Seventh to the Twelfth Century.* Trans. Howard B. Clarke. Ithaca: Cornell University Press, 1974.

Dufeuil, Michel-Marie. "L'oeuvre d'une vie rhythmée: chronographie de Rutebeuf." In *Musique, littérature et société au Moyen Age,* ed. Danielle Buschinger and André Crispin, Actes du Colloque d'Amiens, 279–94. Paris: Honoré Champion, 1981.

Dufournet, Jean. "Adam de la Halle et *Le Jeu de la Feuillée.*" *Romania* 86 (1965): 199–245.

———. *Adam de la Halle à la recherche de lui-même ou le jeu drammatique de la Feuillée.* Paris: Société d'édition d'enseignement supérieur, 1974.

———. "A la recherche de Rutebeuf" and "Un sobriquet ambigu." In *Melanges de langue et de littérature françaises du Moyen Age et de la Renaisance offerts à M. Charles Foulon,* 1:105–10. Rennes: Institut de Français, Université de Haute Bretagne, 1980.

———. "Variations sur un motif—la taverne dans le théâtre arrageois du XIIIe siècle." In *Hommage à Jean-Charles Payen: Farai chansoneta novele,* 161–74. Caen: Centre de Publications de l'Université de Caen, 1989.

———. "*Courtois d'Arras* ou le triple héritage." *Revue des Langues Romanes* 95, no. 1 (1991): 75–114.

———, ed. *Rutebeuf: poèmes de l'infortune.* Paris: Gallimard, 1986.

Eco, Umberto, ed. *On the Medieval Theory of Signs.* Philadelphia: John Benjamins Publishing Co., 1989.

Enders, Jody. *Rhetoric and the Origins of Medieval Drama.* Ithaca: Cornell University Press, 1989.

Esposito, Edoardo. "Les formes d'hospitalité dans le roman courtois (du Roman de Thèbes à Chrétien de Troyes)." *Romania* 103 (1982): 197–234.

Faral, Edmond. *Mimes français du XIIIe siècle.* Paris: Honoré Champion, 1910.

———. *La vie quotidienne au temps de Saint Louis.* Paris: Hachette, 1942.

———. *Les jongleurs en France au Moyen Age.* Paris: Honoré Champion, 1910. Reprint, Geneva: Slatkine Reprints, 1987.

Ferster, Judith. *Chaucer on Interpretation.* Cambridge: Cambridge University Press, 1985.

Foucault, Michel. "What Is an Author?" in *Textual Strategies: Perspectives in Post-structuralist Criticism,* ed. Josué V. Harrari, 141–60. Ithaca: Cornell University Press, 1979.

Foulet, Lucien, and Charles Foulon. "Les scènes de taverne et les comptes du tavernier dans le *Jeu de St. Nicolas* de Jean Bodel." *Romania* 68 (1944): 422–43.

Frank, Grace. *The Medieval French Drama.* New York: Oxford University Press, 1954.

Frappier, Jean. "Rutebeuf, poète du jeu, du guigon et de a misère." In *Du Moyen Age à la Renaissance,* 123–33. Paris: Honoré Champion, 1976.

Fritz, Jean-Marie. *Le discours du fou au Moyen Age, XIIe–XIIIe siècles: Etude comparée des discours littéraire, médical, juridique et théologique.* Paris: PUF, 1992.

Garapon, Robert. *La fantaisie verbale et le comique dans le théâtre français du Moyen Age à la fin du 17e siècle.* Paris: Armand Colin, 1957.

Garrisson, Francis. "Les hôtes et l'hébergement des étrangers au moyen age, quelques solutions de droit comparée." In *Etudes d'Histoire du Droit Privée offertes à Pierre Petot,* 199–222. Paris: Librairie du recueil Sirey, 1959.

Gaunt, Simon. *Gender and Genre in Medieval French Literature.* Cambridge: Cambridge University Press, 1995.

Gautier d'Aupais. Ed. Edmond Faral. CFMA 20. Paris: Honoré Champion, 1919.

Gellrich, Jesse. *The Idea of the Book in the Middle Ages: Language Theory, Mythology, and Fiction.* Ithaca: Cornell University Press, 1985.

Geoffrey of Vinsauf. *Poetria nova.* Trans. Margaret F. Nims. Toronto: Pontifical Institute of Medieval Studies, 1967.

Geremek, Bronislaw. *The Margins of Society in Late Medieval Paris.* Trans. Jean Birrell. Cambridge: Cambridge University Press, 1987.

Gerster, Walter. "Beitrag zur Geshichte einiger Bezeichnungen fur Gasthaus, besonders fr. taverne-hôtel-auberge." *Vox Romanica* 9 (1946): 57–87.

Gilles, Henri. "Lex peregrinorum." In *Le Pèlerinage,* 161–90.

Godefroy, Frédéric. *Dictionnaire de l'ancienne langue française.* Paris: Ministère de l'instruction publique, 1892. Reprint, Vaduz, Liechtenstein: Klaus Reprints, 1965.

Gordon, Barry. *Economic Analysis before Adam Smith: Hesiod to Lessius.* London: Macmillan, 1975.

Gottfried von Strassburg. *Tristan.* Ed. Gottfried Weber. Darmstadt: Wissenschaftliche Buchgesellschaft, 1967.

Goux, Jean-Joseph. *Freud, Marx: economie et symbolique.* Paris: Editions du Seuil, 1973.

Gravdal, Kathryn. *Vilain and Courtois: Transgressive Parody in French Literature of the Twelfth and Thirteenth Centuries.* Lincoln: University of Nebraska Press, 1989.

Greimas, Algirdas Julien. *Dictionnaire de l'ancien français.* Paris: Larousse, 1980.

Guide du pèlerin de Saint-Jacques de Compostelle, Le. Ed. Jeanne Vieillard. 4th ed. Macon: Protat Frères, 1969.

Guiraud, Pierre. *Le jargon de Villon ou le gai savoir de la Coquille.* Paris: Gallimard, 1968.

Guillaume de Lorris and Jean de Meun. *Le roman de la rose.* Ed. Ernest Langlois. Paris: Firmin-Didot et Cie, 1914–24.

Guillaume le clerc de Normandie. *Le besant de Dieu.* Ed. Pierre Ruelle. Brussels: Editions de l'Université de Bruxelles, 1973.

Gurevich, Aron. *Categories of Medieval Culture.* Trans. G. L. Campbell. London: Routledge and Kegan Paul, 1985.

———. *Medieval Popular Culture: Problems of Belief and Perception.* Trans. János M. Bak and Paula A. Hollingsworth. Cambridge: Cambridge University Press, 1988.

Guy, Henry. *Essai sur la vie et les oeuvres littéraires du trouvère Adam de le Hale.* Paris: Hachette, 1898.

Ham, Edward B. "Rutebeuf—Pauper and Polemicist." *Romance Philology* 11, no. 3 (1957): 226–39.

Harris, Roy, and Talbot J. Taylor. *Landmarks in Western Linguistic Thought.* London: Routledge, 1989.

Heldris de Cornuaille. *Le Roman de Silence: A Thirteenth-Century Arthurian Verse Romance.* Ed. Lewis Thorpe. Cambridge, England: Heffer, 1972.

Hélin, Maurice. *A History of Medieval Latin Literature.* New York: William Salloch, 1949.

Hellmuth, Leopold. *Gastfreudschaft und Gastrecht bei den Germanen.* Vienna: Verlag des Osterreichischten Akademie den Wissenschaften, 1984.

Helsinger, Howard. "Pearls in the Swill: Allegory in the French Fabliaux." In *The Humor of the Fabliaux,* ed. Cooke and Honeycutt, 93–106.

Hiltbrunner, Otto. "Gastfreundschaft und Gasthaus in der Antike." In *Gastfreundschaft, Taverne und Gasthaus,* ed. Peyer, 2–20.

Holy Bible, The. Revised Standard Version.

Honeycutt, Benjamin L. "The Knight and His World as an Instrument of Humor in the Fabliaux." In *The Humor of the Fabliaux,* ed. Cooke and Honeycutt, 75–92.

Hugh of St. Victor. *Didascalicon: A Medieval Guide to the Arts.* Ed. and trans. Jerome Taylor. New York: Columbia University Press, 1961.

Hugh Primas and the Archpoet. Ed. Fleur Adcock. Cambridge: Cambridge University Press, 1994.

Huizenga, Johan. *Homo Ludens: A Study of the Play-Element in Culture.* New York: Roy, 1950.

Hult, David F. *Self-Fulfilling Prophecies: Readership and Authority in the First Roman de la Rose.* Cambridge: Cambridge University Press, 1986.

Hunt, Tony. "The Authenticity of the Prologue of Bodel's *Jeu de Saint Nicolas.*" *Romania* 97 (1976): 252–67.

———. "Rhetoric and Poetics in Twelfth-Century France." In *Rhetoric Revalued: Papers from the International Society for the History of Rhetoric,* ed. Brian Vickers, 165–71. Medieval and Renaissance Texts and Studies, vol. 19. Binghampton, N.Y.: Center for Medieval and Early Renaissance Studies, 1982.

Ibanès, Jean. *La doctrine de l'église et les réalités économiques au XIIIe siècle.* Paris: PUF, 1967.

Irvine, Martin. *The Making of Textual Culture: 'Grammatica' and Literary Theory, 350–1100.* Cambridge: Cambridge University Press, 1994.

Jauss, Hans Robert. *Towards an Aesthetic of Reception.* Trans. Timothy Bahti. Minneapolis: University of Minnesota Press, 1982.

Jeanroy, Alfred, ed. *Chansons et dits artésiens.* Bordeaux: Feret, 1898. Reprint, Geneva: Slatkine Reprints, 1976.

Jeanroy, Alfred, and A. Langfors, eds. *Chansons satiriques et bachiques du XIIIe siècle.* CFMA 23. Paris: Honoré Champion, 1921.

Jean [Jehan] le Marchant. *Le livre des miracles de Notre-Dame de Chartres écrit en vers au XIIIe siècle par Jehan le Marchant.* Ed. M. G. Duplessis. Chartres: Garnier, 1855.

Jehan le teinturier d'Arras. *"Le mariage des sept arts" de Jehan le teinturier d'Arras.* Ed. Arthur Langfors. CFMA 31. Paris: Honoré Champion, 1923.

Jones, Charles W. *The St. Nicholas Liturgy and Its Literary Relationships (Ninth to Twelfth Centuries).* Berkeley: University of California Press, 1963.

Jubinal, Achille, ed. *Jongleurs et trouvères: Ou choix de saluts, epîtres, rêveries et autres pièces legères des XIIIe et XIVe siècles.* Paris: A. J. Merklein, 1835.

———. *Nouveau recueil de contes, dits, fabliaux et autres pièces.* 2 vols. Paris: Edouard Pannier, 1839. Reprint (2 vols. in 1), Geneva: Slatkine Reprints, 1975.

Jugnot, G. "Les Chemins de pèlerinage dans la France Médiévale." In *L'Homme et la route occidentale au Moyen Age et aux temps modernes,* ed. Charles Higounet, Deuxième Tournées Internationales d'histoire, 20–22 Sept. 1980, 57–83. Auch: Centre Culturel de l'abbaye de Flaran, 1982.

Jugnot, G., and R. de la Coste-Messeliere. "L'acceuil des pèlerins à Toulouse." In *Le pèlerinage,* 117–36.

Julleville, Petit de. *Histoire du théâtre en France—les mystères.* Paris: Hachette, 1880.

———. *Histoire de la langue et de la littérature française des origines à 1900.* Paris: Armand Colin, 1896.

———. *La comédie et les moeurs en France au Moyen Age.* Paris: Cerf, 1897.

Karras, Ruth. *Common Women: Prostitution and Sex in Medieval England.* New York: Oxford University Press, 1996.

Kellogg, Judith. *Medieval Artistry and Exchange: Economic Institutions, Society, and Literary Form in Old French Narrative.* New York: P. Lang, 1989.

Kelly, Douglas. "La spécialité dans l'invention des topiques." In *Archéologie du signe,* ed. Lucie Brind'Amour and Eugene Vance, 101–25. Toronto: Pontifical Institute for Medieval Studies, 1983.

Kerntke, Wilfried. "Taberna, Ortsherrschaft und Markt-entwicklung in Bayern." In *Gastfreundschaft, Taverne und Gasthaus,* ed. Peyer, 93–100.

———. *Taverne und Markt. Ein Beitrag zur Stadtgeschichtsforschung.* New York: P. Lang, 1987.

Klauenberg, Otto. *Getränke und Trinken in altfranzo-sischer Zeit.* Hannover: Druck von Wilhelm Harzig, 1904.

Kleinhans, Martha. *"Lucidere vault tant a dire comme donnant lumiere": Untersuchung und Edition der Prosaversionen 2, 4 und 5 des Elucidarium.* Beihefte zur *Zeitschrift für romanische Philologie,* no. 248. Tübingen: Max Niemeyer, 1993.

Köhler, Erich. *Ideal und Wirklichkeit in der höfische Epik.* Beihefte zur *Zeitschrift für romanische Philologie,* no. 97. Tübingen: Max Niemeyer, 1970.

Kristeva, Julia. *Semeiotike = recherches pour une semanalyse.* Paris: Editions du Seuil, 1969.

Ladurie, Emmanuel Le Roy. *Montaillou, village occitan de 1294 à 1324.* Paris: Gallimard, 1975.

Langholm, Odd. *Economics in the Medieval Schools: Wealth, Exchange, Value, Money, and Usury according to the Paris Theological Tradition, 1200–1350.* Leiden: E. J. Brill, 1992.

Langlois, Charles Victor. *La vie française au Moyen Age.* 4 vols. Paris: Hachette, 1924–28.

Lanson, Gustave. *Histoire de la littérature française.* Paris: Hachette, 1938.

Le Goff, Jacques. *Pour un autre Moyen Age.* Paris: Gallimard, 1977.

———. *La naissance du Purgatoire.* Paris: Gallimard, 1981.

———. *The Medieval Imagination.* Trans. Arthur Goldhammer. Chicago: University of Chicago Press, 1988.

———. *Your Money or Your Life: Economy and Religion in the Middle Ages.* New York: Zone Books, 1988.

Lejeune, Philippe. *Le pacte autobiographique.* Paris: Editions du Seuil, 1975.

Lekai, Louis J. *The Cistercians: Ideals and Reality.* Kent, Ohio: Kent State University Press, 1977.

Lemke, W. H. "The Angel in *Le Jeu de Saint Nicolas.*" *Romance Notes* 11 (1969): 420–26.

Le Roy, Onésime. *Etudes sur les mystères.* Paris: Hachette, 1837.

Lestocquoy, J. *Aux origines de la bourgeoisie: Les villes de Flandres et d'Italie.* Paris: PUF, 1952.

———. *Etudes d'histoire urbaine, villes et abbayes: Arras au Moyen Age.* Arras: Imprimerie Centrale de l'Artois, 1966.

Leupin, Alexandre. *Barbarolexis: Medieval Writing and Sexuality.* Cambridge: Harvard University Press, 1989.

Little, Lester. *Religious Poverty and the Profit Economy in Medieval Europe.* Ithaca: Cornell University Press, 1978.

Lorcin, Marie-Thérèse. *Façons de sentir et de penser: Les fabliaux français.* Paris: Honoré Champion, 1979.

———. "Manger et boire dans les fabliaux, rites sociaux et hiérarchie des plaisirs." In *Manger et boire au Moyen Age,* ed. Denis Menjot, Actes du Colloque de nice, 15–17 Oct. 1982, 227–37. Paris: Les Belles Lettres, 1984.

MacGregor, Gordon. *The Broken Pot Restored: "Le Jeu de la Feuillée" of Adam de la Halle.* Lexington, Ky.: French Forum, 1991.

Maddox, Donald. *The Semiotics of Deceit: The Pathelin Era.* Lewisburg, Pa.: Bucknell University Press, 1984.

Mannoni, Octave. *Clefs pour l'imaginaire ou l'autre scène.* Paris: Editions du Seuil, 1969.

Marie de France. *Les lais de Marie de France.* Ed. Jean Rychner. CFMA 93. Paris: Honoré Champion, 1983.

Marshall, Mary. "Theater in the Middle Ages: Evidence from Dictionaries and Glossaries." *Symposium* 4, no. 1 (1950): 1–39; 4, no. 2 (1950): 366–89.

Matthew of Vendôme. *The Art of Versification.* Ed. Aubrey Galyon. Ames: Iowa State University Press, 1980.

Mauron, Claude. *Le Jeu de la Feuillée: Etude psychocritique.* Paris: Jose Corti, 1973.

Mauss, Marcel. *The Gift: Forms and Functions of Exchange in Archaic Societies.* Trans. Ian Cunnison. New York: W. W. Norton and Co., 1967.

Ménard, Philippe. "Les Fous dans la société médiéval." *Romania* 98 (1977): 433–59.

———. "Le sens du *Jeu de la Feuillée.*" *Travaux de linguistique et de littérature publiés par le centre de philologie et de littératures romanes de l'université de Strasbourg* 16, no. 1 (1978): 381–93.

———. *Les fabliaux: Contes à rire du Moyen Age.* Paris: PUF, 1983.

———. "Les Emblèmes de la folie dans la littérature et dans l'art (XIIe et XIIIe siècles)." In *Hommage à Jean-Charles Payen: Farai chansoneta novele,* 253–66. Caen: Centre de Publications de l'Université de Caen, 1989.

Méon, Dominique, ed. *Nouveau recueil de fabliaux et contes.* 2 vols. in 1. Paris: Chasseriau, 1823.

Migne, J.-P. *Patrologiae cursus completus, series latina.* 221 vols. Paris: Garnier Frères, 1844–1903.

Minnis, Alastair J. *The Medieval Theory of Authorship: Scholastic Literary Attitudes in the Later Middle Ages.* London: Scholar Press, 1984.

Misch, Georg. *A History of Autobiography in Antiquity.* Trans. E. W. Dickes. London: Routledge and Kegan Paul, 1950.

Moniage Guillaume, Les deux redactions en vers du. Ed. Wilhelm Cloetta. 2 vols. Paris: Fermin-Didot et Cie, 1906–11.

Montaiglon, Anatole de, ed. *Recueil général et complet des fabliaux des XIIIe et XVe siècles.* 6 vols. Paris: Librairie des bibliophiles, 1872.

Morawski, Joseph, ed. *Proverbes français antérieurs au XVe siècle.* CFMA 47. Paris: Honoré Champion, 1925.

Morris, Colin. *The Discovery of the Individual, 1050–1200.* London: S.P.C.K. for the Church Historical Society, 1972.

Muscatine, Charles. *The Old French Fabliaux.* New Haven: Yale University Press, 1986.

Nelson, Benjamin. *The Idea of Usury: From Tribal Brotherhood to Universal Otherhood.* 2d ed. Chicago: University of Chicago Press, 1969.

Newman, Sandra G. *The Boundaries of Charity: Cistercian Culture and Ecclesiastical Reform, 1098–1180.* Stanford: Stanford University Press, 1996.

Nichols, Steven. *Romanesque Signs: Early Medieval Narrative and Iconography.* New Haven: Yale University Press, 1985.

Noomen, Willem, ed. *Nouveau recueil complet des fabliaux.* 10 vols. to date. Assen and Maastricht: Van Gorcum, 1983–.

Noonan, John. *The Scholastic Analysis of Usury.* Cambridge: Harvard University Press, 1957.

Nykrog, Per. *Les fabliaux.* Copenhagen: E. Munksgaard, 1957.

Otis, Leah. *Prostitution in Medieval Society: The History of an Urban Institution in Languedoc.* Chicago: University of Chicago Press, 1985.

Oursel, Raymond. *Pèlerins du Moyen Age: Les Hommes, les Chemins, les Sanctuaires.* Paris: Fayard, 1978.

Passion du Palatinus, La. Ed. Grace Frank. CFMA 30. Paris: Honoré Champion, 1922.

Patch, Howard. *The Goddess Fortuna in Mediaeval Literature.* Cambridge: Harvard University Press, 1927.

Patterson, Lee. *Negotiating the Past: The Historical Understanding of Medieval Literature.* Madison: University of Wisconsin Press, 1987.

Payen, Jean Charles. *Le motif du repentir dans la littérature médiévale.* Geneva: Droz, 1967.

———. "Les Eléments idéologiques dans *Le Jeu de Saint Nicolas.*" *Romania* 94 (1973): 484–505.

———. "Fabliaux et Cocagne." In *Epopée animale fable fabliau,* ed. Bianciotto and Salvat, 435–47.

Pearcy, Roy J. "Modes of Signification and the Humor of Obscene Diction in the Fabliaux." In *The Humor of the Fabliaux,* ed. Cooke and Honeycutt, 163–96.

Pèlerinage, Le. Cahiers de Fanjeaux, 25. Toulouse: Privat Editeur, 1980.

Pesce, L.-G. "Le Portrait de Rutebeuf." *Revue de l'Université d'Ottawa* 28, no. 1 (1958): 55–119.

Peyer, H. C., ed. *Gastfreundschaft, Taverne und Gasthaus im Mittelalter.* Munich: R. Oldenbourg, 1983.

———. *Gastfreundschaft und kommerzielle Gastlichkeit im Mittelalter.* Munich: Stiftung Historisches Kollegs, 1983.

———. *Von der Gastfreundschaft zum Gasthaus: Studien zur Gastlichkeit im Mittelalter.* Hannover: Hahnsche Buchhandlung, 1987.

Plato. *Ion, Gorgias, Phaedrus, and Symposium.* Trans. Lane Cooper. Ithaca: Cornell University Press, 1948.

———. *Laws.* Loeb Classical Series. Cambridge: Harvard University Press, 1968.

Poirion, Daniel. *Précis de la littérature française du moyen age.* Paris: PUF, 1983.

Porter, Lambert. *La fatrasie et le fatras: Essai sur la poésie irrationnelle in France au Moyen Age.* Geneva: Droz, 1960.

Rabecka-Brykczynska, Irena. "Die Taverne im fruhmittelalterlichen Polen." In *Gastfreundschaft, Taverne und Gasthaus,* ed. Peyer, 103–18.

Raoul de Houdenc. *The "Songe d'Enfer" of Raoul de Houdenc.* Ed. Madelyn T. Mihm. Tübingen: Max Niemeyer, 1984.

Raybin, David. "The Court and the Tavern: Bourgeois Discourse in *Li Jeus de Saint Nicolas.*" *Viator* 19 (1988): 177–92.

Regalado, Nancy. "Poets of the Early City." *Yale French Studies* 32 (1964): 12–23.

———. *Poetic Patterns in Rutebeuf: A Study in Noncourtly Poetic Modes of the Thirteenth Century.* New Haven: Yale University Press, 1970.

Rey-Flaud, Henri. *Pour une dramaturgie du Moyen Age.* Paris: PUF, 1980.

Reynolds, Suzanne. *Medieval Reading: Grammar, Rhetoric, and the Classical Text.* Cambridge: Cambridge University Press, 1996.

Reyval, Alfred. *L'église et le théâtre: Essai historique.* Paris: Bloud Gay, 1924.

Richard of Devizes, *Cronicon Richardi Divisensis de tempore regis Richardi Primi.* Ed. J. T. Appleby. London: Thomas Nelson and Sons, 1963.

Robertson, D. W., Jr. *A Preface to Chaucer: Studies in Medieval Perspectives.* Princeton: Princeton University Press, 1962.

Robertson, H. S. "Structure and Comedy in *Le Jeu de Saint Nicolas.*" *Studies in Philology* 64 (1967): 551–63.

Robins, R. H. *Ancient and Mediaeval Grammatical Theory in Europe with Particular Reference to Modern Linguistic Doctrine.* London: Bell, 1951.

———. *A Short History of Linguistics.* 3d ed. New York: Longman, 1990.

Robson, C. A. *Maurice de Sully and the Medieval Vernacular Homily.* Oxford: Basil Blackwell, 1952.

Röhnstrom, Otto. *Etude sur Jean Bodel.* Uppsala: Imprimerie Almqvist et Wiksell, 1920.

Rossiaud, Jacques. *Medieval Prostitution.* Trans. Lydia G. Cochrane. Oxford: Basil Blackwell, 1988.

Rousse, Michel. "Le mariage de Rutebeuf et la fête des fous." *Le Moyen Age* 88 (1982): 435–50.

———. "Le *Jeu de St. Nicolas:* Du clerc au jongleur." In *Hommage à Jean-Charles Payen: Farai chansoneta novele,* 311–21. Caen: Centre de Publications de l'Université de Caen, 1989.

———. "Le Théâtre et les jongleurs." *Revue des Langues Romanes* 95, no. 1 (1991): 1–14.

Roussel, Henri. "Notes sur la littérature arrageoise du XIIIe siècle." *Revue des Sciences Humaines* 88 (1957): 249–86.

Ruck, E. H. *An Index of Themes and Motifs in Twelfth-Century French Arthurian Poetry.* Arthurian Studies, 25. Rochester: D. S. Brewer, 1991.

Ruelle, Pierre, ed. *Les congés d'Arras.* Brussels: Presses Universitaires de Bruxelles, 1965.

Rutebeuf. *Oeuvres complètes de Rutebeuf.* Ed. Edmond Faral and Julia Bastin. 2 vols. Paris: A. and J. Picard, 1959–60.

———. *Oeuvres complètes.* Ed. Michel Zink. 2 vols. Paris: Bordas, 1989.

Rychner, Jean. *Contribution à l'étude des fabliaux.* Neuchâtel: Faculté des lettres, 1960.

Salin, Edgar. "Just Price." In *Encyclopedia of the Social Sciences,* ed. Edwin Seligman, 504–7. New York: Macmillan, 1937.

Santucci, Monique. "Le fou dans les lettres françaises médiévales." *Les lettres romanes* 36, no. 3 (1982): 195–211.

Schmitt, Jean-Claude. *Prêcher d'exemples.* Paris: Stock, 1985.

Schmugge, Ludwig. "Pilgerverkehrs." In *Gastfreundschaft, Taverne und Gasthaus,* ed. Peyer, 37–60.

Schuler, Thomas. "Gastlichkeit in karolingischen Benediktinerklostern: Anspruch und Wirklichkeit." In *Gastfreundschaft, Taverne und Gasthaus,* ed. Peyer, 21–36.

Semrau, Franz. *Wurfel und Wurfelspiel im alten Frankreich.* Beihefte zur *Zeitschrift fur romanishe Philologie,* no. 23. Halle: Max Niemeyer, 1910.

Serper, Arié. *Rutebeuf: Poète satirique.* Paris: Klinksieck, 1969.

Shell, Marc. *The Economy of Literature.* Baltimore: Johns Hopkins University Press, 1978.

———. *Money, Language, and Thought. Literary and Philosophical Economies from the Medieval to the Modern Era.* Berkeley: University of California Press, 1982.

Shoaf, R. A. *Dante, Chaucer, and the Currency of the Word.* Norman, Okla.: Pilgrim Books, 1983.

Siciliano, Italo. *François Villon et les thèmes poétiques du Moyen Age.* Paris: Armand Colin, 1934.

Simpson, James. *Piers Plowman: An Introduction to the B-text.* London: Longman, 1990.

Spence, Sarah. *Texts and the Self in the Twelfth Century.* Cambridge: Cambridge University Press, 1996.

Spencer, Richard. "The Role of Money in the Fabliaux." In *Epopée animale fable fabliau,* ed. Bianciotto and Salvat, 565–75.

Spitzer, Léo. "Note on the Poetical and Empirical 'I' in Medieval Authors." *Traditio* 4 (1946): 414–22.

Spufford, Peter. *Money and Its Use in Medieval Europe.* Cambridge: Cambridge University Press, 1988.

Stock, Brian. *The Implications of Literacy: Written Language and Models of Interpretation in the Eleventh and Twelfth Centuries.* Princeton: Princeton University Press, 1983.

Sturges, Robert S. *Medieval Interpretation: Models of Reading in Literary Narrative, 1100–1500.* Carbondale: Southern Illinois University Press, 1991.

Sutherland, D. R. "Fact and Fiction in the *Jeu de la Feuillée.*" *Romance Philology* 13, no. 4 (1960): 419–28.

Szabo, Thomas. "Xenodochia, Hospitaler und Herbergen-kirchliche und kommerzielle Gastung im mittelalterlichen Italien." In *Gastfreundschaft, Taverne und Gasthaus,* ed. Peyer, 61–92.

Tauber, Walter. *Das Wurfelspiel im Mittelalter und in das fruher Neuzeit.* Frankfurt: Peter Lang, 1987.

Thurston, Herbert, S. J., and Donald Attwater, eds. *Butler's Lives of the Saints.* 4 vols. New York: P. J. Kennedy and Sons, 1956.

Togeby, Knut. "The Nature of the Fabliaux." In *The Humor of the Fabliaux,* ed. Cooke and Honeycutt, 7–14.

Ungureanu, Marie. *La bourgeoisie naissante.* Arras: Commission départementale des monuments historiques du Pas-de-calais, 1955.

Vance, Eugene. "The Functions and Limits of Autobiography in Augustine's *Confessions.*" *Poetics Today* 5, no. 2 (1984): 399–409.

———. *Mervelous Signals: Poetics and Sign Theory in the Middle Ages.* Lincoln: University of Nebraska Press, 1986.

van Houtte, Jan. "Herbergswesen und Gastlichkeit im mittelalterlichen Brugge." In *Gastfreundschaft, Taverne und Gasthaus,* ed. Peyer, 177–88.

Verdon, Jean. *Le plaisir au Moyen Age.* Paris: Perrin, 1996.

Vincent, Patrick R. *The "Jeu de St. Nicolas" of Jean Bodel of Arras: A Literary Analysis.* Johns Hopkins Studies in Romance Literatures and Languages, vol. 49. Baltimore: Johns Hopkins University Press, 1954. Reprint, New York: Johnson Reprint Co., 1973.

Vitz, Evelyn Birge. "Type et individu dans 'l'autobiographie' médiévale." *Poètique* 24 (1975): 426–45.

———. *Medieval Narrative and Modern Narratology: Subjects and Objects of Desire.* New York: New York University Press, 1989.

Wace. *The Life of Saint Nicholas.* Ed. Mary Sinclair. Philadelphia: University of Pennsylvania Dissertation, 1923.

Wace. *Le romon de Brut de Wace.* Ed. Ivor Arnold. 2 vols. Paris: Société des Anciens Textes Français, 1938–40.

Wailes, Stephen L. "Vagrantes and the Fabliaux." In *The Humor of the Fabliaux,* ed. Cooke and Honeycutt, 43–58.

Welter, Jean Thiebaut. *La Tabula Exemplorum.* Paris: Occitania, 1926.

Wetherbee, Winthrop. *Platonism and Poetry in the Twelfth Century.* Princeton: Princeton University Press, 1972.

Whicher, George F., ed. *The Goliard Poets: Medieval Latin Songs and Satires.* New York: New Directions, 1949.

White, Arthur. *Palaces of the People: A Social History of Commercial Hospitality.* New York: Taplinger, 1968.

Wolterbeek, Marc, ed. *Comic Tales of the Middle Ages: An Anthology and Commentary.* New York: Greenwood Press, 1991.

Zink, Michel. "Le Jeu de Saint Nicolas de Jean Bodel, drame spirituel." *Romania* 99 (1978): 31–46.

———. *La subjectivité littéraire autour du siècle de saint Louis.* Paris: PUF, 1985.

———. "Bonheurs de l'inconséquence dans le texte de Rutebeuf." *L'Esprit Créateur* 27, no. 1 (1987): 79–89.

———. *Littérature française du moyen age.* Paris: PUF, 1992.

Zumthor, Paul. "'Roman' et 'Gothique': Deux aspects de la poésie mediévale." In *Studi in Onore di Italo Siciliano,* ed. Leo S. Olschki, 1223–34. Florence: Biblioteca dell'Archivum Romanicum, 1966.

———. *Essai de poétique médiévale.* Paris: Editions du Seuil, 1972.

———. *Langue, texte, énigme.* Paris: Editions du Seuil, 1975.

———. *Speaking of the Middle Ages.* Trans. Sarah White. Lincoln: University of Nebraska Press, 1986.

Index

Abelard, Peter, 162–63, 213
Adam de la Halle, 12, 43, 61, 95, 121,
    125, 172, 186–87, 193, 195, 206,
    212, 214–40, 246, 248–49
Adler, Alfred, 57, 237
Alain de Lille, 23, 80, 101, 106, 116–17,
    130–33, 195–96, 244
Alexander III, Pope, 61
Amadas et Idoine, 196–97
Amplificatio, 99–100, 102–3, 105, 108
Anselm of Canterbury, Saint, 60
Anticlaudianus, 196
Archpoet, the, 4
Arens, Arnold, 94
Aristotle, 65, 87, 203, 223, 226
Artois region, 62
Aube (genre), 120
Augustine, Saint, 4, 7, 17, 18–19, 21,
    23, 26, 66, 78, 80, 84, 92, 101,
    103–4, 108, 144, 147, 211, 214,
    237–38, 242, 248
    Doctrina Christiana, De, 17–21, 23,
    26, 80, 103–4, 124–26, 149–50,
    214
Auxerre, wine of, 73, 165

Bakhtin, Mikhail, 10, 239, 249
Barter economy, 50, 60, 65
Barthes, Roland, 238
Bataille, Georges, 177–78
Bédier, Joseph, 48, 155–56

Benedictines, 27, 59
    Benedictine Rule, 38
Bernard of Cluny, 46, 75
Besant (coin), 103, 164
"Besant de Dieu, Le," 103
Bible, 27, 29, 38, 79, 147, 154, 167,
    244
    Deuteronomy, 38, 58
    Genesis, 68
    Luke, 27, 137
    New Testament, 61
"Blasme des fames, Le," 163
Bloch, R. Howard, 101, 117, 119,
    137–38, 156, 158, 166
Bodel, Jean, 25, 35, 54–110, 126, 172,
    178, 215, 217, 222, 231, 246
Boethius, 87, 226
"Boivin de Provins," 157–65, 167, 169,
    171, 196, 202
Bonaventure, Saint, 65
Boniment, 54, 217
Book of God, 7
Brothels, 1–3, 5, 11, 17, 33, 51, 83, 115,
    118, 126–55, 158–64, 228, 247
"Brunain, La vache au prestre," 170
Burns, Jane, 80, 101, 106, 131

Caesarius of Heisterbach, 60
Caillois, Roger, 247–49
Canon Law, 26, 74, 105, 132–34
Canterbury Tales, 48

Carmina Burana, 42, 88, 115–26. *See also* "Denudata veritate"; "Ego sum abbas Cucaniensis"; "Manus ferens munera"; "Potatores exquisiti"; "Si quis deciorum"
Caupona (Latin term), 28
Cerquiglini, Jacqueline, 182, 187–88
Chanson des Saisnes, 96
Charlemagne, 38, 82
"Charlot le juif," 210
Chartres, 14, 24, 43, 208, 227
Chaucer, Geoffrey, 48, 88, 203
Chivalry, 37–38
Chrétien de Troyes, 31, 46, 100, 109
  Erec et Enide, 31, 34, 35–36, 100
  Lancelot, 36–37
  Perceval, 109
  Yvain, 32
Cistercians, 26–27, 34, 38–39, 45, 60
"Clerc Golias, Le," 126
Cloth industry, 62–63
Cocagne, 145–52
"Complainte de Constantinople, La," 37–38
"Complainte (de Rutebeuf), La," 182–83
Confession, 12, 15, 103, 181, 211, 214, 235, 245
Confrérie (of Arras), 70
Congé (literary genre), 217, 228, 230
"Contre le tens qui devise," 186
Cooke, Thomas, 173
Copeland, Rita, 6
"Coquaigne, Li fabliaus de," 145–51
Courtois d'Arras, 1, 11, 17, 67, 87, 115, 120, 126–55, 161–62, 164, 167, 178, 196, 201, 207, 222, 238, 241, 248
"Credo au ribaut, Le," 1, 17, 126, 168–69
Crusades, 56, 60, 81

Dane, Joseph, 72, 95
Dante Alighieri, 88, 152, 181, 203, 235
  Inferno, 152
  Purgatorio, 235

Decretum (Gratian), 129
"Denudata veritate," 42, 116–18
De planctu Naturae, 23, 117, 130–31, 195–96
"Deux bordeors ribauds, Les," 1, 3, 93, 142
"Devise au lecheor, La," 1, 111–13, 115
Diaconus, 95
"Dit de l'herberie, Le," 226
"Diz des ribaux de Grève, Li," 182
Dominicans, 45, 59
Dragonetti, Roger, 235
Dubois, Michel, 73
Duby, Georges, 34
Dufournet, Jean, 154, 184, 209, 224, 227, 238

"Ego sum abbas Cucaniensis," 121–22
Enseignes (of Tavern), 25, 228
Epic (genre), 2, 12, 38, 48, 52, 81, 98, 102, 106–7, 133, 139, 215–16, 218, 223
"Estat du monde, L'," 76, 184
"Estormi," 170–72
Ethics (Aristotle), 65
Etymologies (Isidore of Seville), 203
Eugenius III, Pope, 60
Exempla, 46, 63, 238

Fabliaux, 1, 11, 32, 35, 72, 97, 115, 126, 155–79, 180, 203, 210, 246
"Fames, les dez et la taverne, Les," 126
Farce de maître Pathelin, La, 245
Fastoul, Baude, 217
Fatrasie (genre), 218–21, 223, 228, 234, 239
Feast of Fools, 150, 189, 192, 210, 215, 225, 227, 242–43
Flanders, 3, 48
Florence, 41
Foliage, as sign of the tavern, 25, 228
Fortuna, the Goddess, 136, 168
  Fortune, 10, 119, 125, 229
  wheel of fortune, 215, 218, 228
Foucault, Michel, 162

Foulques de Neuilly, 63–64, 91
Franciscans, 45, 59
Freud, Sigmund, 163
Fungibles (and nonfungibles), 65

Garapon, Robert, 222
Garrisson, Francis, 49
Gastfreundschaft, 26, 28, 30, 39
Gautier de Coinci, 84
Gautier, Théophile, 152–53
Geoffrey of Vinsauf, 100, 102, 103, 106, 109, 117, 131–32
Gift culture and gift giving, 16, 24, 29, 34–35, 37, 49, 51–52, 88, 154, 217
Gluttony, 16–17, 46, 52, 114, 117, 152–53, 193–94, 232, 239
Golden Age, The, 66, 150–51
Goliard poets, 1, 4, 72, 115–26, 138, 148, 154, 167, 173, 175, 178–79, 185, 229, 239, 246. See also *Carmina Burana*
"Gombert et des deus clers, De" 35
Good Samaritan, 27
Grammar/*Grammatica,* 23, 100, 104, 116, 173, 243
Gratian, 129
"Griesche d'esté, La," 182, 184–86, 191–92, 202–6, 208
"Griesche d'yver, La," 182, 185, 188–89, 197, 201, 207, 214, 221
Guibert de Nogent, 48
Guide du pèlerin de Saint-Jacques de Compostelle, Le, 40, 42
Guillaume de Lorris, 188
Guillaume le clerc de Normandie, 103, 105
Guilt culture, 12, 181, 211–12, 235, 245
Guy, Henry, 234

Hagiography, 52, 96, 98, 106–7, 133, 139, 215
Hasard (dice game), 92–93, 125, 168
Helsinger, Howard, 170
Henry, Albert, 74
Hermas, 78

"Historia calamitatum," 162–63, 213
Honorius d'Autun, 10,18
Hospitalia, 26, 40–41, 243
Hostellagium, 49
Huizenga, Johan, 247, 249
Hult, David, 235

Idolatria, De (Tertullian), 75
"Image du monde, L'," 45
Innocent III, Pope, 60, 63, 65, 205
Inns, 1–3, 5, 16, 24–49, 62, 155, 228, 247
"In taberna quando sumus," 1, 122–25, 178, 185
Interpretatione, De (Aristotle), 87
Irvine, Martin, 245
Isidore of Seville, 203
Isolde (Tristan and Isolde), 24
Italy, 48–49

Jacques de Vitry, 62–63
Jauss, Hans Robert, 120–21
Jean de Meun, 98
Jean le Marchant, 14–24, 43, 46, 57, 83, 87, 111, 114, 137, 145, 168, 208, 227, 238
Jeu de la Feuillée, Le, 1, 95, 139, 195, 207, 214–41, 246
Jeu de Saint Nicolas, Le, 1, 4, 10–11, 25, 50, 54–110, 125–26, 139, 142, 154, 170, 203, 215, 224, 228, 231–32, 241, 246
"Jeu des dez, Le," 126
Jeu parti (genre), 159
John Scotus Eriugena, 7, 211
Joke, concept of, 24
"Jus du pelerin, Li," 43
Just price, 74–76, 105, 243

Karras, Ruth, 133
Kelly, Douglas, 106
Köhler, Erich, 35
Kristeva, Julia, 100–101

Labor theory of value, 68
Langton, Stephen, 63

Lateran Council (Fourth), 103, 211, 235
Law, commercial (concerning exchanges in inns), 49
Law, Germanic, 30–31
Law, Norman customary, 69, 127
Law, Roman, 28, 75
Lecheor/lecher, 14, 16–17, 50, 111–14, 129, 145, 153, 159, 161–62
Le Goff, Jacques, 143, 223
Le Puy (France), 88
Leupin, Alexandre, 101, 240
Liber Sententiarum (Peter Lombard), 60, 89
Literacy, rise of, 50
Livre des Miracles de Notre-Dame de Chartres, Le, 14–24
Lombard, Peter, 60, 63, 89
London, 242
Louis, Saint, 17, 210

Maaille (coin), 86
Maddox, Donald, 245
Magnae derivationes (Uggacione of Pisa), 241
"Manus ferens munera," 88
"Mariages Rutebeuf, Li," 182–83, 185, 189–90, 200, 216, 220
Marie de France, 99–100, 108–9, 167, 217
"Lanval," 217
"Prologue," 99–100, 109, 167
Matthew of Vendome, 100, 109, 158
Maurice de Sully, 143
Mauron, Claude, 229
Mauss, Marcel, 34
McGregor, Gordon, 216, 218–19, 221, 234
Ménard, Philippe, 191, 231
Mendicant friars, 26, 45, 114, 192, 210
Minnis, Alastair, 102–3
"Miracle de Théophile, Le," 49–50
"Miracles de Notre Dame" (Gautier de Coinci), 84
"Miserere," 78–79, 153

Monasteries 16, 26, 38, 41, 48, 50, 243
Moniage Guillaume, Le, 48

Natural Law, 66–67
Nichols, Steven, 7, 18–19, 23, 101
Nicolas, Saint (as quasi-historical personage), 55, 93–94
Noonan, John, 62
Notre Dame de Chartres, 34
Nykrog, Per, 156, 179

"Paix de Rutebeuf, La," 209
Palamedes (inventor of dice), 136
Parable of the prodigal son, 17
Parable of the talants, 103, 144
Paris, 91, 180, 215, 217, 231, 233, 237
University of, 8, 208
Pastourelle (genre), 120
"Patenostre a l'usurier, Le," 64, 90–91
Paul, Saint, 237–38
Payen, Jean-Charles, 150
"Peccatores exquisiti," 115
Pelagianism, 144
Penitence, 12, 103, 214, 235, 245
Penitentials, 129–30, 211
Peraldus, Guilelmus, 192–95, 233
Peter Cantor, 63–64, 79, 84, 91–92, 114, 129, 133, 144, 244
Philippe de Beaumanoir, 69, 127
Pierce, Charles S., 12
Piers Plowman, 178
Pilgrimmage and pilgrims, 14, 16–17, 20–21, 24, 38–40, 42–45, 48, 94, 118, 227
"Plaies du monde, Les," 183, 209
"Plantez, La," 142, 169–70
Plato, 29, 31, 33–34, 46–47, 102, 104, 131
Laws, 29, 34, 46
"Phaedrus," 102, 104
Poetria nova, 100, 102, 106, 113, 117, 131–32, 152
Pompeii, 28
"Potatores exquisiti," 4, 115–16
"Povretei Rutebeuf, La," 182
Preaching, urban, 26, 46, 63, 90, 187

"Prestre et le chevalier, Le," 32–33, 77
Priscian, 99
Prostitution, 3, 11, 28, 114–15, 121,
    126–55, 157–65, 192–93. *See also*
    Brothels
Protocapitalism, 3, 11
"Proverbe au vilain, Li," 1
Purgatory, 9, 143–44
"Putains et les lecheors, Les," 129
Puy (poetic fraternity of Arras), 70,
    228, 236

Raoul de Houdenc, 51
"Renart le bestournei," 210
"Repentance Rutebeuf, La," 181,
    205–9, 214
Rey-Flaud, Henri, 58
Rhetoric, 99–101, 107–8, 110, 136
Richard of Devizes, 242
Robert Courson, 63–64, 91
Robertson, D. W., 7, 9
Romance (genre), 24, 99–100, 106, 109,
    139, 188
Romance of the Rose, 66, 98, 109,
    150–51, 188, 195, 212–13, 235
Romanesque sign theory, 3, 7, 19, 21,
    101, 211, 246
Rome, 150
Rousse, Michel, 189–91
Roussel, H. 225
Rudel, Jaufré, 190
Rutebeuf, 1, 12, 37, 52, 61, 76, 83, 107,
    125, 132–33, 180–216, 220–22,
    224–26, 230, 237, 235–38, 246,
    248–49. *See also* "Charlot le juif";
    "La complainte de Constantino-
    ple"; "La complainte (de
    Rutebeuf)"; "Le dit de l'herberie";
    "Li diz des ribaux de Grève";
    "L'estat du monde"; "La griesche
    d'esté"; "La griesche d'yver"; "Li
    mariages Rutebeuf"; "La paix de
    Rutebeuf"; "Les plaies du monde";
    "La povretei Rutebeuf"; "Renart
    le bestournei"; "La repentance
    Rutebeuf"; "La voie de Paradis"

Rychner, Jean, 156

"Saint Pierre and the Jongleur," 84
Saracens, 56–58, 69–70, 96–97
Saussure, Ferdinand de, 12
Semioticity, of Middle Ages, 5, 211
Sepet, Marius, 225
Servius, 241
Shell, Marc, 142
Shoaf, R. A., 88, 203, 212
"Si quis deciorum," 118–19
Soissons, wine of, 165
Sommeillon, Robert, 236
"Songe d'Enfer, Le," 51
Song of Roland, 82, 211
"Song of Songs," 26
Speculative grammar, 105
Stock, Brian, 50, 77, 245
Sturges, Robert, 100, 211
Sutherland, D. R., 216
Szabo, Thomas, 30

Taberna (Latin), 28
Tacitus, 30
    Germania, 30
"Taverner," 49
Tertullian, 75
Theodosius, 28
Theosis, 3, 18–19, 23, 101, 106–7, 232,
    237–38
Thibaut de Champagne, 186
Thomas Aquinas, Saint, 64–66, 80,
    112–13, 125, 172, 205
Thomas of Cobham, 107, 114, 130,
    133
Toulouse, 16, 40, 42, 44, 88
Translatio imperii, 38
Translatio studii, 45
Tristan, 24
"Trois aveugles de Compiegne, Les,"
    157, 164–69, 247
"Trois dames de Paris, Les," 173–78
Troubadours, 109, 172, 200

Uggacione of Pisa, 241
Urban II, Pope, 61

Vance, Eugene, 101, 172, 214, 221, 230, 239
Venice, 60
Verbum abbreviatorum (Peter Cantor), 79
"Vergier de Paradis, Le," 143
"Vers de la Mort, Les," 61
Villon, François, 73, 81, 83
Virgil, 241
Vita Saint Beraldi, 120
Vitz, Evelyn, 213–14
"Voie de Paradis, La" 52
Vox significativa, 173
Vulgate Cycle, 108, 172

Wace, 93, 193

Brut, 193
Vie de Saint Nicolas, 93
Water, as drink of pilgrims, 42–43, 116–18
William of Auxerre, 66, 75
William IX (Count of Poitiers), 200
Wine, fixed municipal prices of, 54–55, 67, 86
of Auxerre, 73, 165
of Soissons, 165

Xenodochium, 39

Zero sum game, 79, 98, 144, 151, 177
Zink, Michel, 201, 207, 209
Zumthor, Paul, 186–88, 211, 245

DATE DUE

JUL − 1 1999	

UPI 261-2505 G   PRINTED IN U.S.A.